SPSS for Psychologists

SPSS for Psychologists

(and everybody else)

6th edition

Nicola Brace
Senior Lecturer in Psychology, The Open University

Richard Kemp
Associate Professor, School of Psychology, University of New South Wales, Sydney, Australia

Rosemary Snelgar
Principal Lecturer in Psychology, University of Westminster

 macmillan education palgrave

This book is not sponsored or approved by IBM®SPSS®, and any errors are in no way the responsibility of SPSS®.

SPSS is a trademark of SPSS, Inc., an IBM Company, registered in many jurisdictions worldwide.

First edition 2000
Second edition 2003
Third edition 2006
Fourth edition 2009
Fifth edition 2012
Sixth edition 2016

Published by
PALGRAVE

Palgrave Macmillan in the UK is an imprint of Macmillan Publishers Limited, registered in England, company number 785998, of Houndmills, Basingstoke, Hampshire RG21 6XS.

Palgrave Macmillan in the US is a division of St Martin's Press LLC, 175 Fifth Avenue, New York, NY 10010.

Palgrave is a global academic imprint of the above companies and has companies and representatives throughout the world.

Palgrave® and Macmillan® are registered trademarks in the United States, the United Kingdom, Europe and other countries

ISBN 978–1–137–57922–5

This book is printed on paper suitable for recycling and made from fully managed and sustained forest sources. Logging, pulping and manufacturing processes are expected to conform to the environmental regulations of the country of origin.

A catalogue record for this book is available from the British Library.

A catalog record for this book is available from the Library of Congress.

Printed in China

To my granddaughter Alice, who was born while we were writing this edition,
and her wonderful parents Hannah and Matthew
Nicky

To Penelope, Joseph, Francesca, Big Malc and Wilb,
and the people of Cuba, where I spent time while finishing the last sections of this book
'Viva Cuba Libre!'
Richard

To my siblings, Sue, Meg and Tim, and all their descendants!
Rosemary

Contents

Preface

How to use this book

This book is designed to help you analyse psychological data using the software package IBM® SPSS® Statistics software (SPSS).[1] With the exception of the first few sections of Chapter 1, we recommend that you read this book while sitting at a computer that is running SPSS.

Chapter 1 serves as a reminder of some issues related to research design, while Chapter 2 shows you how to enter data into SPSS. In Chapters 3 and 4, we show you how to explore, clean and manage your data. In Chapters 5–12, you will learn how to undertake a variety of statistical procedures using SPSS. The order of these chapters is designed to reflect the way many university psychology departments teach statistics to undergraduates, but the chapters are largely free-standing, so you do not need to read them in sequence. We hope that once you are familiar with the process of data entry, you will use this book as a reference to assist you to undertake the analysis you need. To help you select the most appropriate statistical procedure, we have included a brief description of each test in Chapter 1. The procedures covered in Chapters 5–8 are likely to be taught in most undergraduate psychology research methods courses, whereas those covered in Chapters 9–12 are slightly more advanced. We hope that the statistical procedures described in these later chapters will be of particular help to students undertaking their final-year research project and postgraduate students and researchers.

Within each of the analysis chapters, we briefly describe the procedure, show you how to undertake the analysis, explain some of the options available, and teach you how to obtain suitable graphs and descriptive statistics. Critically, each section ends with an explanation of how to interpret the output produced by SPSS.

Chapter 13 describes the use of syntax to control SPSS and also provides some useful information on topics such as printing and importing and exporting files. Finally, we have included an extensive Glossary of the statistical terms used in this book.

The content of each chapter is now explained in a little more detail.

Chapter 1

Chapter 1 provides a brief overview of the basic concepts and terminology used in psychological research and statistical analysis, and introduces SPSS. We describe some basic methods of data collection and the types of data that are collected in quantitative research. We then consider data analysis and provide you with an introduction to the windows and buttons you will use when analysing your data with SPSS. Finally, we show you how to start and exit SPSS.

Chapters 2–4

Chapter 2 shows you how to set up SPSS to receive your data, and how to create and save a data file. In Chapter 3, you learn how to explore the data you have

---

[1] SPSS Inc. was acquired by IBM in October 2009.

entered to calculate some simple descriptive statistics, how to check and clean your data files, and how to use SPSS to produce useful graphical representations of your data. Chapter 4 introduces you to some useful functions you can use to manage your data set. We show you how to do things such as split the data file or group participants together, and how to recode existing variables or compute new ones.

Chapters 5–8

Chapter 5 covers some simple inferential statistical tests that can be used to determine: whether a sample mean differs from a known population mean; whether there is a difference between the scores from two groups of participants; or whether there is a difference between the scores from participants when tested under two different conditions. Chapters 6 and 7 focus on statistical tests of association, while Chapter 8 describes a family of statistical procedures used to analyse data from more complex experimental designs involving several variables.

Chapters 9–12

Chapters 9–12 look at tests that are appropriate for experiments involving more complex designs or for data obtained using non-experimental methods such as surveys or questionnaires.

In general, each of Chapters 5–12 covers a family of related tests, each of which is described in its own section. We introduce each statistical test with a brief description. This description is not intended to replace that which you will find in a statistics textbook; rather, it is intended to act as a reminder of when and how to use the test. We also include an example of a typical or real piece of research that might be analysed using the test, to give you a concrete example. We then give detailed, step-by-step instructions on how to perform the analysis using SPSS. In the earlier chapters, we include screenshots (pictures) and a full description of every step required to perform the test. In later chapters, we assume that you will have become a little more familiar with the workings of SPSS, and therefore summarise some of the simpler operations. Each chapter includes an annotated example of the output produced by SPSS to help you understand the results of your analyses. Finally, we include a note on how you should report the results of your analyses. The data we use to demonstrate the statistical tests covered in Chapters 5–7 can be found in the Appendix, and all the data can be downloaded from the Palgrave website (he.palgrave.com/psychology/ brace/data.htm).

Chapter 13

Chapter 13 introduces you to syntax and shows how using this text language to control SPSS can increase your efficiency, especially when working on larger, more complex data files. In addition, we describe some useful option settings, how to print files, how to import and export spreadsheet files, and how to incorporate SPSS output into other documents. This chapter also describes how to access the extensive SPSS help libraries.

Differences between versions of SPSS

This book was written using SPSS Version 23, which is quite similar to earlier versions by IBM, and indeed to even earlier versions of SPSS (or PASW as it was briefly known). However, the changes that have been made do not relate much to the tools we introduce in this book. You may see small differences between the dialogue boxes and the output we show and that produced by your version of SPSS, and these may either be cosmetic, affecting only the appearance of the program, or may result from changes made to the option settings in SPSS. We show you how to use these option settings to control SPSS in Chapter 13.

We hope that you find our book useful and that it helps you to enjoy psychological research.

Acknowledgements

Welcome to the sixth edition of *SPSS for Psychologists*. Once again, we would like to take the opportunity to thank the many people who have contributed to this book. In particular, we would like to thank our colleagues, past and present, for their invaluable advice, and the various reviewers who have provided feedback on earlier editions. These contributions have again helped to shape the new edition. We thank you for your time and hope that you can see where we have made amendments or additions in light of your comments. We would also like to thank the various colleagues, supervisors, students and friends who have contributed to our knowledge of statistics and data analysis either through formal teaching, informal discussion or by presenting us with challenging data analysis problems. Some of these people were also kind enough to allow us to utilise their data to illustrate the use of particular statistical techniques. We would particularly like to thank Gini Harrison for providing access to her excellent interactive online resources, which you can find on the website that accompanies this text. Richard would also like to thank Xiang Yan Hong for his help in preparing some of the screenshots in this edition.

We first thought of writing a book about SPSS some 10 years before we got around to doing it. With each new version of SPSS and each new group of students, we revised our teaching notes and talked about what our book would look like. So, when our first edition was published, we were delighted by the positive response it received. Our objective was to enable students to actively engage in the discipline by undertaking their own research. Reading about psychology can be interesting, but the real fun is in doing it, and that inevitably involves the collection and analysis of data and the use of software such as SPSS. We are therefore particularly pleased to hear from students who tell us that our book has enabled them to complete their own research. It is this more than anything else that keeps us motivated to update and expand our text for each new edition. The fact that we are now into the sixth edition has amazed and delighted us (although this demonstrates how even older we now are). Thank you for taking the time to contact us.

Finally, we would like to thank the team at Palgrave for their support. Over the six editions of this book, we have worked with many different members of the Palgrave team. All have contributed greatly to this book, but we would particularly like to thank Paul Stevens, Cathy Scott and Amy Wheeler for their help and support in producing this edition, and Maggie Lythgoe for her copyediting.

Nicola Brace
Richard Kemp
Rosemary Snelgar

1 Introduction

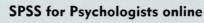

SPSS for Psychologists online
Visit he.palgrave.com/psychology/brace for data sets, online tutorials and exercises.

Section 1: PSYCHOLOGICAL RESEARCH AND SPSS

- IBM SPSS Statistics software (SPSS) is a widely used computer program designed to aid the statistical analysis of data, particularly data collected in the course of research.

- SPSS® has been around in various different forms for many years, and has become the 'industry standard' software for data analysis.

- SPSS is the program most widely used by university researchers, especially those working in psychology and the social sciences. SPSS is also widely used in private and government research organisations and many large private companies and nongovernmental organisations.

- Being able to describe yourself as a competent user of SPSS will enhance your employment prospects considerably.

- Although at first sight SPSS might appear rather complex, it is not difficult to learn how to undertake a wide range of statistical analyses, and once you have mastered these basics, they will enable you to undertake far more sophisticated research than would be possible without the aid of such software.

But I am studying psychology not statistics – why do I need to learn to use SPSS?

This is a common question, and the answer lies in an understanding of the nature of psychology and the type of research that many, if not most, psychologists undertake. Psychology can be considered a science, because it draws on systematic methods from the sciences. The problem is that people are not the easiest of things to study because they vary both between individuals and over time. That is, they differ in terms of how they react in a particular situation, and how a person reacts in a situation today might be quite different from how they react tomorrow. This means that the data collected by psychologists are much more 'noisy' than that collected in some other sciences. Consider, for example, a chemist investigating the properties of magnesium. The chemist knows that, under constant conditions, every bit of magnesium will react in the same way as every other bit of magnesium, and that how the magnesium reacts today will be the same as how it reacts tomorrow. Thus, the chemist might only need to do an experiment once using one piece of magnesium and is unlikely to need to use statistics to help explain the results of the observations. The situation facing the psychologist is quite different, and in order to be able to determine how, in general, people react in a given situation, the psychologist will probably need to test a range of different individuals and then make use of statistical techniques to determine what trends are present in the data. So psychologists are particularly likely to need to use statistics in their research.

In recent years the complexity of the statistical techniques routinely used in psychological research and taught to undergraduate students has increased considerably. This routine reliance on more complex statistical analysis is made possible by the widespread availability of sophisticated statistical analysis software such as SPSS. Thus, in order to be able to undertake psychological research, either as a student or a professional, you need to be able to use software such as SPSS. This book is designed to introduce you to SPSS so that you can use the program to undertake the statistical analyses you need for your course or research.

In the remainder of this section, we will provide a brief overview of some of the concepts relating to research methods, data and statistical analysis that are important to bear in mind when using SPSS to analyse your data. We refer to many of these in later chapters. (You are probably already familiar with many of them from your lectures on research methods.) Additionally, in each chapter we include an overview of some statistical issues, but this book is not intended to be a statistics reference, and you should also refer to a statistics text for full guidance.

Research design and SPSS

A variety of different methods can be used in psychological research. Methods commonly used include questionnaire studies, interviews, observation and experiments. Each of these methods can result in the collection of quantitative data suitable for analysis using SPSS. The experimental method is a particularly important method that allows us to draw conclusions regarding the cause–effect relationship between two variables. The method and design employed will influence how data are entered into SPSS and the choice of statistical test used for analysis.

Related and unrelated designs in psychological research

One important characteristic of any research method is whether it involves a *related* or *unrelated* design – also known as 'correlated' or 'within-participants', and 'uncorrelated' or 'between-participants' designs respectively. In a related research design, two or more measures on a variable are linked in some way – typically because they are measured from the same participant. In contrast, if we make only one measure on each variable from each participant, this would be an unrelated design. This distinction is important because data collected using related and unrelated designs are analysed using different statistical procedures, and thus the data collected using related and unrelated data must be coded differently in SPSS data files (see Chapter 2).

Levels of measurement

SPSS is designed to aid the analysis of quantitative data, which will probably consist of a series of measurements for each of one or more variables. A variable is simply some quantity that varies and can be measured; so, height, time, weight, sex (male or female) and IQ test score are all examples of variables. A typical data set in psychological research will consist of several variables each measured for each of several cases or participants.

We use a scale to make the measurements of a variable, and the characteristics of the scale determine the characteristics of the data we collect and ultimately what descriptive and inferential statistics we legitimately undertake on these data. Many statistics texts written for psychology students describe four different types of scales, or levels of measurement: *nominal, ordinal, interval* and *ratio*. We describe them briefly below. When entering data into SPSS, you will need to classify variables as *nominal, ordinal* or *scale*; SPSS uses the term *scale* to refer to either interval or ratio variables.

1. **Nominal level** Nominal (also referred to as 'categorical') variables are categorised, rather than measured in the strict sense. The value of a nominal variable should not be taken to imply any more than a label (or a name, hence the term 'nominal'). For example, we might decide to record the sex of our participants and to enter these data into SPSS by adopting the coding scheme 1 = Male, 2 = Female. Assigning 1 or 2 allows us to differentiate between these two groups of participants. With nominal data just about the only thing we can do is count or measure frequency. We can report how many men and women we have, but there is little else we can do with these data and it would make no sense to calculate statistics such as the mean sex of our participants.

> SPSS does not automatically know about the level of measurement used to collect your data. It is up to you to make sure that you do not ask SPSS to undertake any inappropriate analysis, such as calculating the mean of nominal data.

2. **Ordinal level** Ordinal variables are measured using a scale that allows us to imply order or rank. An ordinal variable tells you more than a nominal variable; for example, it may be legitimate to say that the student who was

assigned a rank of 1 performed better than the student with rank 2. However, what we can do with these data is still limited because we do not know how much better the rank 1 student performed than the rank 2 student, and because it is unlikely that the difference in ability indicated by ranks 1 and 2 will be the same as that between ranks 2 and 3, or ranks 107 and 108. Thus an ordinal scale is still a rather limited measure of performance.

3. **Interval and ratio levels** Measuring at interval or ratio levels provides us with numbers that are more number-like. If we have an interval or ratio scale, then we can be certain that 3 is more than 2, and 4 is more than 3. Furthermore, we know that the interval between all points on the scale is the same; for example, the difference between 23 and 24 is the same as the difference between 102 and 103.

   An interval scale is a scale that has an arbitrary zero so that a value of zero doesn't indicate that you have none of the quantity being measured. In a ratio scale, zero means that there is none of the quantity being measured. In practice, the difference between these two types of data is not critical and SPSS does not distinguish between them, using the term *scale* to describe both interval and ratio variables. For your research methods modules, however, you probably will need to know the difference between interval and ratio levels of measurement.

Hypotheses

A hypothesis is a prediction about the outcome of the research. The hypothesis, often known as a 'research hypothesis', 'experimental hypothesis' or 'alternative hypothesis', predicts that there will be a difference between conditions, or that there is an association between variables. The null hypothesis, by contrast, expresses the possibility that there is no effect or association.

When analysing data using SPSS you need to be clear about whether your research hypothesis is one-tailed or two-tailed. A one-tailed hypothesis makes predictions about both the presence of an effect (e.g. there will be a difference in the performance of young and old participants on a memory test) and also about the direction of this difference or association (e.g. young participants will obtain a higher score on a memory test than elderly participants). In contrast, a two-tailed hypothesis predicts only the presence of an effect, not its direction. With certain statistical procedures, SPSS will ask you to specify whether your hypothesis is one- or two-tailed.

Populations and samples

When we plan a piece of research, we will have in mind a population. For statistical purposes, a population is the total set of all possible scores for a particular variable. For some research the population might be quite small. For example, if we are researching occupational stress among professional taxidermists, then our population is all professional taxidermists. Given that there are relatively few professional taxidermists, we might be able to interview them all and so measure the entire population of scores. However, for most research, it would never be possible to collect the entire population of all possible scores for a variable, either because the population is too large, or because of practical limitations. In these situations we rely on testing a sample. That is, we collect a smaller subgroup of scores that we hope will be representative of the whole population. A bigger sample has a better chance of being representative of the population, so sample size is an important consideration (see Statistical power later in this section). You will need to seek guidance on this from your statistics text as SPSS will analyse your data even when your sample size is too small for the analysis you want to undertake.

Parameters and statistics

If we measure the entire population of scores for a variable, then we can calculate a *parameter* of the population, such as the mean. However, usually we only sample the population and so can only calculate the mean of the sample. A measure, such as the mean or standard deviation, based on a sample is known as a *statistic*. The important distinction is that we can calculate a statistic, but usually can only estimate a parameter because we cannot measure the entire population of scores. Assuming that our sampling procedure was sound, and our sample was not too small, we would expect the mean of the sample to provide a fairly accurate estimate of the mean of the population. The bigger the sample, the more accurate our estimate is likely to be, but unless we test the entire population we will never know the true population parameter for certain.

Descriptive statistics

Descriptive statistics summarise large volumes of data. The role of descriptive statistics is to provide the reader with an understanding of what the data look like by using a few indicative or typical values. Depending on the type of data, this can involve a measure of central tendency (e.g. mean) and a measure of spread (e.g. standard deviation). In Chapter 3 we cover how to obtain descriptive statistics. Additionally, in each of the chapters covering a statistical procedure we show you how to obtain descriptive statistics; however, you will need to decide which is most appropriate for your data.

Confidence intervals and point estimates

When estimating a statistic such as a mean, there are two approaches we could adopt. In psychological research the most common approach is to cite a single value, or point estimate, which represents the best estimate of the parameter. For example, we might calculate that the mean height of a sample is 1.73 m and we might use this as our estimate of the mean of the population. Clearly, it is unlikely that the true value for the population will be exactly 1.73 m, but this point estimate represents our best guess at the value. Although they are widely employed in psychology, point estimates are limited because they do not tell us anything about the likely accuracy of our estimate. The alternative approach uses a device called a 'confidence interval', which consists of two values, an upper and lower limit, and these two values define the range within which we expect the true value to fall. These values give an indication of how uncertain we are about our estimate of the population parameter; the more widely spread the values, the less certain we are about our estimate. For example, we might calculate that the upper and lower limits of the 95% confidence interval are 1.6 m and 1.8 m. These confidence intervals define the range of values, which is likely to include the unknown population parameter. More precisely, these values tell us that if we took repeated samples from the population and calculated the 95% confidence intervals for each, then in 95% of these samples the calculated interval would include the true population parameter. Thus, we estimate that there is a 95% probability that the true value lies between these two values.

The confidence interval approach has several advantages over the point estimate approach. First, it serves to remind us that the population estimate is just that – an estimate with which is associated a certain level of error. Second, the confidence interval approach conveys information about the likely magnitude of the real value. If we only provide a point estimate value for the population mean, then we have no way of knowing what the likely limits are. Another valuable use of confidence intervals is in the graphing of results. By marking the confidence intervals when plotting means, we provide the reader with a clear indication of the extent to which the estimated means for different conditions overlap. This use of confidence intervals in graphing is illustrated in Chapter 5.

Bootstrapping

Recent versions of SPSS have included a powerful procedure called 'bootstrapping'. The name 'bootstrapping' refers to the impossible idea of picking yourself up off the floor by pulling on your shoelaces, and is used in various contexts to describe a process that achieves something without external assistance; for example, we talk about 'booting' a computer when we start it up. In statistics, the term is used to describe a particular approach to estimating parameters. Normally, when we estimate a parameter such as variance, we make assumptions about the nature of the distribution. Bootstrapping provides an alternative method of estimating these same parameters without making such assumptions.

Imagine that we are interested in the height of a population of people and have measured a sample of 100 individuals. We can now use the bootstrapping method to estimate the mean height of the population. We do this by collecting lots of new samples, each of 100 observations, and then calculate the mean for each of these samples. But where do we get these new samples from? SPSS doesn't collect more data for you; instead it samples from your sample using a procedure called 'random resampling with replacement'. To understand this, imagine that each of your 100 observations are written on a scrap of paper and placed into a tub. Now imagine reaching into the tub, picking out one piece of paper and recording the value on the paper before returning it to the tub. Now repeat this 99 more times to give you a new sample of 100 observations. This is called our 'bootstrap sample'. Note that some of the original values will not be included in the bootstrap sample, while others might appear several times, and as result the mean of this new sample will probably not be the same as the mean of the original sample. If we repeat this whole process lots of times (typically at least 1,000 times), we will end up with a set of means of our bootstrap samples and can use these to estimate the mean of the population from which the original sample was drawn.

Bootstrapping is particularly useful when we don't know about the underlying population distribution or don't want to assume that the distribution is normal. SPSS now includes a bootstrapping option in many statistical procedures to estimate mean, standard deviation, variance, skewness, kurtosis and various other statistics. We will not cover the use of the bootstrapping option here, but once you have familiarised yourself with SPSS, you might like to explore the bootstrapping option and compare the output with that from the conventional method we describe in detail in each chapter.

Inferential statistics and probability

Inferential statistics allow us to go beyond simply describing the data. Through the use of a variety of different inferential statistical tests, we can answer questions such as: 'Is there a difference between the reading ability of the male and the female participants?' or 'Is there a relationship between participants' age and reading ability?' What all these statistical tests have in common is that they use mathematical procedures to attempt to estimate the probability of obtaining the data if the null hypothesis were true.

Inferential statistical tests allow us to decide which of two possible explanations is the most likely: is it more likely that our sample was unrepresentative or is there really a difference between the two groups? Inferential tests do this by calculating the probability that the apparent difference was just down to luck in our sampling; that the pattern of results observed in our data could have arisen by chance alone. For this reason, all inferential statistical tests will result in the computation of a probability value or a p value, which ranges between 0 and 1.

The probability value calculated for a statistical test tells us how likely it is that any patterns we can see in our data are just down to chance fluctuations, and not indicative of a 'real' effect. When using SPSS the output from the inferential tests will include this probability value and this is often labelled the 'Sig. Value'.

But how should you interpret the value? There are two approaches that can be taken here: report the probability level and leave the reader to decide how to interpret this, or set a criterion below which the null hypothesis can be rejected and the research hypothesis accepted. This second approach is the one traditionally adopted in psychological research and is the basis of the concept of statistical significance. Psychologists usually set the criterion (also known as the Type I error rate) at $p = .05$. If the probability, that the pattern we have observed in our data would arise just by chance (if the null hypothesis was true), is less than .05 (or 5%) then we reject the null hypothesis, and declare that we have a *statistically significant* result. In each chapter covering a statistical test, we show you how to report the probability value provided by SPSS.

Adjusting p values for one- and two-tailed hypotheses

By default, SPSS usually calculates the p value for the two-tailed hypothesis, and this is the safest, most conservative option to adopt. However, if before undertaking the research, you established a one-tailed hypothesis, and did so on the basis of sound reasoning or previous research, then it is possible to either request the calculation of a p value appropriate to a one-tailed hypothesis (as you can do for the tests of correlation described in Chapter 6) or to calculate the one-tailed *p* value by halving the two-tailed value.

Exact and asymptotic significance

SPSS provides the option of either exact or asymptotic significance for certain inferential statistical tests. Asymptotic significance is tested against an asymptotic distribution in which the probability of occurrence of extremely high or low values never reaches zero, so in a graph of the distribution the tails never touch the horizontal axis. The normal distribution is an example of an asymptotic distribution. In real distributions such extreme values do not occur, so real distributions are not asymptotic. If we have a large sample, then it is safe to use the asymptotic distribution to calculate probability values. However, with small sample sizes this approach can be problematic. To overcome this problem versions of several inferential statistical tests have been developed, which give what is called the 'exact' significance. One common example is Fisher's exact test, used in chi-square designs that involve small numbers of participants (see Chapter 7, Section 4). If you choose to make use of an exact test, then you should make this clear when reporting the results of your analysis.

The fact that the exact tests allow you to test hypotheses with small numbers of participants does not mean that it is acceptable to test few participants. The statistical power of your design (see below) will be greatly reduced by a small sample size.

Confidence intervals and statistical inference

The confidence interval approach described earlier can also be employed to make statistical inference. SPSS can calculate the *mean difference* (e.g. between two groups or two conditions) – this is an estimate of the real difference between the two population means – and we can state this mean difference using either a point estimate or a confidence interval. For example, if the upper and lower limits of the 95% confidence interval for the mean difference were 1.3 and 2.2, this would tell us that, according to our estimates, there is a probability of .95 (or 95% probability) that the real mean difference will lie somewhere between these two values.

Expressing the significant difference using confidence intervals has the advantage that it also provides an indication of the magnitude of the likely difference between two groups or two conditions, and the variability of the difference. Using the confidence interval approach, a difference is taken to be significant if the upper and lower limits of the confidence interval are either both positive or both negative – that is, if the range of values does not include zero. If the range of values does include zero, this tells us that it is quite likely (more than 5% in the case of 95% confidence intervals) that the true difference between the population means might be zero, and hence any difference we see in our data is just down to sampling error. This is equivalent to saying that the difference is non-significant.

At present, SPSS provides confidence intervals for the mean difference as part of the default output for the *t*-test (see Chapter 5) and in this case these confidence intervals can be used to infer statistical significance. Confidence intervals for the mean are also available as optional output for some tests; for example, ANOVA, ANCOVA and MANOVA. However, the use of confidence intervals to infer statistical significance in these routines is not well supported in SPSS and is beyond the scope of this book. Interested readers are advised to consult Bird (2004), which provides comprehensive coverage of this complex issue.

Effect size

Most psychological journals require that authors quote *effect size* alongside the statement of whether the result is significant. If we are undertaking research into the effectiveness of a new form of psychological treatment for depression, then we will not only want to know whether the new form of treatment is more effective than the old, but also *how much* more effective the new treatment is. This is the role of a measure of effect size; it tells us how big an effect we can expect from an intervention, treatment, manipulation of an independent variable or difference between groups.

Effect sizes are measured and quoted using a variety of scales. The most basic, and sometimes most useful, measure of effect size is a raw difference of means expressed in the same units used to measure the dependent variable. For example, when reporting the results of an intervention for children with reading difficulties, we could report that the mean difference between the treated and untreated group was 8.2 points on a standardised test of reading ability. Researchers familiar with this test of reading ability will be able to determine whether this is a large, medium or small effect size and thus whether the intervention is worthwhile.

Sometimes, it is not very useful to express effect size in the units used to measure the dependent variable. For example, suppose a researcher measures how long it takes a group of elderly and a group of young participants to memorise a piece of text. The dependent variable is time measured in minutes, but the absolute time taken will depend on the passage selected and is therefore rather arbitrary and difficult to interpret. The most widely adopted solution in cases like this is to standardise the effect size measure by expressing it in standard deviation units, a procedure advocated by Cohen (1988). One such measure, called Cohen's *d*, tells us how big the difference in the means is relative to the standard deviation of the scores. Cohen (1988) suggested a classification for effect sizes using this measure. He suggested that an effect size of 0.2 should be regarded as 'small', 0.5 should be regarded as a 'medium' sized effect, and an effect size of 0.8 should be regarded as 'large'. It is important to realise that there is nothing special about these values and the labels attached to them – this is merely the naming convention suggested by Cohen.

Effect size measures, like confidence intervals, are a way of providing the reader with more meaningful information. There are several different measures of effect sizes in addition to Cohen's *d*. We show you how to obtain a measure of effect size in each chapter covering an inferential statistical test.

Statistical power

The power of an inferential statistical procedure is the probability that it will yield statistically significant results. Power is the ability of a procedure to accurately discriminate between situations where the null hypothesis is true and situations where the null hypothesis is false. Statistical power is influenced by several factors, including the effect size (see above) and the sample size (usually the number of participants tested). If we are hoping to find statistically significant evidence for a small effect, then we will need to test a large number of participants. It is possible to calculate, for a given effect size, how many participants we will need in order to have a good chance of achieving statistical significance. Cohen (1988) suggests that, in order to avoid wasting their own time and that of their participants, experimenters should aim to achieve a power of 0.8. That is, we should design our experiments so that we have at least an 80% chance of obtaining a significant result. For this reason, it is good practice to estimate the power that a particular design will achieve, and how many participants will be needed, to have a particular probability of revealing a significant effect, should there be one. Many research funding bodies will only consider applications that include this type of power calculation.

There is another reason to calculate the power of a given design. If we fail to obtain a significant result, there are two possible explanations. It could be that the null hypothesis is true – that is, that there is no difference or no association. Alternatively, it could be that there is a difference or an association but that we failed to detect it because we had insufficient statistical power. Unless you know about the power of your design, there is no way you can distinguish between these two alternatives. However, if you know that your design had a power of about 0.8 to detect a small effect size ($d = 0.2$) and you have not found a significant effect, then you know with a probability of 0.8 that *either* there is no effect *or* if there is an effect, it is very small (d is less than 0.2). Thus, there is only a relatively small probability that there is an effect greater than 0.2, which you did not find.

Practical equivalence of two samples

In advance of undertaking our research, we might decide that we are only interested in an effect that exceeds a certain effect size. For example, if comparing two treatments for depression, we might decide that, given the additional 'costs' associated with our new treatment, we are only interested in an effect size of at least $d = 0.15$. In this situation, we have decided, in advance, that an effect size of less than 0.15 is 'trivial' and that two treatments that differ by less than this amount are of *practical equivalence*. Given this, if our power was 0.8 to detect an effect of size 0.15, then we can confidently conclude, if we fail to find an effect size of at least 0.15, that there is no practical difference between the two treatments. If, on the other hand, the statistical power of our design to detect such a small effect was low, say 0.5, then we should conclude that the issue of whether this new treatment is worthwhile is still undecided (and we should chastise ourselves for having conducted such an important piece of research with such low statistical power!).

Statistical power calculations can appear daunting because they involve the interrelationship between four variables: the statistical power of the design, the sample size, the criterion p value and the effect size. However, there are several specialist software packages available to undertake these calculations for you. We particularly recommend a piece of software called G*Power, which can be downloaded free from www.gpower.hhu.de.

CHAPTER 1

Statistical power and SPSS

As with confidence intervals, recent editions of SPSS have increased the availability of measures of power. For example, measures of 'Observed power' are now available from the 'Options' dialogue box for the ANOVA, ANCOVA and MANOVA routines. Where available, users may like to incorporate this additional information into their research reports.

Section 2 provides a guide to the tests covered in this book, and we then move on to describing SPSS.

Section 2: GUIDE TO THE STATISTICAL TESTS COVERED

Choosing the correct statistical procedures

SPSS will not tell you which descriptive statistic/s you should use to describe your data, or which inferential statistic to use to test your hypothesis. Broadly speaking, you need to consider the nature of the hypothesis being tested, the method and/or experimental design employed, the number of variables manipulated and/or measured, and the type of data collected.

Most of the inferential statistical tests covered in this book are *parametric tests*, and these are inferential tests that have greater statistical power. However, their use is limited to situations where the data meet certain requirements, including the following:

1. The data are measured using an interval or ratio scale.
2. The data are drawn from a population that is normally distributed.
3. The samples being compared are drawn from populations that have the same variance.

As we shall see, in some cases, SPSS includes information that you can use to assess whether the data violate any of these assumptions. Also, certain tests make additional or different assumptions from those listed above, and we alert you to these cases in the relevant chapters.

There are occasions in psychology when we collect data that do not satisfy all these requirements. *Nonparametric* tests are inferential tests that make very few assumptions about the data and in particular its distribution. However, they are less powerful than their parametric equivalents.

Below is a guide to the statistical tests covered in this book.

Chapter 5 Covers tests that look for a difference between two groups or two conditions (or levels) of the independent variable (IV) or factor	**One-sample *t*-test**: determines whether a mean is different from a set value **Independent *t*-test**: suitable for independent groups design **Paired *t*-test**: suitable for repeated measures or matched-subjects designs **Mann–Whitney test**: nonparametric equivalent to the independent *t*-test **Wilcoxon test**: nonparametric equivalent to the paired *t*-test

Chapter 6 Covers tests that look for a relationship between two variables	**Pearson's** r: used to test for correlation between two variables; assumes linear relationship **Spearman's** r_s: nonparametric equivalent to Pearson's r; used to test for correlation between two variables using ranked data
Chapter 7 Covers tests suitable for nominal data	**Multidimensional chi-square**: can be used as test of association or as a test of differences between independent groups **McNemar test**: used to test for differences on a dichotomous variable for related designs
Chapter 8 Covers tests of difference for experimental designs involving more than two levels of the IV and/or more than one IV	**ANOVA**: various versions (one-way; two-way etc.) used to analyse data from complex experimental designs involving independent groups, repeated measures or mixed designs **Kruskal–Wallis**: nonparametric test suitable for independent groups design involving one independent variable with three or more groups or conditions **Friedman**: nonparametric test suitable for repeated measures designs involving one independent variable with three or more conditions
Chapter 9 Covers a test looking at the relationship between several IVs and one dependent variable	**Multiple regression**: allows us to predict a score on one dependent variable (the criterion variable) from a number of independent (or predictor) variables
Chapter 10 Covers two tests related to ANOVA	**ANCOVA**: similar to ANOVA but controls for the effect of one or more covariates **MANOVA**: similar to ANOVA but used when the design includes more than one dependent variable
Chapter 11 Covers two tests looking at the relationship between several IVs and category membership	**Discriminant analysis**: similar to multiple regression but the dependent variable is a categorical (nominal) variable **Logistic regression**: similar to discriminant analysis but makes no assumptions about the distribution of the independent (predictor) variables
Chapter 12 Covers a test looking at the interrelationships among a large number of variables	**Factor analysis**: allows you to identify whether a factor structure underlies correlations between a number of variables and to extract the factors

Section 3: WORKING WITH SPSS

SPSS (originally Statistical Package for the Social Sciences) is an enormously powerful program for statistical analysis. SPSS has been around in various forms for over 40 years, and for a brief period was known as PASW, before being taken over by IBM in 2009. The package is now formally known as IBM SPSS Statistics®. Knowing how to use SPSS will allow you to perform a wide range of statistical analyses, which would otherwise require a great deal of complex calculation.

Data analysis using SPSS

There are three basic steps involved in data analysis using SPSS. First, enter the raw data and save as a data file. Second, select and specify the analysis you require. Third, examine the output produced by SPSS. These steps are illustrated below. The special windows used by SPSS to undertake these steps are described next.

Data Entry The data are entered into the Data Editor window and saved as a data file.	→	**Analysis** An appropriate analysis is selected and specified using the dialogue boxes.	→	**Inspection of Results** The results of the analysis (the output) are inspected in Viewer window. An additional analysis may then be undertaken and/or the results reported.

The different types of window used in SPSS

SPSS utilises several different window types. However, new users of SPSS only need to be familiar with two of these windows: the Data Editor window and the Viewer window. We will be using these two windows in this and the next chapter. The other window types are explained briefly here and will be covered in more detail elsewhere in the book.

The Data Editor window

The Data Editor window (or data window) is the window you see when you start up SPSS. This window looks rather like a spreadsheet and is used to enter all the data that is going to be analysed. You can think of this window as containing a table of all your raw data. We will examine this window in more detail when we start up SPSS.

The Viewer window

The Viewer window is used to display the results or output of your data analysis. For this reason we will sometimes refer to it as the 'Output window'. We will examine this window in more detail when we perform our first simple analysis in Chapter 2.

Some other windows used in SPSS

1. The Syntax Editor window is used to edit special program files called 'syntax files'. The use of this window is explained in Chapter 13 and will be of particular interest to more advanced users.
2. The Chart Editor window is used to edit standard (not interactive) charts or graphs. The use of this window is explained in Chapter 3.
3. The Pivot Table Editor window is used to edit the tables that SPSS uses to present the results of your analysis. The use of this window is explained in Chapter 13.

4. The Text Output Editor window is used to edit the text elements of the output shown in the Viewer window. The use of this window is described briefly in Chapter 13.

Section 4: STARTING SPSS

Start SPSS by double clicking on the icon on your desktop or by selecting **IBM SPSS Statistics 23** (or the latest version you have) from the applications on your machine.

> If you do not have an SPSS icon on your desktop then:
> For PC, click on the Start button at the bottom left-hand corner of the screen, then select **All Programs**. If the SPSS application is not visible in the list, it may be inside a folder; you can use the search field to find it.
> For Mac, select Finder, then Applications.

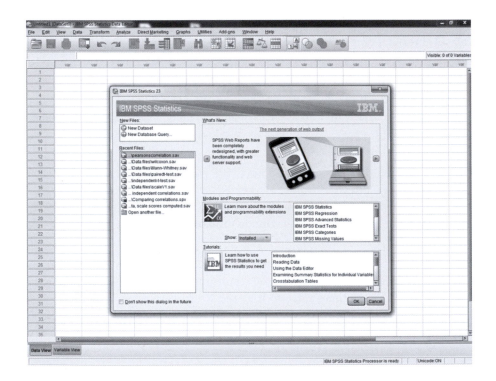

The image above is the opening screen for SPSS Statistics 23. Unless a previous user has switched it off, a box will appear in the centre of the opening screen, as shown above. This box is an example of a dialogue box. SPSS makes extensive use of dialogue boxes to allow you to control the program. This dialogue box is designed to help get new users started, but we aren't going to use it. Click on the Cancel button to close the dialogue box (see below) so that we can see the Data Editor window behind it.

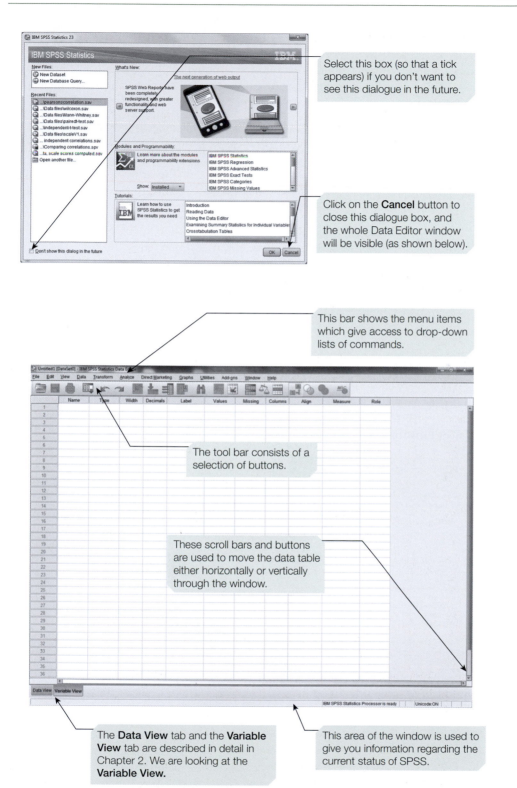

Select this box (so that a tick appears) if you don't want to see this dialogue in the future.

Click on the **Cancel** button to close this dialogue box, and the whole Data Editor window will be visible (as shown below).

This bar shows the menu items which give access to drop-down lists of commands.

The tool bar consists of a selection of buttons.

These scroll bars and buttons are used to move the data table either horizontally or vertically through the window.

The **Data View** tab and the **Variable View** tab are described in detail in Chapter 2. We are looking at the **Variable View.**

This area of the window is used to give you information regarding the current status of SPSS.

The menu and toolbars of the data editor windows

The menu and toolbars from the Data Editor window of SPSS Statistics 23 are shown below. The toolbar buttons duplicate functions that are also available from the menus. Some of the more useful buttons are explained below.

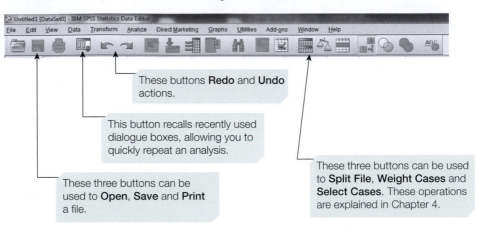

These buttons **Redo** and **Undo** actions.

This button recalls recently used dialogue boxes, allowing you to quickly repeat an analysis.

These three buttons can be used to **Split File**, **Weight Cases** and **Select Cases**. These operations are explained in Chapter 4.

These three buttons can be used to **Open**, **Save** and **Print** a file.

Section 5: HOW TO EXIT FROM SPSS

1. Click on the **File** menu item.
2. Select **Exit** from the **File** menu.

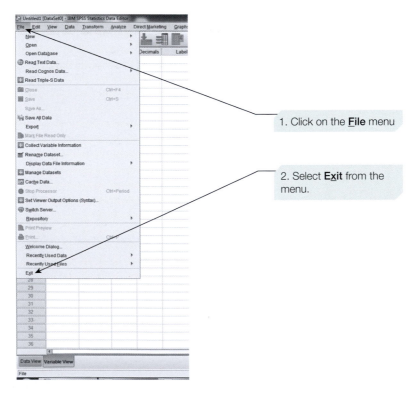

1. Click on the **File** menu

2. Select **Exit** from the menu.

If you have made any changes since you last saved the file, SPSS will ask you if you want to save the file before you exit (see below).

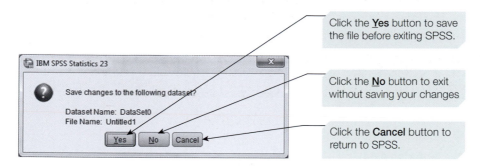

Click the **Yes** button to save the file before exiting SPSS.

Click the **No** button to exit without saving your changes

Click the **Cancel** button to return to SPSS.

Summary

- This chapter provided an overview of some of the statistical concepts you need to understand when using SPSS, and introduced you to SPSS.

- Section 2 gave an overview of the statistical procedures covered in detail in Chapters 5–12. Section 3 outlined the SPSS windows, and Sections 4 and 5 showed you how to start and exit from SPSS.

- Chapter 2 will cover how to enter data into SPSS.

- Chapter 3 will show how to explore your data.

- Chapter 4 will demonstrate different ways of manipulating your data, for example to create new variables.

2 Data entry in SPSS

In this chapter

- The Data Editor window
- Defining a variable in SPSS
- Entering data
- Saving a data file
- Opening a data file
- Data entry exercises
- Answers to data entry exercises
- Checking and cleaning data files

SPSS for Psychologists online
Visit he.palgrave.com/psychology/brace for data sets, online tutorials and exercises.

Section 1: THE DATA EDITOR WINDOW

What is the Data Editor window?

- The Data Editor is the active window when you start SPSS. It is used to record all the data we want to analyse.

- It has two views: the Variable View and the Data View.

- The Variable View allows us to name each column in the Data table and specify what sort of values the column will contain.

- The Data View contains a table with a large number of cells in rows and columns. The table can be very large with only a small part of it visible, in which case use the scroll bars on the edges of the window to move round the table.

- In psychology, we almost always enter data in the same way. Normally, each row represents an individual participant and each column represents a variable.

The arrangement of the data in the Data Editor window

The precise way that the data are entered in the Data Editor window is critical and will depend, in part, on the details of your study. If you are entering data from an experiment, then you need to consider the design employed. In an independent groups design, each participant will provide one measure of performance. In addition, you will need to indicate which of your experimental groups each participant was assigned to. Thus, the most basic independent groups design will require that you use one column of your data table to record which group your participant was in, and a second column to record that participant's score. By comparison, in a repeated measures design, each participant's performance will be assessed several times. Thus, for each participant you will need several variables to record the performance of the participant under each condition.

> In SPSS, the word 'variable' means a column in the data table; it does not have the same meaning as it does in experimental design. For example, in a repeated measures design where there are two levels of the independent variable, we use two columns in the data table to record the values for the single dependent variable.

Section 2: DEFINING A VARIABLE IN SPSS

Our first job is to set up the data file with important information about each of our variables. This process of defining the variables is described here.

The Data View and Variable View

If you look at the bottom left-hand corner of the Data Editor window, you will notice two 'tabs'. One tab is labelled 'Data View' and the other 'Variable View'. You can think of these as the index tabs for two different pages of information. When you first enter the Data Editor window, you will probably find the Variable View tab selected. If you click on the Data View tab, you will be presented with the empty data table. If you click on the Variable View tab, a different screen of information will be displayed. These two views are illustrated below.

The Data View is the screen you will use when entering your data into SPSS. At present, this view shows an empty data table in which each of the variables (columns) is labelled 'var'. Before you can enter your data into this data table, you must set up each variable ready to receive the data. The first thing SPSS needs to know is the name of each of your variables; these names will be inserted at the top of the columns of the data table. In addition, you need to give SPSS other important information about each variable. This process of defining the variables is undertaken in the Variable View. If you click on the Variable View tab, you will notice that in this view the columns are headed **Name**, **Type**, **Width**, **Decimals** etc. In the Variable View of the data table, the variables are arranged down the side of the table and each column gives information about a variable. For example, in the column headed **Name** we will provide the name of each variable, in the **Type** column we are going to tell SPSS what type of variable this is and so on.

> In the Data View of the Data Editor window, each row of the data table represents data from one case and each column contains data from one variable. However, in the Variable View, the columns and rows are used differently. In this view, each row gives information about one variable. Don't let this confuse you; remember, once you have set up all your variables and are ready to enter your data, you will work in the Data View where a row is a case (usually a participant) and a column is a variable.

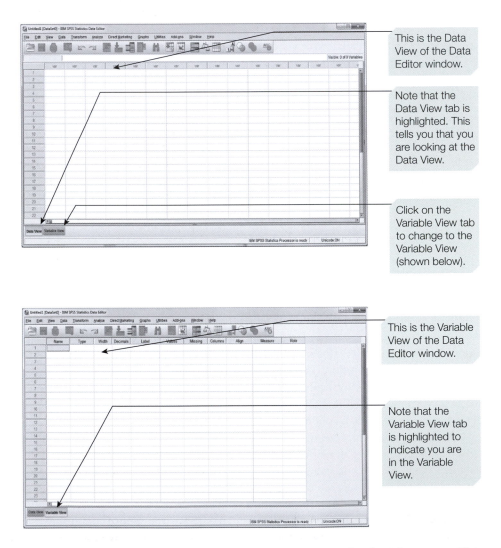

This is the Data View of the Data Editor window.

Note that the Data View tab is highlighted. This tells you that you are looking at the Data View.

Click on the Variable View tab to change to the Variable View (shown below).

This is the Variable View of the Data Editor window.

Note that the Variable View tab is highlighted to indicate you are in the Variable View.

Henceforth, when we refer to 'the Data Editor window' without specifying which view, we will be referring to the Data View.

Setting up your variables

If you are not already in the Variable View of the Data Editor, click on the Variable View tab now. We will now use this view to set up each of the variables we need.

> An alternative way to switch from the Data View to the Variable View is to double-click on the grey header (which will probably be labelled 'var') at the top of the column you wish to define. This will take you to the appropriate row of the Variable View.

Variable name

The first thing we need to do is to give the variable a meaningful name. Type the name of your first variable into the first row of the **Name** column. You should choose a variable name that makes sense to you and which you are not likely to forget. Students often use the variable name 'score'. This is not a good choice as it tells us almost nothing about the variable. Examples of more useful variable names might include 'memscore' (for participants' scores in a memory experiment), 'introver' (a participant's introversion score), 'sex' or 'famfaces' (the number of famous faces named by a participant). Your variable name can be any length, but we suggest you keep it fairly short so it is easy to read. Two points about variable names: they must start with a letter of the alphabet (i.e. not a number); and they cannot contain spaces or some special characters such as colons, semicolons, hyphens or commas (full stops, the @, #, $ and _ characters are allowed). If you enter an invalid variable name, SPSS will warn you when you try to move from the **Name** column.

> The underscore character (_) can be used in place of spaces in variable names. For example, the name 'Q1_1' might be used for the scores from Question 1 Part 1.

We have named the first variable 'Sex', because we are going to use this variable to code the sex of our participants.

Once you have entered the variable name, use either the mouse (point and click) or the tab key to move to the next column of the table. As you move the cursor, several of the other columns of the table will be filled with either words or numbers. These are the default settings for the variable 'Sex'. You can leave these settings as they are, or you can change some or all of them before moving on to define your next variable. Below we explain each of the settings and how to adjust them.

Variable type

The second column in the Variable View table is headed **Type**. SPSS can handle variables of several different types. For example, variables can be numeric (containing numbers) or string (containing letters) or even dates. The **Type** column is used to indicate what type each variable is. The **Type** will now be set to **Numeric** (unless the default settings have been changed on your copy of SPSS). If you want to change the variable type, click on the word **Numeric**, and then click on the button that appears in the cell. This will call up the **Variable Type** dialogue box (see below).

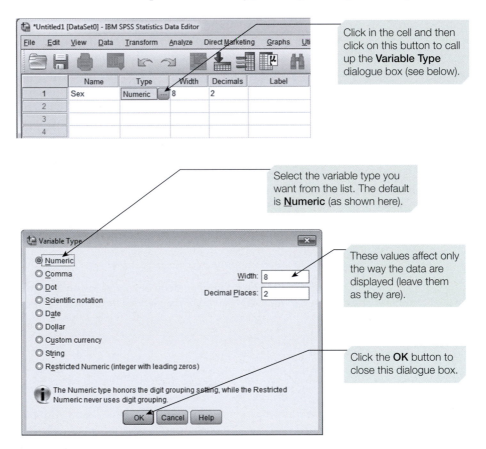

Click in the cell and then click on this button to call up the **Variable Type** dialogue box (see below).

Select the variable type you want from the list. The default is **Numeric** (as shown here).

These values affect only the way the data are displayed (leave them as they are).

Click the **OK** button to close this dialogue box.

We strongly recommend that, until you are an experienced user, you only use numeric variables. It is easy to use numbers to represent categories and this will save you trouble later (e.g. you can use the numbers 1 and 2 rather than 'm' and 'f' to record the sex of your participants). Until you are a much more experienced SPSS user, you are unlikely to need to use any of the other variable types.

As far as possible, avoid using string variables in SPSS – if you ignore this advice, you will regret it later!

Variable width and decimal places

As we saw above, the **Variable Type** dialogue box allows you to set the <u>**Width**</u> and **Decimal <u>Places</u>** of the variable (see above). Alternatively, these settings can be changed in the third and fourth columns of the Variable View (see below).

These settings adjust the width of the column and the number of decimal places used to display the variable in the Data Editor. These settings do not affect the way the value is stored or the number of decimal places used in statistical calculations. Changing decimal places, however, does affect the number of decimal places shown in SPSS output. With numeric data, the default settings are for a total <u>**Width**</u> of 8 with 2 **Decimal <u>Places</u>** (e.g. 12345.78). If you attempt to input a data value that will not fit into the width, then SPSS will round it in order to display the value. However, the actual value you entered is stored by SPSS and used in all calculations. One effect of this is that unless you set **Decimal <u>Places</u>** to zero, all values, even integers (whole numbers without decimal places) will be displayed with 2 decimal places. Thus, if you enter a value of '2' in the Data Editor window, SPSS will display '2.00'. This might look a little untidy, but is of little consequence and it is probably not worth altering these settings to stop this happening.

	Name	Type	Width	Decimals	Label
1	Sex	Numeric	8	2	
2					
3					
4					

*Untitled1 [DataSet0] - IBM SPSS Statistics Data Editor
File   Edit   View   Data   Transform   Analyze   Direct Marketing   Graphs

You can change the variable **Width** and number of **Decimals** places by changing these values. However, this only alters the look of the table.

You can probably leave the **Type**, **Width** and **Decimals** settings at their default values.

Variable label

The fifth column in the Variable View table is headed **Label**. This column is used to enter a variable label.

A variable label is simply a phrase associated with the variable name and which helps you to remember what data this variable contains. If you have called a variable something like 'Sex', then you probably don't need to be reminded about what it is describing. If, however, you have a large number of variables, then variable labels can be useful. For example, if you are entering the data from a questionnaire, you might have a variable named 'q3relbef'. In this case a variable label might be invaluable, as it could remind you that this variable coded the responses to question 3 on your questionnaire, which asked about religious belief. You can type in any phrase using any characters that you like, but it is best to keep it fairly short. SPSS will not try to interpret this label; it will simply insert it into the output next to the appropriate variable name when you perform any analysis. It is also worth remembering that when you have to select variables for inclusion in an analysis, SPSS will list them by these variable labels, not the names. This is another reason to keep the labels short and meaningful. To add a variable label, type it in to the column **Label**.

> Variable labels are included in the output produced by SPSS. Although they are not essential, they act as a reminder about the variables and can be helpful when you are interpreting the output. We recommend you take the time to use them whenever appropriate.

Value labels

A value label is a label assigned to a particular value of a variable. You are most likely to use value labels for nominal or categorical variables. For example, we might want to use value labels to remind ourselves that, when entering values for the religion of our respondents, we used the codes: 1 = Buddhist; 2 = Christian; 3 = Hindu; 4 = Muslim; 5 = Other; 0 = Atheist.

A second use for value labels is with a grouping or independent variable. For example, you might want to compare the reaction time of participants who were tested under one of several different doses of alcohol. You could use a value label to remind yourself that group 1 received no alcohol, group 2 received 1 unit of alcohol and group 3 received 2 units. Value labels will be inserted into the SPSS output to remind you what these values mean.

Value labels are entered using the **Values** column of the Variable View table. At present, this column will probably contain the word **None**. Click the mouse on this cell, or use the tab key to move to this cell. As you do so, a button will appear at the right-hand side of the cell. Click on this button to call up the **Value Labels** dialogue box (see below).

> Value labels can be a great help when interpreting SPSS output. Although they are not essential, we recommend that you use them when appropriate. It would not be appropriate to add value labels to some variables. For example, you would not want to add a label to every possible value of a continuous variable such as reaction time. A good rule of thumb is that you should add value labels to all nominal variables and should consider adding them to ordinal variables. They are unlikely to be needed for interval or ratio variables.

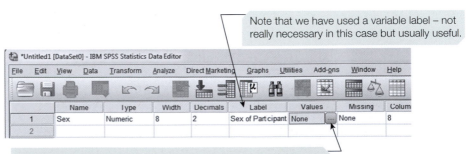

Note that we have used a variable label – not really necessary in this case but usually useful.

To add value labels, click in the **Values** cell, then click on this button. This will call up the **Value Labels** dialogue box (see below).

If you are using value labels, enter the value into the **Value** box, then enter the label for this value into the **Label** box.

Value Labels

Value Labels

Value: 2

Label: Female

Spelling...

1.00 = "Male"

Add

Change

Remove

OK   Cancel   Help

Then click on the **Add** button to add this value label to the list of labels for this variable. Repeat these steps to add additional values and labels.

When you have added all the values and labels for the variable, click on the **OK** button to close the dialogue box and return to the Variable View table.

Missing values

Sometimes you will not have a complete set of data. For example, some participants might decline to tell you their religion or their age, or you might lose or be unable to collect data from some participants, perhaps because of equipment failure. These gaps in the data table are known as 'missing values'.

When we have a missing value, we need to be able to tell SPSS that we do not have valid data for this variable for this participant. We do this by choosing a value that cannot normally occur for this variable. In the religion example above, we might choose to code religion as 9 when the participant does not state their religion. Thus, 9 is the missing value for the variable religion. The missing value can be different for each variable, but does not have to be. The important thing is that this value cannot normally occur for this variable. For age, you could use 99 (unless you are testing very old people). Alternatively, you can use a negative number (e.g. −9), assuming that negative values cannot occur for the variable you have measured.

Before you specify any missing values, the cell in the **Missing** column of the Variable View table will contain the word 'None'. To specify a missing value, click in the **Missing** column of the Variable View table. A button will appear at the right-hand end of the cell. Click on this button to call up the **Missing Values** dialogue box (see below).

Note that we can see the value labels we added in the previous step.

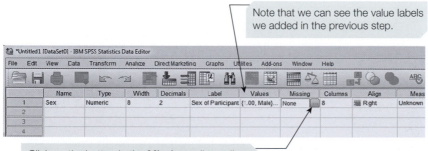

Click on the button in the **Missing** cell to call up the **Missing Values** dialogue box (see below).

Missing Values

○ No missing values
◉ Discrete missing values

[9] [   ] [   ]

○ Range plus one optional discrete missing value

Low: [   ]   High: [   ]

Discrete value: [   ]

[OK] [Cancel] [Help]

1. To include up to three different missing values, select this option then enter your missing value(s) in the box(es).

2. Click on the **OK** button to close the dialogue box and return to the Variable View table.

SPSS allows you to specify the missing values in several ways:

1. **No missing values**: This is the default setting for this dialogue box. If this option is selected, SPSS will treat all values for this variable as valid.

2. **Discrete missing values**: This option allows you to enter up to three discrete values. For example, 7, 9 and 11 could all be set as missing values by selecting this option and entering the values in the three boxes. If you choose to use only one missing value to code your missing data, enter it into the first of the three boxes (as we've done above).

3. **Range plus one optional discrete missing value**: This option allows you to indicate that a range of values is being used as missing values. For example, selecting this option and entering the values 7 and 11 in the **Low** and **High** value boxes would instruct SPSS to treat the values 7, 8, 9, 10 and 11 as missing values. If, in addition to this range of values, the value 0 was typed into the **Discrete value** box, then SPSS would treat the values 7, 8, 9, 10, 11 and 0 as missing.

You should always assign at least one missing value. In most cases this is all you will need, but occasionally we might want to differentiate between several different types of missing data. For example, by assigning different missing values we could distinguish between an unanswered question, an indecipherable answer and an item that was not applicable to this participant.

Select either the **Discrete missing values** or the **Range plus one optional discrete missing value option**, and enter the value(s) you have chosen to represent missing values. If you have only one missing value, enter it into the first of the **Discrete missing values** boxes. Now click on the **OK** button to return to the Variable View table.

> The **Missing Values** dialogue box does not allow you to label the missing values. Once you have entered them, however, you can label them in the **Value Labels** dialogue box if you wish. For example, you could add labels to show that 9 = unanswered; 10 = illegible.

Column format

The next column of the Variable View table is labelled **Columns**. This entry in the table is used to specify the width of the column that the variable occupies in the Data

View table of the Data Editor window. You can leave this value at its default setting unless you want to change the appearance of the Data View table. You may, for example, want to fit more columns onto the screen in order to see more variables without having to scroll. In this case you could reduce the width of each column. To adjust the settings, click on the cell and then use the up and down buttons that will appear at the right-hand end of the cell to adjust the value. You can look at the effect of the change you have made by switching to the Data View.

> You can more easily change the width of a column by dragging it with the mouse. Switch to the Data View and then move the mouse to the top row of the table and hover over the border between two columns. The mouse pointer will change to a double-headed arrow. You can now click and drag to adjust the width of the column. The changes you make here will be reflected in the Variable View settings.

Column alignment

The column of the Variable View labelled **Align** allows you to specify the alignment of the text within the cells of the Data View table. This setting has no effect on the operation of SPSS and only changes the appearance of the Data View table. The default setting is right alignment, in which the decimal points of the values in the column are lined up. In left alignment, the values are flush to the left-hand end of the cell. In centre alignment, the values are centred in the cell (and thus the decimal points will not necessarily line up).

If you wish to change the column alignment, click in the **Align** cell and then click on the menu button that will appear in the cell and select the required alignment from the drop-down list (see below).

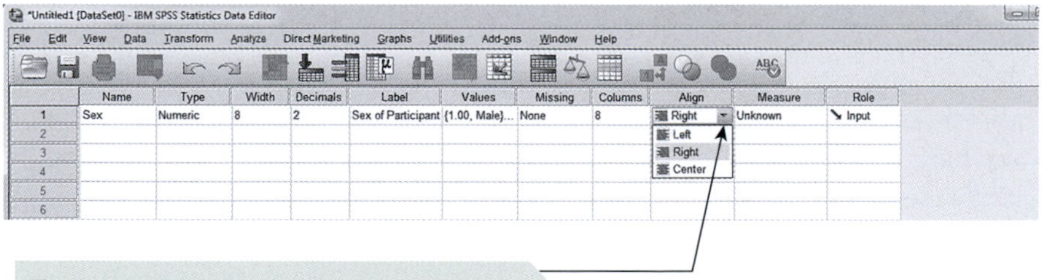

To change the column alignment, click on this button and select from the drop-down list.

Measure

The next column of the Variable View table is labelled **Measure.** This column is used to specify the level of measurement for the variable. SPSS offers three options: **Nominal, Ordinal** and **Scale.** Psychologists usually distinguish four levels of measurement: nominal, ordinal, interval and ratio (see Chapter 1, Section 1). SPSS does not distinguish between interval and ratio data and uses the term **Scale** to describe a variable measured using either of these levels of measurement.

To set the measurement option, click in the **Measure** cell of the Variable View table and then click on the button that appears in the cell and select from the drop-down list (see below). The relevant icons will appear in the SPSS dialogue boxes as a reminder of the level of measurement of this variable.

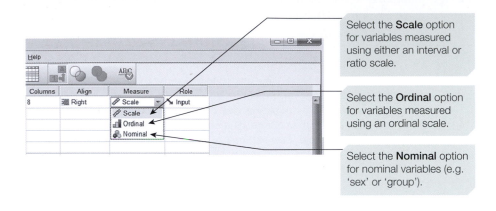

Select the **Scale** option for variables measured using either an interval or ratio scale.

Select the **Ordinal** option for variables measured using an ordinal scale.

Select the **Nominal** option for nominal variables (e.g. 'sex' or 'group').

If you open a data file created using an earlier version of SPSS or some other program, the **Measure** will be set for you – variables with value labels will be set as **Nominal**, while variables with only a small number of values will be set as **Ordinal**. All other variables will be set as **Scale**.

Role

The final column of the Variable View table is called **Role**. This is a fairly recent addition to SPSS, and is intended to help users who are undertaking complex analyses. The idea is that you can identify a group of variables as having a particular role in your analysis. For example, you might have several variables that are going to be used as dependent variables and others that will be independent variables. If you indicate this through the **Role** setting, these variables will be automatically assigned when you come to undertake some kinds of analyses. The six **Role** options are **Input** (for independent variables), **Target** (for dependent variables), **Both** (for variables that may take on either role), **None** (for variables with no role set), **Partition** (used to divide a data set so different parts can be used for different purposes) and **Split** (used by other analysis packages). In practice, this is not likely to be useful for the novice user, and we recommend that you leave **Role** at its default setting of Input.

Remember, for most variables, you can accept most of the default settings. In practice, all you need to do is to enter a variable name, set the level of measurement and, if appropriate, add variable labels and value labels.

CHAPTER 2

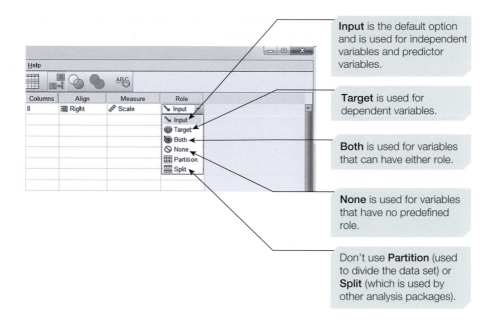

Input is the default option and is used for independent variables and predictor variables.

Target is used for dependent variables.

Both is used for variables that can have either role.

None is used for variables that have no predefined role.

Don't use **Partition** (used to divide the data set) or **Split** (which is used by other analysis packages).

Check your settings

Once you have completed the definition of your first variable, switch to the Data View by clicking on the Data View tab at the bottom left-hand corner of the table. You will now see the name of your new variable appear at the top of the appropriate column of the Data Editor window (see below). If you changed the column width and/or alignment, you will see the effect of these changes.

Now switch back to the Variable View and repeat this process for each of the variables required for your data file.

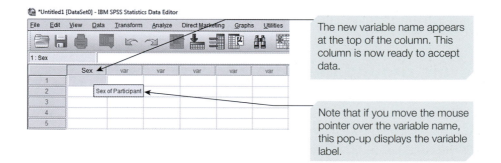

The new variable name appears at the top of the column. This column is now ready to accept data.

Note that if you move the mouse pointer over the variable name, this pop-up displays the variable label.

Copying variable settings

It is easy to copy the settings from one variable and 'paste' these onto one or more new variables.

Suppose, for example, that you have administered a questionnaire that contains 20 items. Each item consists of a printed statement to which the participant is asked to respond by choosing from one of several options, such as 'Strongly Disagree', 'Disagree', 'Neither Agree or Disagree', 'Agree', and 'Strongly Agree'. In our SPSS data table, each question will be represented by a variable, which we might call Q1, Q2 etc. For each of these variables, it would be useful to enter the value labels 1 = 'Strongly Disagree', 2 = 'Disagree' and so on. This would be rather time-consuming. However, if we enter these value labels for the first variable, we can then move the cursor to the Values cell of the Variable View table and select Copy from the Edit menu (or right click and select Copy). If we now click in the cell (or select the range of cells) we want to copy these labels to, and select Paste from the Edit menu (or right click and select Paste), the value labels will be copied to all the selected cells.

Section 3: ENTERING DATA

A first data entry exercise

As a data entry exercise, we will enter the data from a simple study in which we have recorded the sex (coded as 1 = Male, 2 = Female), the age and the memory score (number of words recalled from a list of 20).

Before we can enter these data, we need to define the three variables to be used (see the previous section for details of how to define a variable). Remember that as sex is a nominal variable, we should use value labels to remind ourselves what the values 1 and 2 represent. Once the three variables have been defined, we can begin entering the data. You can copy the data for the first five participants from the screenshot shown below.

Click on the top left-hand cell of the table (ensure that you are at the top left-hand corner of the window by checking the scroll bars). This cell will become highlighted (it will have a bold border). Any number you now type will appear in the bar above the variable names at the top of the window. If you press the Enter key or the Tab key, or use the mouse or cursor keys (up, down, left, and right arrows) to move to another cell, this number will be inserted into the cell.

Moving around the Data Editor window

 Check that you are in Data View before trying to enter data.

You can use either the mouse or the cursor keys to move round the data table. Alternatively, you can press the Enter key to move down to the next participant for the current variable, or the Tab key to move across to the next variable for the current participant.

It is best to enter the data one participant at a time, working across the data table. For example, you should enter the sex, age and memory score for the first participant in row one, then for the second participant in row two and so on. If you enter the data a column at a time working down the columns (e.g. the sex of all the participants

This shows that a value is currently being entered for the fifth participant in the column 'MemScore'.

This value represents the memory score for the fifth participant. As you type in the number, it appears both here and in the cell that was highlighted.

These are the row or case numbers. Normally, you can think of them as participant numbers.

first, then their ages etc.), you may make a mistake and such an error is likely to result in the data from one participant being assigned to another participant.

Once you have entered all your data into the data table, you should carefully check that you have entered it correctly. Cross-checking the data file against the original record of the data is an important stage in the process of analysis. Either cross-check the original records against the data on the screen, or against a printout of the data (see Chapter 13, Section 5 for details of how to print a copy of your data).

> You may accidentally enter an empty row of data, which will appear as a row of cells filled with dots. If this has happened, it is worth taking the time to remove the blank line(s) as SPSS will interpret each blank line as a participant for whom you have no data. Thus, SPSS will tell you it has more cases than you expect. To delete the blank case, click on the case number associated with the extra row; the case will become highlighted. Now either press the delete key, or right click and select **Clear**.

Sometimes, new SPSS users panic that they have 'lost' their data because they cannot see it on the screen. This is often because the data have scrolled out of view. Check that the scroll bars are set to the top left-hand corner of the window.

The value labels button

If you have assigned value labels to one or more of your variables, you can choose whether you want SPSS to display the values you enter, or the labels associated with the values. For example, in this file, we have assigned the value labels 'Male' and 'Female' to the values 1 and 2 of the variable 'Sex'. SPSS can either display the values (i.e. the numerals '1' or '2') or the labels 'Male' or 'Female'. Clicking on the **Value Labels** button on the toolbar of the Data Editor window will toggle between these two display states (see below). This option affects only the way the data are displayed in the Data Editor window, and not the way they are analysed.

Furthermore, if you select to display the variable labels rather than the data values, then SPSS will help with the data entry process by providing a drop-down list of possible values. See below to see how this works.

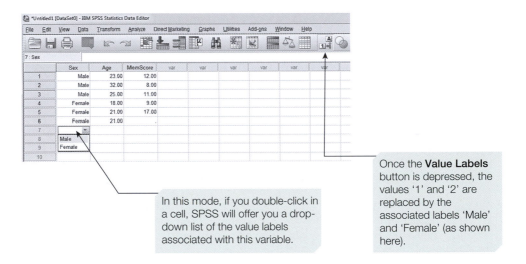

Click on the **Value Labels** button to toggle between displaying the values entered (as shown here) and the associated labels (see below).

In this mode, if you double-click in a cell, SPSS will offer you a drop-down list of the value labels associated with this variable.

Once the **Value Labels** button is depressed, the values '1' and '2' are replaced by the associated labels 'Male' and 'Female' (as shown here).

When you have finished entering your data and have carefully checked it, you should save a copy of the data file. We describe how to save the data file in Section 4.

It is possible to have several data files open at a time; however, this can become confusing, so we recommend that you work with just one data file until you have become familiar with SPSS.

Section 4: SAVING A DATA FILE

You will have spent a lot of time entering your data, so remember to save the data file as soon as you have checked it carefully. If you are entering a large amount of data, it is a good idea to save the file every few minutes.

To save the data to a file

Click on the menu item **File** at the top of the screen. Now click on either **Save** or **Save As**.

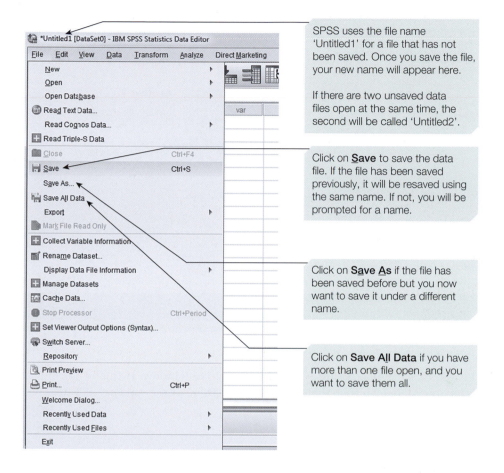

SPSS uses the file name 'Untitled1' for a file that has not been saved. Once you save the file, your new name will appear here.

If there are two unsaved data files open at the same time, the second will be called 'Untitled2'.

Click on **Save** to save the data file. If the file has been saved previously, it will be resaved using the same name. If not, you will be prompted for a name.

Click on **Save As** if the file has been saved before but you now want to save it under a different name.

Click on **Save All Data** if you have more than one file open, and you want to save them all.

Select **Save** to resave the file using the existing name. The resaved file will replace the old version. If the file has not been saved previously, or if you click on **Save As**, you will be presented with the **Save Data As** dialogue box (see below).

Type the name for the file into the **File name:** box. The file name you choose should be reminiscent of the study from which the data originated (for example, 'DataEntryPractice'). You should not use a full stop in the file name and should not attach a suffix to the file name. By default, SPSS will attach the suffix '.sav' to any name you enter. Do not change this suffix, or SPSS might not recognise the file as a data file. Before you click the **Save** button, check which drive and which directory the file is going to be saved to. You may want to save the file to a different drive, or to a USB stick or cloud drive.

We are currently in the folder called 'Data Sets'.

These buttons allow you to move around in folders, create new folders, and change the way the file information is displayed.

Click here and then type your chosen file name.

By default, the file will be saved as an SPSS data file with the suffix '.sav' added to the end of the file name. Don't change this unless you are sure you want to save in some other format, such as Excel.

Section 5: OPENING A DATA FILE

To open a data file, follow the instructions below:

1. Ensure that the Data Editor window is the active window. If this is not the case, select the SPSS icon from the taskbar at the bottom of the screen.

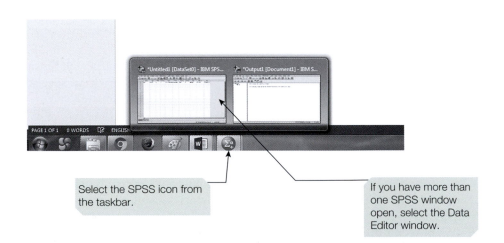

Select the SPSS icon from the taskbar.

If you have more than one SPSS window open, select the Data Editor window.

2. To open a different data file, click on the **File** menu (illustrated on the next page).

3. Select **Open**.

4. Select **Data**. The Open File dialogue box will now appear (see the next page).

2. Click on the **File** menu.

3. Select **Open**.

4. Choose **Data**.

*Untitled1 [DataSet0] - IBM SPSS Statistics Data Editor

File   Edit   View   Data   Transform   Analyze   Direct Marketing   Graphs

New
Open
Open Database
Read Text Data...
Read Cognos Data...
Read Triple-S Data
Close   Ctrl+F4
Save   Ctrl+S
Save As...
Save All Data
Export
Mark File Read Only
Collect Variable Information
Rename Dataset...
Display Data File Information
Manage Datasets
Cache Data...
Stop Processor   Ctrl+Period
Set Viewer Output Options (Syntax)...
Switch Server

Project
Data...
Internet Data
Syntax...
Output...
Script...

Open Data

Look in: DATA SETS

1-Way Between-Subjects Anova.sav   Chi-Square.sav
1-Way Within-Subjects Anova.sav   PracticeEntry.sav
2-Way Between-Subjects Anova.sav
2-Way Within-Subjects Anova.sav
3-Way Mixed Anova.sav
3-Way Within-Subjects Anova.sav
Ancova.sav
Chapter 2 Final Example.sav
Chapter 2 Second Example.sav

File name:

Files of type: SPSS Statistics (*.sav)

Encoding:

Minimize string widths based on observed values

Retrieve File From Repository...

Open
Paste
Cancel
Help

5. Move to the correct folder either using this drop-down list or by selecting the folder from the list below.

6. Click on the name of the file and then click the **Open** button. Alternatively, double-click the name of the file to open.

You can choose which type of file to show in the box above. By default, only SPSS data files will be shown.

SPSS can read and write files of various formats, including Excel spreadsheet files. In Chapter 13 we describe how to import Excel spreadsheets into SPSS and how to save SPSS data files as Excel spreadsheets.

> If the file you are looking for has a suffix other than '.sav', SPSS will not recognise it as a data file and will not display it in the dialogue box. If you can't find the file you are looking for, and think that it may have been saved with some other file name suffix, click on the button at the right-hand end of the **Files of type** box and select 'All files (*.*)' from the list of file types offered. All the files in the current directory, regardless of type or suffix name, will now be displayed in the dialogue box. If you find that your data file was saved with some other suffix, use Windows Folders to make a copy and change the suffix to '.sav'.

Section 6: DATA ENTRY EXERCISES

In this section, we are going to practise entering data from studies with two different types of experimental design. Later in this chapter and in subsequent chapters we will use these data files to demonstrate other procedures. Take the time to complete these exercises, as they will help you to appreciate the way that the design employed in a study influences the shape of the data file. When you have completed these two data files, compare them to the files we made, which are shown in Section 7.

Data from an independent groups design

As explained in Chapter 1, in the independent groups design, we are comparing the performance of two or more groups of different participants. In the example below, we have used this design to investigate the effect of a mnemonic instruction given to a group of participants before they were asked to learn a total of 20 words. The dependent variable was the number of words correctly recalled.

RODENTS IN SPACE: A SIMPLE MEMORY EXPERIMENT

Twenty-one first-year undergraduates participated in a simple memory experiment designed to investigate the effect of a mnemonic strategy on memory for paired words. The participants were randomly divided into two groups. All participants were given two minutes to memorise a list of 20 words presented in pairs. All the participants were told to memorise the words, but those in the mnemonic instruction group were advised to try to form a mental image to link the two words in a pair (e.g. for the word pair Rocket – Hamster, a participant might imagine a small furry rodent being fired into outer space). The participants in the other group, the non-mnemonic group, were not given this instruction. After learning the words for two minutes, the participants were then required to complete some simple mental arithmetic problems for two minutes. Finally, all participants tried to recall the words in any order. The number of words correctly recalled was recorded. The data are summarised below.

Memory scores (out of 20) for the mnemonic instruction group:

> 20, 18, 14, 18, 17, 11, 20, 18, 20, 19, 20

Memory scores (out of 20) for the non-mnemonic group:

> 10, 20, 12, 9, 14, 15, 16, 14, 19, 12

Using these data, attempt to do the following:

1. Set up an SPSS data file to record these data. Give appropriate names to the variables you are using.
2. Apply value and variable labels where appropriate.

3. Enter and check the data, then save the file using an appropriate file name.

4. Ensure that you can reopen the file.

5. Compare the data file you have constructed to the one illustrated in Section 7.

Data from a repeated measures design

In a repeated measures design, every participant is exposed to each condition and thus contributes a data point from each level of the independent variable. This will be reflected in the structure of the data file, which will have a column for each level of the independent variable. In the example below, we have used this experimental design to investigate mental representation.

COMPARING MENTAL IMAGES

If you ask someone the question 'How many windows are there in the front of your home?', most people will report that they attempt to answer the question by 'inspecting' a mental image of their house. Does this mean that we store information in the form of mental images? Some psychologists think not, arguing that information is actually stored in a more abstract form and that our experience of inspecting mental images is illusory. However, several lines of evidence support the idea that we are able to manipulate information utilising a form of representation that shares many qualities with mental images. This experiment is modelled on one such line of evidence.

Imagine you were asked to decide whether or not a lion was bigger than a wolf. You could make your decision by recalling abstract information about the average size of each animal. Alternatively, you could form a mental image of these two animals standing side by side and decide which was the taller. If you adopted the mental imagery approach, then you might expect the decision to take longer when the two animals were of a similar size than when they were of very different sizes. If the decision were based on a more abstract form of representation, then you would expect the relative size of the animals to have no impact on the speed of the decision. Thus, if it takes longer to compare the size of two similar sized animals than two dissimilar sized animals, this will offer some support for the idea that these decisions are based on the manipulation of image-like forms of mental representation.

In our experiment, each of 16 participants undertook 20 trials. In each trial, the participant was presented with a pair of animal names and had to decide as quickly as possible which animal was the largest. The dependent variable was the time to make this decision (in milliseconds – ms). For half of the trials the difference in size between the two animals was large (e.g. Mosquito – Elephant), and for the other half of the trials the difference in size was small (e.g. Horse – Zebra). In the data table on the next page, we have recorded each participant's mean decision time (in ms) for the large and small difference trials.

Participant	Large diff.	Small diff.
1	936	878
2	923	1005
3	896	1010
4	1241	1365
5	1278	1422
6	871	1198
7	1360	1576
8	733	896
9	941	1573
10	1077	1261
11	1438	2237
12	1099	1325
13	1253	1591
14	1930	2742
15	1260	1357
16	1271	1963

1. Set up an SPSS data file to record these data. Give appropriate names to the variables you are using.
2. Apply value and variable labels where appropriate.
3. Enter and check the data, then save the file to disk using an appropriate file name.
4. Ensure that you can reopen the file.
5. Compare the data file you have constructed to the one illustrated in Section 7.

Section 7: ANSWERS TO DATA ENTRY EXERCISES

A data file for an independent groups design

Below is a screenshot of the data file we constructed for this simple memory experiment. Your data table might not look identical, but should have the same basic characteristics. Note that there are two critical variables in this design. The first is a nominal variable (or grouping variable) that we have used to record whether the participant was in the Mnemonic or Non-mnemonic group. Thus, it indicates the level of the independent variable (or factor). The other critical variable is a ratio variable and has been used to record the dependent variable, the number of words each participant recalled. In addition to these two variables, we have also included a variable called 'Participant', which assigns a number to each participant. This is good practice. If you have the **Value Labels** button (on the toolbar) depressed, then the 'Condition' column will display value labels rather than values (i.e. Mnemonic or Non-mnemonic rather than 1 or 2).

*Untitled2 [DataSet1] - IBM SPSS Statistics Data Editor

File   Edit   View   Data   Transform   Analyze   Direct M

	Participant	Condition	NumWords
1	1.00	1	20.00
2	2.00	1	18.00
3	3.00	1	14.00
4	4.00	1	18.00
5	5.00	1	17.00
6	6.00	1	11.00
7	7.00	1	20.00
8	8.00	1	18.00
9	9.00	1	20.00
10	10.00	1	19.00
11	11.00	1	20.00
12	12.00	2	10.00
13	13.00	2	20.00
14	14.00	2	12.00
15	15.00	2	9.00
16	16.00	2	14.00
17	17.00	2	15.00
18	18.00	2	16.00
19	19.00	2	14.00
20	20.00	2	19.00
21	21.00	2	12.00

We have called this variable 'NumWords'. Being lazy, we have left the variable width as 8 with 2 decimal places.

We have used the name 'Condition' for this variable. Because it is a nominal variable, we have used value labels to show that the value 1 indicates the participant was in the mnemonic condition, and the value 2 that they were in the non-mnemonic condition (see screenshot of the Value Labels dialogue box below). We have set the variable width to 1 (with no decimal places) and the column width to 5 (neither of these changes are essential).

For this screenshot, we did not have the **Value Labels** button depressed; if it is depressed on your system, then your screen will show the value labels rather than the values.

We have included a variable called 'Participant', which gives each participant a number. This is not essential but is good practice; we will explain why later.

Value Labels

Value Labels

Value:

Label:

1.00 = "Mnemonic condition"
2.00 = "Non-menemonic condition"

Add

Change

Remove

Spelling...

OK   Cancel   Help

These are the value labels we used for the variable 'Condition'.

> Remember, the data file constructed for an experiment that employed an independent groups design will always require a nominal variable that is used to indicate the condition under which each participant was tested.

The data file for a repeated measures design

Below is a screenshot of the data file we constructed to record the data from our mental imagery experiment. Your data table might not look identical, but should have the same basic characteristics. As with the independent groups design, there are a total of three variables, but in this case two are used to record the performance of the participants when tested under a particular condition. As this is a repeated measures design, each participant was tested under both conditions, so we have two data points for each participant. In this design, there is no need for a nominal variable.

Compare this data file to the one on the previous page. Make sure that you understand why these two files have a different structure.

> Remember, in a data file constructed for a repeated measures design, there must be a variable (and hence a column in the data file) for each condition.

*Untitled3 [DataSet2] - IBM SPSS Statistics Data Editor

File Edit View Data Transform Analyze Direc

17 : SmallDif

	PartNum	LargeDif	SmallDif
1	1.00	936.00	878.00
2	2.00	923.00	1005.00
3	3.00	896.00	1010.00
4	4.00	1241.00	1365.00
5	5.00	1278.00	1422.00
6	6.00	871.00	1198.00
7	7.00	1360.00	1576.00
8	8.00	733.00	896.00
9	9.00	941.00	1573.00
10	10.00	1077.00	1261.00
11	11.00	1438.00	2237.00
12	12.00	1099.00	1325.00
13	13.00	1253.00	1591.00
14	14.00	1930.00	2742.00
15	15.00	1260.00	1357.00
16	16.00	1271.00	1963.00
17			
18			

We have called this variable 'SmallDif' and are using it to record the participants' mean decision times on the small difference trials. As this is a ratio variable, we have not assigned any value labels. We have left the variables Width and Columns at their default values.

We have called this variable 'LargeDif' and are using it to record the participants' mean decision times on the large difference trials. All other variable settings are left at their default values.

We have used the variable name 'PartNum' for the participant number variable. This is not essential but is good practice; we will explain why later.

Participant 16, for example, had a mean decision time of 1271 ms for the large difference trials and 1963 ms for the small difference trials.

Section 8: CHECKING AND CLEANING DATA FILES

In this chapter we have described how to enter and save data in SPSS. Having done that, your next task should always be to carefully check the file and 'clean' it to remove the errors it will inevitably contain.

Never start analysing your data before you have checked and cleaned it. Ignoring this advice could have one of two outcomes. If you don't check the data and later find an error, you will have to repeat all the analyses you have undertaken so far. This can cost you hours, days, or even weeks of work. Alternatively, you may never notice the errors. The consequences of this could include a failed course, a misleading publication, or even an incorrect policy decision. Carpenters have a saying, 'measure twice and cut once'. The equivalent rule in statistics should be 'check your data twice and analyse once'.

Careful data checking should lead to the detection of all the errors in your data. These errors can then be corrected in a process known as 'data cleaning'. Checking and cleaning a data file may be a quick job, or it may take a great deal of time. Checking and cleaning the data file for a simple experiment may only take a few minutes. On the other hand, it may take a researcher weeks of work to check and clean the data files for a big project, which involves combining data from different sources across thousands of participants and hundreds of variables. In many projects, the data checking and cleaning takes much longer than the analysis of the final data set.

The best way to check your data for errors is to use some of the simple descriptive statistics procedures we describe in Chapter 3. These simple analyses will allow you to detect unexpected, implausible and invalid values in your data file and correct them. Because we need to use descriptive statistics commands to check your data, we are going to introduce these commands first before explaining in Chapter 3, Section 6 how to use the commands to check the data. Remember that, in practice, you should always do your data checking and cleaning first before attempting any final statistical analysis of the data.

> To avoid wasting hours of work, always carefully check and clean your data before undertaking any analysis. We describe how to check and clean a data file in Chapter 3, Section 6.

Summary

- This chapter showed you how to create a data file in SPSS.

- Sections 1 and 2 explained the different parts of the Data Editor window and showed how to define a variable.

- Section 3 walked you through the process of setting up a data file, and Sections 4 and 5 showed how to save and open a data file.

- Sections 6 and 7 provided two data entry exercises to highlight differences between the data files used to code the data from independent groups and repeated measures designs. In Chapter 3, we will use these data files to learn how to explore data using descriptive statistics.

- Section 8 described the importance of taking time to check and clean your data file. The procedures for doing this will be described in Chapter 3, after we have introduced you to some of the descriptive statistics commands you will need to use to do this checking.

- For guidance on how to incorporate your data file in a report, or print it, see Chapter 13.

3 Exploring and cleaning data in SPSS

SPSS for Psychologists online
Visit he.palgrave.com/psychology/brace for data sets, online tutorials and exercises.

Section 1: DESCRIPTIVE STATISTICS

- Descriptive statistics allow us to summarise data by using numbers or graphs and charts. Descriptive statistics can help us understand important aspects of a data set, and critically can help identify errors in our data – as described in Section 6.

- Summary descriptives can accurately describe a large volume of data with just a few values. Common summary descriptives include measures of central tendency (e.g. mean, median and mode), confidence intervals, and measures of dispersion (e.g. range, minimum and maximum, interquartile range, standard deviation and variance). In this chapter we show some of the ways to calculate these values using SPSS.

- Data can also be described through the use of graphs or charts. In this chapter we show how to use SPSS to produce some types of graphs, and briefly introduce others that are covered in more detail in subsequent chapters.

- Most inferential commands in SPSS include some optional descriptive statistics.

- SPSS includes several commands specifically designed to produce descriptive statistics. In this chapter we describe the use of three of these commands, **Descriptives**, **Frequencies** and **Explore**.

- The **Descriptives** and **Frequencies** commands produce a variety of useful descriptive statistics, but these are calculated across all participants and cannot easily be presented broken down by one or more grouping variables.

- The **Explore** command can provide descriptive statistics broken down by one or more grouping variables.

- We use the first of these commands, the **Descriptives** command to introduce you to the Viewer window, which displays all the output in SPSS.

- A research report should always include appropriate descriptive statistics to assist the reader to understand the data and any effects reported.

Section 2: THE DESCRIPTIVES COMMAND

In this section we will use the data from the independent groups study of memory, which you entered and saved in Chapter 2, Section 6. Employing this data set we will learn how to use the **Descriptives** command to produce some basic descriptive statistics, to illustrate some principles of working in SPSS, and how the Viewer window is used to study output.

To obtain output from the Descriptives command

1. Once your data are entered, checked and saved, click on the word **Analyze** at the top of the screen (see below).
2. Select **Descriptive Statistics**.
3. Select **Descriptives**.

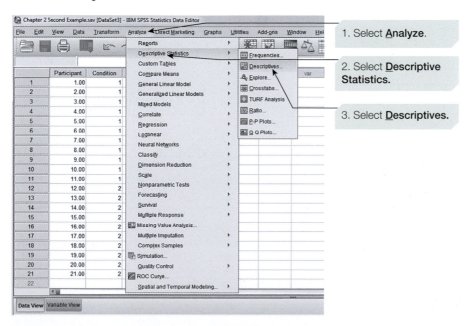

SPSS will now present you with the **Descriptives** dialogue box shown below. This dialogue box follows a basic structure common to most commands in SPSS. Within the dialogue, there are two boxes. The left-hand box lists all the variables in the data file (listed either by variable name or variable label), while the right-hand box, which will be empty when you first use the command, lists the variables that will be analysed (i.e. for which the output will be produced).

4. Select the first variable you want included in the analysis (the variable you want to describe) by clicking on the variable in the left-hand box.

5. The arrow button between the two boxes will now be highlighted and pointing towards the right-hand **Variable(s)** box. Click on this arrow to move the variable into the right-hand box. Repeat this procedure for each of the variables you want included in the analysis. Alternatively, you can drag and drop the variable(s) from the left-hand to the right-hand boxes.

6. When you have selected all the variables you are interested in, click on the **Options** button. This will reveal the **Descriptives: Options** dialogue box (shown on the next page), which lists all the descriptive statistics available in the **Descriptives** command.

7. If you select the **Save standardized values as variables** option, SPSS will add a new variable to your data file, which will give the scores expressed as *z*-scores or standard scores, in which values are expressed as a number of standard deviations from the mean. This is illustrated at the end of this section.

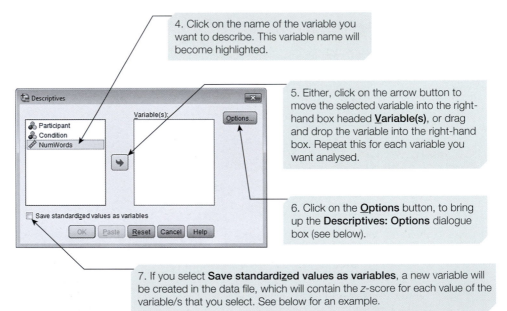

4. Click on the name of the variable you want to describe. This variable name will become highlighted.

5. Either, click on the arrow button to move the selected variable into the right-hand box headed **Variable(s)**, or drag and drop the variable into the right-hand box. Repeat this for each variable you want analysed.

6. Click on the **Options** button, to bring up the **Descriptives: Options** dialogue box (see below).

7. If you select **Save standardized values as variables**, a new variable will be created in the data file, which will contain the *z*-score for each value of the variable/s that you select. See below for an example.

You can select more than one variable by holding down either the <shift> key or the <Ctrl> key while clicking on the names of the variables. If you <shift> click the first and last variables in a list, all the variables in between will be selected. If you hold down the <Ctrl> key while clicking on the name of a variable, that variable will be selected or deselected.

8. In the **Descriptives: Options** dialogue box (below), select the descriptive statistics you require by clicking in the boxes so that a tick appears.

9. When you have selected all the statistics you require, click on the **Continue** button (Continue) to return you to the **Descriptives** dialogue box (see bottom of page).

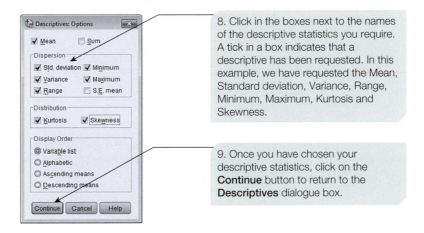

8. Click in the boxes next to the names of the descriptive statistics you require. A tick in a box indicates that a descriptive has been requested. In this example, we have requested the Mean, Standard deviation, Variance, Range, Minimum, Maximum, Kurtosis and Skewness.

9. Once you have chosen your descriptive statistics, click on the **Continue** button to return to the **Descriptives** dialogue box.

10. Finally, click on the OK button to execute the **<u>D</u>escriptives** command.

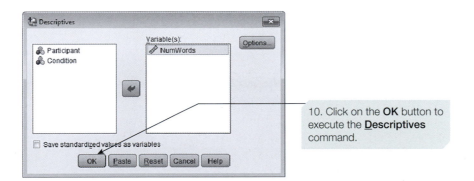

10. Click on the **OK** button to execute the **<u>D</u>escriptives** command.

We have chosen to calculate descriptive statistics only for 'NumWords' which was the dependent variable in our study. Sometimes students also request descriptive variables for independent or grouping variables, but few of the descriptive statistics available in the **Descriptives** command are suitable for use with these nominal or ordinal variables. The **Frequencies** command (see Section 4 of this chapter) includes several descriptive statistics which are more appropriate for nominal and ordinal variables.

Most of the results of the **<u>D</u>escriptives** analysis will be presented in the Viewer window, which we will explore in Section 3. However, if you selected the **<u>S</u>ave standardized values as variables** option (see step 7 above), a change will also be made to your data file, as shown below.

	Participant	Condition	NumWords	ZNumWords
1	1.00	1	20.00	1.09682
2	2.00	1	18.00	.54841
3	3.00	1	14.00	-.54841
4	4.00	1	18.00	.54841
5	5.00	1	17.00	.27420
6	6.00	1	11.00	-1.37102
7	7.00	1	20.00	1.09682
8	8.00	1	18.00	.54841
9	9.00	1	20.00	1.09682
10	10.00	1	19.00	.82261
11	11.00	1	20.00	1.09682
12	12.00	2	10.00	-1.64523

If we selected the option **Save standardized values as variables** (see step 7 above), then this new variable will be added to our data file.

A z-score is a useful way of describing performance on a test. The z-score indicates by how many standard deviations a score differs from the mean score. A z-score of 0 indicates that the participant's test score is equal to the mean for the test, while a z-score of +1 indicates that the test score is one standard deviation above the mean, and a z-score of –2 indicates performance is two standard deviations below the mean. In the example above, we can see that participant 12 recalled 10 words. This is hard to interpret, but the z-score of –1.65 tells us that this performance is 1.64 standard deviations below the mean performance on this test. Z-scores are useful for three reasons. First, they allow us to easily identify participants who are scoring above or below a threshold value, second, they allow us to compare performance across different tests, and, third, they allow us to track changes in the performance over time.

In Section 3, we will explain the workings of the Viewer window before examining the output of the **Descriptives** command.

Section 3: THE VIEWER WINDOW

Once you click on the [OK] button to execute a command, SPSS will open a new window called the Viewer window. The Viewer window is the SPSS window in which the results of all analyses are presented. If a Viewer window is already open, SPSS will append the output to the bottom of the window. If there isn't a Viewer window open, SPSS will open one for you.

The Viewer window comprises two distinct parts or 'panes'. The left-hand pane acts as a 'navigator' or 'outline'. This is a bit like a table of contents that lists all the components of the output that are shown in the larger pane. Clicking on an icon in the navigator pane moves you to that part of the output in the main or 'display' pane. This is useful when you have used a command that produces large amounts of output, or when you have executed several different commands.

Before examining the output in detail, we need to highlight several characteristics of the Viewer window.

This is the navigator pane of the Viewer window. The arrow (which is red on your screen) indicates the part of the output we are currently looking at in the main pane.

This display pane shows the output produced by SPSS. For longer outputs, a scroll bar will appear on the right, which allows you to scroll up and down. You can navigate through the output by clicking on the icons in the smaller pane.

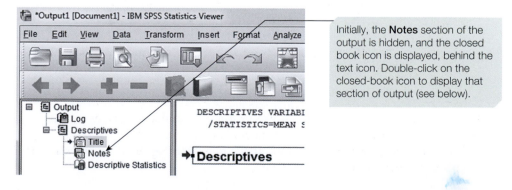

Points to note about the two panes of the Viewer window

1. Output can be hidden or displayed. A closed book icon represents a hidden section of output and an open book represents a section of output that is being displayed. Double-click on a book icon to either open or close it and either display or hide the associated section of output.

2. Click on one of the minus signs to collapse and hide all the output from a command (here, **Descriptives** is the command). Click on a plus sign to expand and display all the output from a command.

Initially, the **Notes** section of the output is hidden, and the closed book icon is displayed, behind the text icon. Double-click on the closed-book icon to display that section of output (see below).

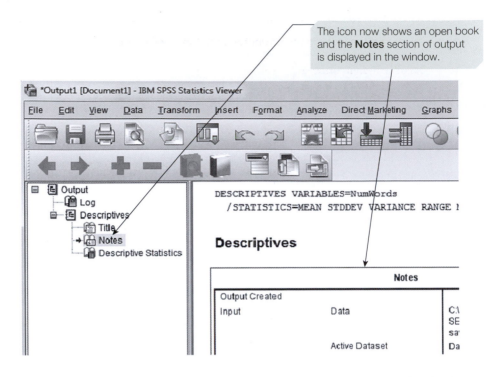

The icon now shows an open book and the **Notes** section of output is displayed in the window.

3. Most of the output produced by the SPSS commands is in the form of tables known as 'pivot tables'. The **Descriptives Statistics** table in the output above is an example of a pivot table. Pivot tables can be edited in various ways – see Chapter 13, Section 4 for full details.

4. Some parts of the output are in the form of plain text. The title **Descriptives** is an example of text output.

5. You can select output either by dragging the mouse over the section in the main pane or by clicking on the appropriate icons in the navigator pane. In the navigator pane, click on the name of a command to select all the output from that command. You can select all output in the Viewer window by clicking on the top icon in the navigation pane (labelled **Output**). Lower level icons (e.g. **Descriptive Statistics**) select only that particular part of the output.

6. Selected output can be cut, copied and pasted using the relevant options on the **Edit** menu or by right clicking and selecting the desired operation. Output can be printed using the **Print** command available under the **File** menu (see Chapter 13, Section 5 for details of printing output).

Sometimes, you will want to delete all the output in the Viewer window. The easiest way to do this is to click on the **Output** icon in the navigator pane and then press the Delete key on your keyboard. You can now start a new analysis with a blank output window.

7. You can change the relative width of the two panes by clicking on and dragging the line that separates the two panes.

If you find the icons in the navigator pane too small to see clearly, you can enlarge them by selecting **Outline Size** from the **View** menu. Now select **Small**, **Medium** or **Large**.

Points to note about the output

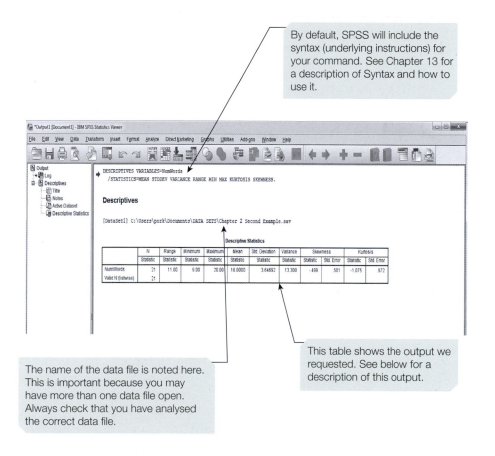

By default, SPSS will include the syntax (underlying instructions) for your command. See Chapter 13 for a description of Syntax and how to use it.

This table shows the output we requested. See below for a description of this output.

The name of the data file is noted here. This is important because you may have more than one data file open. Always check that you have analysed the correct data file.

Points to note about the Descriptives output

1. The descriptive statistics shown in the output of the **Descriptives** command are based on all cases. For example, the mean value of 16.00 shown is calculated across all 21 participants in the data file. It is likely that you would want many of these statistics calculated separately for each condition. This is more easily done using the **Explore** command, which is introduced in Section 5.

2. If you want descriptive statistics for more than one variable, move each variable name into the **Variable(s)** box in the **Descriptives** dialogue box (see step 5 on page 44).

Section 4: THE FREQUENCIES COMMAND

The **Frequencies** command generates frequency distribution tables showing the number of cases (participants) with a particular score on each variable. For example, a frequency distribution table of the variable age would tell you how many of your participants were 20-year-olds, how many 21 and so on, for each of the ages represented in the group of participants. In addition, the **Frequencies** command will also produce a range of summary descriptives, including measures of central tendency and measures of dispersion, and some charts. One limitation is that the **Frequencies** command calculates descriptive statistics for all cases and will not give descriptives for subgroups broken down by some other variable (unless we use it in combination with commands such as **Select Cases or Split File**; see Chapter 4, Section 4).

To obtain a Frequencies output

1. Once your data are entered, checked and saved, click on the word **Analyze** at the top of the screen (see below).
2. Select **Descriptive Statistics**.
3. Select **Frequencies** to bring up the **Frequencies** dialogue box (shown below).

1. Click on **Analyze**.
2. Select **Descriptive Statistics**.
3. Select **Frequencies**.

4. Select the variable(s) you want included in the frequency analysis and move them into the **Variable(s)** box either by clicking the arrow button or by dragging and dropping the variable(s).
5. Click on the **Statistics** button to bring up the **Frequencies: Statistics** dialogue box (shown below), which lists all the descriptive statistics available with the **Frequencies** command.

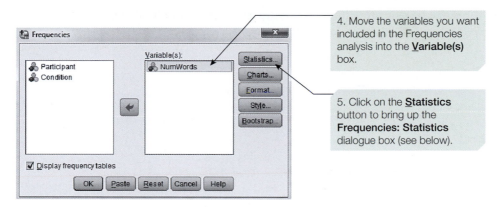

6. In the **Frequencies: Statistics** dialogue box select all the descriptive statistics you require.

7. Click on the **Continue** button to return you to the **Frequencies** dialogue box.

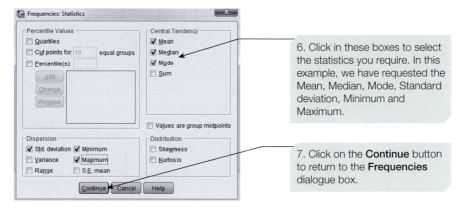

8. Now click on the **Charts** button. The **Frequencies: Charts** dialogue box will appear (see below).

9. Select the chart type that you would like; it should be appropriate for the type of data (see Section 7). In this example, we have requested a histogram.

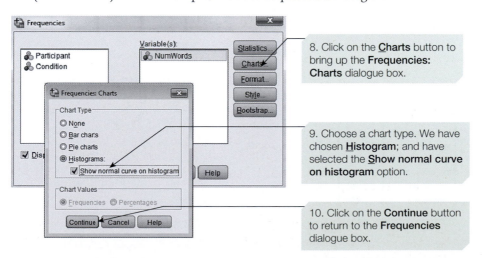

10. Click on **Continue** button to return to the **Frequencies** dialogue box (see below).

11. Click on the **OK** button to execute the **Frequencies** command.

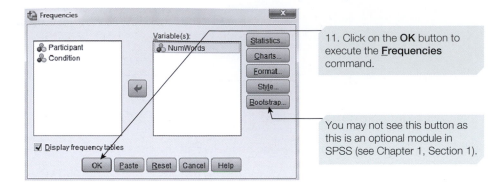

11. Click on the **OK** button to execute the **Frequencies** command.

You may not see this button as this is an optional module in SPSS (see Chapter 1, Section 1).

The results of the Frequencies analysis are described below.

Clicking on the **Format** button in the **Frequencies** dialogue box will allow you to adjust the way the output appears on the page. Experiment with these settings to discover the different ways of organising the output.

The output produced by the Frequencies command

This is the title for the output produced by the **Frequencies** command.

This table lists all the descriptive statistics we requested. The column gives these figures for the number of words recalled (ignoring the condition participants were assigned to). We can see that the mean number of words recalled was 16 and that the maximum number recalled, 20, was also the mode.

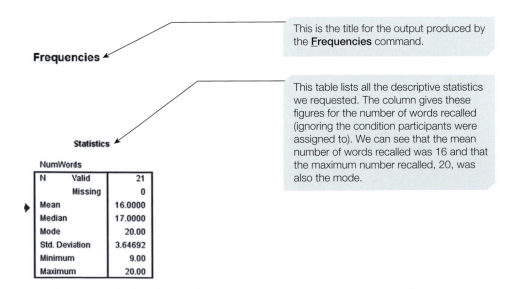

Frequencies

Statistics

NumWords

N	Valid	21
	Missing	0
Mean		16.0000
Median		17.0000
Mode		20.00
Std. Deviation		3.64692
Minimum		9.00
Maximum		20.00

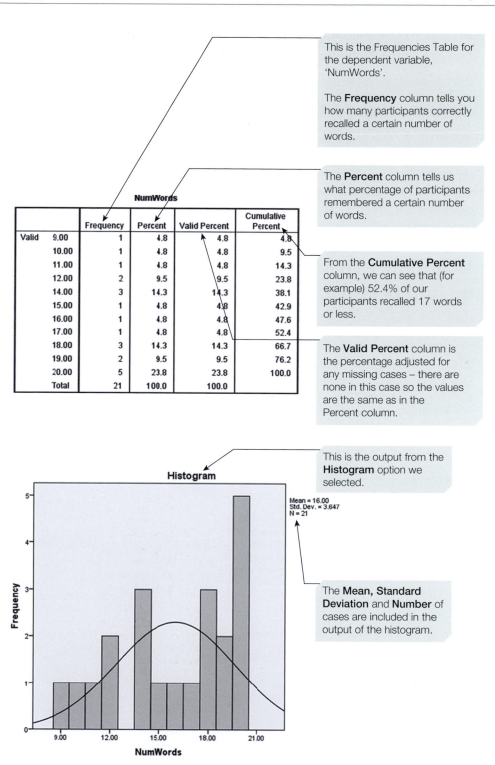

This is the Frequencies Table for the dependent variable, 'NumWords'.

The **Frequency** column tells you how many participants correctly recalled a certain number of words.

The **Percent** column tells us what percentage of participants remembered a certain number of words.

NumWords

		Frequency	Percent	Valid Percent	Cumulative Percent
Valid	9.00	1	4.8	4.8	4.8
	10.00	1	4.8	4.8	9.5
	11.00	1	4.8	4.8	14.3
	12.00	2	9.5	9.5	23.8
	14.00	3	14.3	14.3	38.1
	15.00	1	4.8	4.8	42.9
	16.00	1	4.8	4.8	47.6
	17.00	1	4.8	4.8	52.4
	18.00	3	14.3	14.3	66.7
	19.00	2	9.5	9.5	76.2
	20.00	5	23.8	23.8	100.0
	Total	21	100.0	100.0	

From the **Cumulative Percent** column, we can see that (for example) 52.4% of our participants recalled 17 words or less.

The **Valid Percent** column is the percentage adjusted for any missing cases – there are none in this case so the values are the same as in the Percent column.

This is the output from the **Histogram** option we selected.

Histogram

Mean = 16.00
Std. Dev. = 3.647
N = 21

The **Mean, Standard Deviation** and **Number** of cases are included in the output of the histogram.

So far in this chapter we have looked at the **Descriptives** command and the **Frequencies** command. These commands provide useful output, but are limited, in that they cannot easily produce descriptive statistics separately for different groups of participants. In Section 5, we will introduce the **Explore** command, which is designed for use in these situations.

Section 5: THE EXPLORE COMMAND

Unlike the **Descriptives** or the **Frequencies** command, using the **Explore** command makes it easy to obtain descriptive statistics for separate groups of participants. For example, in the case of our memory experiment, we could use the **Explore** command to calculate summary statistics, such as the mean memory score, separately for the participants in the Mnemonic and Non-mnemonic groups. We can also use **Explore** to obtain some simple graphs.

Using the Explore command to analyse data from an independent groups design

1. Once your data are entered, checked and saved, click on the menu item **Analyze** (see below).

2. Select **Descriptive** Statistics.

3. Select **Explore**.

1. Select **Analyze**.

2. Select **Descriptive Statistics**.

3. Select **Explore**.

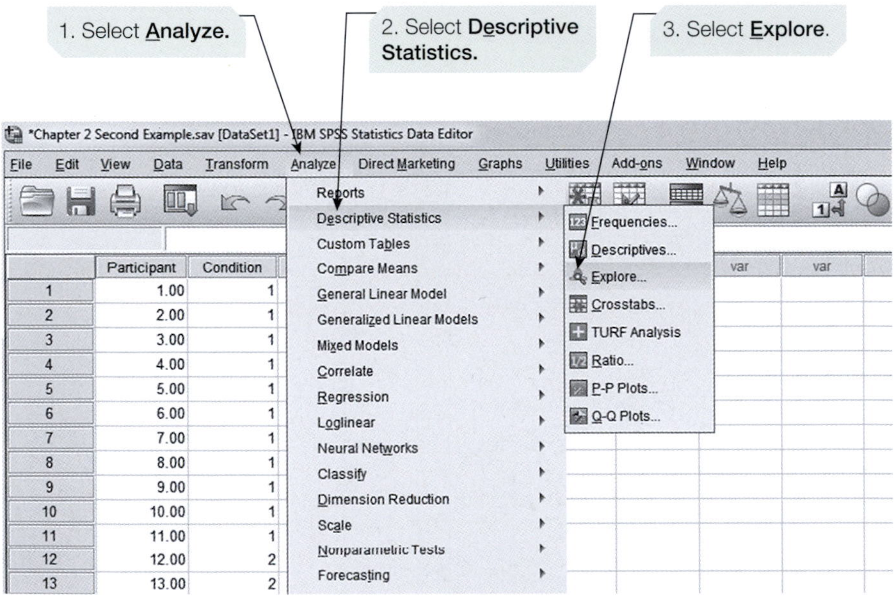

4. SPSS will now present you with the **Explore** dialogue box (shown on the next page). This has a similar structure to the **Descriptives** dialogue box. Select the variable(s) you want to analyse (e.g. 'NumWords') from the left-hand box and then click the top arrow button (which will be pointing to the right). This will move the

selected variable(s) to the uppermost box called the **Dependent List**. Alternatively, drag and drop the variable.

5. Select the grouping variable (e.g. 'Condition') from the left-hand box and move it to the **Factor List** box either by clicking the middle arrow button or by dragging and dropping the variable.

6. Finally, click on the OK button to execute the **Explore** command.

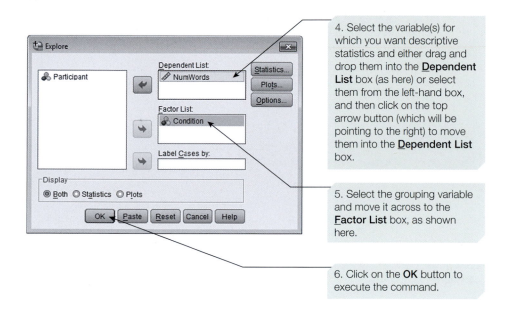

4. Select the variable(s) for which you want descriptive statistics and either drag and drop them into the **Dependent List** box (as here) or select them from the left-hand box, and then click on the top arrow button (which will be pointing to the right) to move them into the **Dependent List** box.

5. Select the grouping variable and move it across to the **Factor List** box, as shown here.

6. Click on the **OK** button to execute the command.

You could also click on the **Plots** button to change the type of graph requested. We will explain some of the plot options when analysing the data from our repeated measures design later in this section.

The Viewer window will now become the active window; if not, select it from the taskbar menu at the foot of the screen. The output of the **Explore** analysis using the data from the memory experiment is presented next.

The output produced by the Explore command for an independent groups design

The output of the **Explore** command will appear in the Viewer window, as shown below. We will now examine each part of this output in detail.

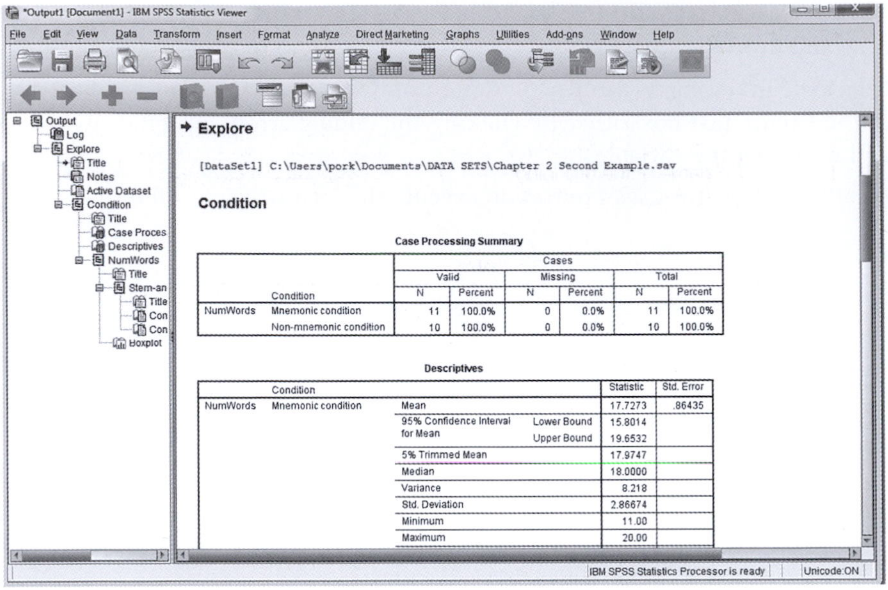

CHAPTER 3

→ **Explore**

[DataSet1] C:\Users\pork\Documents\DATA SETS\Chapter 2 Second Example.sav

Condition

Case Processing Summary

		Cases					
		Valid		Missing		Total	
	Condition	N	Percent	N	Percent	N	Percent
NumWords	Mnemonic condition	11	100.0%	0	0.0%	11	100.0%
	Non-mnemonic condition	10	100.0%	0	0.0%	10	100.0%

Descriptives

				Statistic	Std. Error
NumWords	Mnemonic condition	Mean		17.7273	.86435
		95% Confidence Interval for Mean	Lower Bound	15.8014	
			Upper Bound	19.6532	
		5% Trimmed Mean		17.9747	
		Median		18.0000	
		Variance		8.218	
		Std. Deviation		2.86674	
		Minimum		11.00	
		Maximum		20.00	

IBM SPSS Statistics Processor is ready   Unicode:ON

These titles are the first part of the output from the **Explore** command.

This table provides information about the cases that were processed, listing both valid and missing cases. Check that this information is correct.

Explore

Condition

Case Processing Summary

		Cases					
		Valid		Missing		Total	
	Condition	N	Percent	N	Percent	N	Percent
NumWords	Mnemonic condition	11	100.0%	0	0.0%	11	100.0%
	Non-rrnemonic condition	10	100.0%	0	0.0%	10	100.0%

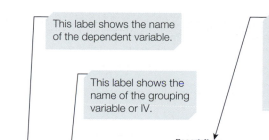

This label shows the name of the dependent variable.

This label shows the name of the grouping variable or IV.

This table shows the descriptive statistics for the participants in each condition. The statistics given include the mean, the 95% confidence interval, the median, variance, standard deviation (SD) and other information.

Descriptives

Condition				Statistic	Std. Error
NumWords	Mnemonic condition	Mean		17.7273	.86435
		95% Confidence Interval for Mean	Lower Bound	15.8014	
			Upper Bound	19.6532	
		5% Trimmed Mean		17.9747	
		Median		18.0000	
		Variance		8.218	
		Std. Deviation		2.86674	
		Minimum		11.00	
		Maximum		20.00	
		Range		9.00	
		Interquartile Range		3.00	
		Skewness		-1.595	.661
		Kurtosis		2.214	1.279
	Non-mnemonic condition	Mean		14.1000	1.12990
		95% Confidence Interval for Mean	Lower Bound	11.5440	
			Upper Bound	16.6560	
		5% Trimmed Mean		14.0556	
		Median		14.0000	
		Variance		12.767	
		Std. Deviation		3.57305	
		Minimum		9.00	
		Maximum		20.00	
		Range		11.00	
		Interquartile Range		5.25	
		Skewness		.337	.687
		Kurtosis		-.590	1.334

These are the two levels of the IV. The text is taken from the value labels we assigned to the variable.

The mean (and SD) for the Mnemonic and Non-Mnemonic conditions were 17.73 (2.87) and 14.1 (3.57) respectively.

Explore calculates the skewness and kurtosis for each condition. For small sample sizes, as here, these values are not very useful. For larger samples, you should consider what these values indicate about the distribution of the data.

Before writing up your results, consider how many decimal places you should report. In the example above, we have reported values rounded to two decimal places in line with the *Publication Manual of the American Psychological Association* (APA, 2009).

Stem-and-Leaf Plots

```
NumWords Stem-and-Leaf Plot for
Condition= Mnemonic condition

Frequency     Stem &  Leaf

    1.00 Extremes      (=<11)
    1.00        1 .  4
    5.00        1 .  78889
    4.00        2 .  0000

Stem width:      10.00
Each leaf:        1 case(s)
```

The default **Explore** output includes Stem-and-Leaf plots, as shown here. Each plot can be thought of as a histogram on its side. The advantage over a histogram is that all the individual data values can be seen. These plots can help you understand your data, but boxplots or histograms are more commonly used in psychology reports (see below).

```
NumWords Stem-and-Leaf Plot for
Condition= Non-mnemonic condition

Frequency     Stem &  Leaf

    1.00        0 .  9
    5.00        1 .  02244
    3.00        1 .  569
    1.00        2 .  0

Stem width:      10.00
Each leaf:        1 case(s)
```

This is the Stem-and-Leaf plot for the Non-mnemonic condition. The data are represented in two parts, the leaf, which contains the last digit of the value and the stem, which contains the other digits. In this case, the stem has a value of 10. The number 9 is represented as a stem of 0 plus a leaf of 9, while 12 is a stem of 1 plus a leaf of 2, and 20 is a stem of 2 and a leaf of 0.

The plot allows us to see the number of words recalled by the participants in the Non-mnemonic condition. We can see that our data include 1 participant who recalled 9 words, 5 participants who recalled between 10 and 14 words (10, 12, 12, 14 and 14); 3 participants who recalled between 15 and 19 words (15, 16 and 19); and 1 participant who recalled 20 words.

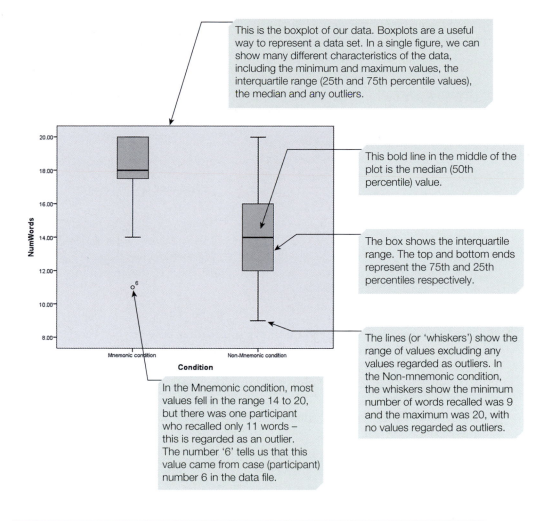

This is the boxplot of our data. Boxplots are a useful way to represent a data set. In a single figure, we can show many different characteristics of the data, including the minimum and maximum values, the interquartile range (25th and 75th percentile values), the median and any outliers.

This bold line in the middle of the plot is the median (50th percentile) value.

The box shows the interquartile range. The top and bottom ends represent the 75th and 25th percentiles respectively.

The lines (or 'whiskers') show the range of values excluding any values regarded as outliers. In the Non-mnemonic condition, the whiskers show the minimum number of words recalled was 9 and the maximum was 20, with no values regarded as outliers.

In the Mnemonic condition, most values fell in the range 14 to 20, but there was one participant who recalled only 11 words – this is regarded as an outlier. The number '6' tells us that this value came from case (participant) number 6 in the data file.

The boxplot provides a powerful way of summarising our data and showing a range of descriptive statistics all in one plot. In this case, the boxplot clearly shows there is a ceiling effect for the Mnemonic condition, with many participants recalling either the maximum possible 20 words or close to this value.

Using the Explore command to analyse data from a repeated measures design

To illustrate how to use the **Explore** command to analyse repeated measures data, we will use the data file we made and saved in Chapter 2, Section 6.

Follow steps 1 to 3 shown on page 54 for an independent groups design.

4. For an experiment involving a repeated measures design, there will be at least two variables for which descriptives will be required – move both of these into the **Dependent List** box.

5. In a repeated measures design, such as this, there will be no grouping variable, so nothing is moved to the **Factor List** box.

6. In this example we will show you how to alter the default settings for the plots obtained. Click on the **Plots** button to bring up the **Explore: Plots** dialogue box (shown below).

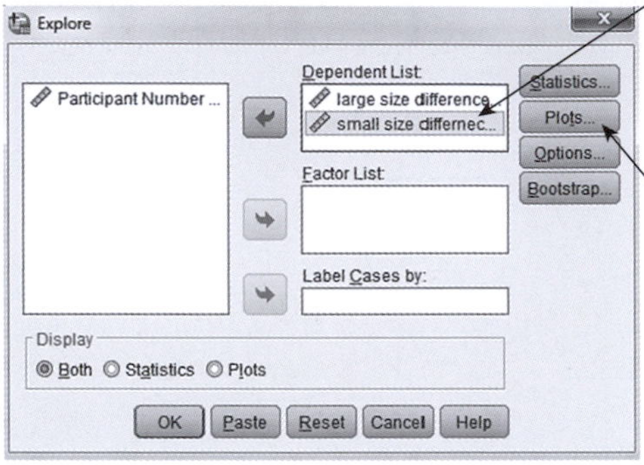

4. As this is a repeated measures design, we need descriptive statistics for each of these two variables. Select them both and move them into the **Dependent List** box as shown here.

6. Click on the **Plots** button, to bring up the **Explore: Plots** dialogue box (see below).

7. The **Explore: Plots** dialogue box allows you to alter how boxplots are produced. We need to change the setting to **Dependents together**. This change is needed because in the data file for a simple repeated measures design, there is no SPSS variable that denotes the factor (IV). Instead, the levels of the independent variable are represented by separate columns of data (i.e. separate SPSS variables). SPSS calls these variables 'dependents', hence we need to select the **Dependents together** option (see below).

8. Once you have selected the plots you want, click on the **Continue** button to return to the **Explore** dialogue box, then click on the **OK** button.

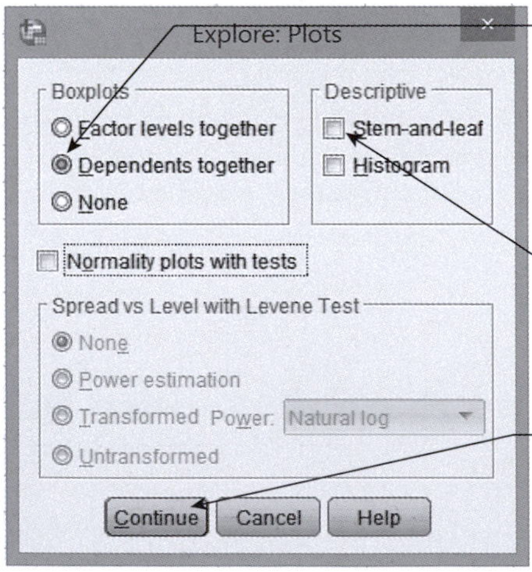

7. The default setting for Boxplots is **Factor levels together**, but this is only useful for an independent groups design. For a repeated measures design, change this to **Dependents together**.

You can also select the type of descriptive. The default is **Stem-and-leaf** but you can also request a **Histogram** if desired. In this example, we will deselect Stem-and-leaf.

8. Click on the **Continue** button to return to the **Explore** dialogue box, then click on the **OK** button to execute the command.

The boxplots produced by the Explore command for a repeated measures design

The boxplot below allows us to visually compare the performance of participants in our two conditions. Looking at this figure, it is apparent that participants in the large size difference condition often responded more quickly than those in the small size difference condition, and this is reflected in the relative median values, marked by the bold horizontal lines in the figure. We can also see that participant 14 responded slowly in both conditions.

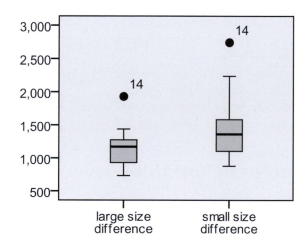

It is worth noting how this figure would have looked if we hadn't changed the default setting of **Factor levels together** in the **Explore: Plots** dialogue box. This setting would produce two separate boxplots, as shown below (for this demonstration we have positioned the graphs alongside each other and resized them – see Section 7).

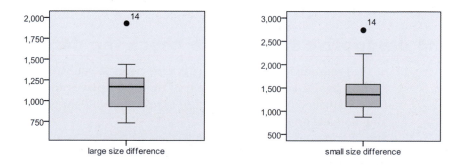

Presented this way, the performance of the participants in the two conditions appears to be quite similar; however, this is an artefact of the way SPSS sets the values of the axes of a chart to fit its contents. If you look carefully, you will see that the scales of the y-axes of the two graphs are different. This is why it is better to use the **Dependents together** option as this ensures the two conditions are graphed in a way that allows easy comparison.

Section 6: USING DESCRIPTIVE STATISTICS TO CHECK YOUR DATA

As we explained at the end of Chapter 2, before undertaking any analysis, it is critical to carefully check your data and correct any errors. This data checking and cleaning is most easily performed using the descriptive statistics commands, **Descriptives**, **Frequencies** and **Explore**, outlined above in Sections 2, 4 and 5.

To illustrate this process, we will use a file that we will be exploring in more detail in Chapter 4. For the purposes of this exercise, we have deliberately included errors in this file. If you would like to follow along as we check and clean this file, you can download your own copy (see below). Alternatively, use the procedures we describe here to check your own files.

The file we will be using is called 'adoption_survey with errors' and can be downloaded from he.palgrave.com/psychology/brace.

You may need to refer back to the instructions in Chapter 2 and in the earlier sections of this chapter to help you follow these steps.

Checking variables in Variable View

First check the format of your data file:

- Open your data file and go to Variable View. Check that you set Value labels for any nominal or ordinal variables, and remind yourself what values you used. For example, in the case of Sex, what values did you use to represent Male and Female? This will remind you what values to expect for these variables.

- Next check the Missing Values. Did you set at least one missing value for each variable, and if so what value(s) did you use?

- Switch to Data View and check there aren't any rows of cells with dots. This is especially likely to occur below your last participant. If you find any such rows, delete them (see below for an example of this).

Using descriptive statistics to check the data

Next, we will use the **Frequencies** command to check for errors in your data file. The same process could be completed using the output of the **Descriptives** and **Explore** commands, but the frequency tables of the **Frequencies** command are particularly useful for checking nominal or ordinal variables.

Following the instructions in Section 4, undertake a Frequencies analysis, for each of the variables in your data file. Select options to give you Mean, Median and Mode values, together with Minimum and Maximum values and Range. Some of the output from this analysis of our data file is reproduced below.

This is the first part of the output from the **Frequencies** command. This table reports each of the statistics we requested for each of the variables.

The first thing to look at is the **Number** of cases (N). Two values are given; the number of **Valid** cases (excluding missing cases) and the number of **Missing** cases. How many cases (participants) do you think are in your data set, and is this the same as the number reported here?

➡ **Frequencies**

Statistics

		ID	sex	ethnicity	religion	adopted	q1	q2	q3
N	Valid	19	20	21	20	19	19	20	
	Missing	2	1	0	1	2	2	1	
Mean		10.58	2.7500	7.2857	3.6500	1.5789	2.6316	2.4500	9.83
Median		11.00	2.0000	3.0000	3.0000	1.0000	2.0000	2.0000	3.00
Mode		1ᵃ	2.00	2.00ᵃ	3.00	.00	1.00	1.00	1.0
Range		19	23.00	98.00	6.00	4.00	4.00	4.00	129.
Minimum		1	1.00	1.00	1.00	.00	1.00	1.00	1.
Maximum		20	24.00	99.00	7.00	4.00	5.00	5.00	130.

a. Multiple modes exist. The smallest value is shown

We collected data from 20 participants, so we should expect a total of 20 cases. However, our first variable (ID) shows 19 valid cases and 2 missing cases, a total of 21 cases. Furthermore, given that this variable is the participant identifier number we allocated, we shouldn't expect any missing values for this variable. We must have made one or more errors here.

Now look at the data file (see below) and see if you can spot the errors for this variable.

File	Edit	View	Data	Transform	Analyze	Direct Marketing	Graph

11 : q3   5.00

	ID	sex	ethnicity	religion	adopt
1	1	2.00	2.00	3.00	
2	2	1.00	2.00	7.00	
3	3	24.00	4.00	2.00	
4	4	2.00	3.00	2.00	
5	5	2.00	2.00	6.00	
6	6	2.00	99.00	5.00	
7	7	1.00	4.00	3.00	
8	8	1.00	1.00	6.00	
9	9	2.00	2.00	3.00	
10	10	2.00	3.00	3.00	
11	11	2.00	4.00	5.00	
12	12	1.00	4.00	5.00	
13	13	2.00	4.00	3.00	
14	14	1.00	1.00	5.00	
15	15	1.00	3.00	3.00	
16	16	2.00	4.00	1.00	
17	17	2.00	5.00	2.00	
18	18	1.00	1.00	3.00	
19	19	2.00	1.00	2.00	
20	20	2.00	2.00	3.00	
21	.	.	2.00	.	
22					

We set the value 9 as the missing value for all variables, forgetting that 9 was a legitimate value for the participant 'ID' variable. The solution is to change the missing value for this variable to 99 or 0, for example.

Because we accidently entered an extra value for the variable, 'ethnicity', SPSS has created an extra 'phantom' participant and set all other variables for this participant to system missing (shown by dots in the cells).

The first error is quite easy to spot. We have an additional row of data for a phantom participant (row 21 of the data table). This occurred because we accidently entered an extra value for the variable 'ethnicity'. SPSS has then set all the other variables for this row to system missing – shown by dots in the cells. Importantly, this single error will have resulted in a missing case being recorded for every variable. It is also important to think about how this error occurred and whether it might indicate other problems. For example, does it suggest that the ethnicity data are out of sequence with the other variables, and if so, is it possible that we have assigned the wrong ethnicity to some of our participants. You may need to go back to your original data records to check how this error occurred. For the purposes of this exercise, we are going to assume that it was just a typing error and doesn't indicate anything more worrying. The solution is simple – click on the row number 21 to highlight the whole row and press the delete key to remove it from the file. Then resave the data file.

The second error for the variable 'ID' is harder to spot. When we set up the data file, we assigned the missing value of 9 to all the variables, including this one. However for this variable, the value 9 is legitimate as there was a 9th participant. As a result, SPSS has treated our 9th participant as having a missing value for the variable 'ID'. The solution is to go to the Variable View of the data file and change the missing value for this variable. In this case, we could set it to 99 as we only have 20 participants. An alternative would be to set it to 0 as we would never use this value as a participant ID number. When you have made the change, save the data file again.

Having fixed these two errors, save the corrected data file and rerun the **Frequencies** command. You will note that when you select Frequencies, all the options will be set as before, so all you need to do is click on the OK button. Now check the output to make sure you have fixed the problem with the ID variable.

The new output is shown below. We now have the correct number of participants, with no missing values for the variables 'ID', 'sex', 'ethnicity' and 'religion'. The variables, 'adopted' and 'q1' each show 1 missing value, and 'q3' shows 2 missing values, but checking our records reveals that this is correct as some participants didn't respond to each of these questions.

Frequencies

Statistics

		ID	sex	ethnicity	religion	adopted	q1	q2	q3	q4
N	Valid	20	20	20	20	19	19	20	18	
	Missing	0	0	0	0	1	1	0	2	
Mean		10.50	2.7500	7.5500	3.6500	1.5789	2.6316	2.4500	9.8333	2.75
Median		10.50	2.0000	3.0000	3.0000	1.0000	2.0000	2.0000	3.0000	2.00
Mode		1^a	2.00	4.00	3.00	.00	1.00	1.00	1.00^a	2.
Range		19	23.00	98.00	6.00	4.00	4.00	4.00	129.00	4.
Minimum		1	1.00	1.00	1.00	.00	1.00	1.00	1.00	1.
Maximum		20	24.00	99.00	7.00	4.00	5.00	5.00	130.00	5.

a. Multiple modes exist. The smallest value is shown

Next look at the **Minimum** and **Maximum** values for these variables. Can you see any errors here? The variable 'sex' has a maximum value of 24. This doesn't look right as sex was coded using 1 = Male and 2 = Female. To investigate this further, scroll down the Frequencies output to the Frequencies table for the variable 'sex' (shown below).

sex		Frequency	Percent	Valid Percent	Cumulative Percent
Valid	Male	7	35.0	35.0	35.0
	Female	12	60.0	60.0	95.0
	24.00	1	5.0	5.0	100.0
	Total	20	100.0	100.0	

From this table we can see we have 7 male participants and 12 female participants in our data file, and one person who has been coded with a value of 24. Checking the data file shows that participant 3 is the one with the value 24, and checking our records shows that we actually had 13 female respondents, not 12, so we can safely assume that we accidently typed '24' instead of '2' for this participant. Make the change and resave the data file.

Now look at frequencies tables for the next two variables, 'ethnicity' and 'religion' (below). In the 'ethnicity' variable, we appear to have one erroneous value of 99 and in the 'religion' variable one erroneous value of 7. If we can identify what the correct values should have been, we can correct the data file. Alternatively, if we were not certain what the true values should have been, we could change these values to 9, the missing value for these two variables.

ethnicity		Frequency	Percent	Valid Percent	Cumulative Percent
Valid	Asian	4	20.0	20.0	20.0
	African	5	25.0	25.0	45.0
	Chinese	3	15.0	15.0	60.0
	European	6	30.0	30.0	90.0
	Other	1	5.0	5.0	95.0
	99.00	1	5.0	5.0	100.0
	Total	20	100.0	100.0	

religion		Frequency	Percent	Valid Percent	Cumulative Percent
Valid	Atheist	1	5.0	5.0	5.0
	Buddhist	4	20.0	20.0	25.0
	Christian	8	40.0	40.0	65.0
	Islam	3	15.0	15.0	80.0
	Other	3	15.0	15.0	95.0
	7.00	1	5.0	5.0	100.0
	Total	20	100.0	100.0	

After locating and correcting each error, resave your data file. We recommend using a slightly different name each time you save the file, so that the previous version isn't overwritten and is available in case you make a mistake. For example, we could use the names 'adoption_survey v2', 'adoption_survey v3' and so on.

Following this process of carefully examining the output of the descriptive statistics commands such as Frequencies and Explore, we can check each variable in our data file looking for implausible or impossible values.

Checking scale variables

So far we have checked nominal or ordinal variables. When checking scale variables, the **Frequencies** command may be less useful. For example, imagine a file containing data from 100 participants where one of the variables was reaction time measured in milliseconds. In this case, it is likely each participant will have a unique value for the 'reaction time' variable, so the **Frequencies** command will produce output including a long and relatively uninformative frequency table. In these cases, you may find it simpler to use the **Descriptives** command, and carefully check the mean, median, mode, minimum and maximum values of the variable to ensure that all are plausible. A useful alternative is to check the boxplot produced by the **Explore** command looking for unexpected values or outliers.

Finish cleaning the file

Now work through the remaining variables in your file and check each one. Once you are satisfied that you have identified and corrected all the errors, resave the data file one last time using a new file name to indicate that this is the cleaned version of the data file, for example 'adoption_survey_cleaned'.

> The two most common sources of errors in data files are 'finger errors' where a simple typing mistake results in the wrong value being recorded, and errors relating to the use of missing values. Always think carefully about what missing values to set for a variable and make sure you use these values correctly when entering your data.

In the remaining sections we will introduce the topic of how to produce some simple graphs using SPSS.

Section 7: INTRODUCING GRAPHING IN SPSS

Producing graphs in SPSS

There are several ways to create graphs using SPSS. Many of the statistical commands accessed from the **Analyze** menu include graphing options in their output. We have already seen examples of graphs produced this way in Sections 4 and 5 covering the **Explore** and **Frequencies** commands. Many other statistical commands also include graphing options, and these will be covered in later chapters. However, SPSS also includes separate graphing commands. In the remaining sections of this chapter we will introduce you to these graphing commands, but first we will briefly describe some of the graphs types available in SPSS.

Graph types

Boxplots

Boxplots are useful when initially exploring your data, as described in Section 5. Boxplots provide a visual representation of the median and the dispersion (interquartile range and outliers) of the data in each condition of a study.

Histogram

Histograms are used to plot the frequency distribution of data measured on an ordinal, interval or ratio level of measurement. For an independent groups design, data should be plotted separately for each condition. We saw an example of a histogram produced by the **Frequencies** command in Section 4.

Bar charts

Bar charts are used to summarise data collected for different groups and are suitable for nominal and ordinal data. For example, we could use a bar chart to plot responses to a survey question about religious belief. Each bar would show the number of respondents (the frequency) who were followers of each religion.

Bar charts can also be used to summarise data across several levels of an independent variable or factor. In this case, the dependent variable should be of ordinal, interval or ratio level of measurement and each bar could represent the mean (or some other summary statistic) of the dependent variable. The different bars would represent the different levels of the independent variable.

Error bar chart

Error bar charts can be thought of as a simpler version of a boxplot. The central point marks the mean (or another measure of central tendency) and the error bars show a suitable measure of dispersion. For example, you could display the mean and standard deviation, or the mean and the 95% confidence intervals, or the median and the interquartile range. See Chapter 8, Section 3 for an example of this type of graph.

Line charts

Line charts are used to plot a series of data points that are joined together with a line. This is most appropriate when plotting the value on one variable (on the Y-axis) against a second variable which is measured on an interval or ratio scale (on the X-axis). However, in psychology, it is quite common to use line charts to plot the data from more complex designs where we want to illustrate an interaction between factors. In this situation, the line chart has the advantage of clearly linking together related data points. We refer to these as 'interaction graphs' and give examples in Chapter 8, Sections 3 and 5.

Scattergram

Scattergrams are used to illustrate the relationship between two variables. Each variable should be of ordinal, interval, or ratio level of measurement.

The table below shows where you can find examples of each of these types of graph.

Graph type	Chapter and Section
Boxplots	This chapter, Sections 5 and 8
Histogram	This chapter, Sections 4 and 9
Bar charts	Chapter 7, Sections 4 and 5
Error bar graph	Chapter 5, Section 3 Chapter 8, Section 3
Line charts/interaction graphs	Chapter 8, Section 5
Scattergram	Chapter 6, Section 2

Section 8: CHART BUILDER

To use Chart Builder

We will demonstrate how to use <u>C</u>hart Builder by producing a boxplot for the memory study described in Chapter 2, Section 6. The result will be very similar to the boxplot we produced as an option when using the <u>E</u>xplore command in Section 5 of this chapter. As we shall see, <u>C</u>hart Builder is slightly more flexible, allowing us to alter the look of the chart. In addition, we will show how you can edit a chart after it has been produced.

1. Click on <u>G</u>raphs menu at the top of the window.

2. Click on <u>C</u>hart Builder to bring up the **Chart Builder** dialogue box (see below).

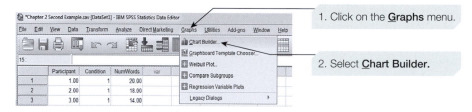

1. Click on the <u>Graphs</u> menu.

2. Select <u>C</u>hart Builder.

3. Before allowing you to proceed, SPSS gives you this reminder. To be able to use **Chart Builder** correctly, two properties of the variables must be set in the Variables view of the data window. You must set the level of measurement for each variable and for nominal or ordinal variables you should give value labels. If you haven't already done this, do it now by closing this dialogue box and going to the Variable View of the data window. If the variables are set up correctly, then click on the **OK** button.

If you need to set the level of measurement or the value labels for a variable it is easiest to close this dialogue and go back to the Variable view of the data window to set these characteristics. However, it is also possible to do this using the **Define Variable Properties** button on the dialogue box, but novice users will probably find this method confusing.

SPSS will now present you with two linked dialogue boxes, the Chart Builder and the Element Properties (see below). We will examine the **Chart Builder** dialogue box first.

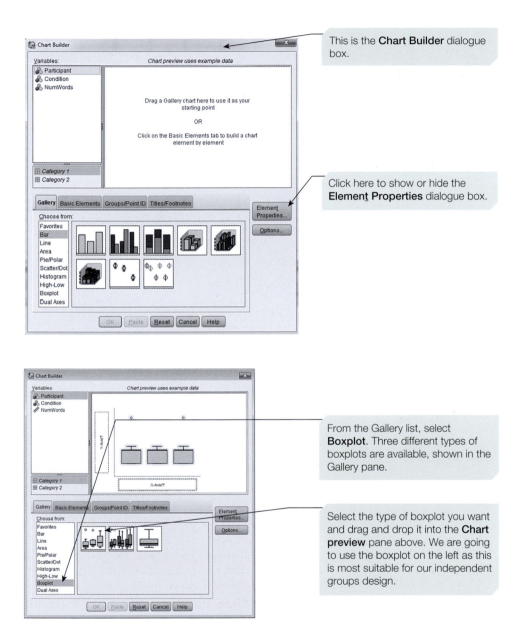

This is the **Chart Builder** dialogue box.

Click here to show or hide the **Element Properties** dialogue box.

From the Gallery list, select **Boxplot**. Three different types of boxplots are available, shown in the Gallery pane.

Select the type of boxplot you want and drag and drop it into the **Chart preview** pane above. We are going to use the boxplot on the left as this is most suitable for our independent groups design.

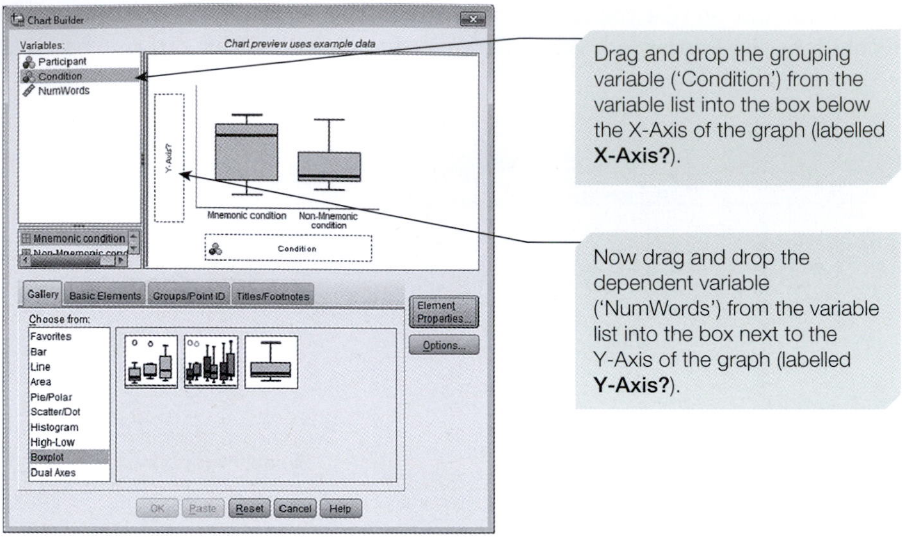

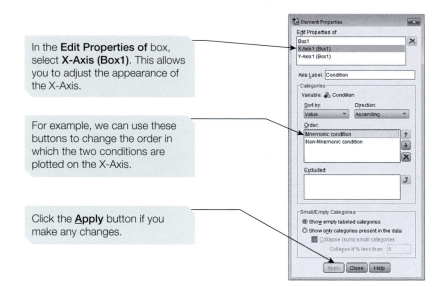

Chart Builder
Variables:
Participant
Condition
NumWords
Chart preview uses example data
Y-Axis?
Mnemonic condition
Non-Mnemonic condition
Condition
Gallery
Basic Elements
Groups/Point ID
Titles/Footnotes
Element Properties...
Options...
Choose from:
Favorites
Bar
Line
Area
Pie/Polar
Scatter/Dot
Histogram
High-Low
Boxplot
Dual Axes
OK
Paste
Reset
Cancel
Help
Drag and drop the grouping variable ('Condition') from the variable list into the box below the X-Axis of the graph (labelled **X-Axis?**).
Now drag and drop the dependent variable ('NumWords') from the variable list into the box next to the Y-Axis of the graph (labelled **Y-Axis?**).

We can now adjust some of the settings for our graph in the **Element Properties** dialogue box.

In the **Edit Properties of** box, select **X-Axis (Box1)**. This allows you to adjust the appearance of the X-Axis.
For example, we can use these buttons to change the order in which the two conditions are plotted on the X-Axis.
Click the **Apply** button if you make any changes.
Element Properties
Edit Properties of:
Box1
X-Axis1 (Box1)
Y-Axis1 (Box1)
Axis Label: Condition
Categories
Variable: Condition
Sort by:
Value
Direction:
Ascending
Order:
Mnemonic condition
Non-Mnemonic condition
Excluded:
Small/Empty Categories
Show empty labeled categories
Show only categories present in the data
Collapse (sum) small categories
Collapse if % less than: 5
Apply
Close
Help

Finally, click on the **OK** button on the **Chart Builder** dialogue box to produce your chart. The output is shown below.

GGraph

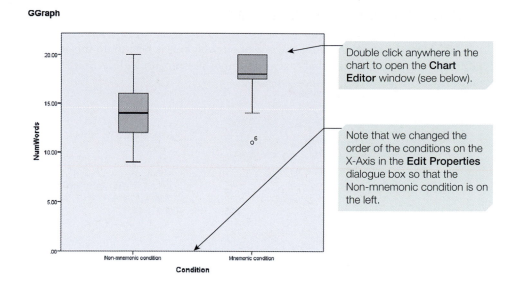

Double click anywhere in the chart to open the **Chart Editor** window (see below).

Note that we changed the order of the conditions on the X-Axis in the **Edit Properties** dialogue box so that the Non-mnemonic condition is on the left.

Editing charts in the Chart Editor window

Once a chart has been produced, it can be edited. In the Output window, double-click anywhere inside the chart to open the Chart Editor window, shown below.

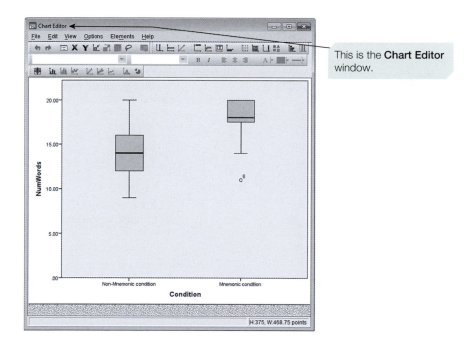

This is the **Chart Editor** window.

The menus and toolbars in the Chart Editor window can be used to improve the initial appearance of the chart. Items such as chart titles, subtitles, legends, axis titles, labels, line characteristics and markers can all be altered. Changes can be made through the menus, or by double-clicking directly on the item, or by clicking on the toolbar icons or buttons. If you hover your cursor over an icon or button, a pop-up message indicates its function.

For example, we will reduce the size of our chart. It is best to do this in the Chart Editor commands to ensure that text and symbol size remain legible. Start by clicking on **Edit** then **Properties**, as shown below.

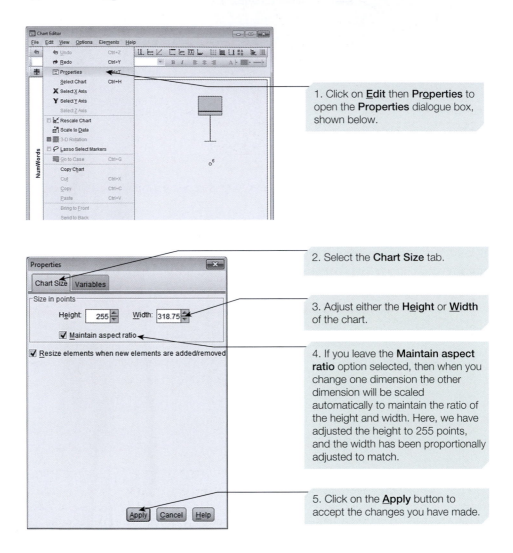

1. Click on **Edit** then **Properties** to open the **Properties** dialogue box, shown below.

2. Select the **Chart Size** tab.

3. Adjust either the **Height** or **Width** of the chart.

4. If you leave the **Maintain aspect ratio** option selected, then when you change one dimension the other dimension will be scaled automatically to maintain the ratio of the height and width. Here, we have adjusted the height to 255 points, and the width has been proportionally adjusted to match.

5. Click on the **Apply** button to accept the changes you have made.

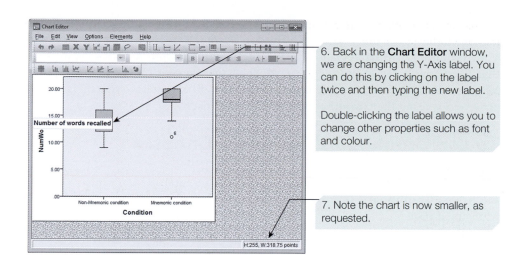

6. Back in the **Chart Editor** window, we are changing the Y-Axis label. You can do this by clicking on the label twice and then typing the new label.

Double-clicking the label allows you to change other properties such as font and colour.

7. Note the chart is now smaller, as requested.

Finally, close the **Chart Editor** window. The changes you have made will now be reflected in the output window.

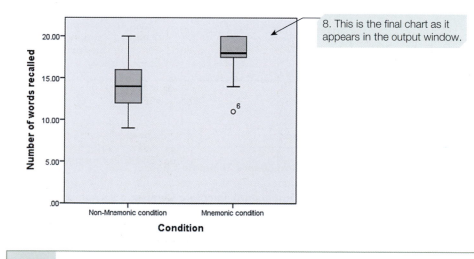

8. This is the final chart as it appears in the output window.

The Chart Editor window is used to edit charts produced from Chart Builder, and also to edit charts produced from commands on the Analyze menu. For charts produced using Graphboard Template Chooser, there is a separate editor, shown in Section 9.

Section 9: GRAPHBOARD TEMPLATE CHOOSER

The **Graphboard Template Chooser** is an alternative way to produce high-quality charts and includes innovative features such as an animation option, which could be useful in presentations. However, it does not currently include all the graph types we cover in this book.

We will demonstrate how to use **Graphboard Template Chooser** by producing histograms for the memory study described in Chapter 2, Section 6. Earlier, in Section 4, we produced a histogram using the **Frequencies** command. At that time we noted that we couldn't easily produce a separate histogram plot for participants in the Mnemonic and Non-mnemonic conditions. We will now show that it is easy to achieve this using the **Graphboard Template Chooser**.

To use Graphboard Template Chooser

1. Click on the **Graphs** menu item.
2. Click on **Graphboard Template Chooser**. The dialogue box appears, as shown on the next page.

1. Click on the **Graphs** menu item.

2. Select **Graphboard Template Chooser**. This will bring up the **Graphboard Template Chooser** dialogue box (see below).

	Participant	Condition	NumWords	var
1	1.00	1	20.00	
2	2.00	1	18.00	
3	3.00	1	14.00	
4	4.00	1	18.00	
5	5.00	1	17.00	
6	6.00	1	11.00	
7	7.00	1	20.00	
8	8.00	1	18.00	
9	9.00	1	20.00	

As with **Chart Builder**, **Graphboard Template Chooser** requires the level of measurement and value labels to be set for each of the variables you are going to use. However, **Graphboard Template Chooser** does not remind you of this.

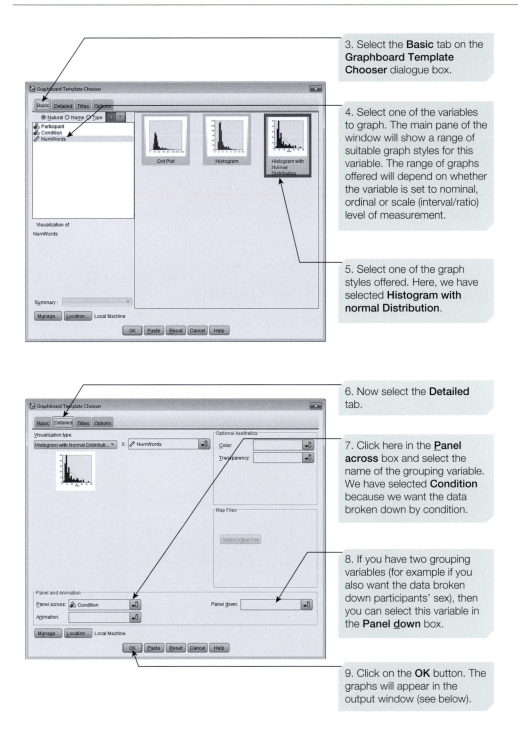

3. Select the **Basic** tab on the **Graphboard Template Chooser** dialogue box.

4. Select one of the variables to graph. The main pane of the window will show a range of suitable graph styles for this variable. The range of graphs offered will depend on whether the variable is set to nominal, ordinal or scale (interval/ratio) level of measurement.

5. Select one of the graph styles offered. Here, we have selected **Histogram with normal Distribution**.

6. Now select the **Detailed** tab.

7. Click here in the **Panel across** box and select the name of the grouping variable. We have selected **Condition** because we want the data broken down by condition.

8. If you have two grouping variables (for example if you also want the data broken down participants' sex), then you can select this variable in the **Panel down** box.

9. Click on the **OK** button. The graphs will appear in the output window (see below).

The two histograms produced by **Graphboard Template Chooser** are shown below.

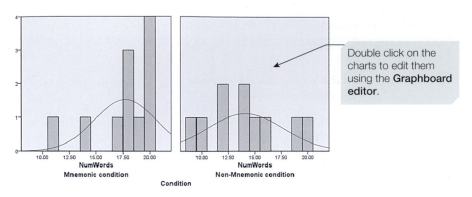

Double click on the charts to edit them using the **Graphboard editor**.

The Graphboard Editor window

The **Graphboard Editor** window allows you to change many aspects of the graphs you have produced. Explore the menus and buttons to discover what you can do.

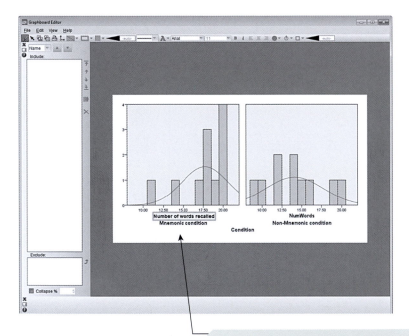

Here in the **Graphboard Editor** window we are changing the X-Axis label. Double click on the existing label and type in the new label. This wouldn't be necessary if we had given the variable a variable label when we set it up.

Summary

- This chapter introduced you to several statistical commands that can be used to produce a range of descriptive statistics in SPSS and demonstrated various ways of producing graphs.

- Section 3 introduced the Viewer window, which is the SPSS window in which the results of all analyses are displayed.

- Descriptive statistics can be obtained in several different ways. Sections 2, 4 and 5 demonstrated the **Descriptives**, **Frequencies** and **Explore** commands.

- It is vital to check and clean data files. Section 6 illustrated how to use the **Descriptives**, **Frequencies** and **Explore** commands to check and clean your data file.

- Graphs can be created in SPSS as options in many of the statistical analysis commands found under the **Analyze** menu. In addition, graphs can be produced using the **Graphs** menu.

- The **Graphs** menu includes **Chart Builder** and **Graphboard Template Chooser**. These methods of producing graphs were demonstrated in Sections 7–9.

4 Data handling

In this chapter

- An introduction to data handling
- Sorting a file
- Splitting a file
- Selecting cases
- Recoding values
- Computing new variables
- Counting values
- Ranking cases
- Data transformation
- Data file for scales or questionnaires

SPSS for Psychologists online
Visit he.palgrave.com/psychology/brace data sets, online tutorials and exercises.

Section 1: AN INTRODUCTION TO DATA HANDLING

- SPSS includes a series of commands that can be used to modify, manipulate or transform the data. We refer to these as the Data Handling commands.

- These commands are very useful, especially when working with large data files containing many variables for each participant. Files such as these often arise from survey or questionnaire research.

- Questionnaires often contain items (questions) that can be grouped into a number of subscores. We can use certain Data Handling commands to calculate the subscores.

- Data Handling commands can also be used to transform variables, for example a log transformation converts a variable from a raw score to a log score. This type of transformation can reduce distortions, such as skewness, which might otherwise invalidate some analyses.

An example data file

To illustrate the use of these commands, we have created a small data file, which is printed in the Appendix and available from he.palgrave.com/psychology/brace. The data file contains the results of a fictitious survey of people's attitudes to cross-racial adoption. The data file contains participant number, demographic data, such as the participant's age, sex, ethnic origin, religious belief and experience of adoption, together with their responses to 10 statements concerning aspects of adoption. These responses were made using a 5-point scale ranging from 'Strongly Agree' (1) to 'Strongly Disagree' (5). The response to each of these items has been recorded in variables q1 to q10.

Section 2: SORTING A FILE

Students who are new to SPSS sometimes worry about the order in which participants' data are entered into the SPSS data file. For example, do you have to enter all the data from participants in one condition before entering the data from the other condition? Normally, the order of the cases does not matter, but there are occasions when you might want to sort a data file so that the cases are in some meaningful order, perhaps to make it easier to check the accuracy of the data file. One situation in which order of cases does become relevant is when you are 'splitting' a file (see the **Split File** command in Section 3 below).

> If you are likely to change the order of the cases in a file by using either the **Sort Cases** or **Split File** commands, then you will not be able to rely on the SPSS case numbers (the numbers on the extreme left of the data window) to identify participants. For this reason, it is always best to create your own participant identification variable and record this number both in the data file and on your original records so that you can check the data later if necessary.

The Sort Cases command

In this example we will sort the data by two variables, first by participants' sex, and then, within sex, we will sort by ethnicity.

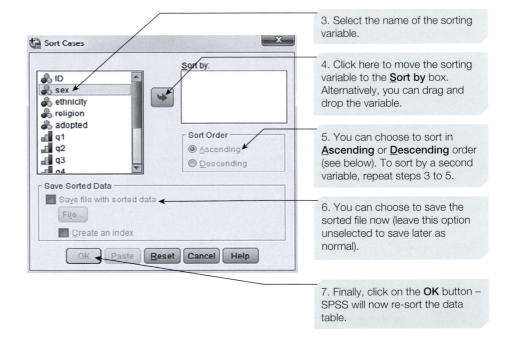

1. Click on the menu item **Data.**

2. Select **Sort Cases** to call up the Sort Cases dialogue box shown below.

3. Select the name of the sorting variable.

4. Click here to move the sorting variable to the **Sort by** box. Alternatively, you can drag and drop the variable.

5. You can choose to sort in **Ascending** or **Descending** order (see below). To sort by a second variable, repeat steps 3 to 5.

6. You can choose to save the sorted file now (leave this option unselected to save later as normal).

7. Finally, click on the **OK** button – SPSS will now re-sort the data table.

You can sort in either ascending or descending order. **Ascending** order puts participants with a low value on the sort variable before participants with a higher value (e.g. Male before Female if we used the code Male = 1, Female = 2). **Descending** would sort in the reverse order. You will probably want **Ascending** order.

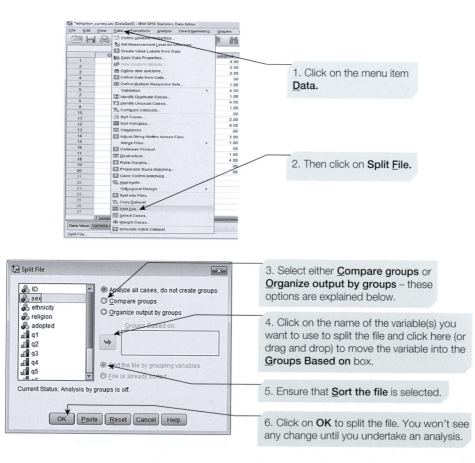

Looking at the data file we can see the file is now sorted by sex and ethnicity.

Note that after sorting the file, the participant number ('ID') no longer matches the case number. This is why we recommend including a variable for participant number.

Section 3: SPLITTING A FILE

The **Split File** function is a particularly useful feature of SPSS. **Split File** semi-permanently splits a data file into groups, and in subsequent analysis the output can be organised according to these groups. For example, you can request SPSS to organise all subsequent output so that statistics are presented separately for male and female participants. To split a file, follow the steps shown below.

1. Click on the menu item **Data.**

2. Then click on **Split File.**

3. Select either **Compare groups** or **Organize output by groups** – these options are explained below.

4. Click on the name of the variable(s) you want to use to split the file and click here (or drag and drop) to move the variable into the **Groups Based on** box.

5. Ensure that **Sort the file** is selected.

6. Click on **OK** to split the file. You won't see any change until you undertake an analysis.

Options

The difference between the options **Compare groups** and **Organize output by groups** is worth exploring. The former contrasts the two groups within one section of output, whereas the latter produces two different sections of output. We usually find **Organize output by groups** more useful, but try each so that you understand the difference.

Output

Initially, the only consequence of the **Split File** command is that two lines of text are added to the output window. This text serves as a reminder that the **Split File** is active. It tells you that the file has been sorted (this is a necessary first step that SPSS undertakes for you) and split using the separate output option. Subsequently, any command will be performed separately for each of the two groups. For example, if we **Split File** by sex, and then use the **Frequencies** command (see Chapter 3, Section 2) to obtain some information about the variable 'adopted' (which codes experience of adoption), the output will be shown first for the Male participants and then for the Female participants.

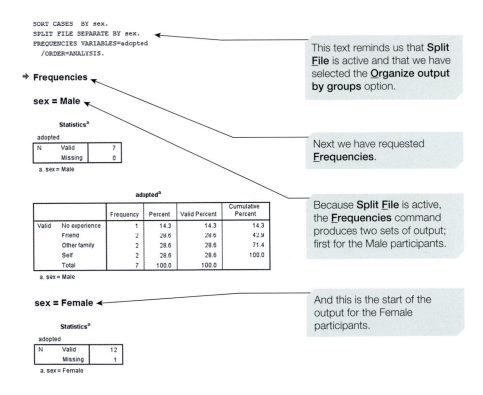

```
SORT CASES BY sex.
SPLIT FILE SEPARATE BY sex.
FREQUENCIES VARIABLES=adopted
  /ORDER=ANALYSIS.
```

This text reminds us that **Split File** is active and that we have selected the **Organize output by groups** option.

→ **Frequencies**

sex = Male

Statistics[a]

adopted		
N	Valid	7
	Missing	0

a. sex = Male

Next we have requested **Frequencies**.

adopted[a]

		Frequency	Percent	Valid Percent	Cumulative Percent
Valid	No experience	1	14.3	14.3	14.3
	Friend	2	28.6	28.6	42.9
	Other family	2	28.6	28.6	71.4
	Self	2	28.6	28.6	100.0
	Total	7	100.0	100.0	

a. sex = Male

Because **Split File** is active, the **Frequencies** command produces two sets of output; first for the Male participants.

sex = Female

Statistics[a]

adopted		
N	Valid	12
	Missing	1

a. sex = Female

And this is the start of the output for the Female participants.

Unsplitting a file

Remember that **Split File** is a semi-permanent change. Once you have executed the **Split File** command, the output from all other commands will be broken down by the selected variable. This will remain in force until you reverse the process by unsplit-ting the file. To do this, first repeat steps 1 and 2 above and then select the option **Analyze** all cases, do not create groups. Then click the ⬚ᵒᵏ button. From this point onwards, all the output will return to the normal format.

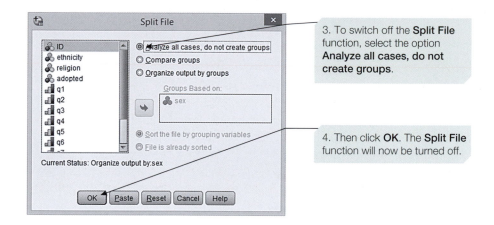

3. To switch off the **Split File** function, select the option **Analyze all cases, do not create groups**.

4. Then click **OK**. The **Split File** function will now be turned off.

Another option under the **Data** menu item is **Split into Files**. As the name implies, this allows you to divide the data file on the basis of one variable (e.g. sex) and save the different parts of the data set in separate data files. Although this might sound useful, in practice it is usually more efficient to keep the data together in a single file and use **Split File** or **Select Cases** (described in the next section) to achieve the analysis you want.

Section 4: SELECTING CASES

An alternative to splitting a file is to select certain cases and use only these in subse-quent analyses. For example, we might be particularly interested in the survey responses made by our Atheist respondents. **Select Cases** will allow us to analyse just these participants' responses. All other data will be temporarily suppressed.

Comparing the Select Cases and Split File commands

Select Cases is different from **Split File**. **Select Cases** suppresses analysis of non-selected cases, whereas **Split File** analyses all cases but arranges output by the sort-ing variable. Use **Select Cases** when you want to consider only some of your data. Use **Split File** when you want to contrast two or more groups of participants.

The Select Cases command

To <u>**Select Cases**</u>, perform the following steps.

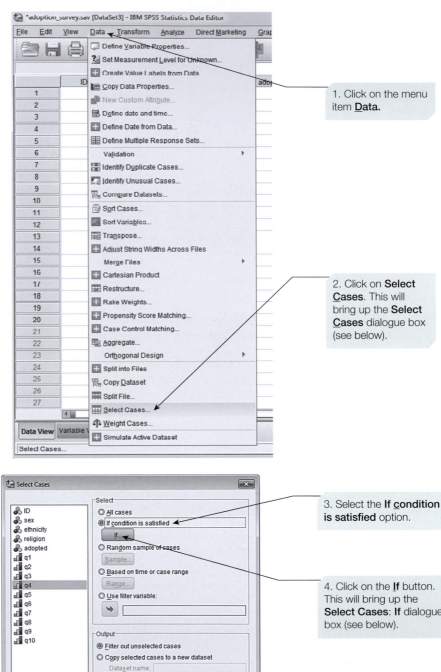

1. Click on the menu item **Data.**

2. Click on **Select Cases**. This will bring up the **Select Cases** dialogue box (see below).

3. Select the **If condition is satisfied** option.

4. Click on the **If** button. This will bring up the **Select Cases: If** dialogue box (see below).

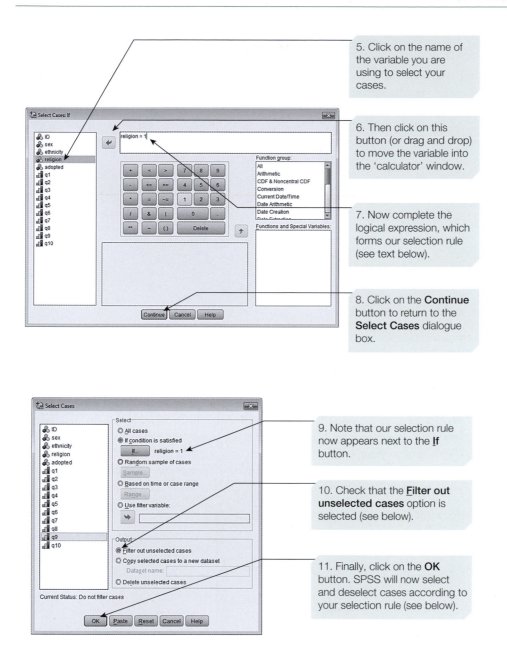

5. Click on the name of the variable you are using to select your cases.

6. Then click on this button (or drag and drop) to move the variable into the 'calculator' window.

7. Now complete the logical expression, which forms our selection rule (see text below).

8. Click on the **Continue** button to return to the **Select Cases** dialogue box.

9. Note that our selection rule now appears next to the **If** button.

10. Check that the **Filter out unselected cases** option is selected (see below).

11. Finally, click on the **OK** button. SPSS will now select and deselect cases according to your selection rule (see below).

In step 10 above, there are three options. The default is **Filter out unselected cases**. The second alternative, **Copy selected cases to a new dataset**, allows us to open a new data file that we can use to save just the selected cases. This is useful if we want to draw out a small subset of cases for separate analysis, leaving the original file unchanged. The third option, **Delete unselected cases**, will permanently delete the unselected cases from your data file. If you use this option, make certain that you have a backup copy of your data file.

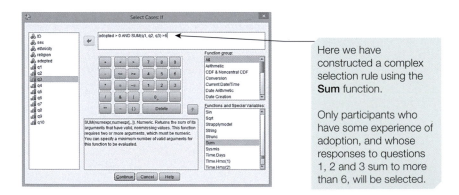

SPSS has put a line through the case number of the deselected cases. Note that only case 16 (an atheist) has been selected.

SPSS has created a new variable called 'filter_$', which it uses to choose which cases are selected.

Selection rules

You can construct very complex selection rules by using the logical operators AND, OR and NOT. The selection rules can either be typed in using the keyboard or can be built up using the calculator keypad that appears in the dialogue box. For example, if we wanted to select only Chinese Christians who had some experience of adoption, we could construct the following expression: **religion = 3 and ethnicity = 3 and adopted > 0**. The **Select Cases: If** dialogue box also contains useful functions you can use in constructing your selection rule. The functions are organised into groups; for example, there is a Statistical group containing various functions to calculate the mean, standard deviation and related values. Click on a group to see the available functions. If you click on a function name, a description will appear in the box next to the functions.

Here we have constructed a complex selection rule using the **Sum** function.

Only participants who have some experience of adoption, and whose responses to questions 1, 2 and 3 sum to more than 6, will be selected.

Selection methods

The **Select Cases** dialogue box offers a total of four methods of selecting cases (see step 3 on page 84). These are:

1. The default **If Condition is satisfied** method is the most useful method.

2. The **Random sample of cases** method allows you to sample cases at random from your data file, and SPSS allows you to specify either the number or percentage of cases to be selected.

3. The **<u>B</u>ased on time or case range** method allows you to select cases either by case number or on the basis of a time or date range.

4. In the **<u>U</u>se filter variable** method, a case is selected if the value of the chosen variable is not zero (and is not missing) – this option can be useful if you have a yes/no variable coded as 1/0. Using this method, you could easily select only the 'yes' responses.

It is useful to note that a line of text at the bottom of the **Select Cases** dialogue box indicates the current selection rule. Finally, remember to reselect **<u>A</u>ll cases** after you have completed your analysis of the selected cases.

Reselecting all cases

The **Select Cases** function can be very useful, but it is important to remember that it is semi-permanent. **Select Cases** will stay in force until you either make some other selection or choose the **<u>A</u>ll cases** option in the **Select Cases** dialogue box (see step 3 on page 84).

(see step 3 on page 84).

Section 5: RECODING VALUES

There are many occasions when you need to recode some of your data. This might be because you made an error when entering the data, but it is more likely that you will want to recode your data in light of results from a preliminary analysis, or in order to allow you to undertake an additional analysis.

For example, early analysis of our adoption survey might reveal that we have very few participants who report experience of adoption through either 'immediate family' or 'other family'. In light of this, we might decide to collapse these two categories together into one new category. We could do this manually but for a large data set that would be time-consuming. SPSS provides the **Recode** command for this purpose.

SPSS offers two **Recode** options. We can either change the values in the existing variable, or we can create a new variable for our recoded data. These two options are called **Recode into <u>S</u>ame Variables** and **Recode into Different Variables** respectively. It is usually safer to recode into a different (new) variable rather than overwriting the original data – that way, if you make a mistake, you will be able to go back to the original values and try again. To recode a variable, follow the steps outlined below.

Recode into Different Variables

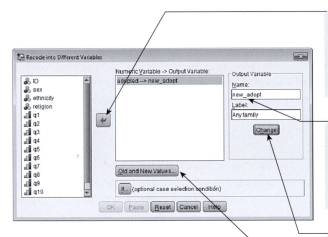

1. Click on the menu item **Transform**.

2. Choose which type of recode you want to perform – **Recode into Different Variables** is the safest.

3. Select the variable to be recoded and then click on this button to move it into the **Numeric Variable -> Output Variable** box (or drag and drop the variable).

4. Enter the name for the new variable for the recoded values. We have used the name 'new_adopt'. Add a label to help you remember the change.

5. Click the **Change** button.

6. Click here to bring up the **Old and New Values** dialogue box (see below).

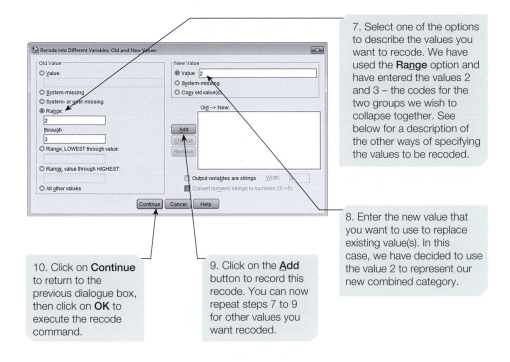

7. Select one of the options to describe the values you want to recode. We have used the **Range** option and have entered the values 2 and 3 – the codes for the two groups we wish to collapse together. See below for a description of the other ways of specifying the values to be recoded.

8. Enter the new value that you want to use to replace existing value(s). In this case, we have decided to use the value 2 to represent our new combined category.

9. Click on the **Add** button to record this recode. You can now repeat steps 7 to 9 for other values you want recoded.

10. Click on **Continue** to return to the previous dialogue box, then click on **OK** to execute the recode command.

Specifying the values to be recoded

In the **Recode into Different Variables: Old and New Values** dialogue box (see step 7 above), you are offered seven different methods of specifying the values you want to recode, and you can use a combination of these methods if required. The **Range, LOWEST through value:** and the **Range, value through HIGHEST:** are often very useful – for example if you want to collapse together all categories 6 and above, you could use the **Range, value through HIGHEST:** option entering the value 6 in the box. When specifying the values to be recoded, you should give careful consideration to your missing values. If, for example, you used 9 as the missing value, then recoding using the **Range, value through HIGHEST:** would result in the missing observation being included in the new category, which you may not want.

The **Value:** option allows you to specify a single value that you want to recode. The **All other values** option translates as 'and for everything I haven't yet specified' and allows you to tell SPSS how to recode all the values not covered by one of the previous recode instructions.

The **System-missing** and the **System- or user-missing** options are very powerful. System-missing values are rather like user-missing values (what, in Chapter 2, we simply called missing values). Both are used to indicate that there is no valid value for a variable. However, a system-missing value indicates that SPSS rather than you (the 'user') has declared a value non-valid – perhaps, for example, because, for this participant, it is not possible to calculate a valid value for the variable. These two options allow you to recode these two types of missing values but before you use them, think carefully about the implications of your actions.

Note if you enter a value into the **New Value** box, which has previously been specified as a missing value (see step 8 above), you can effectively remove a range of values from an analysis by recoding valid responses into missing values. Similarly, by clicking on the **System-missing** option in the **New Value** box, you can instruct SPSS to regard any value or range of values as system-missing from this point onwards.

The **Copy old value(s)** option is very useful, as it allows you to specify a range of values that should remain unchanged.

Remember: the big advantage of using **Recode into Different Variables** (rather than **Recode into Same Variables** described below) is that you do not lose anything. If you make an error, the original data are still available in the old variable and you can simply try again.

Recode into Same Variables

If you are certain that you know what you are doing, and you have a backup of your data file, you might decide that you can overwrite the existing data rather than create a new variable. To do this, select **Recode into Same Variables** at step 2 described on page 88. From this point onwards, the procedure is very similar to that described above except that you omit steps 4–6 as there is no new variable to name. The results of this recode will overwrite the original data in the data table.

Conditional recode

On some occasions, you might want to recode a variable only if a particular condition is satisfied for that participant. For example, you might want to perform the recode described above, but only for the female participants. This can be achieved by using the **If** button, which appears in both the **Recode into Different Variables** and the **Recode into Same Variables** dialogue boxes. Follow the procedure described on pages 88–9 up to step 10. At step 10 click **Continue**, then follow the steps described below.

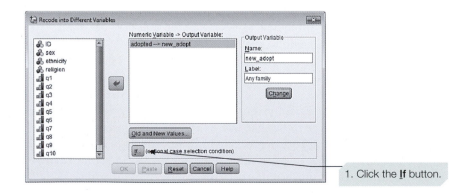

1. Click the **If** button.

2. Click here to indicate that you want to perform a conditional recode.

3. Select the name of the variable around which you are going to build your conditional rule, then click the arrow (or drag and drop) to move this variable into the box (as shown here).

4. Now complete your conditional statement using either your computer keyboard or the keypad or functions listed in the dialogue box.

5. Once you have written your conditional statement, click on **Continue** to return to the previous dialogue box (see below).

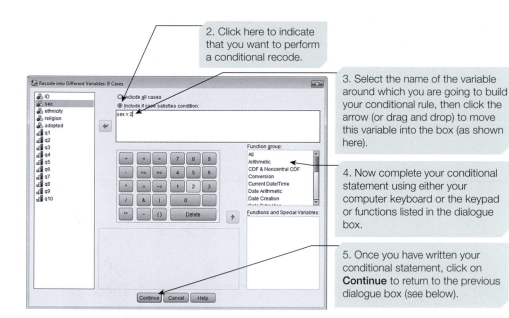

6. Note that your conditional rule is listed here.

7. Click **OK** to complete the conditional recode.

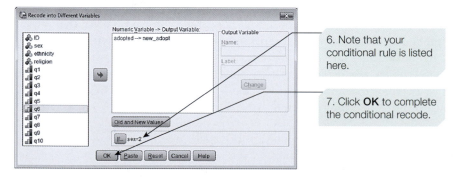

8. As a result of this **Recode into Different Variables** command, a new variable has been added to the data file ('new_adopted').

Note that most of the values for this variable have been set to system-missing (dot in the cell), indicating a value couldn't be computed. This happened because in step 3 above, we specified that we wanted this recode only to apply to females who had experience of adoption in their family (adopted values of 2 or 3).

CHAPTER 4

The rules for constructing the conditional statement (or logical expression) are the same as in the **Select If** command described earlier. You can construct quite complex logical expressions by using a combination of the functions provided and the operators (add, subtract etc.) available on the calculator style buttons. Some of the less obvious buttons are listed below:

**	Raise to the power (for example, '3**2' is equivalent to $3^2 = 9$)
<=	Less than or equal to
>=	Greater than or equal to
~=	Not equal to
&	And
|	Or
~	Not

Section 6: COMPUTING NEW VARIABLES

Sometimes we need to calculate a new variable based on the values of existing variables. For example, you may have entered the response given by each participant to each question in a questionnaire. You could now use SPSS to calculate the overall score for the questionnaire or several separate scores for subscales within the questionnaire. In our fictitious survey of attitudes to adoption, we administered a 10-item questionnaire, which was made up of two subscales. We therefore need to sum the responses to the items that contribute to each of the subscales. SPSS can do this for us using the **Compute Variable** command.

*adoption_survey.sav [DataSet3] - IBM SPSS Statistics Data Editor

File   Edit   View   Data   Transform   Analyze   Direct Marketing   Graphs

28 : q4

	religion	ad
1	3.00	
2	3.00	
3	2.00	
4	2.00	
5	6.00	
6	5.00	
7	3.00	
8	6.00	
9	3.00	
10	3.00	
11	5.00	

Compute Variable...
Programmability Transformation...
Count Values within Cases...
Shift Values...
Recode into Same Variables...
Recode into Different Variables...
Automatic Recode...
Create Dummy Variables
Visual Binning...
Optimal Binning...
Anonymize Variables
Prepare Data for Modeling   ▶
Rank Cases...

1. Click on menu item **Transform.**

2. Select **Compute Variable**.

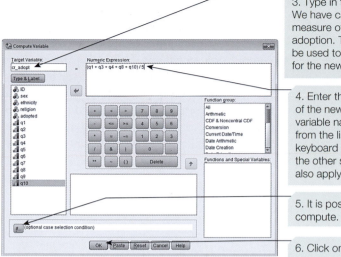

3. Type in the name of the new variable. We have called it 'cr_adopt', as it is a measure of attitudes to cross-racial adoption. The **Type & Label** button can be used to add labels and set the type for the new variable.

4. Enter the formula for the computation of the new variable here. Either type variable names or drag and drop them from the list on the left. Use the keyboard or the screen buttons to add the other symbols you need. You can also apply functions.

5. It is possible to perform a conditional compute.

6. Click on **OK**.

When entering the name of the new variable (see step 3 above), it is possible to enter a variable label to act as a reminder of what the new variable means. Do this by clicking on the **Type & Label** button. You can then either type in a text label, or by selecting the **Use expression as label** option, you can ask SPSS to use your numeric expression as the variable label. In this case, the label would be 'COMPUTE cr_adopt=(q1+q3+q4+q8+q10) / 5'.

*adoption_survey.sav [DataSet3] - IBM SPSS Statistics Data

File   Edit   View   Data   Transform   Analyze   Di

6 : new_adopt

	adopted	q1	q2	q10	cr_adopt
1	1.00	4.00	4.00	2.00	4.00
2	.00	4.00	1.00	5.00	4.40
3	1.00	2.00	3.00	1.00	1.60
4	.00	2.00	1.00	1.00	1.60
5	.00	4.00	5.00	3.00	3.80
6	.00	2.00	1.00	1.00	
7	4.00	1.00	1.00	5.00	2.40
8	4.00	1.00	2.00	1.00	1.40
9	2.00	1.00	1.00	1.00	1.20
10	3.00	2.00	2.00	2.00	2.00
11	.00	5.00	4.00	5.00	5.00
12	1.00	4.00	4.00	3.00	3.00
13	1.00	3.00	3.00	4.00	3.00
14	2.00	2.00	3.00	5.00	3.40
15	1.00	9.00	1.00	2.00	.
16	4.00	1.00	2.00	2.00	1.60
17	.00	5.00	4.00	5.00	4.40
18	2.00	5.00	4.00	4.00	.
19	4.00	1.00	1.00	1.00	1.20
20	9.00	1.00	2.00	3.00	2.20
21					
22					

7. This is our new variable 'cr_adopt' – the average of the scores on items 1, 3, 4, 8 and 10.

8. Note that SPSS has put a dot in this cell to represent a system-missing value. SPSS cannot calculate a valid value (see step 9).

9. SPSS can't calculate a valid value because participant 15 did not respond to question 1 and we therefore entered a missing value (9). See below.

CHAPTER 4

Compute and Missing Values

When using **Compute Variable**, it is important to think carefully about missing values. SPSS will not be able to compute the value of the new variable if any of the values for the variables involved in the compute statement are missing. In the example above, participant 15 had not answered question 1 (q1) and we had entered a missing value (9) in this cell of the data table. As a result, SPSS is unable to compute a value for the new variable 'cr_adopt' for this participant. With complex compute statements involving lots of variables, this can be a major problem. One way round this is to make use of functions such as **Mean**, which make automatic allowances for missing values. This is illustrated below.

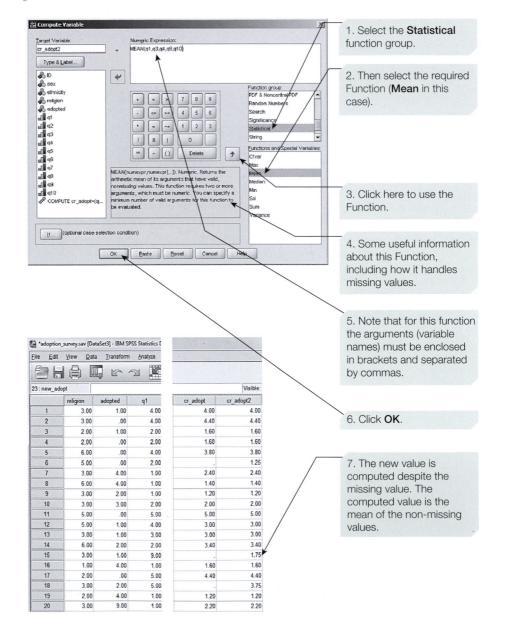

1. Select the **Statistical** function group.

2. Then select the required Function (**Mean** in this case).

3. Click here to use the Function.

4. Some useful information about this Function, including how it handles missing values.

5. Note that for this function the arguments (variable names) must be enclosed in brackets and separated by commas.

6. Click **OK**.

7. The new value is computed despite the missing value. The computed value is the mean of the non-missing values.

It is important to consider whether the new values computed using functions in this way are legitimate. For example, if you use the **Sum** function, then in cases where one or more values are missing, the total will be made up of fewer values. This may or may not be what you want. Before undertaking a **C̲ompute Variable** command, think carefully about what will happen in cases with missing values.

Section 7: COUNTING VALUES

Sometimes it is useful to be able to count for each participant how many times a particular value occurs over a range of variables. If, as in our example data set, you have a series of variables that represent the responses to questionnaire items, you might want to find out how many times each participant has answered 'Strongly Agree'. You could do this by asking SPSS to count the number of times the value 1 (the value used to code the response 'Strongly Agree') has occurred in variables 'q1' to 'q10'. Using **C̲ount Values within Cases**, SPSS will create a new variable that will contain a value representing the number of times the value 1 occurs in variables 'q1' to 'q10'.

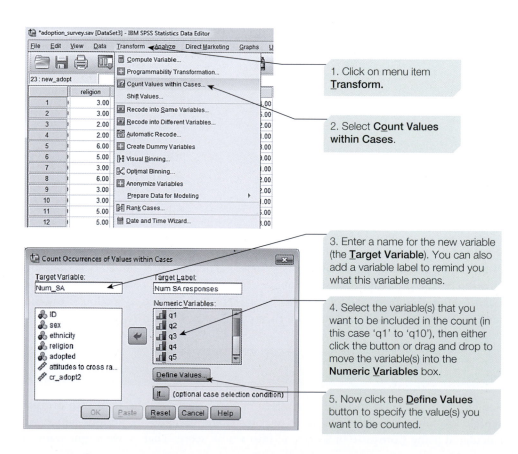

1. Click on menu item **Transform.**

2. Select **C̲ount Values within Cases**.

3. Enter a name for the new variable (the **Target Variable**). You can also add a variable label to remind you what this variable means.

4. Select the variable(s) that you want to be included in the count (in this case 'q1' to 'q10'), then either click the button or drag and drop to move the variable(s) into the **Numeric V̲ariables** box.

5. Now click the **Define Values** button to specify the value(s) you want to be counted.

When selecting more than one variable – as in step 4 above – you can select them all in one go by holding down the <shift> key and clicking on the first and then the last of the variables. You can then use the mouse to drag and drop the variables as a block.

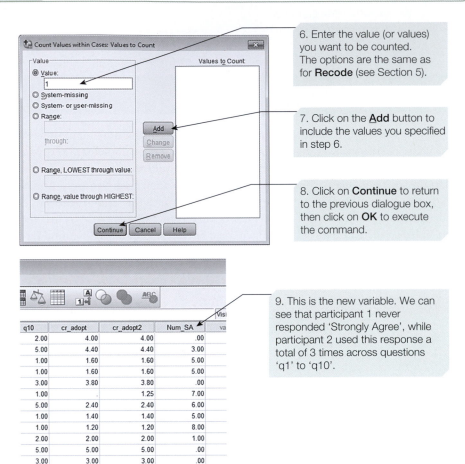

6. Enter the value (or values) you want to be counted. The options are the same as for **Recode** (see Section 5).

7. Click on the **Add** button to include the values you specified in step 6.

8. Click on **Continue** to return to the previous dialogue box, then click on **OK** to execute the command.

9. This is the new variable. We can see that participant 1 never responded 'Strongly Agree', while participant 2 used this response a total of 3 times across questions 'q1' to 'q10'.

q10	cr_adopt	cr_adopt2	Num_SA	va
2.00	4.00	4.00	.00	
5.00	4.40	4.40	3.00	
1.00	1.60	1.60	5.00	
1.00	1.60	1.60	5.00	
3.00	3.80	3.80	.00	
1.00	.	1.25	7.00	
5.00	2.40	2.40	6.00	
1.00	1.40	1.40	5.00	
1.00	1.20	1.20	8.00	
2.00	2.00	2.00	1.00	
5.00	5.00	5.00	.00	
3.00	3.00	3.00	.00	

Conditional Count

It is possible to perform a conditional count – where we only count the occurrences of a value(s) for participants who satisfy some particular criterion. This is done by clicking on the **If** button after step 5 above. This will bring up a dialogue box almost identical to the one we used for the conditional recode described in Section 5. You can now specify your conditional rule and then click on the **Continue** button.

Section 8: RANKING CASES

Sometimes it is useful to convert interval or ratio scores (scale data) into ordinal scores. We might, for example, want to convert the variable 'cr_adopt', which we calculated using **Compute** in Section 6, into a rank score. That is, we might want to rank all our participants on the basis of their score on this variable. The participant who had the highest overall 'cr_adopt' score would be given a rank of 1, the next highest a rank of 2 and so on. The **Rank Cases** command calculates the ranks for us and generates a new variable to contain the ranks. We can rank in either ascending or descending order, and can even rank on the basis of more than one variable.

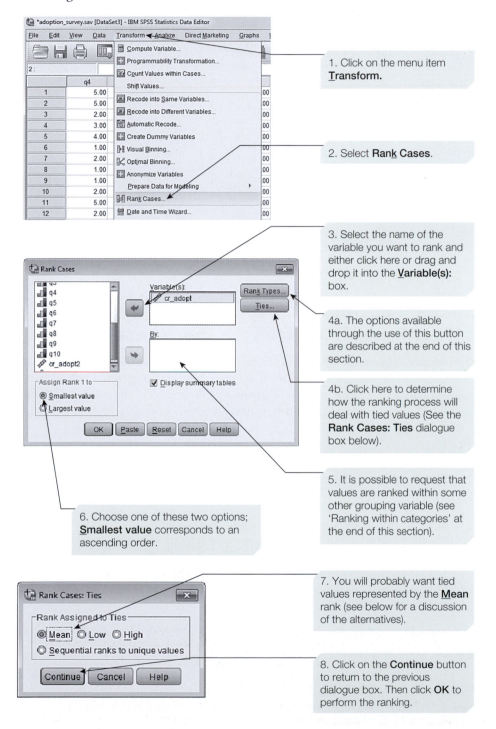

1. Click on the menu item **Transform.**

2. Select **Rank Cases**.

3. Select the name of the variable you want to rank and either click here or drag and drop it into the **Variable(s):** box.

4a. The options available through the use of this button are described at the end of this section.

4b. Click here to determine how the ranking process will deal with tied values (See the **Rank Cases: Ties** dialogue box below).

5. It is possible to request that values are ranked within some other grouping variable (see 'Ranking within categories' at the end of this section).

6. Choose one of these two options; **Smallest value** corresponds to an ascending order.

7. You will probably want tied values represented by the **Mean** rank (see below for a discussion of the alternatives).

8. Click on the **Continue** button to return to the previous dialogue box. Then click **OK** to perform the ranking.

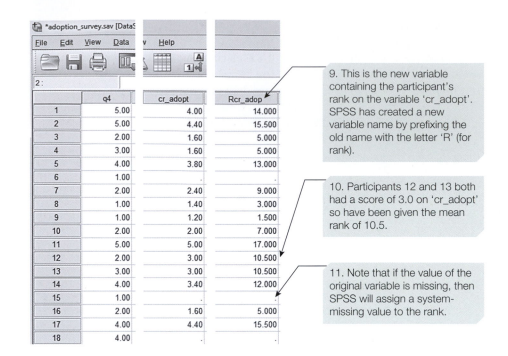

9. This is the new variable containing the participant's rank on the variable 'cr_adopt'. SPSS has created a new variable name by prefixing the old name with the letter 'R' (for rank).

10. Participants 12 and 13 both had a score of 3.0 on 'cr_adopt' so have been given the mean rank of 10.5.

11. Note that if the value of the original variable is missing, then SPSS will assign a system-missing value to the rank.

Ranking tied values

SPSS provides four alternative methods of dealing with tied values:

1. The default, **Mean** method, gives the tied values the mean of the available ranks. You can see this option in operation above where participants 12 and 13 both scored 3.0 on 'cr_adopt' and were given a rank of 10.5 – the mean of ranks 10 and 11. This is the ranking method described in most introductory statistics books.

2. The **Low** option assigns the tied participants the lowest of the available ranks – so in this case both would have been ranked 10.

3. The **High** option would award both participants the highest of the available ranks – 11 in this case.

4. The **Sequential ranks to unique values** option would assign a rank of 10 to both participant 12 and 13, but would then assign a rank of 11 to the next highest scoring participant, thus ensuring that all the sequential ranks are awarded – this means that the highest rank will *not* be equal to the number of valid cases (as it would for the other three methods).

Types of ranking

SPSS provides a wide range of different ranking methods. These are available by clicking on the **Rank Types** button (see step 4a above). Use the help button for more information about these options. If in doubt leave the **Mean** option selected.

Ranking within categories

By specifying a second variable in the **By**: box (see step 5 on page 97), it is possible to request SPSS to rank the scores on the first variable within categories formed by the second variable. For example, if we specified the variable 'sex' in this box, then SPSS would first rank all the male participants and then rank all the female participants. Thus, in this case, we would have two participants (one male and one female) with a rank of 1.

Section 9: DATA TRANSFORMATION

Data transformation involves applying a mathematical function to every value in a data set to systematically change the values. At its simplest, data transformation could involve adding a constant, or converting from a raw score into a percentage score. For example, we might give students a simple statistics test scored out of 11. We could then transform these raw scores into percentage values by applying the formula PercentScore = (RawScore/11)*100.

One of the most common data transformations used in psychology is the log transformation. Log transformations (or log transforms) involve replacing every value in a data set with the log of the value. You will remember from your secondary school maths classes that the logarithm of a value is the exponent to which the base must be raised to produce that number. Common logs (written as $\log_{10}$) use a base of 10, while natural logs ($\log_e$, sometimes written as ln) use the mathematical constant, e (approximately 2.71828), as their base. For example, because $10^2 = 100$, the common log of 100 is 2. This is written as $\log_{10}(100) = 2$. The natural log of 100 is approximately 4.605. That is, $\log_e(100) = 4.605$, and $e^{4.605} = 100$.

The table below shows the relationship between raw values (x), and the $\log_{10}$ and $\log_e$ of these values.

x	1	10	100	1000	10000	100000	1000000
$\log_{10}(x)$	0	1	2	3	4	5	6
$\log_e(x)$	0	2.30	4.61	6.91	9.21	11.51	13.82

Looking at this table, we can see one useful characteristic of logs. With each order of magnitude increase in the value x, the log of this value increases by a much smaller constant amount (in the case of common logs increasing by just 1). We can use this characteristic of logs to our advantage to rescale certain types of data. Often data are not normally distributed, showing either a positive or a negative skew. For example, a data set in which most values are close to the mean value, with a few much higher values, is said to have a 'positive skew' and when plotted in a histogram will appear asymmetric around the mean, with a longer tail to the right than the left. Skewed data such as these can invalidate certain inferential statistical tests. A simple solution is to undertake a log transform of the data by calculating the log of each raw value. This is often enough to reduce the skew in the data, allowing us to proceed with our analysis using the transformed data. We demonstrate this process below.

CHAPTER 4

Log transformation of decision latency data

To illustrate the use of log transformations, we will work with a file containing decision latency data from 129 trials in which participants were required to decide whether two photographs were of the same or different people. The time taken to reach this decision was recorded. Time-based data such as these are often positively skewed because there is no upper limit to how long participants can take to respond. Participants need a finite minimum amount of time to respond to a stimulus, but they could lose concentration and take seconds, minutes or even hours to respond. As a result, decision time data typically have a strong positive skew.

To follow this example, download the data file called 'LogTransformDemo.sav' from he.palgrave.com/psychology/brace.

First, we will use the **Explore** command to check whether the raw data are normally distributed.

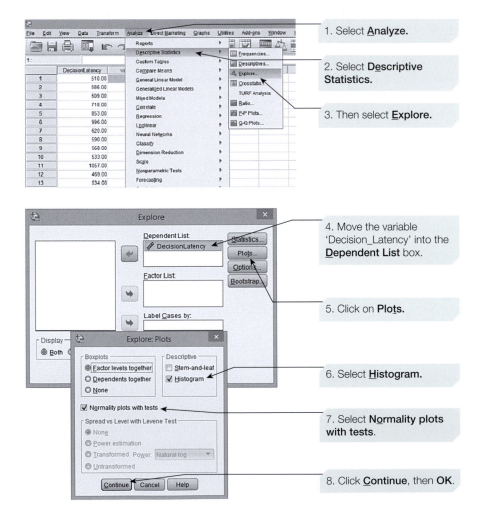

Tests of Normality

	Kolmogorov-Smirnov[a]			Shapiro-Wilk		
	Statistic	df	Sig.	Statistic	df	Sig.
DecisionLatency	.084	129	.025	.959	129	.001

a. Lilliefors Significance Correction

This table reports two tests of the 'normality' of the distribution (the Kolmogorov-Smirnov and Shapiro-Wilk tests). Both are significant (Sig value less than .05), indicating that this distribution is significantly different from a normal distribution.

DecisionLatency

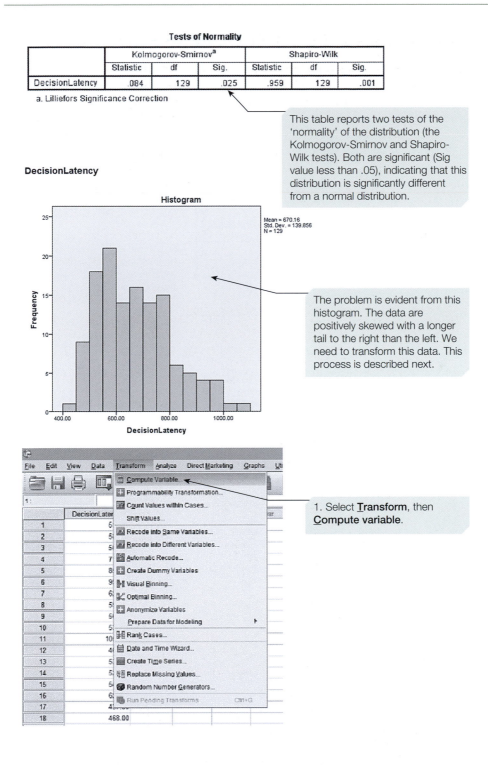

Histogram

Mean = 670.16
Std. Dev. = 139.856
N = 129

The problem is evident from this histogram. The data are positively skewed with a longer tail to the right than the left. We need to transform this data. This process is described next.

1. Select **Transform**, then **Compute variable**.

CHAPTER 4

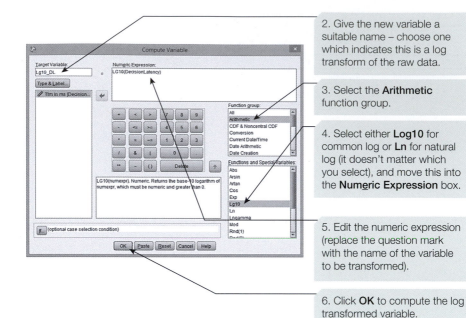

2. Give the new variable a suitable name – choose one which indicates this is a log transform of the raw data.

3. Select the **Arithmetic** function group.

4. Select either **Log10** for common log or **Ln** for natural log (it doesn't matter which you select), and move this into the **Numeric Expression** box.

5. Edit the numeric expression (replace the question mark with the name of the variable to be transformed).

6. Click **OK** to compute the log transformed variable.

The new variable is added to the data file. To illustrate this process, we have computed two new variables, the first is a $\log_{10}$ transform, the other a $\log_e$ transform. Note that these two transformations have different values, but as we will see shortly, they produce similar shaped distributions.

	DecisionLatency	Lg10_DL	Ln_DL
1	510.00	2.71	6.23
2	586.00	2.77	6.37
3	509.00	2.71	6.23
4	718.00	2.86	6.58
5	853.00	2.93	6.75
6	996.00	3.00	6.90
7	620.00	2.79	6.43
8	590.00	2.77	6.38
9	568.00	2.75	6.34
10	533.00	2.73	6.28
11	1057.00	3.02	6.96
12	469.00	2.67	6.15
13	534.00	2.73	6.28
14	520.00	2.72	6.25
15	549.00	2.74	6.31
16	629.00	2.80	6.44
17	437.00	2.64	6.08
18	468.00	2.67	6.15

Now repeat the Explore analysis described above. This time include both the original variable and the transformed variable.

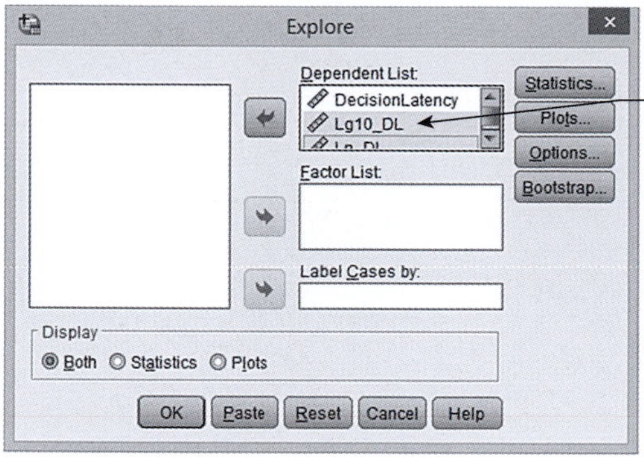

Repeat the **Explore** analysis with the new transformed variable included in the **Dependent List**.

Sections of the output are shown below. If you look at the second table of output (not shown here), you will see that the descriptive statistics for the original raw data and the transformed variables are quite different. However, despite this, the skew and kurtosis values that provide measures of the shape of the distribution are the same.

Tests of Normality

	Kolmogorov-Smirnov[a]			Shapiro-Wilk		
	Statistic	df	Sig.	Statistic	df	Sig.
DecisionLatency	.084	129	.025	.959	129	.001
Lg10_DL	.064	129	.200*	.981	129	.070
Ln_DL	.064	129	.200*	.981	129	.070

*. This is a lower bound of the true significance.

a. Lilliefors Significance Correction

Note that although the raw data (first line of this table) are not normally distributed, the two log transformations have both successfully normalized the data. The Kolmogorov-Smirnov and Shapiro-Wilk tests show no significant deviation from normality. Note also that these two transformations give rise to identical values for these two statistics.

CHAPTER 4

DecisionLatency

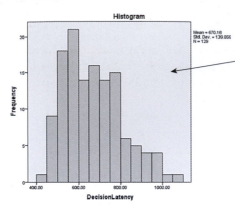

This is the histogram of the raw data we saw earlier. The positive skew (longer tail to the right) is apparent.

Lg10_DL

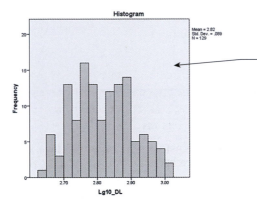

This is the histogram of the data after a $\log_{10}$ transformation. Compared to the raw data above, it is apparent that the distribution is now much more symmetric around the mean.

Ln_DL

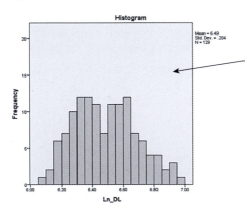

This is the histogram of the data after a $\log_e$ transformation. Although the two transformed variables have different means and standard deviations, both transformations have been equally effective in normalizing the data.

Section 10: DATA FILE FOR SCALES OR QUESTIONNAIRES

In this section, we demonstrate how SPSS can be used to help you handle data obtained using scales or questionnaires. We describe a simple data check, and how to recode responses from reversed items. Checking the reliability and dimensionality of a scale are covered in Chapter 12, Sections 4 and 5.

We have entered data obtained with Larsen's (1995) Attitudes Toward Recycling (ATR) scale, used for a research methods exercise with first-year psychology students at University of Westminster. There are 20 items, used in the order they are printed in Larsen (1995, Table 1). Two changes were made, as Larsen developed his scale in the USA: 'styrofoam' was replaced with 'polystyrene'; 'sorting garbage' was replaced with 'sorting rubbish into different containers'. We used a Likert-type scale with responses from 1 (strongly agree) to 5 (strongly disagree). The data file 'ScaleV1.sav' (available from the Appendix or he.palgrave.com/psychology/brace) includes data from 50 cases, which we will use to demonstrate some issues around use of scales in psychology. Normally one would need many more cases.

Open the data file and note that:

1. 'Qnum' (Questionnaire Number) is the identification number we wrote on the paper copies of the questionnaires as we entered the data. We have included it so we can check our data file against our paper records, even if the order of cases in the data file is changed by sorting the file (see Section 2).

2. The responses to each item have been entered separately: 'q_a' to 'q_t'. Students often prefer to calculate the total or mean score by hand and then enter these values only. However, it is better practice to enter the response to each item. This allows us to undertake various checks on the data before using **Compute** to calculate the total or mean response for each participant.

3. In this data set we have used 9 as the missing value for each of the scale items.

A simple check on data entry

Using the process described in Chapter 3, Section 6, check the data using the **Descriptives** command. A section of the output is shown below. Inspect the minimum and maximum values of each item. In this case, you will note that for 'q_c' the maximum value is 6, yet the responses were from 1 to 5. Note any such oddities.

Descriptive Statistics

	N	Minimum	Maximum	Mean	Std. Deviation
q_a	50	2	5	3.96	.832
q_b	50	1	5	2.06	.913
q_c	50	2	6	3.94	1.058
q_d	50	2	5	4.34	.688

This error in data entry can be found and corrected in the following way:

1. In Data View, click on the 'q_c' variable name.

2. Click on menu items **Edit** ⇒ **Find**. This will bring up the **Find and Replace - Data view** dialogue box.

3. Enter the value 6 in the **Find** field and click on the **Find Next** button.

4. With each click on the **Find Next** button, SPSS will locate the next instance of the value 6 for this variable.

5. Make the necessary correction to these values. In this data file there is only one error: the response on questionnaire 2 to item c should be 5 not 6. Correct that response, and save the data file as 'ScaleV2.sav', so that you can use it in the next exercise.

Reversals

Good scales or questionnaires often include items that are reverse coded to avoid a participant response bias. We can use SPSS to reverse the coding of these items. First consider which direction you want a high score to indicate. For example, consider these two items from a library satisfaction questionnaire:

1. The university library is an excellent place to make notes for coursework.

2. I find it very difficult to study in the university library.

With responses on a scale of 1 (strongly agree) to 5 (strongly disagree), an individual with a strong positive view of the library should respond in opposite directions to those two items. Consider whether you want your final score to represent overall *satisfaction* with the library or overall *dissatisfaction*. This will determine which items you reverse.

This type of data can be scored in either direction. Use the variable label to keep a note of the direction of the scoring.

In the case of the 'ScaleV2.sav' data file, we want a high score to indicate that the participant has positive attitudes towards recycling and related environmental issues, so items b, g, h, i, k, l, m, p, q and r need to be reversed. We can do this using the **Recode** command in the following way (also see Section 5 above).

1. Click on menu items **Transform** ⇒ **Recode into Different Variables**.

2. In the **Recode into Different Variables** dialogue box, select the first variable that needs to be reverse coded (q_b) and provide a new name for the output variable: we suggest q_bR (the R indicates the variable has been reversed). Click on the **Change** button.

3. Repeat this process for each of the variables that need to be reversed.

4. Click on the **Old and New Values** button.

5. In the **Recode into Different Variables: Old and New Values** dialogue box, enter the old and new values one at a time. In this case, we want to recode a value of 5 as 1, 4 as 2, 2 as 4 and 1 as 5. The value 3 remains unchanged (see below). In

addition, you can recode any missing values into System-missing values. An alternative is to use the **Copy old value(s)** option, but you would need to remember to set 9 as missing for the new variables.

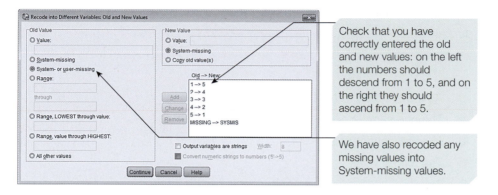

Check that you have correctly entered the old and new values: on the left the numbers should descend from 1 to 5, and on the right they should ascend from 1 to 5.

We have also recoded any missing values into System-missing values.

6. Click on **Continue**, then on **OK**. The new variables will be added at the right-hand end of the data file.

7. Once you have checked the **Recode** has worked correctly, you can delete the original variables. This will prevent you from using the old version by mistake; however, only do this after you have saved a backup copy of your original data file.

8. Save the data file as 'ScaleV3.sav'. The variables and the first case should be as shown below. The file is now ready to use in other exercises on assessing the reliability and dimensionality of the scale (Chapter 12, Sections 4 and 5).

Qnum	q_a	q_c	q_d	q_e	q_f	q_j	q_n	q_o	q_s	q_t	q_bR	q_gR	q_hR	q_iR	q_kR	q_lR	q_mR	q_pR	q_qR	q_rR
1	4	3	4	4	4	4	5	4	3	5	4	4	4	4	4	4	3	3	1	3

Summary

- This chapter demonstrated a series of useful commands that allow us to manipulate the contents of the data file.

- Using these commands, it is possible to change the coding of variables, to compute new variables, or to select only certain cases for subsequent analysis.

- These commands are particularly valuable when managing large data sets such as those produced in survey research.

- The compute command can also be used to transform data so they meet the assumptions of inferential tests. One of the most common transformations, the log transform, was demonstrated and we saw how this normalized a set of previously skewed data.

- Section 10 illustrated the use of some of these commands in a survey study.

5

Tests of difference for one- and two-sample designs

In this chapter

- An introduction to *t*-tests
- The one-sample *t*-test
- The independent *t*-test
- The paired *t*-test
- An introduction to nonparametric tests of difference
- The Mann–Whitney test
- The Wilcoxon test

SPSS for Psychologists online
Visit he.palgrave.com/psychology/brace for data sets,
online tutorials and exercises.

Section 1: AN INTRODUCTION TO *t*-TESTS

- The *t*-test is used to determine whether two means are significantly different from one another.

- There are three types of *t*-test:

  ○ The one-sample *t*-test, which is the simplest, determines whether the observed mean is different from a population mean.

  ○ The independent *t*-test is used when comparing means from two independent groups of individuals.

  ○ The paired *t*-test is used when comparing the means of two sets of observations from the same individuals (e.g. repeated measures design) or from pairs of individuals (e.g. when using a matched-subjects design).

- All forms of the *t*-test are parametric tests and make certain assumptions about the data: that they are measured at interval or ratio level, meet the assumption of homogeneity of variance, and are drawn from a population that has a normal distribution (see Chapter 1, Section 2).

- When reporting descriptive statistics to accompany the results of the *t*-test, you should give the mean and standard deviation as the measures of central tendency and dispersion.

- In some textbooks you might find this test referred to as the Student's *t*-test. This is because William Gossett, who devised the test, worked for the Guinness Brewing Company, which did not permit him to publish under his own name, so he wrote under the pseudonym of 'Student'.

Section 2: THE ONE-SAMPLE *t*-TEST

We mentioned in Section 1 that the *t*-test is used to determine whether two means are significantly different from one another. The one-sample *t*-test allows us to compare the sample mean against a known population mean. For example, we might want to see whether the mean from a group of participants differs from a predefined value, such as the population mean IQ score, or an expected value based on previous research. This test should be used when the data meet the assumptions for a parametric test.

Example study: assessing memory

For the purposes of demonstrating how to perform the one-sample *t*-test, we will use fictitious data from a made-up study. An enthusiastic teacher, who also happens to be a psychology graduate, noticed that some of the children in the final year of primary school class consistently forgot to bring in their sports kit, their lunch box or their homework, and frequently forgot the instructions given to them in class. She wondered if this was because they were generally more forgetful due to poorer memory skills. She therefore asked permission to administer a standardised test of long-term memory, which had a published norm of 75% for children of this age group. She performed the one-sample *t*-test on the data she collected to test the hypothesis that the mean of her sample differed from the expected value of 75%. This was a two-tailed hypothesis as she was unable to find any previous relevant literature or theory to suggest there would be a difference. The results showed that her sample mean was significantly lower than the expected value.

If you use this fictitious data set and follow the instructions given next, you will be able to compare the output you produce with the annotated output we give at the end of this section. (These data are available in the Appendix or from he.palgrave.com/psychology/brace.)

CHAPTER 5

To perform a one-sample *t*-test

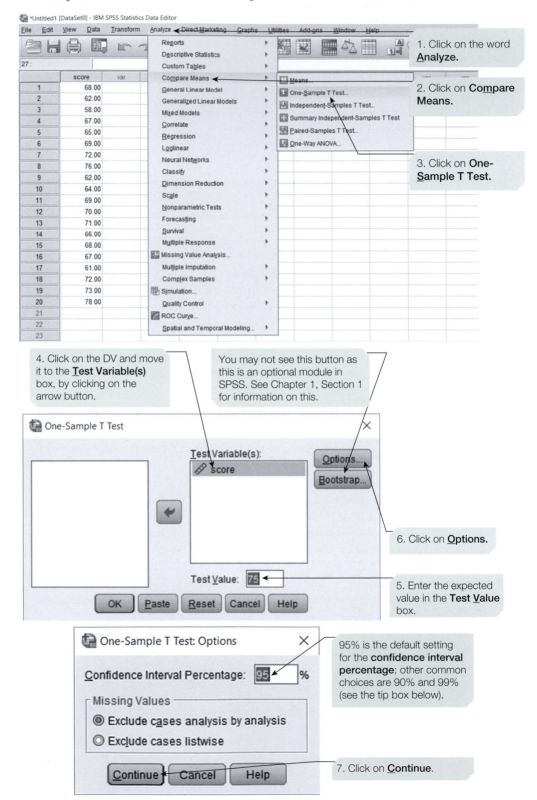

CHAPTER 5

1. Click on the word **Analyze.**

2. Click on **Compare Means.**

3. Click on **One-Sample T Test.**

4. Click on the DV and move it to the **Test Variable(s)** box, by clicking on the arrow button.

You may not see this button as this is an optional module in SPSS. See Chapter 1, Section 1 for information on this.

6. Click on **Options.**

5. Enter the expected value in the **Test Value** box.

95% is the default setting for the **confidence interval percentage**; other common choices are 90% and 99% (see the tip box below).

7. Click on **Continue.**

8. Finally, click on [OK] in the **One-Sample T Test** dialogue box. The output of the *t*-test will appear in the Output window, and we show this with annotations below. We also show you how you would describe the results of the test, were you to write a report on this study.

Confidence intervals describe the limits within which the population mean is likely to fall (see Chapter 1, Section 1). The default, 95%, indicates that there is a 95% probability of the population mean falling between the limits shown in the output. SPSS allows us to make these confidence intervals narrower or wider. For example, if we are conducting a study with important clinical implications, where we want to estimate the population mean with a higher degree of precision, we might choose 99% confidence intervals.

SPSS output for one-sample *t*-test

Obtained using menu items: Compare Means > One-Sample T Test

T-Test

[DataSet0]

Useful descriptives showing the number of children and their mean score (*M*) and standard deviation (*SD*) on the memory test.

One-Sample Statistics

	N	Mean	Std. Deviation	Std. Error Mean
score	20	67.9000	5.06692	1.13300

One-Sample Test

	Test Value = 75					
					95% Confidence Interval of the Difference	
	t	df	Sig. (2-tailed)	Mean Difference	Lower	Upper
score	-6.267	19	.000	-7.10000	-9.4714	-4.7286

So, *t* = 6.27 and note that we ignore the minus sign.

The degrees of freedom (df) = 19.

Sig. (2-tailed) is the *p*-value for a two-tailed test. This needs to be smaller than .05 for the result to be significant. A *p* value can never equal zero. SPSS rounds to three decimal places, so here *p* must be less than .0005 (see the tip box below on reporting *p* values).

Reporting the results

In a report you might write:

Performance on a memory test by a group of forgetful children was on average lower ($M = 67.9\%$, $SD = 5.07$) compared to the expected value of 75%. A one-sample t-test showed that this difference was significant ($t = 6.27$, df = 19, $p < .001$, two-tailed).

Guidance provided by the American Psychological Association recommends that we report statistics such as t to two decimal places, and p values less than .001 as $p < .001$. If p values are greater than .001, the exact value should be reported up to two or three decimal places. NB: A leading zero is not used when reporting values that can never be greater than 1, such as p values.

Section 3: THE INDEPENDENT t-TEST

The independent t-test compares the performance of the participants in group A with the performance of the participants in group B. This test should be used when the data meet the assumptions for a parametric test and are obtained using an independent groups design. These two groups could constitute a male and a female group because we wish to examine sex differences, or they could constitute two groups of participants who undergo different drug conditions: one a low dose drug condition and one a high dose drug condition. This type of t-test is often also called an *unrelated* t-test.

Example study: the memory experiment

In the example shown next, we use the data from the memory experiment used in the data entry exercise in Chapter 2, Section 6. It was hypothesised that the group receiving mnemonic instructions would remember more words than the group who did not receive any specific mnemonic instructions. If you use these data and follow the instructions given next, you will be able to compare the output you produce with the annotated output we give at the end of this section.

To perform an independent *t*-test

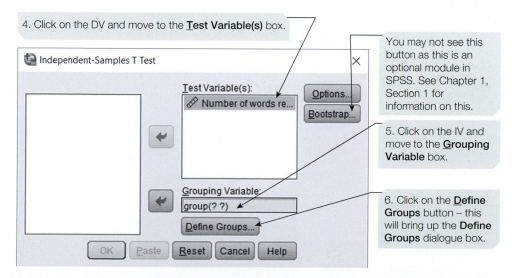

4. You will now be presented with the **Independent-Samples T Test** dialogue box (see below). As is typical in the IBM SPSS Statistics software (SPSS), the box on the left lists all the variables in your data file. Click on the name of the dependent variable (DV) in your analysis and then click on the arrow button to move this variable name into the box marked **Test Variable(s)**.

5. Now click on the name of the independent variable (IV) and then click on the arrow button to move this into the box marked **Grouping Variable**.

Once you have entered the dependent and independent variables into their appropriate boxes, the dialogue box will look like this:

CHAPTER 5

6. Click on the **Define Groups** button to bring up the **Define Groups** dialogue box (see below). This dialogue box is used to specify which two groups you are comparing. For example, if your independent variable is 'sex', which you have coded as 1 = Male, 2 = Female, then you need to enter the values 1 and 2 into the boxes marked Group 1 and Group 2 respectively. This might seem rather pointless, but you might not always be comparing groups that you had coded as 1 and 2. For example, you might want to compare two groups who were defined on the basis of their religious belief (Atheists and Christians, who could be coded as 0 and 2 respectively – see Chapter 2, Section 2, on value labels). In this case, we would enter the values 0 and 2 into the two boxes in this dialogue box. (We will not be describing the use of the **Cut point** option here.)

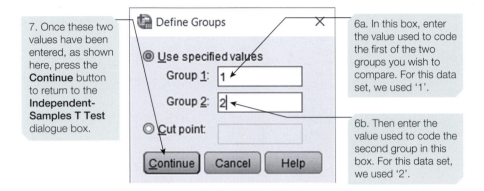

7. Once these two values have been entered, as shown here, press the **Continue** button to return to the **Independent-Samples T Test** dialogue box.

6a. In this box, enter the value used to code the first of the two groups you wish to compare. For this data set, we used '1'.

6b. Then enter the value used to code the second group in this box. For this data set, we used '2'.

7. Clicking on the **Continue** button in the **Define Groups** dialogue box will return you to the **Independent-Samples T Test** dialogue box. You will see that your two values have been entered into the brackets following the name of your independent variable (you may have noticed that previously there were question marks inside these brackets).

8. Finally, click on OK in the **Independent-Samples T Test** dialogue box. The output of the *t*-test will appear in the Output window.

The output from this independent *t*-test is shown, with annotations, below. We also show you how you would describe the results of the test, were you to write a report on this experiment.

SPSS output for independent groups *t*-test

Obtained using menu items: Compare Means > Independent-Samples T Test

T-Test

Useful descriptives showing that those in the mnemonic condition remembered the most words. You can calculate the effect size from these descriptives (see next page).

Group Statistics

	Condition	N	Mean	Std. Deviation	Std. Error Mean
Number of words recalled	Mnemonic condition	11	17.7273	2.86674	.86435
	No mnemonic condition	10	14.1000	3.57305	1.12990

These lower and upper confidence limits enclose the confidence interval. There is a 95% probability that the difference between the means for the population will fall between 0.68 and 6.57. Note, 0 is not within those limits: remember that indicates a significant difference (Chapter 1, Section 1).

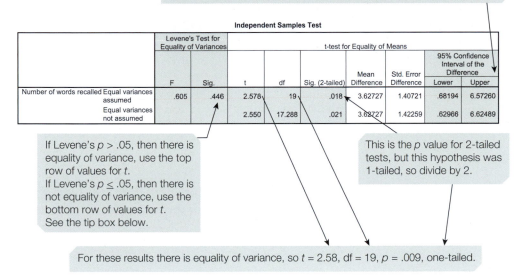

Independent Samples Test

		Levene's Test for Equality of Variances		t-test for Equality of Means					95% Confidence Interval of the Difference	
		F	Sig.	t	df	Sig. (2-tailed)	Mean Difference	Std. Error Difference	Lower	Upper
Number of words recalled	Equal variances assumed	.605	.446	2.578	19	.018	3.62727	1.40721	.68194	6.57260
	Equal variances not assumed			2.550	17.288	.021	3.62727	1.42259	.62966	6.62489

If Levene's $p > .05$, then there is equality of variance, use the top row of values for t.
If Levene's $p \leq .05$, then there is not equality of variance, use the bottom row of values for t.
See the tip box below.

This is the p value for 2-tailed tests, but this hypothesis was 1-tailed, so divide by 2.

For these results there is equality of variance, so $t = 2.58$, df = 19, $p = .009$, one-tailed.

Equality (or at least similarity) of variance is one of the requirements for using parametric statistical tests. SPSS, however, carries out two versions of the independent groups t-test: the top row for when there is equality of variance and the bottom row for when the variances are unequal. If you use the latter in a report, you must note that fact.

Measure of effect size

The output for the independent groups t-test does not include an estimate of the size of the effect and this is not an option on SPSS that you can select. However, from the output you can calculate this and we show you how to do so next.

Cohen's d (see Chapter 1, Section 1) is a measure of effect size that is frequently reported in journal articles when reporting t-tests (Fritz, Morris and Richler, 2012). Essentially, this involves working out the difference between the two means from each condition and dividing this by the two standard deviations (SD) combined. You use the following formula to calculate d when the number of participants in each condition (N) is identical or similar. Consult a statistics text on an alternative way of combining standard deviations if there is a large discrepancy in N in your data.

$$d = \frac{x_1 - x_2}{\text{mean } SD}$$

This formula requires you to carry out the following steps:

1. Look at the SPSS output and identify the mean and standard deviation for each condition, provided in a table called **Group Statistics**. For the data set used in this section:

   The mean for the mnemonic condition, $x_{1,}$ = 17.73 and the SD = 2.87.

   The mean for the no mnemonic condition, $x_{2,}$ = 14.10 and the SD = 3.57.

2. Take the mean of one condition from the mean of the other condition (it is not important which mean to take from which, so you can ignore the sign). For the data set in this section:

   $$17.73 - 14.10 = 3.63.$$

3. Find the mean SD by adding the SD for each condition together and dividing by two (SD of condition 1 + SD of condition 2) / 2. For the data set in this section:

   $$(2.87 + 3.57)/2 = 3.22.$$

4. Use the formula to calculate d. For the data set in this section:

   $$d = (17.73 - 14.10)/3.22 = 3.63/3.22 = 1.13.$$

This would be considered to be a large effect size. Cohen (1988) provided the following guidance on how to interpret d:

- Small effect size: 0.2 (or more)

- Moderate effect size: 0.5 (or more)

- Large effect size: 0.8 (or more).

 Reporting the results

In a report you might write:
More words were recalled in the mnemonic condition (M = 17.73) than in the no mnemonic condition (M = 14.10). An independent t-test showed that the difference between conditions was significant, and the size of this effect was large (t = 2.58, df = 19, p = .009, one-tailed, d = 1.13).

It would be helpful in your report to include more than just the descriptive statistics that are automatically generated as part of the independent t-test output. In Chapter 3, Section 5 we showed you how to use the **Explore** command, and the output using this command with the data from the memory experiment is included at the end of that section. This output provides you with the 95% confidence interval for the mean of each condition. Our estimate of the population mean for the mnemonic condition (based on our sample) is 17.73 and the confidence intervals tell us that there is a 95% probability that the true value will fall between 15.80 and 19.65. Our estimate of the population mean for the non-mnemonic condition is 14.10 and the confidence intervals tell us that there is a 95% probability that the true value will fall between 11.54 and 16.66. A useful way of presenting this information in your report is to show it graphically using an error bar graph. Next, we show you how to create such a graph using SPSS.

Creating an error bar graph: independent groups design

To obtain an error bar graph using Chart Builder

1. On the menu bar, click on **Graphs**.
2. Click on **Chart Builder**.
3. Close the top **Chart Builder** dialogue box, which reminds you that measurement level should be set properly for each variable in your chart (see Chapter 3, Section 7). The **Chart Builder** dialogue box below will be visible.

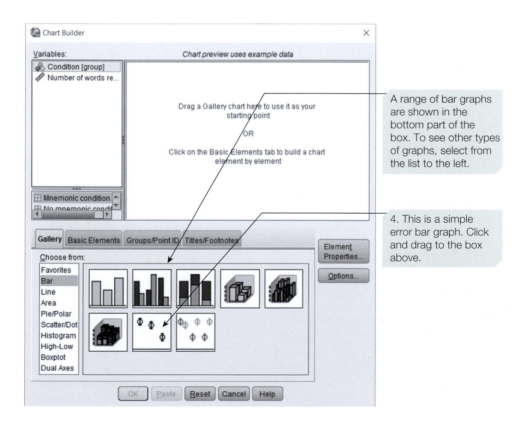

A range of bar graphs are shown in the bottom part of the box. To see other types of graphs, select from the list to the left.

4. This is a simple error bar graph. Click and drag to the box above.

We are showing you how to create an error bar graph, where the error bars are selected to represent the 95% confidence intervals. The confidence interval tells us the limits within which the population mean (the true value of the mean) is likely to fall. SPSS allows alternative options where the bars represent a measure of dispersion such as the standard deviation (see below).

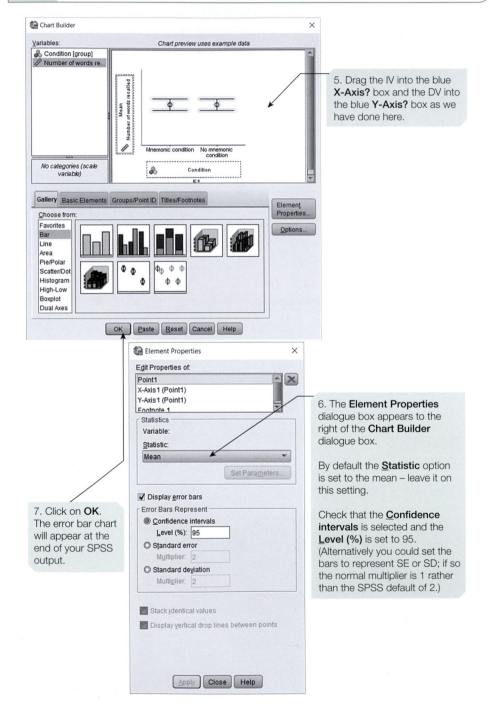

5. Drag the IV into the blue **X-Axis?** box and the DV into the blue **Y-Axis?** box as we have done here.

6. The **Element Properties** dialogue box appears to the right of the **Chart Builder** dialogue box.

By default the <u>**Statistic**</u> option is set to the mean – leave it on this setting.

Check that the **Confidence intervals** is selected and the **Level (%)** is set to 95. (Alternatively you could set the bars to represent SE or SD; if so the normal multiplier is 1 rather than the SPSS default of 2.)

7. Click on **OK**. The error bar chart will appear at the end of your SPSS output.

SPSS output for error bar chart

There is some overlap between the two bars for each group, although the extent of the overlap is quite small.

If the sample means of two groups of people are so different to suggest that they came from a different population – the bars do not overlap – then this is because our experimental manipulation brought about a difference between the samples.

So, no or little overlap is indicative of a significant difference between groups.

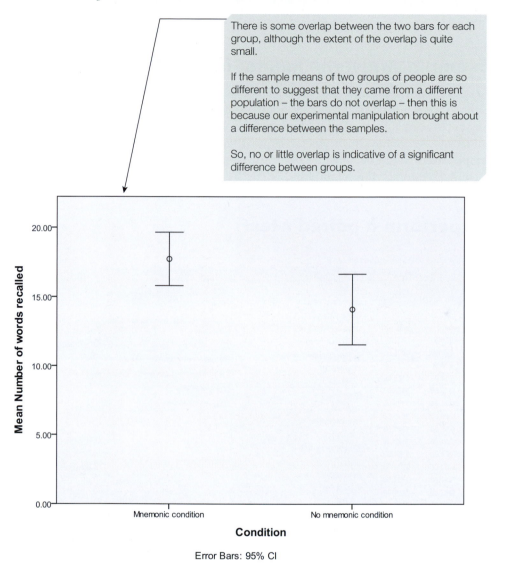

Error Bars: 95% CI

Section 4: THE PAIRED *t*-TEST

In the repeated measures design, data are collected from each participant in all levels of the independent variable. For example, we might compare participant 1's memory performance under noisy conditions with participant 1's memory performance under quiet conditions. In this situation, it is likely that the data from participants will be correlated; for example, if participant A has a good memory, then their scores on a memory test will be high regardless of condition. It is for this reason that a repeated measures *t*-test is often called a *correlated t-*test. With a repeated measures design, it is essential that the data are kept in the correct order, so that participant 1's data on variable A are indeed compared with participant 1's data on variable B. The test itself considers pairs of data together, and for this reason this test is also known as a *paired t-test*.

Example study: the mental imagery experiment

To demonstrate the use of the paired *t*-test, we are going to analyse the data from the mental imagery experiment, the second data entry exercise in Chapter 2, Section 6. It was hypothesised that, as participants would compare their mental images of the two animals to determine which was the larger, their decision times for the small size difference trials would be longer than for the large size difference trials. A paired *t*-test is conducted to test this hypothesis.

To perform a paired *t*-test

paired t-test.sav [DataSet2] - IBM SPSS Statistics Data Editor

File Edit View Data Transform Analyze Direct Marketing Graphs Utilities Add-ons Window Help

	large	small
1	936.00	878.00
2	923.00	1005.00
3	896.00	1010.00
4	1241.00	1365.00
5	1278.00	1422.00
6	871.00	1198.00
7	1360.00	1576.00
8	733.00	896.00
9	941.00	1573.00
10	1077.00	1261.00
11	1438.00	2237.00
12	1099.00	1325.00
13	1253.00	1591.00
14	1930.00	2742.00
15	1260.00	1357.00
16	1271.00	1963.00
17		
18		
19		
20		
21		
22		
23		

Analyze menu:
Reports
Descriptive Statistics
Custom Tables
Compare Means
General Linear Model
Generalized Linear Models
Mixed Models
Correlate
Regression
Loglinear
Neural Networks
Classify
Dimension Reduction
Scale
Nonparametric Tests
Forecasting
Survival
Multiple Response
Missing Value Analysis...
Multiple Imputation
Complex Samples
Simulation...
Quality Control
ROC Curve...
Spatial and Temporal Modeling...

Compare Means submenu:
Means...
One-Sample T Test...
Independent-Samples T Test...
Summary Independent-Samples T Test
Paired-Samples T Test...
One-Way ANOVA...

1. Click on the word **Analyze.**

2. Click on **Compare Means.**

3. Click on the words **Paired-Samples T Test.**

4. You will now see the **Paired-Samples T Test** dialogue box (see below). You need to choose the names of the two variables you want to compare. As before, all the variables in your data file are listed in the left-hand box. Click on each of the two variables you want to compare. These variable names will now be highlighted.

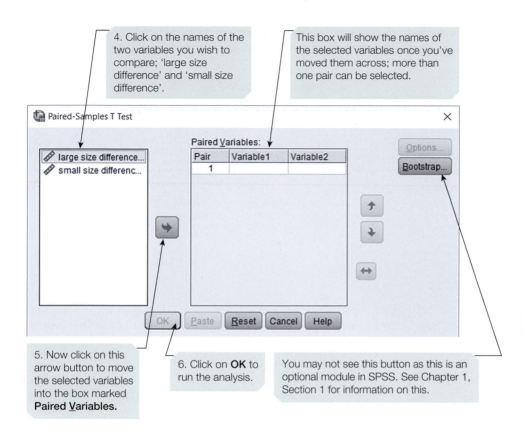

4. Click on the names of the two variables you wish to compare; 'large size difference' and 'small size difference'.

This box will show the names of the selected variables once you've moved them across; more than one pair can be selected.

5. Now click on this arrow button to move the selected variables into the box marked **Paired Variables.**

6. Click on **OK** to run the analysis.

You may not see this button as this is an optional module in SPSS. See Chapter 1, Section 1 for information on this.

SPSS will perform the paired *t*-test. The annotated output is shown below.

SPSS output for paired (or related) *t*-test
Obtained using menu items: > Compare Means > Paired-Samples T Test

T-Test

You can do several paired *t*-tests at once, so SPSS labels each pair. Next, it puts the variable labels, if you entered them; if not, it puts the variable names.

Useful descriptives showing that the mean decision time was fastest for large difference trials. It is worth noting the much larger *SD* for the 'small size difference' condition.

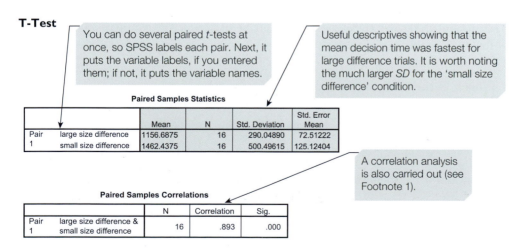

Paired Samples Statistics

		Mean	N	Std. Deviation	Std. Error Mean
Pair 1	large size difference	1156.6875	16	290.04890	72.51222
	small size difference	1462.4375	16	500.49615	125.12404

A correlation analysis is also carried out (see Footnote 1).

Paired Samples Correlations

		N	Correlation	Sig.
Pair 1	large size difference & small size difference	16	.893	.000

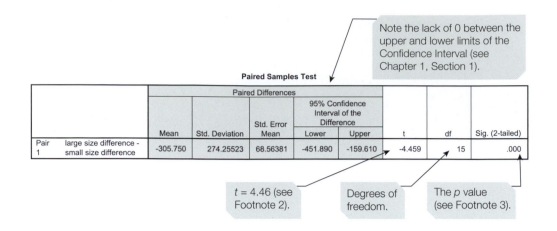

Note the lack of 0 between the upper and lower limits of the Confidence Interval (see Chapter 1, Section 1).

Paired Samples Test

		Paired Differences							
		Mean	Std. Deviation	Std. Error Mean	95% Confidence Interval of the Difference		t	df	Sig. (2-tailed)
					Lower	Upper			
Pair 1	large size difference - small size difference	-305.750	274.25523	68.56381	-451.890	-159.610	-4.459	15	.000

$t = 4.46$ (see Footnote 2).

Degrees of freedom.

The p value (see Footnote 3).

Footnotes

1. SPSS performs a Pearson's correlation (see Chapter 6, Section 3) but you can ignore it if you only want a t-test. A significant positive correlation tells you that participants who were fast on large size difference trials were also fast on small size difference trials. It does not mean that the scores are significantly different.

2. The minus sign tells you that the mean value for the first variable name in the **Paired Variables** box is lower on average than the mean value for the second variable name.

3. A p value can never equal zero. SPSS rounds to three decimal places, so p must be less than .001 or it would appear as .001. In a report, put $p < .001$ if the hypothesis was two-tailed. Here, the hypothesis was one-tailed, so divide by 2, which gives $p < .0005$. However, as we report p values less than .001 as $p < .001$, we would write: $p < .001$, one-tailed.

Measure of effect size

As with the independent t-test, the output for the paired t-test does not include an estimate of the size of the effect and this is not an option on SPSS that you can select. However, from the output, you can calculate Cohen's d, which we described in Section 3, using the formula: $d = (x_1 - x_2) / \text{mean } SD$.

1. Look at the SPSS output and identify the mean and standard deviation (SD) for each condition, which are provided in a table called **Paired Sample Statistics**. For the data set used in this section:

The mean for the large size difference condition, $x_1 = 1156.69$ and the $SD = 290.05$.

The mean for the small size difference condition, $x_2 = 1462.44$ and the $SD = 500.50$.

CHAPTER 5

2. Take the mean of one condition from the mean of the other condition (it is not important which mean to take from which, so you can ignore the sign). For the data set used in this section:

$$1156.69 - 1462.44 = 305.75.$$

3. Find the mean *SD* by adding the *SD* for each condition together and dividing by two (*SD* of condition 1 + *SD* of condition 2) / 2. For the data set used in this section:

$$(290.05 + 500.50)/2 = 395.28.$$

4. Use the formula to calculate *d*. For the data set used in this section:

$$d = (1156.69 - 1462.44)/30.95.28 = 305.75/395.28 = 0.77.$$

This is a moderate to large effect size. Cohen (1988) provided the following guidance on how to interpret *d*:

- Small effect size: 0.2 (or more)
- Moderate effect size: 0.5 (or more)
- Large effect size: 0.8 (or more).

 Reporting the results

In a report you might write:

The average time to decide which of the pair of animals was larger was longer for small size difference trials than for large size difference trials (1462.44 ms and 1156.69 ms, respectively). A paired *t*-test showed that the difference between conditions was significant, and the size of this effect was moderate to large ($t = 4.46$, df = 15, $p < .001$, one-tailed, $d = 0.77$).

We will not show you how to create an error bar with SPSS for the data analysed with the paired *t*-test. Unfortunately, SPSS does not allow Chart Builder to create error bar graphs for data from a repeated measures design. With a repeated measures design the same participants complete both conditions, so this must be taken into account. Brysbaert (2011, 233–4) explains how the confidence intervals from experiments using such a design can be 'corrected' to allow them to be interpreted appropriately, in line with an independent groups design.

CHAPTER 5

Section 5: AN INTRODUCTION TO NONPARAMETRIC TESTS OF DIFFERENCE

■ The Mann–Whitney test and the Wilcoxon matched-pairs signed-ranks test are nonparametric tests of difference and are used to explore whether two data samples are different.

■ The Wilcoxon test is the nonparametric equivalent of the paired *t*-test, and is used for data gathered in experiments involving repeated measures and matched-pairs designs.

■ The Mann–Whitney test is the nonparametric equivalent of the independent *t*-test, and is used to compare data collected in an experiment involving an independent groups design.

■ These nonparametric tests should be used in preference to the equivalent *t*-tests when data are only of ordinal level of measurement or do not meet the other assumptions required for parametric tests.

■ Both tests involve ranking the data, and the calculations are carried out on the ranks. In the annotated output pages for these tests, there is a brief explanation of how each test is performed.

■ When reporting descriptive statistics to accompany the results of a nonparametric test of difference, such as the Mann–Whitney or Wilcoxon test, you should normally give the median and range (not the mean and standard deviation) as the measures of central tendency and dispersion. The median and range are more appropriate descriptives for nonparametric tests because these are distribution-free tests and do not assume normal distribution.

Section 6: THE MANN–WHITNEY TEST

Example study: sex differences and emphasis on physical attractiveness

To demonstrate how to perform the Mann–Whitney test, we shall use the data from an experiment based on research conducted by one of our past students, which was designed to determine whether males and females differ in the emphasis they place on the importance of the physical attractiveness of their partner. Previous research has reported that men are more concerned than women about the physical attractiveness of their heterosexual partner. However, current advertising trends and societal pressure may have altered the emphasis placed on physical attractiveness and, more specifically, the importance they attach to 'body' or physique compared with other characteristics of their ideal partner.

The hypothesis tested is two-tailed: that men and women will differ in the importance they attach to physique. The design employed was an independent groups design. The independent variable was whether the participant was male or female, operationalised by asking equal numbers of males and females to take part in the experiment (only one partner from a relationship participated). The dependent variable was the importance attached to body shape, operationalised by asking participants to rank order 10 characteristics of an ideal partner, one of these being body shape. (These data are available in the Appendix or from he.palgrave.com/psychology/brace.)

How to do it

1. Click on the word **Analyze.**

2. Click on **Nonparametric Tests.**

3. Click on **Legacy Dialogs.**

4. Click on **2 Independent Samples.**

We are recommend you use **Legacy Dialogs** as this gives you more information in the output compared with the new alternative.

The data have been entered with the variable names 'sex' and 'rating'. Follow steps 5 to 11, shown in the shaded boxes below, then click on **OK**. The SPSS output, which will appear after a short delay, is shown on the following page with explanatory comments.

CHAPTER 5

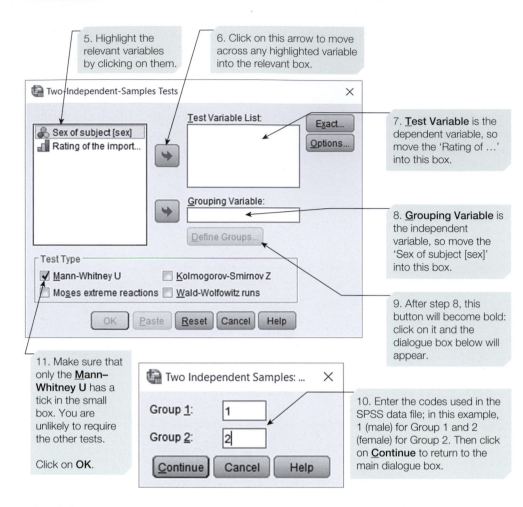

5. Highlight the relevant variables by clicking on them.

6. Click on this arrow to move across any highlighted variable into the relevant box.

7. **Test Variable** is the dependent variable, so move the 'Rating of …' into this box.

8. **Grouping Variable** is the independent variable, so move the 'Sex of subject [sex]' into this box.

9. After step 8, this button will become bold: click on it and the dialogue box below will appear.

10. Enter the codes used in the SPSS data file; in this example, 1 (male) for Group 1 and 2 (female) for Group 2. Then click on **Continue** to return to the main dialogue box.

11. Make sure that only the **Mann–Whitney U** has a tick in the small box. You are unlikely to require the other tests.

Click on **OK**.

SPSS output for Mann–Whitney U test

Obtained using menu items: Nonparametric Tests > Legacy Dialogs > 2 Independent Samples

NPAR TESTS
MANN–WHITNEY TEST

Ranks

	Sex of subject	N	Mean Rank	Sum of Ranks
Rating of the importance of body as characteristic in a partner	Male	20	17.88	357.50
	Female	20	23.13	462.50
	Total	40		

You do not need this part of the output for your Results section, but it gives you some information about the calculations for the Mann–Whitney U test: first, all the data from both groups combined are assigned ranks from the lowest to the highest; then, the ranks given to one group are compared with the ranks given to the other group; the mean ranks shown here indicate whether there are more high ranks in one group than in the other.

Test Statistics[b]

	Rating of the importance of body as characteristic in a partner
Mann-Whitney U	147.500
Wilcoxon W	357.500
Z	-1.441
Asymp. Sig. (2-tailed)	.150
Exact Sig. [2*(1-tailed Sig.)]	.157[a]

a. Not corrected for ties.

b. Grouping Variable: Sex of subject

> The calculated value of U for the Mann–Whitney U Test. You will report this value in your results section.

> SPSS also gives the calculated value of an independent groups version of the Wilcoxon test. You do not need this for writing your results section.

> Depending on the size of your data file, the output may or may not include the Exact Sig. (NB: The value shown here is not from the Exact option button, but produced automatically by SPSS.)

Reporting the results

In a report you might write:

There was no significant difference between men and women in the importance they attached to body shape in a partner ($U = 147.50$, $N_1 = 20$, $N_2 = 20$, $p = .157$, two-tailed).

> If you are reporting descriptive statistics, you should avoid reporting the mean rank or sum of ranks given in this SPSS output and that for the Wilcoxon test described next. Instead, obtain the median and range for the two conditions by using the **Explore** command.

Section 7: THE WILCOXON TEST

Example study: quality of E-FIT images

The police frequently use a computerised facial composite system to help eyewitnesses recall the face of a perpetrator. One such system is E-FIT (Electronic Facial Identification Technique). In a study by Newlands (1997), participants were shown a short video clip of a mock crime scenario depicting an instance of petty theft. Participants were then asked to generate an E-FIT composite of the perpetrator. On completion, they were asked to rate the likeness of their E-FIT image to the person they remember seeing in the video. They were then shown a photo of the perpetrator and again asked to rate the likeness of their E-FIT to that person.

The hypothesis tested was one-tailed: that the likeness ratings of the E-FIT to the perpetrator would be more favourable when recalling the perpetrator from memory than when seeing a photograph of the perpetrator. The design employed was a repeated measures design. The independent variable was the presence or absence of a photograph of the perpetrator, operationalised by asking participants to rate the likeness of their E-FIT, first to their recall of the perpetrator and then to a photo of the perpetrator. The dependent variable was measured on an ordinal scale and was the likeness rating, operationalised by the response on a 7-point scale, where point 1 was 'very good likeness' and point 7 'no likeness'.

For the purposes of this book, we have created a data file that will reproduce some of the findings of this study. (These data are available in the Appendix or from he.palgrave.com/psychology/brace.)

How to do it

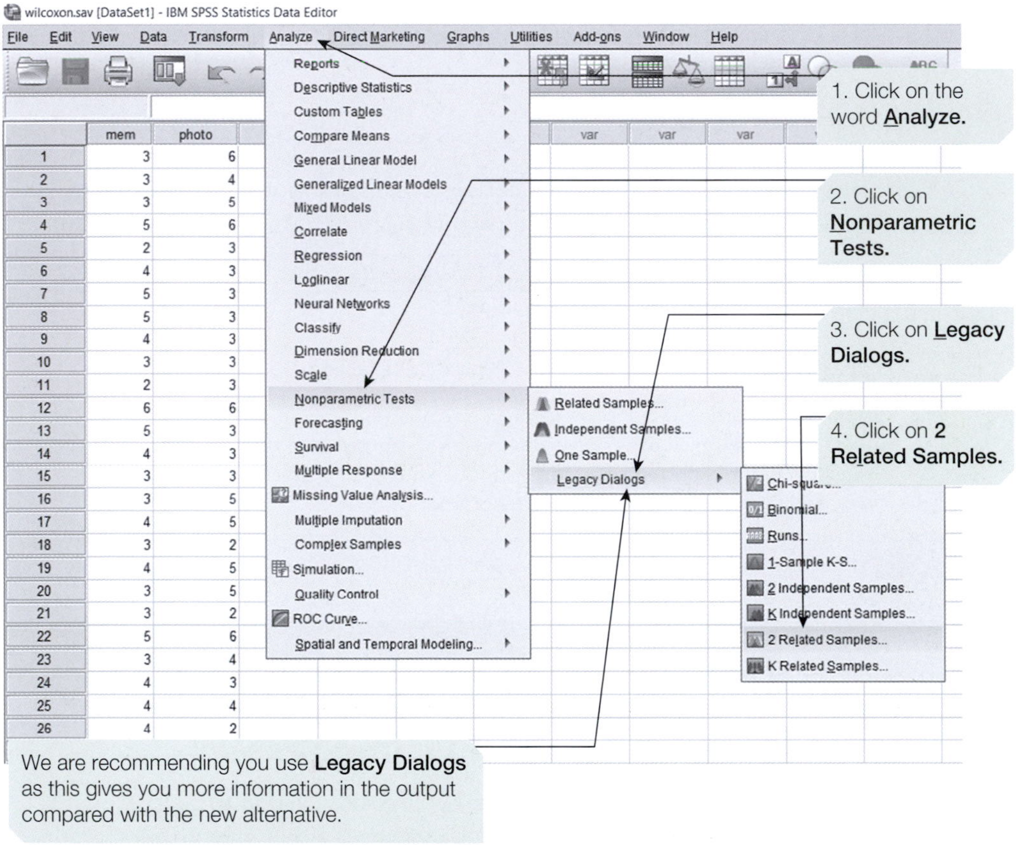

wilcoxon.sav [DataSet1] - IBM SPSS Statistics Data Editor
1. Click on the word Analyze.
2. Click on Nonparametric Tests.
3. Click on Legacy Dialogs.
4. Click on 2 Related Samples.
We are recommending you use Legacy Dialogs as this gives you more information in the output compared with the new alternative.

The dialogue box shown below will appear. The variable labels, and the variable names ('mem' and 'photo'), used in the data file appear in the left-hand box. Follow steps 5 to 7, shown in the shaded boxes, then click on OK. The SPSS output, which will appear after a short delay, is shown below with explanatory comments.

5. The list of variable labels from the data file appears here. Highlight the two variables you want to enter into the analysis by clicking on them.

6. Click on this arrow to move the highlighted variables across to the **Test Pairs** box.

7. Ensure that there is a tick in the Wilcoxon box, and that the other boxes are blank. Click on **OK**.

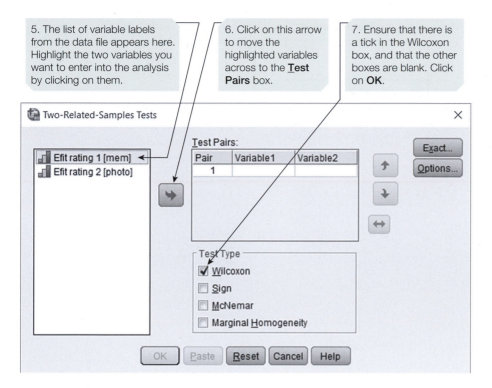

SPSS output for Wilcoxon matched-pairs signed-ranks test

Obtained using menu items: Nonparametric Tests > Legacy Dialogs > 2 Related Samples

NPAR TESTS
WILCOXON SIGNED RANKS TEST

Ranks

		N	Mean Rank	Sum of Ranks
Efit rating 2 - Efit rating 1	Negative Ranks	19[a]	20.26	385.00
	Positive Ranks	20[b]	19.75	395.00
	Ties	9[c]		
	Total	48		

a. Efit rating 2 < Efit rating 1
b. Efit rating 2 > Efit rating 1
c. Efit rating 2 = Efit rating 1

These are the variable labels. If you did not enter variable labels, then the variable names will appear here.

This section gives you some information about the calculations for the Wilcoxon test. You don't need this for your results section; but, first, for each subject the score for one level of the independent variable is subtracted from the score for the other level; then those differences are ranked, ignoring the sign (whether negative or positive) and omitting ties. Once ranking is completed, the signs are reattached. The mean ranks indicate whether there are more high ranks for the positive differences, or for the negative differences, or whether there is a fairly equal spread of ranks, as in this example.

Test Statistics[b]

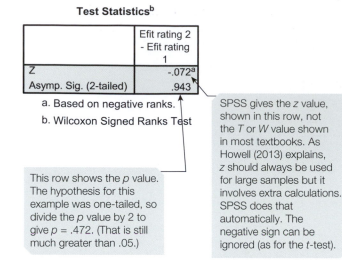

	Efit rating 2 - Efit rating 1
Z	-.072[a]
Asymp. Sig. (2-tailed)	.943

a. Based on negative ranks.

b. Wilcoxon Signed Ranks Test

SPSS gives the z value, shown in this row, not the T or W value shown in most textbooks. As Howell (2013) explains, z should always be used for large samples but it involves extra calculations. SPSS does that automatically. The negative sign can be ignored (as for the t-test).

This row shows the p value. The hypothesis for this example was one-tailed, so divide the p value by 2 to give p = .472. (That is still much greater than .05.)

 Reporting the results

In a report you might write:

There was no significant difference in the likeness ratings of the E-FITs that were made with a photo of the perpetrator visible when compared with those made from the memory of the perpetrator ($z = 0.07$, $N -$ Ties $= 39$, $p = .472$, one-tailed).

Summary

- This chapter introduced you to statistical tests that will tell you if there is a significant difference between two means.

- This could involve comparing one group of participants to a known population mean, or comparing the performance of two groups of participants such as in an independent groups design, or comparing the performance of one group participants who perform in two conditions such as in a repeated measures design.

- Your choice of which test to use will depend on the design of your experiment, and whether the data are parametric.

- Remember our advice on the appropriate descriptive statistics to accompany the results of these tests. See Chapter 3 for guidance on obtaining these.

- If your dependent variable is a total or mean score from several raw scores that have already been entered into your data file, see Chapter 4 for guidance on how to create such a total or mean score in SPSS.

- For guidance on incorporating SPSS output into a report, or on printing the output, see Chapter 13.

- Chapter 8 introduces you to Analysis of Variance (ANOVA), a test of difference that is appropriate for designs that involve more than two groups or conditions, or more than one independent variable.

CHAPTER 5

6 Tests of correlation and bivariate regression

In this chapter

- An introduction to tests of correlation
- Producing a scattergram
- Pearson's r: parametric test of correlation
- Spearman's r_s: nonparametric test of correlation
- Comparing the strength of correlation coefficients
- Brief introduction to regression
- Bivariate regression

SPSS for Psychologists online
Visit he.palgrave.com/psychology/brace for data sets, online tutorials and exercises.

Section 1: AN INTRODUCTION TO TESTS OF CORRELATION

- Researchers often wish to measure the degree of relationship between two variables. For example, there is likely to be a relationship between age and reading ability in children. A test of correlation will provide you with a measure of the strength and direction of such a relationship.

- In a correlation, there is no independent variable: you simply measure two variables. So, if someone wished to investigate the relationship between smoking and respiratory function, they could measure how many cigarettes people smoke and their respiratory function, and then test for a correlation between these two variables.

- Correlation does not imply causation. In any correlation, there could be a third variable, which explains the association between the two variables you measured. For example, there may be a correlation between the number of ice creams sold and the number of people who drown. Here, temperature is the third variable, which could explain the relationship between the measured variables. Even when there seems to be a clear cause-and-effect relationship, a correlation alone is not sufficient evidence for a causal relationship.

- Francis Galton carried out early work on correlation, and one of his colleagues, Pearson, developed a method of calculating correlation coefficients for parametric data: Pearson's product moment correlation coefficient (Pearson's r). If the data are not parametric, or if the relationship is not linear, a nonparametric test of correlation, such as Spearman's r_s should be used.

- Note that for a correlation to be acceptable, one should normally test at least 100 participants; otherwise a small number of participants with extreme scores could skew the data and either prevent a correlation from being revealed when it does exist or cause an apparent correlation that does not really exist. The scattergram is a useful tool for checking such eventualities and for checking that the relationship is linear.

Section 2: PRODUCING A SCATTERGRAM

A scattergram (or scatterplot) will give a good indication of whether two items are related in a linear fashion. Figure 6.1 shows a hypothetical example. Each point on the scattergram represents the age and the reading ability of one child. The line running through the data points is called a 'regression line'. It represents the 'best fit' of a straight line to the data points. The line in Figure 6.1 slopes upwards from left to right: as one variable increases in value, the other variable also increases in value and this is called a *positive correlation*. The closer the points are to being on the line itself, the stronger the correlation. If all the points fall along the straight line, then it is said to be a *perfect correlation*. The scattergram will also show you any outliers.

In the scattergram shown in Figure 6.2, the dots are scattered randomly, all over the graph. It is not possible to draw any meaningful best fit line at all, and the correlation would be close to zero: that is, there is no relationship between the two variables.

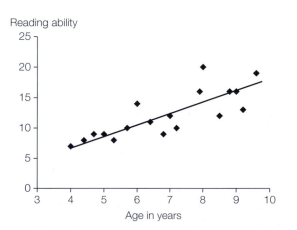

Figure 6.1 Scattergram illustrating a positive correlation: hypothetical data for the relationship between age and reading ability in children

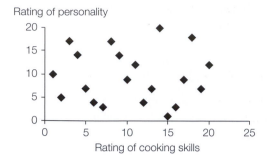

Figure 6.2 Scattergram showing two variables with a relationship close to zero

It is often the case that as one variable increases in value, the other variable decreases in value: this is called a *negative correlation*. In the following example of how to produce a scattergram with SPSS software, we are going to use data that give a negative correlation.

In this book we will only show procedures for dealing with linear relationships, like that shown in Figure 6.1, and also the relationship in the example study below. Sometimes relationships are nonlinear, for example, an inverted U-shape relationship, illustrated in Figure 6.3, which might be found between two variables such as stress and exam performance. For procedures to deal with nonlinear relationships, read the appropriate textbooks.

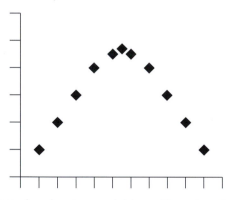

Figure 6.3 Scattergram showing two variables with an inverted U-shape relationship

Example study: relationship between age and CFF

A paper by Mason et al. (1982) described an investigation of (among other things) whether the negative correlation between age and critical flicker frequency (CFF) is different for people with multiple sclerosis than for control participants. For this example, we have created a data file that will reproduce some of the findings for the control participants. CFF can be described briefly and somewhat simplistically as follows. If a light is flickering on and off at a low frequency, most people can detect the flicker. If the frequency of flicker is increased, eventually it looks like a steady light.

The frequency at which someone can no longer perceive flicker is called the *critical flicker frequency* (CFF). (These data are available in the Appendix or from he.palgrave. com/psychology/brace.)

How to obtain a scattergram using Legacy Dialogs

1. On the menu bar, click on **Graphs**.

2. Click on **Legacy Dialogs**.

3. Click on **Scatter/Dot**, and the **Scatter/Dot** dialogue box will appear.

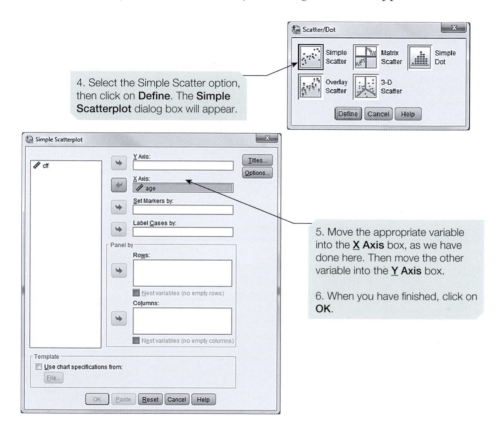

4. Select the Simple Scatter option, then click on **Define**. The **Simple Scatterplot** dialog box will appear.

5. Move the appropriate variable into the **X Axis** box, as we have done here. Then move the other variable into the **Y Axis** box.

6. When you have finished, click on **OK**.

The scattergram will appear in the SPSS output window. You can edit it, including adding the regression line, in the way we describe below. First, we will tell you how to obtain a scattergram with the SPSS command **Chart Builder**.

How to obtain a scattergram using Chart Builder

1. On the menu bar, click on **Graphs**.

2. Click on **Chart Builder**.

3. A **Chart Builder** dialogue box will remind you that measurement level should be set properly for each variable in your chart (see Chapter 3, Section 7). If you are sure that they are set correctly, just click on OK. (If you want to add a regression line to the scattergram, then both variables must be set at Scale in the Measure column of Variable View.)

CHAPTER 6

The **Chart Builder** dialogue box shown below will now be visible.

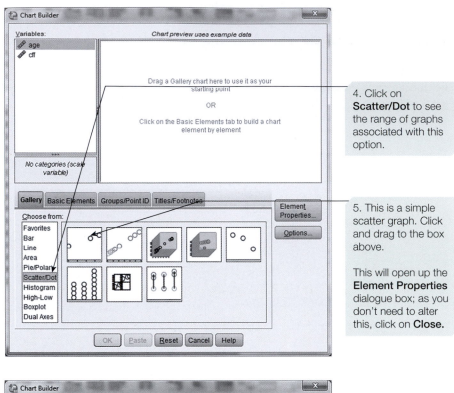

4. Click on **Scatter/Dot** to see the range of graphs associated with this option.

5. This is a simple scatter graph. Click and drag to the box above.

This will open up the **Element Properties** dialogue box; as you don't need to alter this, click on **Close**.

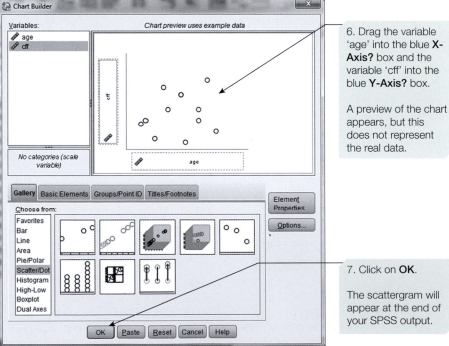

6. Drag the variable 'age' into the blue **X-Axis?** box and the variable 'cff' into the blue **Y-Axis?** box.

A preview of the chart appears, but this does not represent the real data.

7. Click on **OK**.

The scattergram will appear at the end of your SPSS output.

How to add a regression line to the scattergram

To add the regression line, whether the scattergram was produced using **Legacy Dialogs** or **Chart Builder**, you have to edit the graph. Start by double-clicking in the scattergram, and the SPSS Chart Editor window, shown below, will appear.

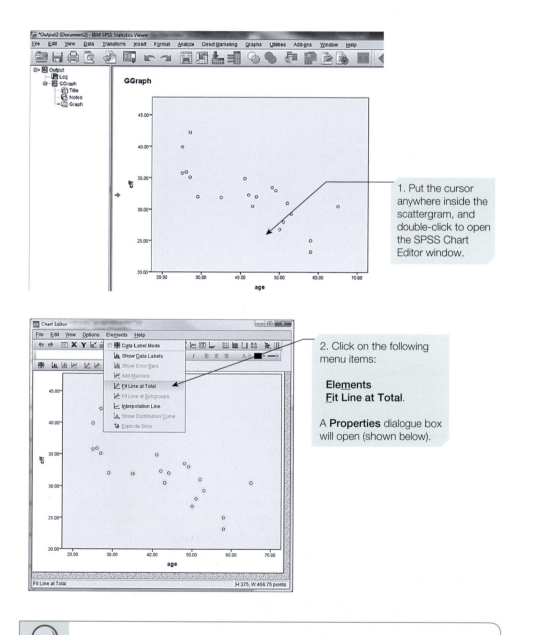

1. Put the cursor anywhere inside the scattergram, and double-click to open the SPSS Chart Editor window.

2. Click on the following menu items:

Elements
Fit Line at Total.

A **Properties** dialogue box will open (shown below).

If you find that **Fit Line at Total** is not available, in your data file check that both variables are set to **Scale** in the **Measure** column, then start again.

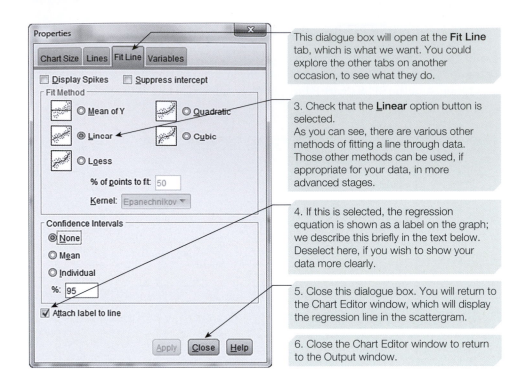

This dialogue box will open at the **Fit Line** tab, which is what we want. You could explore the other tabs on another occasion, to see what they do.

3. Check that the **Linear** option button is selected.
As you can see, there are various other methods of fitting a line through data. Those other methods can be used, if appropriate for your data, in more advanced stages.

4. If this is selected, the regression equation is shown as a label on the graph; we describe this briefly in the text below. Deselect here, if you wish to show your data more clearly.

5. Close this dialogue box. You will return to the Chart Editor window, which will display the regression line in the scattergram.

6. Close the Chart Editor window to return to the Output window.

You can copy the scattergram and paste it into a report, adding a suitable figure legend. For example, see Figure 6.4.

Figure legends should be suitable for the work into which you are incorporating the figure. The legend to Figure 6.4 might be suitable for a report about the study into age and CFF. The legends to Figures 6.1, 6.2, and 6.3, however, are intended to help you follow the explanation in this book, and would not be suitable for a report.

In addition to adding the regression line, you can edit other elements of the chart, to improve appearance. For example, SPSS charts are usually rather large. If you leave them large, the report will be spread over more pages than necessary, which can hinder the ease with which the reader follows your argument. You can shrink charts easily in a program such as MS Word, but it is much better to change the size in Chart Editor, because then the font and symbol size will automatically be adjusted for legibility. We show you how to do this in Chapter 7, Section 5. Editing would also be useful when a number of cases all fall at the same point. The data we use to illustrate the use of Spearman's r_s (Section 3) demonstrate that situation. To clearly illustrate the data you can edit the data symbols in Chart Editor, so that they vary in size according to the number of cases at each point. Guidelines on the appearance of figures are given in APA (2009).

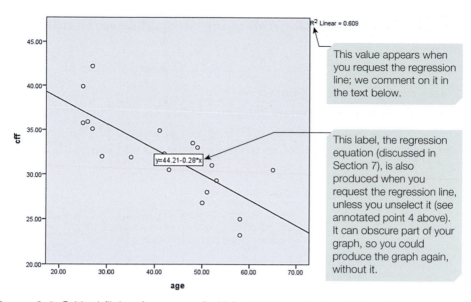

R^2 Linear = 0.609

This value appears when you request the regression line; we comment on it in the text below.

$y=44.21-0.28*x$

This label, the regression equation (discussed in Section 7), is also produced when you request the regression line, unless you unselect it (see annotated point 4 above). It can obscure part of your graph, so you could produce the graph again, without it.

Figure 6.4 Critical flicker frequency (in Hz) plotted against participant's age (in years)

A scattergram is a descriptive statistic that illustrates the data, which can be used to check whether the data are suitable for analysis using a test of correlation. For example, if there are a few cases in one corner of the scattergram, and most of the other cases are clustered together at the opposite end of the regression line, those outliers may produce a significant correlation even though there is no real relationship. A scattergram would also indicate if there is a relationship but it is nonlinear; for example, if the relationship is U-shaped. If there does appear to be a linear relationship (and Pearson's r makes the assumption that any relationship will be linear), we can find out whether or not it is significant with an inferential statistical test of correlation. A test of correlation will give the significance value and the strength of the correlation. The strength of correlation is indicated by the value of the correlation coefficient, which varies between 1 and 0. A perfect negative correlation would have a coefficient of -1, and a perfect positive correlation would have a coefficient of $+1$. In psychology, perfect correlations (in which all the points fall exactly on the regression line) are extremely rare and rather suspect.

Note the R^2 Linear value that appears next to the scattergram above. This is not the correlation coefficient itself; it is the square of Pearson's r and is itself a useful statistic (described in Section 3). You can remove the R^2 legend if you wish: in the Chart Editor window double-click on the legend, so that it is selected, then press delete key.

Next, we show you how to obtain a scattergram using **Graphboard Template Chooser**, which has been available since Version 17. It is not yet possible to add a regression line using this relatively new SPSS graphing option or to edit the size of the graph.

How to obtain a scattergram using Graphboard Template Chooser

<u>G</u>raphboard Template Chooser was described in Chapter 3, Section 8.

1. On the menu bar, click on <u>G</u>raphs.

2. Click on <u>G</u>raphboard Template Chooser.

3. In the dialogue box, ensure that the variables you want to plot are indicated as ordinal or scale. If they are not, go to your data file and set them.

4. Select the two variables that you want. The top variable will be plotted on the X axis. To reorder, use the up or down arrow. Remember to select both variables again.

5. Select the Scatterplot icon at the bottom. You may have to scroll down to see it.

6. Click on **OK**.

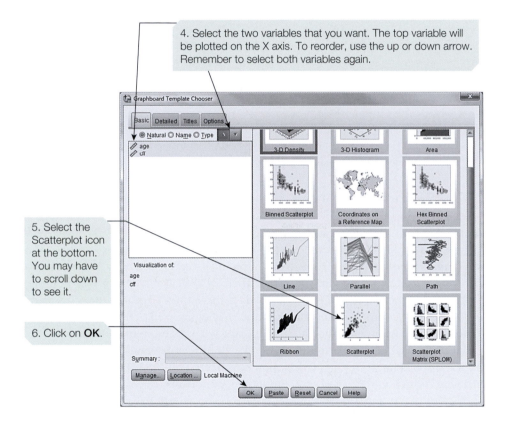

Here we have shown you how to produce the scattergram using the **Basic** tab. You could instead use the **Detailed** tab, described in Chapter 3, Section 8. You would select **Scatterplot** from the **Choose** list, and then set the X and Y variables.

The graph will appear in the Viewer window. Unlike other scatterplot commands, Graphboard does not add R^2 Linear. Double-click in the scattergram if you wish to edit it, and the Graphboard Editor window will appear. However, currently you cannot add a regression line in Graphboard Editor.

Section 3: PEARSON'S *r*: PARAMETRIC TEST OF CORRELATION

Example study: critical flicker frequency and age

To illustrate how to carry out this parametric test of correlation, we will continue using the CFF and age data. Note that the data do not meet the guidelines for correlation of a sample size of around 100. The hypothesis tested was that there would be a negative correlation between CFF and age.

The study employed a correlational design. Two variables were measured. The first was age, operationalised by recruiting volunteer participants who ranged in age from 25 to 66. The second variable was CFF, operationalised by using a flicker generator to measure CFF for each participant; six measures were made, and the mean taken to give a single CFF score for each participant.

How to perform a Pearson's *r*

pearsonscorrelation.sav [DataSet1] - IBM SPSS Statistics Data Editor

File   Edit   View   Data   Transform   Analyze   Direct Marketing   Graphs   Utilities   Add-ons   Window   Help

	age	cff
1	41.00	34.90
2	43.00	30.50
3	25.00	35.75
4	42.00	32.30
5	51.00	28.00
6	27.00	42.20
7	27.00	35.10
8	48.00	33.50
9	58.00	25.00
10	52.00	31.00
11	58.00	23.20
12	50.00	26.80
13	44.00	32.00
14	53.00	29.30
15	26.00	35.90
16	65.00	30.50
17	35.00	31.90
18	29.00	32.00
19	25.00	39.90
20	49.00	33.00
21		

Analyze menu:
Reports
Descriptive Statistics
Custom Tables
Compare Means
General Linear Model
Generalized Linear Models
Mixed Models
Correlate
Regression
Loglinear
Neural Networks
Classify
Dimension Reduction
Scale
Nonparametric Tests
Forecasting
Survival
Multiple Response
Missing Value Analysis...
Multiple Imputation
Complex Samples
Simulation...
Quality Control
ROC Curve...

Correlate submenu:
Bivariate...
Partial...
Distances...
Canonical Correlation

1. Click on **Analyze**.

2. Click on **Correlate**.

3. Click on **Bivariate**. The **Bivariate Correlations** dialogue box will appear (see below).

SPSS will correlate each variable you include with every other variable you include. Thus, if you included three variables A, B and C, it will calculate the correlation coefficient for A * B, A * C and B * C. In the Pearson's *r* example we have just two variables, but in the Spearman's r_s example (in Section 4), we include three variables so that you can see what a larger correlation matrix looks like.

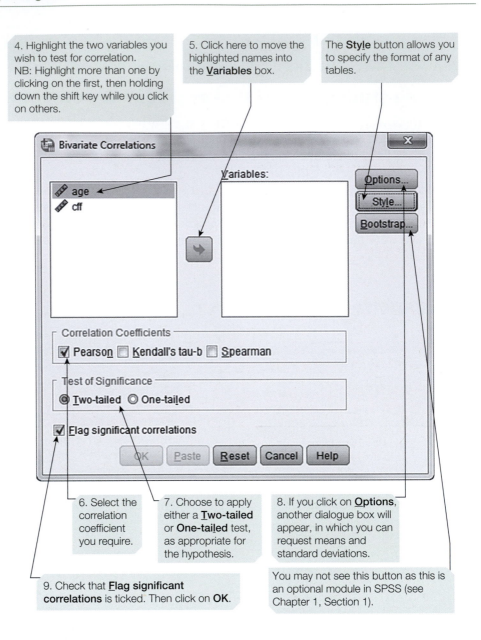

4. Highlight the two variables you wish to test for correlation. NB: Highlight more than one by clicking on the first, then holding down the shift key while you click on others.

5. Click here to move the highlighted names into the **Variables** box.

The **Style** button allows you to specify the format of any tables.

6. Select the correlation coefficient you require.

7. Choose to apply either a **Two-tailed** or **One-tailed** test, as appropriate for the hypothesis.

8. If you click on **Options**, another dialogue box will appear, in which you can request means and standard deviations.

9. Check that **Flag significant correlations** is ticked. Then click on **OK**.

You may not see this button as this is an optional module in SPSS (see Chapter 1, Section 1).

In the **Bivariate Correlations** dialogue box, you have the option of choosing either a one- or two-tailed test, and SPSS will then print the appropriate value of p. Here, we selected two-tailed. In the statistical tests we have covered previously, SPSS will only print the two-tailed p value, and if you have a one-tailed hypothesis, you halve that value to give the one-tailed p value.

The annotated output for Pearson's r is shown on the next page.

SPSS output for Pearson's *r*
Obtained using menu item: Correlate > Bivariate

CORRELATIONS

Descriptive Statistics

Useful descriptives obtained by using the **Options** button in the **Bivariate Correlations** dialogue box.

	Mean	Std. Deviation	N
age	42.4000	12.55891	20
cff	32.1375	4.58249	20

Correlations

		age	cff
age	Pearson Correlation	1	-.780[**]
	Sig. (1-tailed)		.000
	N	20	20
cff	Pearson Correlation	-.780[**]	1
	Sig. (1-tailed)	.000	
	N	20	20

The Pearson's correlation coefficient or Pearson's *r*.

The *p* value. (See Chapter 5, Section 3, Footnote 3).

N, the number of cases.

[**]. Correlation is significant at the 0.01 level (1-tailed).

A complete matrix is printed.

Two of the cells are for each variable with itself (for these cells, *p* is not calculated). The other two cells contain the same information about the correlation between the two variables.

In addition to the *p* value/s in the matrix, SPSS prints this message. Significant correlations are flagged by asterisks; this is particularly useful if you have entered several variables and so have a large correlation matrix.

What you might write in a report is given below, after we tell you about effect sizes in correlation.

For correlations, the sign of the coefficient indicates whether the correlation is positive or negative, so you must report it (unlike the sign in a *t*-test analysis).

CHAPTER 6

Effect sizes in correlation

The value of r indicates the strength of the correlation, and it is a measure of effect size (see Chapter 1, Section 1). As a rule of thumb, r values of 0 to .2 are generally considered weak, .3 to .6 moderate, and .7 to 1 strong. The strength of the correlation alone is not necessarily an indication of whether it is an important correlation: normally, the significance value should also be considered. With small sample sizes this is crucial, as strong correlations may easily occur by chance. With large to very large sample sizes, however, even a small correlation can be highly statistically significant. To illustrate that, look at a table of the critical values of r (in the back of most statistics textbooks). For example, if you carry out a correlational study with a sample of 100 and obtain r of .20, it is significant at the .05 level, two-tailed. Yet .2 is only a weak correlation. Thus, we recommend you report the effect size, the statistical significance and the proportion of variation, which we explain next.

The concept of 'proportion of variation explained' is described in Chapter 8, Section 1. Briefly, a correlation coefficient allows us to estimate the proportion of variation within our data that is explained by the relationship between the two variables. (The remaining variation is down to extraneous variables, situational and participant.) The proportion of variation explained is given by r^2. Thus, for the age and CFF example in which $r = .78$, $r^2 = 0.6084$ and we can say that 60% of the variation in the CFF data can be attributed to age. Note that, logically, we can just as easily say that 60% of the variation in the age data can be attributed to CFF. The latter statement should make it clear that we are not implying a causal relationship: we cannot do so with correlation. The important practical point is that the two variables have quite a lot of variation in common, and one could use a person's age to predict what their CFF might be. If their measured CFF is outside the lower confidence limit for their age, we could investigate further.

Note that the proportion of variation explained does not have to be large to be important. How important it is may depend on the purpose of the study (see Howell, 2013, 312–13). Chapter 9, on multiple regression, also considers the proportion of variance explained in correlational designs.

 Reporting the results

In a report you might write:

There was a significant negative correlation between age and CFF ($r = -.78$, $N = 20$, $p < .001$, one-tailed). It is a fairly strong correlation: 60.8% of the variation is explained. The scattergram (Figure 6.3) shows that the data points are reasonably well distributed along the regression line, in a linear relationship with no outliers.

Section 4: SPEARMAN'S r_s: NONPARAMETRIC TEST OF CORRELATION

When the data for one or both of the variables are not parametric, for example they are measured at ordinal level, or if the scattergram suggests that the relationship between the two variables is not linear, then we use a nonparametric measure of correlation. Here, we describe two such tests, Spearman's r_s and Kendall's tau-b. The s on Spearman's r_s is to distinguish it from Pearson's r. This test was originally called Spearman's ρ (the Greek letter rho), and SPSS still calls the output Spearman's rho.

Example study: the relationships between attractiveness, believability and confidence

Previous research using mock juries has shown that attractive defendants are less likely to be found guilty than unattractive defendants, and that attractive individuals are frequently rated more highly on other desirable traits, such as intelligence. In a study undertaken by one of our students, participants saw the testimony of a woman in a real case of alleged rape. They were asked to rate her, on a scale of 1–7, in terms of how much confidence they placed in her testimony, how believable she was and how attractive she was. (These data are available in the Appendix or from he.palgrave.com/psychology/brace.)

The design employed was correlational, with three variables each measured on a 7-point scale. Although it often accepted that such data could be considered interval in nature (see Chapter 1, Section 1), for the purpose of this section we will consider it as ordinal data. The hypotheses tested were that:

1. There would be a positive relationship between attractiveness and confidence placed in testimony.

2. There would be a positive relationship between attractiveness and believability.

3. There would be a positive relationship between confidence placed in testimony and believability.

 We are using this study to illustrate use of Spearman's r_s and some other aspects of correlation. However, multiple regression (Chapter 9) would usually be more appropriate for three or more variables in a correlational design.

CHAPTER 6

How to perform Spearman's r_s

Carry out steps 1 to 5 as for the Pearson's r (previous section). At step 6, select **Spearman** instead of **Pearson** (see the **Bivariate Correlations** dialogue box below). This example also illustrates the fact that you can carry out more than one correlation at once. There are three variables, and we want to investigate the relationship between each variable with each of the other two. To do this, you simply highlight all three variable names and move them all into the **Variables** box.

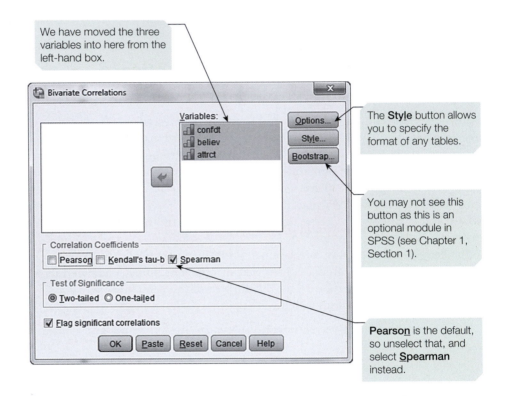

We have moved the three variables into here from the left-hand box.

The **Style** button allows you to specify the format of any tables.

You may not see this button as this is an optional module in SPSS (see Chapter 1, Section 1).

Pearson is the default, so unselect that, and select **Spearman** instead.

The SPSS output for Spearman's r_s is shown on the next page.

SPSS output for Spearman's r_s
Obtained using menu item: Correlate > Bivariate

NONPARAMETRIC CORRELATIONS

Correlations

			confdt	believ	attrct
Spearman's rho	confdt	Correlation Coefficient	1.000	.372**	.157
		Sig. (2-tailed)	.	.000	.143
		N	89	89	89
	believ	Correlation Coefficient	.372**	1.000	.359**
		Sig. (2-tailed)	.000	.	.001
		N	89	89	89
	attrct	Correlation Coefficient	.157	.359**	1.000
		Sig. (2-tailed)	.143	.001	.
		N	89	89	89

**. Correlation is significant at the 0.01 level (2-tailed).

This cell contains the values for the correlation between variables 'confdt' and 'believ':
.372	is r_s
.000	is p
89	is number of cases.

As in the Pearson's output, a complete matrix is printed, but this matrix is larger because three variables were entered.

Look for the diagonal: the output for each bivariate correlation is given twice, once below the diagonal and once above it.

Reporting the results

When reporting the outcome for each correlation, at the appropriate points, you would write:

There was a significant positive correlation between confidence in testimony and believability (r_s = .37, N = 89, p < .001, two-tailed).

There was no significant correlation between confidence in testimony and attractiveness (r_s = .16, N = 89, p = .143, two-tailed).

There was a significant positive correlation between attractiveness and believability (r_s = .36, N = 89, p = .001, two-tailed).

You could illustrate each pair of variables in a scattergram (see Section 1). Note that the R^2 Linear value, given in the scattergram when you add a regression line, is the square of Pearson's r (r^2) and not the square of Spearman's r_s. As described in Section 2, r^2 indicates the proportion of variation explained, but this may not be appropriate for ordinal data.

CHAPTER 6

How to perform Kendall's tau-b

Some researchers prefer to use Kendall's tau instead of Spearman's r_s. To undertake a Kendall's tau-b, follow the same steps as for Pearson's r, but at step 6 select **Kendall's tau-b**. The output takes the same form as that for Spearman's r_s. Kendall's tau-b takes ties into account. Kendall's tau-c, which ignores ties, is available in **Crosstabs** (see Chapter 7, Section 4).

Section 5: COMPARING THE STRENGTH OF CORRELATION COEFFICIENTS

Sometimes you may have data on the same variables for participants from each of two populations that differ on one nominal variable. We may have reason to hypothesise that the correlation between two variables will differ between the two populations. To illustrate this, we will use a study we carried out with student participants as part of a module. It is in the area of environmental psychology, and for this purpose we will use three of the variables we recorded. These were: 'threat', the response to a question about the perceived threat from environmental problems to the participant's own health and wellbeing; 'recycling score', the mean of self-reported recycling rates for a range of materials; and 'gender'. Below, we show the SPSS output for the correlation between the two variables for all participants, for the female group, and for the male group.

Correlations

		threat	Recycle_score
threat	Pearson Correlation	1	.401**
	Sig. (2-tailed)		.000
	N	219	219
Recycle_score	Pearson Correlation	.401**	1
	Sig. (2-tailed)	.000	
	N	219	220

**. Correlation is significant at the 0.01 level (2-tailed).

For all participants.

Note: the male N and female N do not sum to the total N as two participants did not record their gender on the questionnaire.

Correlations

		threat	Recycle_score
threat	Pearson Correlation	1	.279**
	Sig. (2-tailed)		.004
	N	105	105
Recycle_score	Pearson Correlation	.279**	1
	Sig. (2-tailed)	.004	
	N	105	105

**. Correlation is significant at the 0.01 level (2-tailed).

For female participants.

Correlations

For male participants.

		threat	Recycle_score
threat	Pearson Correlation	1	.452**
	Sig. (2-tailed)		.000
	N	112	112
Recycle_score	Pearson Correlation	.452**	1
	Sig. (2-tailed)	.000	
	N	112	113

**. Correlation is significant at the 0.01 level (2-tailed).

You should have a rationale for any comparison of correlation coefficients you make. For this example, differences between the genders are often reported in the area of environmental psychology. The differences may, however, be due to differences in other variables such as age, social class, type of residence area, level of education and so on. Thus, if you do find a difference between correlation coefficients for samples that are not matched on other variables, you should check whether your two samples differ on other variables which might explain your finding.

A test that Fisher devised (e.g. see Howell, 2013, 284–5) allows use of the z tables to assess whether the difference between two r values is significant. There are three stages to applying this test:

1. Transform each r value to a value called r' (pronounced 'r prime'). This is required because the distribution of the difference between two r values is used to assess whether a particular difference is significant; that distribution can be skewed and then use of z would not be valid.

2. Use the r' values to calculate the z value.

3. Use z to determine whether or not there is a significant difference between the two r values.

You can do this yourself using the formulae shown here, or by a SPSS syntax procedure, described in Chapter 13, Section 2.

Using equations

Equation 1
$$r' = (0.5) \log_e \left| \frac{1 + r}{1 - r} \right|$$

Equation 2
$$z = \frac{r_1' - r_2'}{\sqrt{\dfrac{1}{N_1 - 3} + \dfrac{1}{N_2 - 3}}}$$

CHAPTER 6

First, calculate r' from each r:

r_1 (for women) $= .279$ $\qquad\qquad$ r_2 (for men) $= .452$

$$r_1' = (0.5)\log_e\left|\frac{1 + .279}{1 - .279}\right| \qquad\qquad r_2' = (0.5)\log_e\left|\frac{1 + .452}{1 - .452}\right|$$

$$r_1' = (0.5)\log_e\left|\frac{1.279}{0.721}\right| \qquad\qquad r_2' = (0.5)\log_e\left|\frac{1.452}{0.548}\right|$$

$$r_1' = (0.5)\log_e 1.774 \qquad\qquad r_2' = (0.5)\log_e 2.649$$

$$r_1' = (0.5)\,0.573 \qquad\qquad r_2' = (0.5)\,0.974$$

$$r_1' = 0.287 \qquad\qquad r_2' = 0.487$$

Second, calculate z:

$$z = \frac{r_1' - r_2'}{\sqrt{\dfrac{1}{N_1 - 3} + \dfrac{1}{N_2 - 3}}}$$

$$z = \frac{.287 - .487}{\sqrt{\dfrac{1}{105 - 3} + \dfrac{1}{112 - 3}}}$$

$$z = \frac{-.200}{\sqrt{0.010 + 0.009}}$$

$$z = \frac{-.200}{0.138}$$

$$z = -1.451$$

Note that the sign of the z simply indicates whether r_1' is larger or smaller than r_2'.

Third, compare our observed z with the critical z of 1.96. We use the absolute value (that is, ignore the sign). If our observed z is less than 1.96, the difference between the two r values is not significant ($p > .05$); whereas if the observed z is greater than 1.96, the difference is significant ($p < .05$).

In our example, the absolute value of the observed z is 1.451, and therefore $p > .05$.

⚬ Reporting the results

When reporting the outcome of the comparison, if you have only used the critical value of *z*, you would write:

There was no significant difference between the correlation coefficients of .287 for women and .487 for men ($z = 1.45$, $p > .05$).

If you used *z* tables to find *p* more specifically, you would report:

There was no significant difference between the correlation coefficients of .287 for women and .487 for men ($z = 1.45$, $p \simeq .147$).

Section 6: BRIEF INTRODUCTION TO REGRESSION

■ Regression is a statistical technique that allows us to predict someone's score on one variable from their scores on one or more other variables.

■ Unlike the situation with correlation, in regression we attempt to specify the variables in terms of being dependent or independent variables.

■ Regression involves one dependent variable, which we term the 'criterion variable', and one or more independent variables, which we refer to as the 'predictor variables'.

■ With only one predictor variable, we have bivariate regression; multiple regression (see Chapter 9) involves two or more predictor variables.

■ The predictor variable can be measured using a range of scales, although ideally at interval or ratio level, but the criterion variable should be measured using a ratio or interval scale.

■ Human behaviour is inherently noisy and therefore it is not possible to produce totally accurate predictions; however, regression allows us to assess how useful the predictor variable is in estimating a participant's likely score on the criterion variable.

■ As with bivariate correlation, bivariate regression does not imply causal relationships unless a variable has been manipulated.

Regression as a model

As we discuss in Chapter 8, Section 1, human behaviour is variable and therefore difficult to predict. A model is an attempt to explain and simplify data we have measured, in a way that allows prediction of future cases. Say, for example, that we have measured how confident each student feels about how to use SPSS after they have completed a module. The simplest model is the mean; if the mean confidence is 4.1 (on a scale of 1.0 to 5.0), then we can predict that other students who complete the module the following year will have a confidence score of 4.1. However, there will be much error! The difference between each observed value and the predicted value (the mean) will be large for many students. Of course, students vary in other ways, and other variables can affect their confidence in using SPSS; for example, how much time they have spent practising with SPSS. If we measure that as well as confidence, we can use the technique of regression to model the relationship between those two variables. We can then predict how confident a student will be from how much time they have spent practising. There will still be error, but it will be less than in the situation when we only used the mean confidence. The amount of error in the model is indicated by the residuals (the difference between the observed value and predicted value for each case). We describe residuals below.

Section 7: BIVARIATE REGRESSION

From bivariate correlation to bivariate regression

Earlier sections covered correlation between two variables. Here, we use the term 'bivariate', which indicates that only two variables are involved, to distinguish from 'multiple', which indicates that there are more than two variables. To illustrate this section, we will use the example previously used when obtaining a scattergram with a regression line, and also for Pearson's correlation coefficient. Age and CFF were measured; the study is described in Section 2.

In bivariate correlation, we consider the strength of association between two variables, and do not consider whether one might be independent and the other a dependent variable. The technique of regression, however, allows prediction of one variable from another; thus we do need to distinguish between the two variables. Some authorities use the terms 'independent' and 'dependent variable'; however, prediction does not necessarily mean direct causation and other authorities use a different labelling system, which we prefer. In this system, the terms are the 'predictor variable' and the 'criterion variable'. The criterion variable is said to be predicted by the predictor variable. Another labelling system, used in equations and graphs, is X and Y. The predictor variable is denoted X, and the criterion variable is denoted Y. A scattergram with regression line for the example data is shown again below. Age is classified as the predictor, or X, variable, and CFF as the criterion, or Y, variable. It is that way round because we assume that something to do with the ageing process affects CFF, rather than that CFF affects age or ageing. There can often be a logical reason such as that for classifying the variables. Mathematically, however, regression works equally well in the opposite direction; if we used CFF as the predictor and age as the criterion, we can predict someone's age from their CFF with the same degree of accuracy.

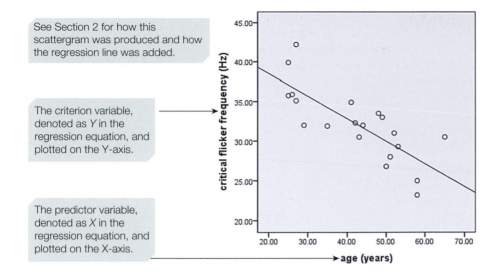

See Section 2 for how this scattergram was produced and how the regression line was added.

The criterion variable, denoted as *Y* in the regression equation, and plotted on the Y-axis.

The predictor variable, denoted as *X* in the regression equation, and plotted on the X-axis.

The bivariate regression equation

In Section 2 we introduced the regression line that can be added to the scattergram (using the **Fit Line at Total** option, see pages 137–138), and we will now explain the equation underlying the regression line. The relationship between any two variables that have a linear relationship is given by the equation for a straight line:

$$Y = a + bX$$

- *Y* is the criterion variable. When we use the equation to predict values of *Y* from observed values of *X*, we can use the symbol *Y′* (pronounced Y prime).

- *X* is the predictor variable.

- *a* is the intercept; it is the value of *Y′* when *X* = 0; when the regression line is added to the scattergram, *a* is the value of *Y* at the point where the line intercepts the Y-axis (if the X-axis starts at 0). Thus, in our example, *a* is the CFF in Hz for someone who is aged 0 years. For purposes of prediction, you should not try to extrapolate much beyond the range of values you measured. Nonetheless, for purposes of the equation, *a* is the value of *Y′* when *X* = 0. Remember that, as default, SPSS applies axis scales around the values occurring in the data as in the example above, so scattergram axes may not include 0. In such cases, *a* cannot be read from the graph; however, SPSS will provide the value of *a*, and also of *b*, as we show below.

- *b* is the slope of the line, known as the 'regression coefficient' (or regression weight); it is the value by which *Y′* will change when *X* is changed by one unit. So, it is the difference in predicted CFF between two people who differ in age by one year. We return to regression coefficients in Chapter 9, for multiple regression.

The regression process involves finding a solution to the equation (that is, identifying values of *a* and *b*) for which the residuals are at a minimum, as described next.

CHAPTER 6

Residuals

A residual is the difference between the observed value of Y for a participant and the value predicted for them by the regression equation (Y'). This section of the scatter-gram illustrates that.

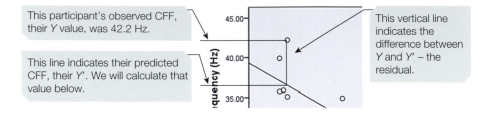

This participant's observed CFF, their Y value, was 42.2 Hz.

This line indicates their predicted CFF, their Y'. We will calculate that value below.

This vertical line indicates the difference between Y and Y' – the residual.

If the two variables are perfectly correlated, then all the points will fall exactly along the straight line and the residuals will all equal zero. It is unlikely, however, that two variables measured in psychological research will be perfectly correlated; normally, there will be a difference between most Y values and their Y'. The difference, $Y-Y'$, is considered error, and known as the 'residual' for each case. Note that residuals can be negative or positive, so they are usually squared when used (see next paragraph). There is error for a number of reasons. There is always error in measurement; this may be due to error in the scale (for example, questionnaires are unlikely ever to be perfect measures of a construct), but it is also due to individual or situational irrelevant variables. In addition, the criterion variable is likely to be affected not just by the predictor variable but also by variables we have not measured.

The best solution to the regression equation will involve values of a and b that minimise residuals – that is, the predicted values are as close as possible to the observed values, on average. The least squares criterion is most commonly used to find the best solution; in this criterion $\Sigma(Y-Y')^2$ (the sum of the squared differences between observed and predicted scores) is at a minimum.

Proportion of variance explained

In regression, we wish to explain the degree of dispersion in the data, usually stated as the variance in the data; we can ask: 'How much of the variance in the criterion variable is explained, or accounted for, by the predictor variable?' For bivariate relationships, r^2 gives the proportion of variance explained as described in Section 3, Effect sizes in correlation. We will return to the concept of variance explained when describing ANOVA in Chapter 8, Section 1, and for multiple regression in Chapter 9.

How to perform bivariate regression in SPSS

For this purpose, we will continue to use the age and CFF data. Click on **Analyze**, **Regression**, **Curve Estimation**. You will be presented with the **Curve Estimation** dialogue box (shown below). You now select *Y*, the criterion (dependent) variable, and *X*, the predictor (independent) variable. SPSS allows you to add more than one *Y* variable, but we currently wish to predict a single *Y* ('cff') from the *X* ('age').

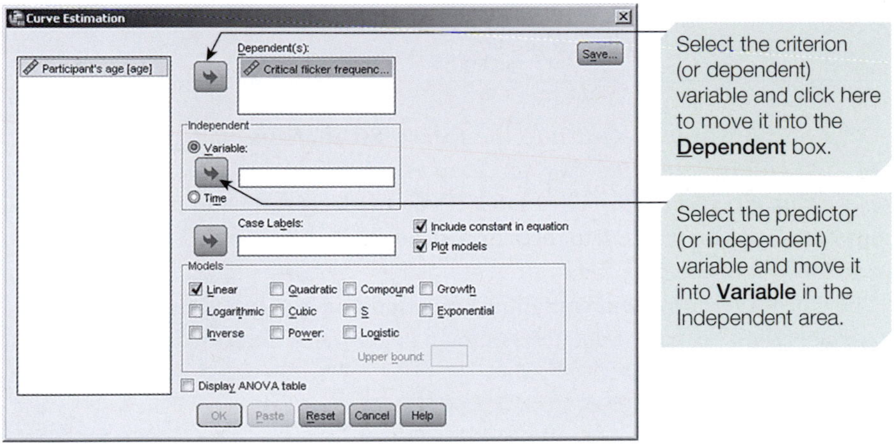

Select the criterion (or dependent) variable and click here to move it into the **Dependent** box.

Select the predictor (or independent) variable and move it into **Variable** in the Independent area.

You can enter two or more *Y* variables into the **Dependent box**, and then SPSS will carry out the bivariate regression procedure separately for each *Y* with the *X*. If you do have more than one *Y*, to obtain all the output for all the *Y*s, you must select **Display ANOVA table** in the dialogue box.

We leave the other settings in the **Curve Estimation** dialogue box as they are. In the Models area of the dialogue box, the default is **Linear**, which applies a bivariate linear regression model and is appropriate for the example we are using. In the future, if you have data with nonlinear relationships, you could explore the other types of curve.

Next click on the **Save** button (top right) to obtain the **Curve Estimation: Save** dialogue box (shown below). SPSS calculates certain values for each case, and the **Save** command allows you to save these to your data file. We have selected **Predicted values** and **Residuals**.

Select **Predicted values** and **Residuals** to add these to your data file.

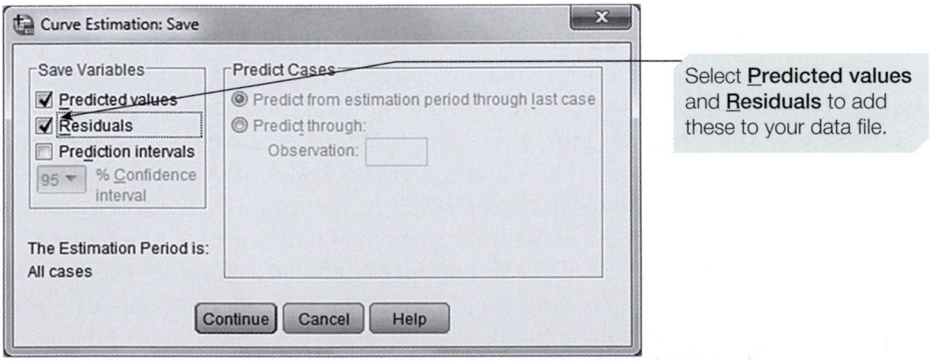

Selecting **Prediction intervals** in the **Curve Estimation: Save** dialogue box will give you two other variables, the upper and lower values for confidence intervals of the predicted values. If you select this, the % Confidence interval box will no longer be greyed out, and you can change from 95% to 90% or 99% if you wish. See Chapter 5 for information about why you might change the confidence interval.

Click on **Continue** to return to the **Curve Estimation** dialogue box, then click on **OK**. You will be reminded that you have asked to add variables to your data file – if you are sure all is well, then click **OK**. (If you inadvertently add unwanted variables to your data file, you can delete them or just not save the amended file; SPSS does not automatically save the data file.)

The Output window will contain information and a graph (described below). The new variables will be in the Data file (as shown below), and described in the annotations.

	age	cff	FIT_1	ERR_1
1	41.00	34.90	32.53616	2.36384
2	43.00	30.50	31.96665	-1.46665
3	25.00	35.75	37.09222	-1.34222
4	42.00	32.30	32.25140	.04860
5	51.00	28.00	29.68862	-1.68862
6	27.00	42.20	36.52271	5.67729
7	27.00	35.10	36.52271	-1.42271
8	48.00	33.50	30.54288	2.95712
9	58.00	25.00	27.69534	-2.69534
10	52.00	31.00	29.40386	1.59614
11	58.00	23.20	27.69534	-4.49534

*pearsonscorrelation.sav [DataSet1] – IBM SPSS Statistics Data Editor

File   Edit   View   Data   Transform   Analyze   Direct Marketing   Graphs   U

1 : FIT_1   32.53615523224773

The new variable 'FIT_1' holds the predicted values, Y'. Thus, for participant 1, who is 41 years old, CFF is predicted from the regression equation to be 32.5 Hz.

The second new variable 'ERR_1' holds the residual (Y, the observed value, minus Y', the predicted value). See below for an explanation.

If you selected **Prediction intervals** in the **Curve Estimation: Save** dialogue box, the upper and lower values for confidence intervals of the predicted values will also be added to the data file. We show these on the last page of this chapter.

The residual is equal to Y (the observed value) minus Y' (the predicted value). It is sometime called the 'error' (indicated by the SPSS variable name 'ERR_1') as it can be considered the amount of error in the prediction. The residual values can be interesting, as we will explain now, but they are not necessarily useful for our purposes. In this example, the residual 'ERR_1' = 'cff' – 'FIT_1'. For participant 1, the predicted value is 2.4 Hz less than their observed value of 34.9. If you scan the 'ERR_1' column, you will see that the absolute value (that is, ignoring whether they are negative or positive) of the residuals varies from effectively 0 to nearly 6. The mean of the absolute residuals is indicative of the strength of the relationship between the two variables, but residuals are unstandardised. That is, they are on the same scale as the original data and not standardised (z-scores are an example of a standardised measure, as described in Chapter 3). Thus, residuals can be difficult to interpret because you must consider the scale on which the variable is measured.

As mentioned above, you can enter more than one *Y* in the **Curve Estimation** dialogue box, in order to carry out separate bivariate regressions of *X* with each *Y*. For example, in addition to CFF, you may have a memory score for the same participants. If you do enter two *Y*s, then the new variables for the second *Y* will be called 'FIT_2' and 'ERR_2'.

In addition to the new variables in the data file, SPSS will also give output with information about the bivariate regression, and the output obtained for the bivariate regression of CFF with age is shown below.

SPSS output

Obtained using: Analyze, Regression, Curve Estimation

Curve Fit

Model Description

Model Name		MOD_1
Dependent Variable	1	cff
Equation	1	Linear
Independent Variable		age
Constant		Included
Variable Whose Values Label Observations in Plots		Unspecified

This table gives information about the model you requested.

Case Processing Summary

	N
Total Cases	20
Excluded Cases[a]	0
Forecasted Cases	0
Newly Created Cases	0

a. Cases with a missing value in any variable are excluded from the analysis.

The **Variable Processing Summary** table shows information about cases for each variable.

Variable Processing Summary

		Variables	
		Dependent	Independent
		cff	age
Number of Positive Values		20	20
Number of Zeros		0	0
Number of Negative Values		0	0
Number of Missing Values	User-Missing	0	0
	System-Missing	0	0

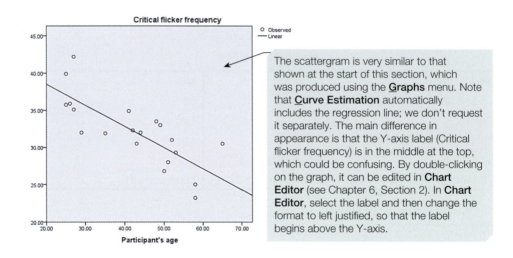

This is r^2, the square of r, which we have seen before. SPSS adds r^2 to the scattergram when we request a regression line (see Chapter 6, Section 2).

Parameter Estimates give values from the regression equation for these data: the constant is a, the intercept; b1 is b, the slope. See text below.

Model Summary and Parameter Estimates

Dependent Variable: cff

| Equation | Model Summary | | | | | Parameter Estimates | |
	R Square	F	df1	df2	Sig.	Constant	b1
Linear	.609	28.040	1	18	.000	44.211	-.285

The independent variable is age.

Whether r^2 is significantly different from 0 is tested using F. This is rarely used for bivariate regression, as we simply use the correlation. We explain the use of F in Chapter 9.

The scattergram is very similar to that shown at the start of this section, which was produced using the **Graphs** menu. Note that **Curve Estimation** automatically includes the regression line; we don't request it separately. The main difference in appearance is that the Y-axis label (Critical flicker frequency) is in the middle at the top, which could be confusing. By double-clicking on the graph, it can be edited in **Chart Editor** (see Chapter 6, Section 2). In **Chart Editor**, select the label and then change the format to left justified, so that the label begins above the Y-axis.

The Parameter Estimates section of the Model Summary and Parameter Estimates table (above) shows:

1. The constant or a, the intercept. Thus, when the modelling process was applied to the values in the data set, the CFF value for someone who is 0 years old was estimated to be 44.21 Hz.

2. b1 or b, the slope or the regression coefficient. For these data b is negative; thus, if age increases by one year, the CFF reduces by 0.285 Hz. More usefully for a report, we could instead say that when people are 10 years older, their CFF would be expected to have reduced by 2.85 Hz. This is, of course, the typical reduction predicted from these data.

Thus, the straight line equation for these data is:

$$\text{CFF} = 44.21 + -.285 \times \text{age, or CFF} = 44.21 - .285 \times \text{age}$$

Using the procedure to predict *Y* for new cases

If you wish to predict *Y* for new cases without using the equation yourself, simply enter the new case/s into the data file and run the procedure again. As an example, we added two hypothetical new cases, with 'age' data only, to the data file and ran the procedure again. In this run, we also selected **Prediction intervals** to obtain confidence intervals for 95% CI. The section of the data file with these new cases is shown below.

An inspection of the output viewer will show you that the two new cases, without observed values for the *Y* variable, affect the excluded cases and missing values, but not the other output.

*pearsonscorrelation.sav [DataSet1] - IBM SPSS Statistics Data Editor

File   Edit   View   Data   Transform   Analyze   Direct Marketing   Graphs   Utilities   Add-ons   Window   Help

9:

	age	cff	FIT_1	ERR_1	LCL_1	UCL_1
1	41.00	34.90	32.53616	2.36384	26.19670	38.87561
2	43.00	30.50	31.96665	-1.46665	25.62881	38.30449
3	25.00	35.75	37.09222	-1.34222	30.45685	43.72758
19	25.00	39.90	37.09222	2.80778	30.45685	43.72758
20	49.00	33.00	30.25813	2.74187	23.87693	36.63932
21	32.00	.	35.09894	.	28.65346	41.54442
22	62.00	.	26.55633	.	19.84313	33.26952
23						

The new case aged 32 years has predicted CFF (shown in 'FIT_1') of 35.1 Hz, while the case aged 62 years has predicted CFF of 26.6 Hz.

The last two columns, 'LCL_1' and 'UCL_1', give the lower and upper limits for the confidence interval requested (95% in this example). For case 20, aged 49, the limits are 23.9 and 36.6. These values can be used as a guide to how serious is a difference of an observed value from the predicted value.

Remember that for the purposes of prediction, you should not try to extrapolate much beyond the range of values that you measured. The two new cases we have added are within the age range of the participants in the study.

Summary

- This chapter introduced you to statistical tests of correlation that will tell you if there is a significant relationship between two variables, and provide you with information on the strength and nature of this relationship.

- Your choice of test of correlation will depend on whether the data are parametric and whether the relationship between the variables is linear.

- You should first obtain a scattergram to observe any general trend in your data and to see if any relationship is linear.

- You can add a regression line to the scattergram.

- The value of the correlation coefficient indicates the strength of the correlation, and is a measure of effect size.

- The sign of the correlation coefficient is important as it indicates whether the relationship is positive or negative.

- It is not possible to infer a causal relationship from a correlation.

- We also introduced how to compare the strength of two correlation coefficients.

- Comparing the strength of two correlation coefficients can be useful if there are grounds to hypothesise that the correlation between two variables will differ for two groups (such as men and women).

- When comparing correlations, you should check whether the groups differ on variables other than the grouping variable (gender, in our example). If they do differ on other variables, you will not know if any difference between the correlations is due to gender or those other variables.

- We also introduced bivariate regression, which allows us to predict one variable (the criterion) from another (the predictor).

- In Chapter 9, we discuss multiple regression, which allows use of more than one predictor variable, in the same model, to predict the criterion variable.

- For guidance on incorporating SPSS output into a report, or on printing the output, see Chapter 13.

7 Tests for nominal data

In this chapter

- Nominal data and dichotomous variables
- Chi-square test versus the chi-square distribution
- The goodness of fit chi-square
- The multidimensional chi-square
- The McNemar test for repeated measures

SPSS for Psychologists online
Visit he.palgrave.com/psychology/brace for data sets, online tutorials and exercises.

Section 1: NOMINAL DATA AND DICHOTOMOUS VARIABLES

- Nominal data, also referred to as 'categorical data', are data measured using scales that only categorise the observations or responses, for example being male or female.

- For convenience, each category is allocated a number when entering data into the IBM SPSS Statistics software (SPSS). These are numbers that cannot be put into any meaningful order; if they could, they would be ordinal data.

- With nominal data, the numbers only represent the category of which the participant is a member. That is why nominal data are sometimes called 'qualitative data' and, by contrast, the ordinal, interval and ratio levels of measurement are called 'quantitative data'. The use of these terms in this way is different from the use in qualitative and quantitative research. Quantitative research can include all levels of measurement, including nominal.

- The independent variable, whether in related designs or independent groups designs, and for true or natural groups experiments, can be thought of as a nominal variable. For example, in the paired *t*-test example in Chapter 5, Section 4, the IV had two levels: large difference and small difference. It is only when both variables are nominal that we must use a test devised for nominal data.

- Nominal variables can have more than two values. For example, if you recorded the smoking status of your participants, you could use three categories: smoker, never smoked and ex-smoker. If you recorded nationality or culture, there may be a huge number of categories among your participants (in a cosmopolitan city such as London, for example). Each of those categories would be represented by a number in a package such as SPSS.

■   Some nominal variables can only have two values, however, and they are known as 'dichotomous variables'.

■   A dichotomous variable is a nominal variable that can *only* take one of two values. For example, if you classify smoking status as smoker or non-smoker, then someone who smokes only very occasionally would be classified as a smoker, whereas an ex-chain smoker would be classified as a non-smoker.

Descriptives for nominal data

An important point for you to think about is which summary descriptives are appropriate for nominal data. If you have recorded your participant's sex, then finding the mean is *meaningless*. So is the median, and any measure of dispersion.

The only summary descriptives suitable for nominal data are counts, or frequencies, and percentages. Thus, we could say that of 20 participants, 15 (75%) are women and 5 (25%) are men. We can display those counts and percentages in a table, as will be shown with chi-square. We can also illustrate them using a bar chart, also shown with chi-square. Note that histograms should be used for displaying data of at least ordinal level of measurement, and not for nominal data.

Entering nominal data into SPSS

When students first consider chi-square (covered below), they think that the data entry will be more complex than it actually is. For any variable measured on a nominal scale, you simply enter the number chosen to represent the category. So we still enter data on one row for each participant. For the participant's sex, we have a column with variable name 'sex', in which we could enter a 1 if that participant is a male or a 2 if she is female. In a 'smoking status' column, the participants could be given a 1 for 'smoker', a 2 for 'never smoked', or a 3 for 'ex-smoker'. We can enter as many nominal variables as we like, and each one will contain numbers that are codes for the categories. Each column is independent of all the others, so you can use the same numbers to represent different things in different columns, as for the sex and smoking status examples. More examples can be seen in Sections 4 and 5, and in Chapter 4, where some nominal variables are used in the data handling exercises.

Section 2: CHI-SQUARE TEST VERSUS THE CHI-SQUARE DISTRIBUTION

- There are two different forms of the chi-square test: the goodness of fit chi-square test and the multidimensional chi-square test.

- The goodness of fit chi-square is used to test whether an observed pattern of events differs significantly from what would be expected by chance alone.

- The multidimensional chi-square test can be used either as a test of association or as a test of difference between independent groups.

The chi-square *test* makes use of the chi-square *distribution* to test for significance. The distinction between 'test' and 'distribution' is made clear by, for example, Howell (2013). In this book we cover the chi-square inferential test, and do not give any details of the chi-square distribution. However, it is worth noting that for some other statistical tests, including some for data with a level of measurement other than nominal, a chi-square distribution is used to test for significance; for example, the Kruskal–Wallis and Friedman tests covered in Chapter 8, Sections 2 and 4, respectively. Also note that the chi-square distribution does not have to be used to test for significance in all inferential tests that are applied to nominal data. Thus, for the McNemar test (Section 5), SPSS uses the binomial distribution.

Section 3: THE GOODNESS OF FIT CHI-SQUARE

In this type of chi-square test – often referred to as either a 'one-dimensional chi' or a 'goodness of fit test' – we are testing whether the observed pattern of events differs significantly from what we might have expected by chance alone. For example, we might ask whether a group of smokers choose brand A cigarettes more often than brand B. Here, we are effectively asking the question: 'Do significantly more than 50% of our smokers choose one brand over the other brand?' In practice, this form of the chi-square test is not often used in psychology. This example of cigarette brands relates to one of the few times the authors have ever used this form of the test. An undergraduate student undertook a project examining the effect of cigarette advertising on cigarette choice. As part of this project, she listed a series of personality characteristics that were implied by cigarette adverts. For example, some cigarette advertisements might imply a sophisticated personality. These personality statements were then presented to smokers who were asked to indicate to which of five brands of cigarettes they thought the statement best applied. The responses for each statement were analysed using the chi-square goodness of fit test to compare the observed distribution against that predicted by the null hypothesis (that the five brands would be equally often selected). This is an interesting, but rare, example of the use of this form of the chi-square test in psychology. Much more common is the second form of this test, described later in this chapter, which allows us to consider whether two variables are independent of one another.

To perform the goodness of fit chi-square test

Note that this type of chi-square test is accessed via the chi-square command that can be found under **Nonparametric tests** in the **Analyze** menu. However, as this form of the test is used infrequently in psychology, we will not be demonstrating it here.

An error that some students make is to use the goodness of fit version of the test when they actually want the multidimensional chi-square test, accessed in a different way, as explained next.

Section 4: THE MULTIDIMENSIONAL CHI-SQUARE

The multidimensional chi-square test can be thought of in two ways: as a test of association or as a test of difference between independent groups.

It can be thought of as a test of association because it allows us to test whether two variables are associated or whether they are independent of each other. For example, let us modify our cigarette example and say that 50 smokers and 50 non-smokers were asked to choose which of two cigarette adverts they preferred. The multidimensional chi-square test would allow us to ask the question: 'Is the pattern of brand choice independent of whether the participant was a smoker or not?' Another example would be to determine whether receiving or not receiving a particular treatment was associated with living or dying. Yet another might be to see whether a person's sex was independent of their choice of favourite colour. In psychology, we often need to test whether nominal variables are, or are not, independent of each other. The experimental hypothesis would be that the two variables are not independent of each other; for example, we could hypothesise that people receiving a particular treatment are less likely to die than those not receiving the treatment.

Note that another way of phrasing that last hypothesis is that there will be differences between the number of people who die under each treatment condition. Thus, the multidimensional chi-square can also be thought of as a test of difference. Whichever way you think of it, the type of data and the way chi-square assesses that data are both the same.

General issues for chi-square
Causal relationships

If you have only measured existing variables, and not manipulated them, then you cannot claim to have shown a causal relationship. You can show an association, as in correlation, and you can show a difference between groups, as in natural/independent groups design (see the Glossary for an explanation). The smoking status and preferred cigarette advert is an example of a study from which you could not draw conclusions about causation. If, however, you have manipulated one of the variables, and used the normal controls required for independent groups designs, then you can draw conclusions about causation. The type of treatment and likelihood of dying is an example of such a study.

Type of data

In order to use chi-square, our data must satisfy the following criteria:

1. The variables must be measured on a nominal level of measurement, giving frequency data. In other words, our data must be able to tell us the number of times some event has occurred. We can, of course, convert other types of data into nominal data. For example, suppose we have IQ scores – we could recode these data, scoring each participant as either 'High IQ' or 'Low IQ' depending on their score. We could then count to give frequency data – the *number* of high and low IQ participants we have observed. (See Chapter 4, Section 5 for information on how to recode in this way.)

2. For multidimensional chi-square, we must have collected data of this sort on at least two variables. For example, in addition to the high/low IQ data above, we might also know whether each of these participants is a smoker or not.

3. The categorisations of each of the variables must be mutually exclusive. In other words, each participant must be *either* a smoker *or* a non-smoker, and *either* high IQ *or* low IQ. Thus, each variable is an independent groups variable. Another way of thinking about this is to say that each participant must fall into one and only one of the cells of the contingency table (see below).

4. Every observation must be independent of every other observation. This will not be the case if you have more than one observation per participant. (Nominal data from a repeated measures design can be analysed by means of the McNemar test, see Section 5.)

The N*N contingency table

When we have nominal data of this form, we can best display the frequencies or counts in a contingency table. If we have two variables, each with two levels (as in the example above), then we draw what is called a 2*2 (pronounced two by two) contingency table. So, if we had 100 participants in our example data set, the contingency table might look like Table 7.1.

Table 7.1 An example of a 2*2 contingency table

	High IQ	Low IQ	Row totals
Smokers	10	20	30
Non-smokers	35	35	70
Column totals	45	55	100 (Grand total)

Contingency tables can be produced by SPSS from nominal data, as we explain next. The numbers in this table represent the numbers of participants who fall into each cell of the table (and remember that each participant can be in only one cell). So we can see that of the 30 smokers in our study, 10 are high IQ and 20 are low IQ. Similarly, we can see that of the low IQ group, 20 are smokers and 35 are non-smokers.

CHAPTER 7

Thus, the contingency table is useful to describe the data. The rationale for the chi-square inferential test is explained below.

Rationale for chi-square test

If there was no association between smoking and IQ, then we would expect the proportion of smokers in the high IQ group to be the same as the proportion in the total sample. That is, we would expect 45/100 or 45% of the smokers to be high IQ. As there were 30 smokers in total, we would expect (45% of 30) = 13.5 of the smokers to be in the high IQ group. In this way, we can work out the expected frequencies for each cell. The general formula is:

$$\text{expected frequency} = \frac{\text{row total} \times \text{column total}}{\text{grand total}}$$

What chi-square does is calculate the expected frequency for each cell and then compare the expected frequencies with the observed frequencies. If the observed and expected frequencies are significantly different, it would appear that the distribution of observations across the cells is not random. We can, therefore, conclude that there is a significant association between the two variables: IQ and smoking behaviour are not independent for our sample of (fictitious) participants.

Chi-square will actually allow us to calculate whether more than two variables are independent of each other. However, it is very difficult to interpret the results of such an analysis, so we would recommend that you resist the temptation to add extra variables unless you are sure you know what you are doing. It is, however, perfectly reasonable to have more than two categories of each variable – for example a 3*3 chi-square is quite acceptable.

Example study: investigating tendency towards anorexia

To illustrate the use of chi-square, we will use some fictitious data based on research conducted by one of our past students. Eighty young women completed an eating questionnaire, which allowed them to be classified as either high or low anorexia (participants with high scores are more likely to develop anorexia). In addition, the questionnaire asked for the employment status of the women's mother (full time, part time or unemployed) and their cultural background (Caucasian, Asian or other) and type of school they attended (private or state comprehensive). Previous research has suggested that the incidence of anorexia is higher among girls attending private schools than state schools, and higher among girls whose mothers are not in full-time employment. In addition, the incidence seems to be higher in Caucasian girls than non-Caucasian girls. We therefore hypothesised that there would be an association between these factors and the classification on the eating questionnaire. To test this hypothesis, we conducted a series of chi-square analyses. (These data are available in the Appendix or from he.palgrave.com/psychology/brace).

To perform the multidimensional chi-square test

The multidimensional chi-square is accessed under the **Crosstabs** command. **Crosstabs** draws up contingency tables and chi-square is an optional inferential statistic within this command.

1. Click on **Analyze**.

2. Select **Descriptive Statistics**.

Chi-Square.sav [DataSet1] - IBM SPSS Statistics Data Editor

File	Edit	View	Data	Transform	Analyze	Direct Marketing	Graphs	Utilities	Add-ons	Window

Reports ▶
Descriptive Statistics ▶   Frequencies...
Custom Tables ▶   Descriptives...
Compare Means ▶   Explore...
General Linear Model ▶   Crosstabs...
Generalized Linear Models ▶   TURF Analysis
Mixed Models ▶   Ratio...
Correlate ▶   P-P Plots...
Regression ▶   Q-Q Plots...
Loglinear ▶
Neural Networks ▶
Classify ▶
Dimension Reduction ▶
Scale ▶
Nonparametric Tests ▶
Forecasting ▶
Survival ▶
Multiple Response ▶
Missing Value Analysis...
Multiple Imputation ▶
Complex Samples ▶
Simulation...
Quality Control ▶
ROC Curve...
Spatial and Temporal Modeling... ▶

	backgrnd	employ				va
1	2	1				
2	2	1				
3	2	1				
4	2	3				
5	2	3				
6	2	3				
7	2	2				
8	2	2				
9	2	2				
10	2	1				
11	2	1				
12	2	1				
13	2	3				
14	2	3				
15	2	3				
16	2	3				
17	2	2				
18	2	2				
19	2	2				
20	2	2				
21	2	3				
22	2	3				
23	1	3	2	1	2	
24	1	1	2	1	2	

Note: Do NOT use the chi-square command available under **Nonparametric Tests**. That is for one-dimensional, goodness of fit, chi-square.

3. Select **Crosstabs** and the dialogue box will appear (shown on the next page).

4. Select the name of the variable that you want to form the row of your contingency table and then click here to move it into the **Row(s)** box.

5. Now repeat this procedure to move your column variable into the **Column(s)** box.

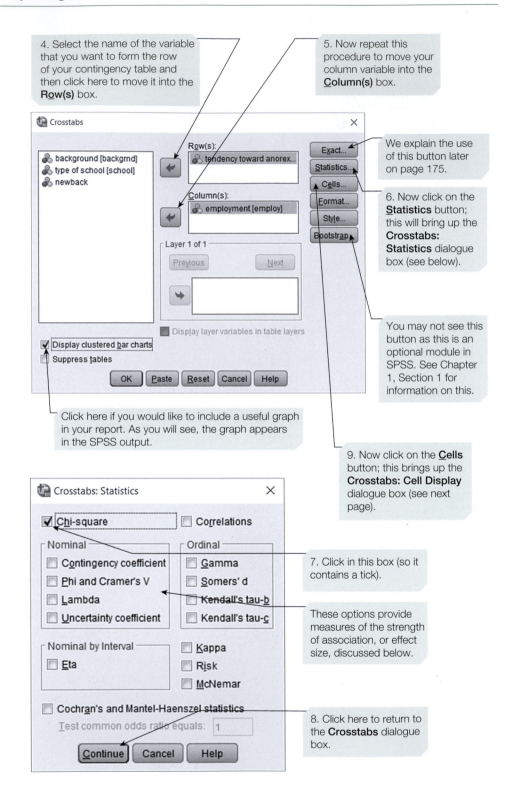

We explain the use of this button later on page 175.

6. Now click on the **Statistics** button; this will bring up the **Crosstabs: Statistics** dialogue box (see below).

You may not see this button as this is an optional module in SPSS. See Chapter 1, Section 1 for information on this.

Click here if you would like to include a useful graph in your report. As you will see, the graph appears in the SPSS output.

9. Now click on the **Cells** button; this brings up the **Crosstabs: Cell Display** dialogue box (see next page).

7. Click in this box (so it contains a tick).

These options provide measures of the strength of association, or effect size, discussed below.

8. Click here to return to the **Crosstabs** dialogue box.

CHAPTER 7

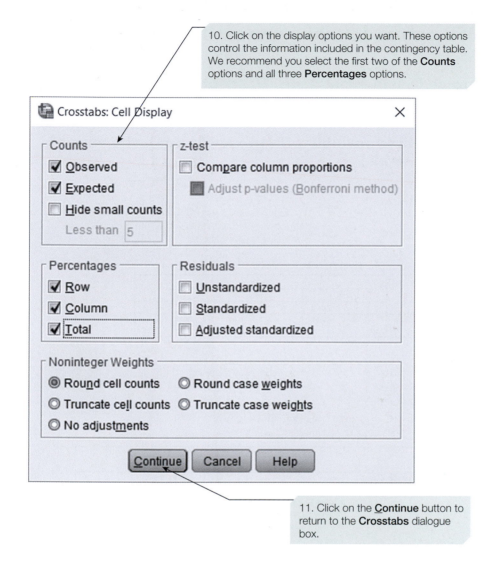

10. Click on the display options you want. These options control the information included in the contingency table. We recommend you select the first two of the **Counts** options and all three **Percentages** options.

11. Click on the **Continue** button to return to the **Crosstabs** dialogue box.

Finally, click on the [ok] button in the **Crosstabs** dialogue box. SPSS will now switch to the Output window and display the contingency table and the chi-square results. Two sets of annotated output are given below. The first is from the 2*3 chi-square exploring the association between the tendency towards anorexia and the mother's employment status (the one shown above in the **Crosstabs** dialogue box). The second is from the 2*2 chi-square exploring the association between tendency towards anorexia and type of school attended.

SPSS output for chi-square without using Exact option

Obtained using menu items: Descriptive Statistics > Crosstabs

Output for first chi-square: tendency towards anorexia * employment (a variable with two levels against a variable with three levels)

CROSSTABS

In this table, SPSS reminds you of the variables entered into the analysis and gives you some summary information about the cases in your data file.

Case Processing Summary

	Cases					
	Valid		Missing		Total	
	N	Percent	N	Percent	N	Percent
tendency toward anorexia * employment	80	100.0%	0	0.0%	80	100.0%

This is the variable that we put into the rows of the table, and these are its two levels.

This table gives you some simple descriptive statistics: counts and percentages for the crosstabulation of the two variables.

This is the variable put into the columns, and these are its three levels.

tendency toward anorexia * employment Crosstabulation

			employment			Total
			f/t	none	p/t	
tendency toward anorexia	high	Count	14	13	11	38
		Expected Count	14.7	11.9	11.4	38.0
		% within tendency toward anorexia	36.8%	34.2%	28.9%	100.0%
		% within employment	45.2%	52.0%	45.8%	47.5%
		% of Total	17.5%	16.2%	13.8%	47.5%
	low	Count	17	12	13	42
		Expected Count	16.3	13.1	12.6	42.0
		% within tendency toward anorexia	40.5%	28.6%	31.0%	100.0%
		% within employment	54.8%	48.0%	54.2%	52.5%
		% of Total	21.2%	15.0%	16.2%	52.5%
Total		Count	31	25	24	80
		Expected Count	31.0	25.0	24.0	80.0
		% within tendency toward anorexia	38.8%	31.2%	30.0%	100.0%
		% within employment	100.0%	100.0%	100.0%	100.0%
		% of Total	38.8%	31.2%	30.0%	100.0%

If you clicked on all the **Counts** and **Percentages** we suggested in the **Crosstabs: Cell Display** dialogue box, all these descriptives are given in each cell. The contents of the cells are described in the Crosstabulation table for the second chi-square (see below).

The Chi-Square Tests table contains the results: if either variable has more than two levels (as here), then SPSS reports these three chi-squares.

Pearson's Chi-Square is used most often, so report this row. (Whichever chi-square test you use, you should give its name when describing the statistical test used.)

Chi-Square Tests

	Value	df	Asymp. Sig. (2-sided)
Pearson Chi-Square	.298[a]	2	.862
Likelihood Ratio	.298	2	.862
Linear-by-Linear Association	.008	1	.930
N of Valid Cases	80		

a. 0 cells (.0%) have expected count less than 5. The minimum expected count is 11.40.

If you used the **Exact** option, available on the **Crosstabs** dialogue box, the table above would have three extra columns: we will describe these later in this section.

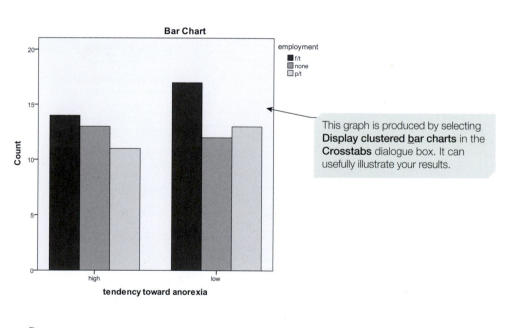

Bar Chart

employment
■ f/t
■ none
□ p/t

Count

tendency toward anorexia

This graph is produced by selecting **Display clustered bar charts** in the **Crosstabs** dialogue box. It can usefully illustrate your results.

Reporting the results

In a report you might write:

There was no relationship between tendency towards anorexia and the employ-ment status of the mother: $\chi^2(2, N = 80) = 0.29$, $p = .862$.

We will discuss reporting the outcome of chi-square in more detail, but first we explain the output for the second chi-square, which explores the association between tendency towards anorexia and type of school attended.

Output for second chi-square: tendency towards anorexia * education (two variables each with two levels)

A row gives information about each level of the column variable; e.g. this row gives information for girls in the 'high' group. It shows the figures for those in comprehensive education separately from those in private education. The total is for all girls in the 'high' group. We can see that of the total of 38 'high' girls, 4 were in comprehensive education and 34 were in private education.

tendency toward anorexia * type of school Crosstabulation

			type of school		Total
			comp	private	
tendency toward anorexia	high	Count	4	34	38
		Expected Count	15.7	22.3	38.0
		% within tendency toward anorexia	10.5%	89.5%	100.0%
		% within type of school	12.1%	72.3%	47.5%
		% of Total	5.0%	42.5%	47.5%
	low	Count	29	13	42
		Expected Count	17.3	24.7	42.0
		% within tendency toward anorexia	69.0%	31.0%	100.0%
		% within type of school	87.9%	27.7%	52.5%
		% of Total	36.2%	16.2%	52.5%
Total		Count	33	47	80
		Expected Count	33.0	47.0	80.0
		% within tendency toward anorexia	41.2%	58.8%	100.0%
		% within type of school	100.0%	100.0%	100.0%
		% of Total	41.2%	58.8%	100.0%

Within each cell, we are given:

Count = the number of participants falling into the cell; i.e. the number of girls who are 'low' and attended comprehensive education (the observed frequency).

Expected Count: the number expected for this cell assuming no association (see below).

% within tendency toward anorexia: the cases in this cell as a % of row total; i.e. % of 'low' girls who attend comprehensive school

% within type of school: the cases in this cell as a % of the column total; i.e. the % of girls who attend comprehensive school who are 'low'.

% of Total: the cases in this cell as a % of the total number of participants.

A column gives information about each level of the row variable. This column shows figures for girls in private schools. Figures are given separately for those in the 'high' and 'low' groups and for the total for all girls in private education. Of the total of 47 girls in private education, 34 of them were 'high' and 13 of them were 'low'.

If each variable has only two levels (a 2*2 chi-square), SPSS reports five tests in the Chi-Square Tests table.

Chi-Square Tests

	Value	df	Asymp. Sig. (2-sided)	Exact Sig. (2-sided)	Exact Sig. (1-sided)
Pearson Chi-Square	28.193[a]	1	.000		
Continuity Correction[b]	25.830	1	.000		
Likelihood Ratio	30.895	1	.000		
Fisher's Exact Test				.000	.000
Linear-by-Linear Association	27.840	1	.000		
N of Valid Cases	80				

a. 0 cells (.0%) have expected count less than 5. The minimum expected count is 15.68.

b. Computed only for a 2x2 table

Continuity correction is the Yates's corrected chi-square (see below).

You can ignore Fisher's Exact Test, unless any cells have an expected count of less than five (see below).

If you used the **Exact** option, available on the **Crosstabs** dialogue box, the table above would have one extra column: we will describe it later in this section.

Interpreting and reporting results from chi-square

SPSS reports several different measures of p. It is probably best to use Pearson's (the chi-square test was developed by Karl Pearson). Note that for chi-square, the value of df (degrees of freedom) is not related to the number of participants. It is the number of levels in each variable minus one multiplied together. So, for a 2*2 chi-square, df = $(2-1)(2-1)$, which equals 1. When reporting the outcome, we also provide the value of N. That should be the number of valid cases (see Chi-Square Tests table), not necessarily the same number as originally tested.

For a 2*2 table, SPSS also calculates the result with and without the continuity correction, or Yates's correction. This is a statistical correction used in cases with relatively few participants or in which you have reason to believe that your sample is not a very good approximation to the total population. There is disagreement about whether to use it, but the Exact test, described below, can be used instead for small samples.

It is important to understand that the chi-square result on its own cannot tell you about the pattern of your results. For that, you have to look at the contingency table. For example, when reporting the results of the second chi-square result (see above), you might write: 'Within the comprehensive school a minority (only 12%) of pupils scored high on the scale, whereas in the private school the majority (72%) scored high on the scale.' If you made a specific one-tailed prediction about the direction of the relationship between the two variables (here we predicted that there will be a higher tendency towards anorexia in the private school pupils) and the pattern of results revealed by the contingency is compatible with this prediction (as here), then you can use the chi-square results to assess whether this particular association is significant.

The strength of the association between the two variables can also be obtained: in the **Crosstabs: Statistics** dialogue box select Phi and Cramer's V. The Symmetric Measures table will appear after the Chi-Square Tests table.

Symmetric Measures

		Value	Approx. Sig.
Nominal by Nominal	Phi	-.594	.000
	Cramer's V	.594	.000
	N of Valid Cases	80	

The value of ϕ (phi) indicates the magnitude of the association; it can be considered equivalent to Pearson's r (see Chapter 6, Section 3).

Just as we can square r to give an estimate of the proportion of variation that is common to the two variables, so we can square ϕ. For these data $\phi^2 = .35$, so 35% of the variation in the tendency towards anorexia score is accounted for by the type of school attended. Just as in the correlation examples, none of the variables in this example study were manipulated: thus, the chi-square results do not imply causation. You will see that the Symmetric Measures table provides a significance value for ϕ: it can be used to assess significance of the relationship between two variables. χ^2, however, is most commonly reported for that purpose.

Reporting the results

In a report you might write:

The relationship between tendency towards anorexia and the type of school attended was significant: $\chi^2(1, N = 80) = 28.19$, $p < .001$. The association was of moderate strength: $\phi = .59$ and thus the type of school attended accounted for 35% of the variance in the score on tendency towards anorexia scale.

You could also include a table of counts and expected frequencies, bar charts and other information as appropriate.

Use of exact tests in chi-square

Look at the Chi-Square Tests tables in the preceding pages. There is a note at the bottom of each, informing you of the number of cells with expected frequencies (what SPSS calls expected counts) of less than 5. It is important that you always check this note. For both chi-square analyses above, there are no cells with this problem. However, if you do perform a chi-square analysis and SPSS reports that there are one or more cells with an expected frequency of less than 5, then you must take some action. If you are performing a 2*2 chi-square, SPSS reports an additional statistic called Fisher's Exact test. This test can be used when cells have low expected frequencies (Siegel and Castellan, 1988, 103–11). However, this test is only available for 2*2 tables. If you are performing something other than a 2*2 chi-square and encounter this problem, then you can use the **Ex**act option.

To demonstrate this for you, we have undertaken a further chi-square analysis, exploring a possible association between cultural background and tendency towards anorexia. In the third SPSS output (see below), two cells have an expected frequency of less than 5.

Output for third chi-square: tendency towards anorexia * cultural background (a variable with two levels against a variable with three levels)

Chi-Square Tests

	Value	df	Asymp. Sig. (2-sided)
Pearson Chi-Square	7.866[a]	2	.020
Likelihood Ratio	8.078	2	.018
Linear-by-Linear Association	2.016	1	.156
N of Valid Cases	80		

a. 2 cells (33.3%) have expected count less than 5. The minimum expected count is 2.85.

For the analysis of tendency toward anorexia against background, we have omitted all the output except this table.

A chi-square is not valid if any of the expected frequencies are less than 5. If SPSS prints a message like this, then look for the relevant cells in the Crosstabulations table. You could then use the **Ex**act option (see text below).

As this was a 2*3 chi-square, there is no Fisher's Exact test. Instead, we use the **Exact** button on the **Crosstabs** dialogue box. Depending on your research hypothesis, you might consider combining groups; here, for example, we could use the **Recode** command (see Chapter 4, Section 5) to combine the 'Asian' and 'Other' groups into one 'Non-Caucasian' group. That would turn our 2*3 into a 2*2 analysis and Fisher's Exact test would be reported.

Using the Exact option for chi-square

If you click on the **Exact** button in the **Crosstabs** dialogue box (above), then the **Exact Tests** dialogue box will appear (see below).

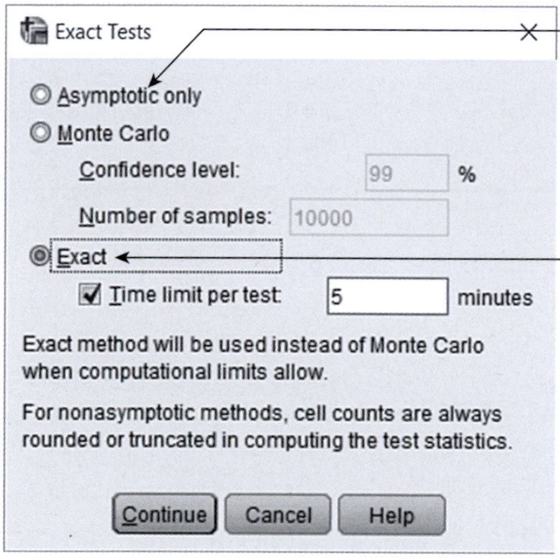

Exact Tests

○ Asymptotic only
○ Monte Carlo
   Confidence level: 99 %
   Number of samples: 10000
◉ Exact ◄
   ☑ Time limit per test: 5   minutes

Exact method will be used instead of Monte Carlo when computational limits allow.

For nonasymptotic methods, cell counts are always rounded or truncated in computing the test statistics.

[Continue] [Cancel] [Help]

Asymptotic only is the default setting: it gives the output shown above. We recommend you leave it on this setting if you are not using Exact tests, and do not use the **Monte Carlo** option.

Click here to select **Exact** tests: you will then get the type of output shown below.

Output for third chi-square (2*3) with Exact option

Chi-Square Tests

	Value	df	Asymp. Sig. (2-sided)	Exact Sig. (2-sided)	Exact Sig. (1-sided)	Point Probability
Pearson Chi-Square	7.866ᵃ	2	.020	.015		
Likelihood Ratio	8.078	2	.018	.037		
Fisher's Exact Test	7.765			.017		
Linear-by-Linear Association	2.016ᵇ	1	.156	.191	.114	.065
N of Valid Cases	80					

a. 2 cells (33.3%) have expected count less than 5. The minimum expected count is 2.85.

b. The standardized statistic is -1.420.

You can now report the Pearson's chi-square, as we show next.

These three extra columns are printed when you select the **Exact** option (see below).

Reporting the results

In a report you might write:

The analysis showed that two cells had expected count less than 5, so an exact significance test was selected for Pearson's chi-square. There was a relationship between tendency towards anorexia and cultural background: $\chi^2(2, N = 80) = 7.87$, exact $p = .015$).

Output for second chi-square (2*2) with Exact option

Chi-Square Tests

	Value	df	Asymp. Sig. (2-sided)	Exact Sig. (2-sided)	Exact Sig. (1-sided)	Point Probability
Pearson Chi-Square	28.193[a]	1	.000	.000	.000	
Continuity Correction[b]	25.030	1	.000			
Likelihood Ratic	30.895	1	.000	.000	.000	
Fisher's Exact Test				.000	.000	
Linear-by-Linear Association	27.840[c]	1	.000	.000	.000	.000
N of Valid Cases	80					

a. 0 cells (.0%) have expected count less than 5. The minimum expected count is 15.68.

b. Computed only for a 2x2 table

c. The standardized statistic is -5.276.

For a 2*2 chi-square, these two columns are printed by default. However, *without* **Exact** option, only *p* value for the Fisher's Exact Test appeared in these columns, whereas *with* **Exact** option, *p* values for other tests, including Pearson's chi-square, are given.

With the **Exact** option, the Point Probability column appears. As in the third chi-square (2*3), the only value in this column is for Linear-by-Linear Association, which is not for nominal data, so we can ignore it.

This example has no cells with expected counts less than 5: we have simply used it to illustrate the output obtained from a 2*2 chi-square with the **Exact** option.

Performing a chi-square using the Weight Cases option

Imagine that you have an eager research assistant who has collected the data for you and diligently calculated the observed frequencies and set these out in a table. Instead of entering each data point into SPSS to perform the chi-square test, you can instead enter just these observed frequencies, and we finish this section by demonstrating how to do this using the **Weight Cases** option.

Table 7.2 gives the observed frequencies for the data we analysed previously in this chapter. The 80 young women who completed an eating questionnaire were classified as either high or low anorexia and the type of school they attended was private or state comprehensive.

Table 7.2 The observed frequencies

	High anorexia	Low anorexia
Private	34	13
Comprehensive	4	35

1. In order to enter these frequencies, you first need to set up a data file as shown below, creating three variables.

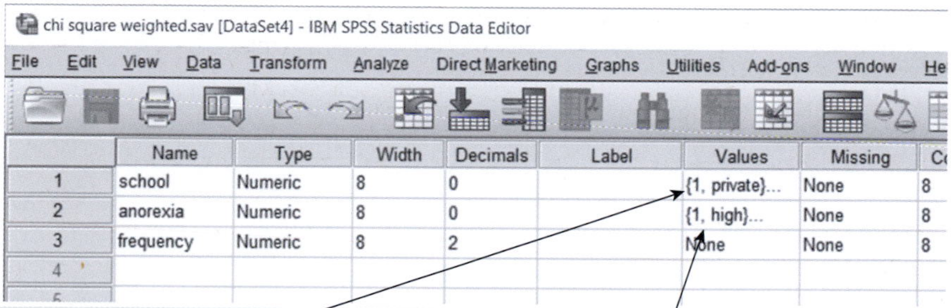

	Name	Type	Width	Decimals	Label	Values	Missing	C
1	school	Numeric	8	0		{1, private}...	None	8
2	anorexia	Numeric	8	0		{1, high}...	None	8
3	frequency	Numeric	8	2		None	None	8
4								
5								

For the variable 'school', we entered value labels '1' for private and '2' for comprehensive.

For the variable 'anorexla', we entered value labels '1' for high and '2' for low.

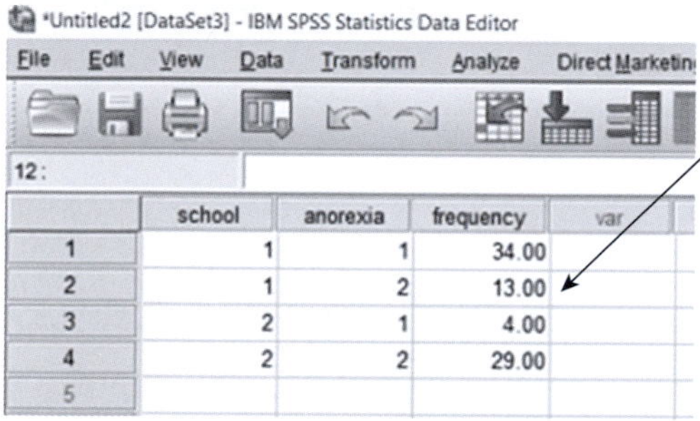

	school	anorexia	frequency	var
1	1	1	34.00	
2	1	2	13.00	
3	2	1	4.00	
4	2	2	29.00	
5				

2. In Data View, enter the appropriate values for 'school' and 'anorexia', along with the corresponding observed frequency, as shown here.

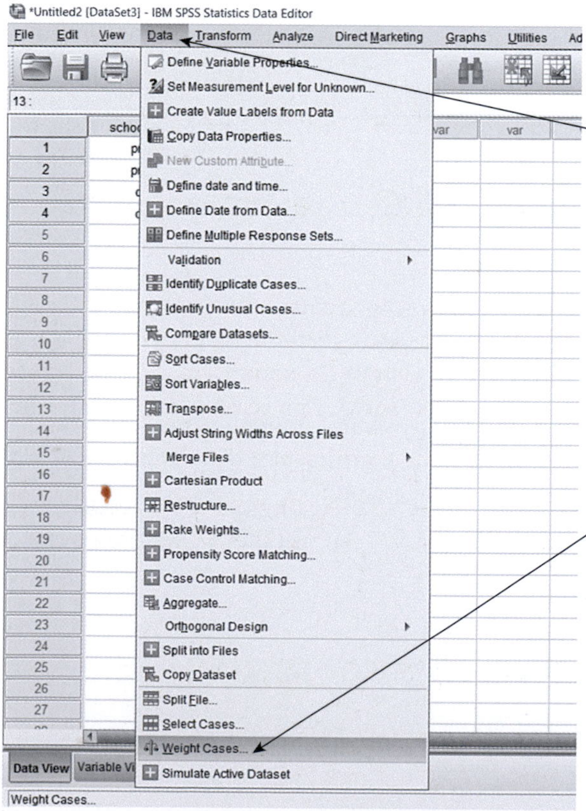

3. Select the **Data** tab.

4. Select the **Weight Cases** option. This brings up the **Weight Cases** dialogue box (see below).

CHAPTER 7

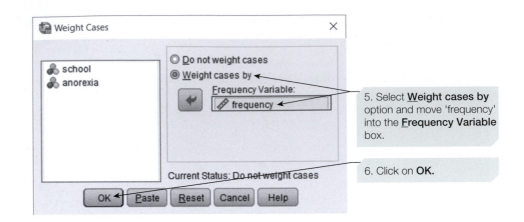

7. Click on **Analyze** ⇒ **Descriptive** Statistics ⇒ **Crosstabs** to bring up the **Crosstabs** dialogue box (shown below).

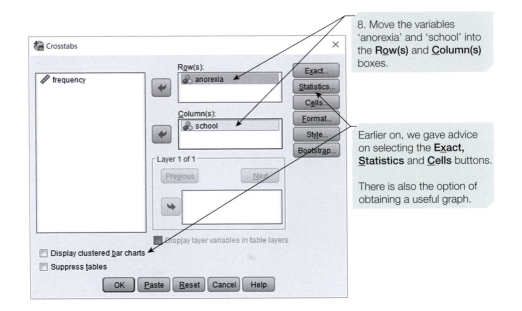

Finally, click on the [OK] button in the **Crosstabs** dialogue box. SPSS will now switch to the Output window and display the contingency table and the chi-square results, identical to those shown earlier in the chapter.

Section 5: THE MCNEMAR TEST FOR REPEATED MEASURES

- The McNemar test is used to analyse data obtained by measuring a dichotomous variable for related designs. The difference between this and the 2*2 chi-square test is that the chi-square test is for independent groups designs.

- Further, the chi-square test can be used to test for association between two variables (as described in Section 4), whereas the McNemar test cannot be used in that way as it can only be used as a test of difference.

- Remember that a dichotomous variable, by definition, can only take one of two values (e.g. yes or no). Thus, the McNemar test is for a situation where you measure the same thing twice; for example, a 'before treatment' yes/no response, and an 'after treatment' yes/no response.

- If you measure more than two values (e.g. yes/uncertain/no), SPSS will automatically apply the McNemar–Bowker test instead. We will not cover that test here.

Example study: gender and handwriting

To illustrate the use of the McNemar test, we will describe an experiment we carried out with students. It is well established that roughly two-thirds of handwriting samples can be correctly judged as being written by a man or a woman. This is significantly above the chance level of 50% correct; the implication is that many (but not all) men and women tend to write in a gender-stereotyped manner. Very briefly, male handwriting is irregular and untidy, whereas female handwriting is rounded and neat. If this is the case, do people have a choice in their writing style? Hartley (1991) investigated this by asking children to try to imitate the handwriting of the opposite sex. We carried out a similar study, but with first-year psychology students.

The experimental hypothesis was that the number of correct identifications of the writer's sex, from the handwriting samples, will be different when the writers were mimicking the opposite sex than when they were writing normally. The independent variable was handwriting style with two levels: one level was the students' normal handwriting (before they knew the hypothesis) and the other level was their writing as if they were of the opposite sex. Each student then recruited a participant to act as judge of the writer's sex for both handwriting samples; the design was, therefore, repeated measures. The order of presentation of the handwriting samples was counterbalanced across participants. The dependent variable was whether the participant's judgement of the writer's sex was correct or incorrect: it was correct if they judged the *real* sex of the writer correctly. Hypothetical data are available in the Appendix or from he.palgrave.com/psychology/brace. Note that the writer's sex is not recorded in these data; we simply recorded, for each handwriting sample, whether their sex was judged correctly or not.

How to perform the McNemar test

The McNemar test can be accessed in two ways: via the **Descriptive Statistics** > **Crosstabs** command, or via the **Nonparametric Tests** > **Legacy Dialogs** > **2 Related**

Samples command. The former command has an advantage over the latter. The **2 Related Samples** command allows you to obtain means and standard deviations as an option, but these descriptives, remember, are completely inappropriate (in fact meaningless) to use with nominal data. The **Crosstabs** command does not have that option, so you are less likely to make a mistake. Thus, we will only cover the **Crosstabs** command.

Via the Crosstabs command

Crosstabs draws up contingency tables and the McNemar test is an optional inferential statistic within this command. Follow steps 1 to 6 in the instructions on performing a multidimensional chi-square (Section 4). The **Crosstabs: Statistics** dialogue box will then appear (see below).

In the **Crosstabs** dialogue box, click on ⬛ OK ⬛ – see output below.

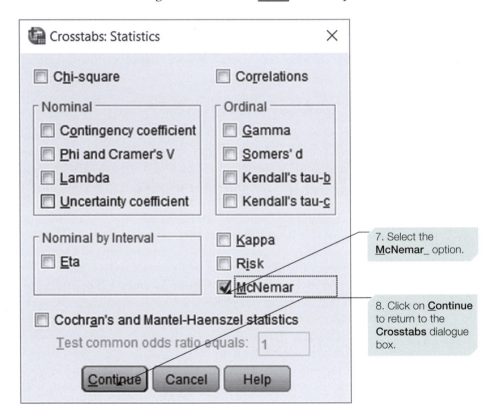

SPSS output for the McNemar test

Obtained using menu items: Descriptive Statistics > Crosstabs

Case Processing Summary

	Cases					
	Valid		Missing		Total	
	N	Percent	N	Percent	N	Percent
normal handwriting * handwriting as if opposite sex	49	100.0%	0	.0%	49	100.0%

normal handwriting * handwriting as if opposite sex Crosstabulation

Count

		handwriting as if opposite sex		
		correct	incorrect	Total
normal handwriting	correct	17	16	33
	incorrect	2	14	16
	Total	19	30	49

The table of observed counts: you can also request expected frequencies and the various percentages, as we did in chi-square above.

Chi-Square Tests

	Value	Exact Sig. (2-sided)
McNemar Test		.001[a]
N of Valid Cases	49	

a. Binomial distribution used.

The outcome of the McNemar test: SPSS assesses its significance using the binomial distribution, and gives the value of p and N only. Notice that this is an exact p, even though we did not use the **Exact** option.

When the **Exact** option is used, this table has two more columns: however, that option is not normally required because SPSS automatically uses an exact significance test for McNemar.

It would be useful to illustrate the results. For data from a related design, rather than using Clustered bar charts in the **Crosstabs** dialogue box, it is probably better to illustrate the findings with two separate bar charts obtained through the **Graphs** menu and suitably edited (as shown below).

How to obtain a bar chart using Chart Builder

1. On the menu bar, click on **Graphs**.
2. Click on **Chart Builder**.
3. Close the top **Chart Builder** dialogue box reminding you that measurement level should be set properly for each variable in your chart (see Chapter 3, Section 7). The **Chart Builder** dialogue box will be visible.

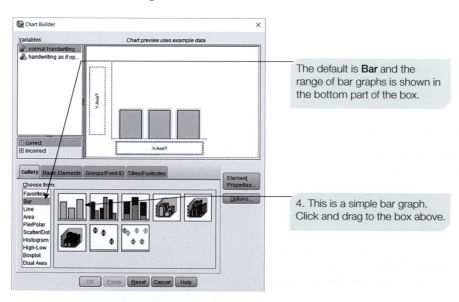

The default is **Bar** and the range of bar graphs is shown in the bottom part of the box.

4. This is a simple bar graph. Click and drag to the box above.

5. The **Element Properties** dialogue box appears to the right of the above dialogue box. Check that **Statistic** is set to **Count** and **Bar Style** to **Bar**.

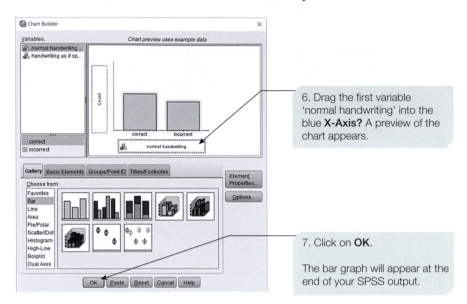

6. Drag the first variable 'normal handwriting' into the blue **X-Axis?** A preview of the chart appears.

7. Click on **OK**.

The bar graph will appear at the end of your SPSS output.

To obtain a second bar graph showing the second variable, repeat steps 1–3 above, drag 'handwriting as if opposite sex' in the x-axis box and click on the ⬚ ok ⬚ button. The following bar graphs will be included at the end of the SPSS output, but one under the other instead of side by side as we have shown them here.

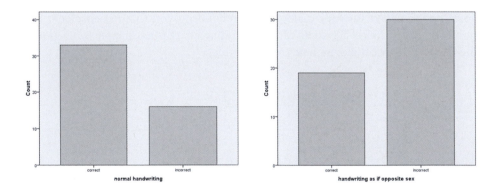

Ideally, you would want both to have the same y-axis scale. Check which has the shortest scale – here it is the second. Double-click on that chart in the SPSS output to bring up the **Chart Editor** window.

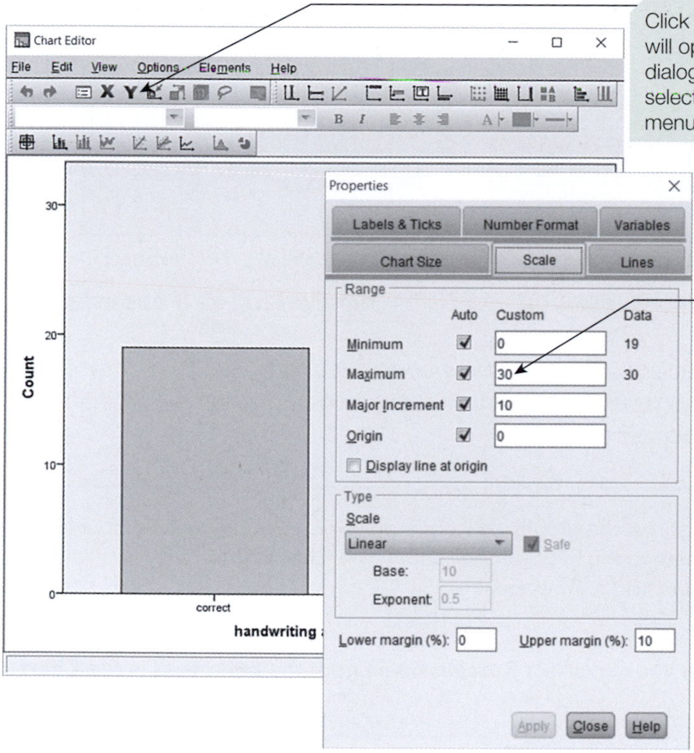

Click here on the **Y** icon, which will open the **Properties** dialogue box. (Alternatively, select this from the **Edit** menu.)

Change the **Maximum** to 40 and check that the **Major Increment** remains at 10 and the **Minimum** at 0. Click on **Apply** and then **Close** buttons.

Close the **Chart Editor** window and the two graphs in the SPSS output should now have the same y-axis scale.

Reporting the results

In a report you might write:

The McNemar test using binomial distribution showed a significant difference in the number of correct judgements, between the two conditions of handwriting style ($N = 49$, exact $p = .001$).

It would also be useful to explain the pattern of results in the following way: Of the 49 participants, 33 (67%) correctly identified the handwriter's sex for the normal handwriting. Of those 33, 17 of them correctly identified the handwriter's sex for the 'opposite handwriting' and 16 of them incorrectly identified it. Of the 16 (33%) who were incorrect for the normal handwriting, 2 of them correctly identified the handwriter's sex for the 'opposite handwriting' and 14 of them incorrectly identified it. In brief, there were more incorrect responses when the writer had written as if they were of the opposite sex. This pattern of results is illustrated in Figure 7.1.

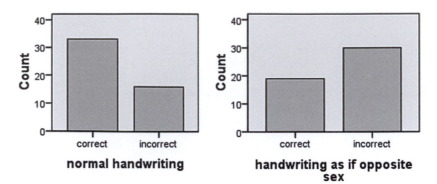

Figure 7.1 The pattern of correct and incorrect identification of handwriter's sex, when the writing was their normal handwriting and when they mimicked the writing of the opposite sex

Rather than shrink the graphs as we did on the previous page, we double-clicked on them in the SPSS output and in the **Chart Editor** window clicked on the rescale chart icon: page.

(Alternatively you can select **Rescale Chart** from the **Edit** menu in the **Chart Editor** window).

Next, we show you how to create a bar chart using **Graphboard Template Chooser**.

How to obtain a bar chart using Graphboard Template Chooser

1. On the menu bar, click on **Graphs**.
2. Click on **Graphboard Template Chooser**.
3. In the dialogue box, ensure that the variables you want to use are set at the correct level of measurement.

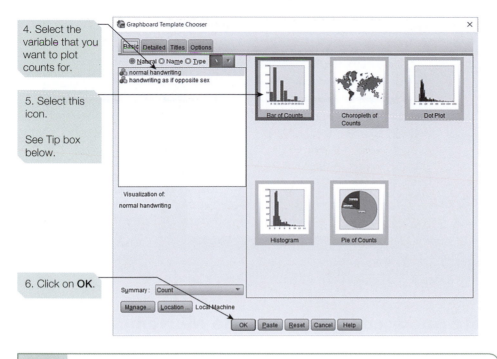

4. Select the variable that you want to plot counts for.

5. Select this icon.

See Tip box below.

6. Click on **OK**.

> Graphboard distinguishes between a 'bar of counts' suitable for nominal data, and 'bar' that will plot a summary descriptive for a variable of at least ordinal level of measurement.

To obtain a second bar graph showing the second variable, repeat the steps above, for 'handwriting as if opposite sex'. As described above, for **Chart Builder**, the graphs should be edited so that the y-axes have the same scale. Double-click in the second chart, which has the shortest scale, to bring up the **Graphboard Editor** dialogue box (shown below). Once you have edited the charts, use them as described elsewhere in this section.

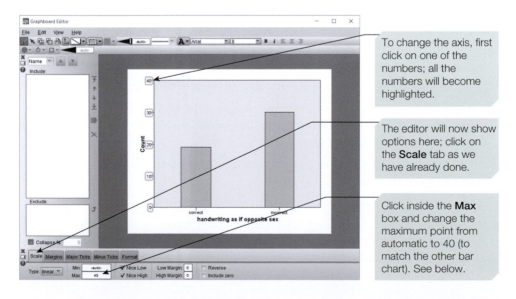

To change the axis, first click on one of the numbers; all the numbers will become highlighted.

The editor will now show options here; click on the **Scale** tab as we have already done.

Click inside the **Max** box and change the maximum point from automatic to 40 (to match the other bar chart). See below.

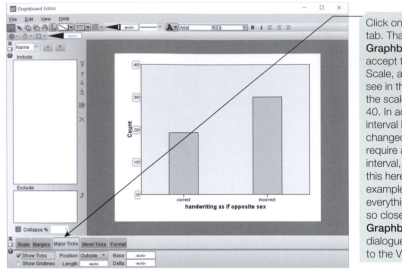

Click on **Major Ticks** tab. That has made **Graphboard Editor** accept the change to Scale, and as you will see in the graph pane, the scale is now 0 to 40. In addition, the tick interval has been changed to 10. If you require a different tick interval, you can amend this here. For this example, however, everything is complete, so close the **Graphboard Editor** dialogue box to return to the Viewer window.

Note about causation and the McNemar test

In related designs, you manipulate an independent variable and either collect data for both of its levels from the same participants (repeated measures) or collect data from matched participants (matched pairs). If you have carried out the normal controls for the design, then you can draw conclusions about causation from the McNemar test output.

Summary

- This chapter introduced you to nominal data and the tests that can be performed on nominal data.

- A contingency table is the best way of displaying nominal data.

- Remember our advice about descriptive statistics for nominal data; calculating the mean or median is inappropriate, as is any measure of dispersion.

- The chi-square test is a nonparametric test often used to analyse nominal data.

- The multidimensional chi-square nevertheless requires that the data satisfy certain criteria. The observations must be independent, so each participant should contribute only one data point.

- The McNemar test is used to analyse data obtained by measuring a dichotomous variable for related designs.

- For guidance on recoding values, see Chapter 4, Section 5.

- For guidance on incorporating SPSS output into a report, or on printing the output, see Chapter 13.

8 Analysis of variance

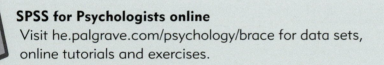

SPSS for Psychologists online
Visit he.palgrave.com/psychology/brace for data sets, online tutorials and exercises.

CHAPTER 8

Section 1: AN INTRODUCTION TO ANALYSIS OF VARIANCE (ANOVA)

- ANOVA is an enormously useful statistical procedure that is widely used to test for differences in experimental designs involving more than two groups or conditions and/or more than one independent variable (IV).

- For IVs involving more than two groups or conditions, ANOVA will tell us whether the scores significantly vary across those conditions, but not precisely which pairs of conditions are significantly different (e.g. whether condition 1 is significantly different from condition 2, whether condition 2 is significantly different from condition 3, or whether condition 1 is significantly different from condition 3). Such comparisons require some additional statistical procedures called *planned* and *unplanned comparisons*.

- ANOVA also allows us to investigate the effect of more than one IV. For example, we could examine the effect of participants' sex as well as their age on their memory for a list of words. Here, we have two IVs (sex and age) and one dependent variable (DV) (memory score). A single ANOVA test will allow us simultaneously to examine the effect of these two IVs. In fact, ANOVA can handle any number of IVs in a single experiment, but, in practice, we rarely include more than three or four for reasons that will become apparent shortly.

■ A major advantage of ANOVA is that it allows us to investigate how these IVs combine to affect the DV. For example, we can ask questions about how the sex *and* the age of a participant *combine* to affect memory score – it might be that male participants' performances decline with age but that female participants' performances improve with age. Such an *interaction* between these two variables is of theoretical importance, and it is only by investigating both variables in one design that we can discover this interaction.

When can we use ANOVA?

As ANOVA is a parametric test, check that:

1. The dependent variable comprises data measured at interval or ratio level.
2. The data are drawn from a population that is normally distributed.
3. There is homogeneity of variance; that is, the samples being compared are drawn from populations that have similar variances.
4. In the case of independent groups designs, independent random samples must have been taken from each population.

It is not essential to have equal numbers of scores in each group or condition comprising the independent variable.

How does it work?

We all know that humans vary in performance, both between individuals and within individuals over time. For these reasons, if we conduct a simple experiment comparing, say, the time it takes to learn a list of short words, medium length words and long words, we would not expect all the participants within a condition to take the same amount of time. We naturally accept that some participants will be faster than others (i.e. there will be variation between individuals). We also know that any one participant might take less or more time on one occasion than on other occasions (i.e. there will be variation within individuals). Remember that we can measure the amount of variation within a set of scores with measures of dispersion, such as the standard deviation or the *variance*.

Now let us imagine for a moment that we were robopsychologists; that is, we were interested in the psychology of robots (rather than robots interested in psychology). If we repeated our learning experiment with a group of R2D2 robots, we would expect all the robots in one condition to react at exactly the same speed. Table 8.1 shows some hypothetical data for robots and for humans.

Let us first consider the data from the humans shown in this table. If we asked you to 'eyeball' the raw data and guess whether there was a difference in learning times for the three lists, you would probably have no problem saying that the difference did appear to be significant. In making this judgement, you are actually doing something quite sophisticated. What you are doing is deciding whether the natural variation between individuals within the conditions is large or small compared to the variation between individuals across the different conditions. That is, you are asking: 'OK, so not all the participants in the List A condition took the same time, and not all the participants in the List B or List C condition took the same time, but is this natural variation (or noise) large or small compared to the difference in times between the three conditions?' In this case, participants within each condition might vary from each other by several seconds, but this is small compared to the larger differences between the times produced under the three different list conditions.

Table 8.1 Time (in seconds) taken to learn three different lists of words for a group of robot and human participants

ROBOTS		
List A	List B	List C
10	20	30
10	20	30
10	20	30
10	20	30
10	20	30
10	20	30
10	20	30
10	20	30
Mean = 10	Mean = 20	Mean = 30	Grand mean = 20

HUMANS		
List A	List B	List C
30	54	68
40	58	75
35	45	80
45	60	75
38	52	85
42	56	90
36	65	75
25	52	88
Mean = 36.38	Mean = 55.25	Mean = 79.50	Grand mean = 57.04

CHAPTER 8

Let us look at the robots' data. Robots perform identically under identical conditions (or at least our robots do), so within each condition every robot has exactly the same learning time. Thus, the variance within each condition is zero. But if we compare the performance between the three conditions, it is clear that all the robots were fastest at learning the short words and all took longest to learn the long words. You might conclude that you want to switch from psychology to robopsychology, but there is also a more important point here. What we want to do is make our human participants' data more like the robots' data; that is, we want to reduce the variance within conditions down towards zero. In fact, all the practices of good experimental design, such as giving all participants the same instructions and testing under identical conditions, are designed to do just this – reduce the variance within each condition. This good experimental practice will reduce the variance but will not eliminate it – our participants will never behave exactly like the robots. So, if we cannot eliminate the variance, perhaps we can account for it. What we need is a statistical procedure that takes account of the variance within the conditions and compares this to the variance between conditions. If the variance between conditions is much larger than the variance within conditions, surely we can say that the IV is having a larger effect on the scores than the individual differences are. Clearly, for the robots, the variance within the conditions is zero and the variance between the conditions is quite large. For our humans, the situation is not quite so clear-cut, but if we calculate the variances, we will find the same basic pattern applies:

Variance between conditions > variance within conditions

This concept of calculating the variance due to nuisance factors such as individual differences and comparing it to the variance due to our manipulation of the IV is central to ANOVA. Exactly how we calculate these variances can get rather complex for some designs, but this does not alter the basic principle that we simply want to ask whether or not the variance in the data brought about by our manipulation of the IV is larger than that brought about by the other nuisance factors such as individual differences. The variance brought about by these nuisance variables is usually referred to as the *error variance*, so we ask whether the error variance is less than the variance due to the manipulation of the IV.

A convenient way of expressing this is to calculate the ratio of the variance due to our manipulation of the IV and the error variance. This ratio is known as the *F*-ratio (named after Fisher). The *F*-ratio is:

F = Variance due to manipulation of IV/Error variance

If the error variance is small compared to the variance due to the IV, then the *F*-ratio will be a number greater than 1 (a large number divided by a smaller number always gives rise to a number greater than 1). If, on the other hand, the effect of the IV is small, and/or the error variance is large (perhaps because our participants varied considerably or because we did not adequately control the experiment), then the *F*-ratio will be a number less than 1 (a small number divided by larger number will always result in a number less than 1). Thus, we can now say that the effect of the IV is definitely not significant, if the F-ratio is less than 1. This is because the error variance is actually larger than the variance caused by our manipulation of the IV.

So, the F-ratio is simply the ratio of these two estimates of variance. The larger the F-ratio, the greater the effect of the IV compared to the 'noise' (error variance) in the data. An F-ratio equal to or less than 1 indicates a non-significant result, as it shows that the scores were equally affected or more affected by the nuisance variables (such as individual differences) as they were by the manipulation of the IV.

How do we find out if the *F*-ratio is significant?

Once we have calculated the value of the F-ratio and found it is larger than 1, we need to determine whether it is large enough to be regarded as significant. That is, we ask whether the effect of the IV is sufficiently larger than the effect of the nuisance variables to regard the result as significant. When calculating the F-ratio with a calculator, we consult F tables to discover, given the number of observations we made, what value F had to exceed to be considered as significant. When using the IBM SPSS Statistics software (SPSS) to perform ANOVA, the output reports the exact p value for that particular F-ratio. This p value is the probability of getting this F-ratio by chance alone and it needs to be less than .05 for the F-ratio to be regarded as significant.

What about degrees of freedom?

You will remember from performing a t-test, another test of difference, that we need to calculate and report the degrees of freedom associated with our analysis. One complication with ANOVA is that for each F value, we must report two sets of degrees of freedom. This is because we need to remember how many observations went into our calculation of the error variance and also how many went into our calculation of the variance due to the manipulation of the IV. As these are the bottom and top halves of the F-ratio equation, these are sometimes referred to as the 'denominator' and 'numerator' degrees of freedom respectively. A good statistics text will explain the calculation of degrees of freedom in detail, but as SPSS calculates and reports these for you, all you need to know is to expect two values for each F-ratio. We will show you how to report these degrees of freedom and the F-ratio in subsequent sections.

What terms are used with ANOVA?

Different textbooks tend to use slightly different terminologies to describe ANOVA. To avoid the problems this can create, we are going to use what we consider to be the simplest terminology.

Factors

Factors are the independent variables, but as there may well be more than one of them per study, it makes sense to call them factors from now on.

CHAPTER 8

Levels of factors

Levels of factors are similar to conditions. In the experiments we considered earlier, we had a single IV, which was manipulated to create two conditions. We would now describe this as a single factor with two levels. In ANOVA designs, a factor can have as many levels as we like. For example, we might have a factor of 'Drug dose', which might be manipulated to create four levels of 0 mg, 10 mg, 20 mg and 30 mg.

Between-subjects factors

Between-subjects factors are factors whose levels vary between participants, so that each participant will experience only one level of a factor. For example, a participant can be administered either 0 mg, 10 mg, 20 mg or 30 mg. This is a factor that is manipulated using an independent groups design, which we will now refer to as a *between-subjects design*.

Within-subjects factors

Within-subjects factors are factors whose levels vary within a participant, so that each participant will experience two or more levels of a factor. For example, a participant might be administered all four different drug dosages. This is a factor that is manipulated using a repeated measures design, which we will now refer to as a *within-subjects design*.

Mixed ANOVA designs

The term 'mixed ANOVA design' is used when a design includes one or more within-subjects factors and one or more between-subjects factors.

How do we describe ANOVA designs?

When describing an ANOVA design, we need to specify three things:

1. The number of factors involved in the design.
2. How many levels there are of each factor.
3. Whether each factor is a within- or a between-subjects factor.

The number of factors is described by talking about a one-way ANOVA (where there is one factor), a two-way ANOVA (two factors) and so on (e.g. a six-way ANOVA would have six factors). What this does not tell you is how many levels each factor has. You could describe this in longhand, but there is an easier convention. For example, a three-way ANOVA, in which the first factor, 'Sex', had two levels, the second factor, 'Age', had three levels and the third factor, 'Drug dose', had five levels, could be described more simply as a 2*3*5 ANOVA design. Note that in this terminology, the number of numerals (three in this case) describes the number of factors, and the values of the numerals indicate the number of levels of each of these factors. Using this terminology, we just need to make it clear whether the factors were within- or between-subject factors. We could do this by writing:

*A 2*3*5 (Sex*Age*Drug dose) mixed ANOVA design was employed where Sex and Age were between-subjects factors and Drug dose was a within-subjects factor.*

Main effects and interactions

Using ANOVA, we can analyse data from studies that incorporate more than one factor. We can assess the effect of each of these factors on their own and the interaction between the factors. The term 'main effect' is used to describe the independent effect of a factor. For example, in the 2*3*5 ANOVA described above, three main effects will be reported. The main effect of 'Sex' will tell us whether men performed significantly differently from women, irrespective of their age or drug dose. The main effect of 'Age' will tell us whether age affects performance, irrespective of sex or drug dose. Finally, the main effect of 'Drug dose' will tell us whether drug dosage affects performance, irrespective of the sex or age of the participants. These main effects simply compare the mean for one level of a factor with the mean of the other level(s) of that factor; for example, comparing mean male performance levels to mean female performance levels. Interactions, on the other hand, assess the combined effect of the factors. An interaction that assesses how two factors combine to affect performance is called a *two-way interaction*. When three factors are involved, the interaction is known as a *three-way interaction*.

When attempting to understand the output from the ANOVA command in SPSS, it is helpful if you know in advance how many results you are looking for:

1. *A one-way ANOVA*, where the single factor is called A, will give rise to just a single main effect of A.

2. *A two-way ANOVA*, where the factors are called A and B, will give rise to two main effects (main effect of A and main effect of B), and a single two-way interaction (A*B). This is a total of three results (3 *F*-ratios).

3. *A three-way ANOVA*, where the factors are called A, B and C, will give rise to three main effects (main effect of A, main effect of B and main effect of C), three two-way interactions (A*B, A*C and B*C) and a single three-way interaction (A*B*C). This is a total of seven results.

4. *A four-way ANOVA*, where the factors are called A, B, C and D, will give rise to four main effects (main effect of A, main effect of B, main effect of C and main effect of D), six two-way interactions (A*B, A*C, A*D, B*C, B*D and C*D), four three-way interactions (A*B*C, A*B*D, A*C*D and B*C*D), and a single four-way interaction (A*B*C*D). This is a total of 15 results.

You can now see why it is unusual to include more than four factors in a design. The number of possible interactions rises steeply as the number of factors increases. Furthermore, it is unlikely that you hypothesised about the shape of these higher order interactions and if they are significant, they can be hard to describe and/or explain. Using SPSS, it is easy to undertake a four- or even five-way ANOVA, but rather more difficult to explain the results. Our advice is to try to limit yourself to a maximum of three factors.

How is the *F*-ratio calculated?

You do not need to know how to calculate the *F*-ratio, as SPSS will do this for you. However, to fully appreciate the output that SPSS generates, it would be helpful to

CHAPTER 8

read this section and realise why the calculation is dependent on the type of factor manipulated. We show this below with reference to a one-way design.

Between-subjects one-way ANOVA design

Let us go back to our word list learning experiment, and imagine that there are different humans taking part in each condition; that eight participants were asked to learn list A, another eight to learn list B and another eight to learn list C.

Table 8.2 Time (in seconds) taken to learn three different lists of words by three groups of human participants in a between-subjects design

HUMANS		
List A	List B	List C
30	54	68
40	58	75
35	45	80
45	60	75
38	52	85
42	56	90
36	65	75
25	52	88
Mean = 36.38	Mean = 55.25	Mean = 79.50	Grand mean = 57.04

There are two sources of variance of interest here:

1. How do the scores in one group vary from those in the other groups? We can look at how the mean of each column deviates from the grand mean. This provides us with a measure of the variance due to the factor.

2. How do the scores vary within each group? We can look at how each score within a column deviates from the mean for that condition. This provides us with a measure of noise.

Together, these two sources of variance must add up to the total variance (the variance between each single score and the grand mean). That is:

$$\text{Var}_{(\text{Total})} = \text{Var}_{(\text{Between Groups})} + \text{Var}_{(\text{Within Groups})}$$

Within-subjects one-way ANOVA design

Imagine that in our learning experiment, eight participants took part and each performed in each level of the factor. We would be able to calculate a mean score for each list and a mean score for each participant; see Table 8.3 (shown on the next page).

The calculation of F for the within-subjects design is more complicated than for between-subjects design. Again, we want to determine the sources of variance. However, with this design, we have repeated observations of each participant as every person performs in every level of the factor. This allows us to distinguish between variation caused by individual differences and variation caused by different participants performing differently across the different conditions, and therefore separate out participant variance from error variance.

Table 8.3 Time (in seconds) taken to learn three different lists of words for the group of human participants in a within-subjects design

HUMANS			
Participant number	List A	List B	List C	Participant mean
1	35	42	64	47
2	48	60	90	66
3	36	65	75	58.67
4	40	55	70	55
5	38	52	85	58.33
6	25	42	58	41.67
7	30	42	60	44
8	42	60	90	64
	Mean = 36.75	Mean = 52.25	Mean = 74.0	Grand mean = 54.33

So, we have three sources of variance and we can ask:

1. How do the scores in one condition vary from those in the other? We can compare overall differences between the three lists. As before, we can look at how the mean of each column deviates from the grand mean. This provides us with a measure of the variance due to our manipulation of the factor.

2. How do participants vary in their average scores? We can get an indication of how much individuals differ from each other by looking at how much each participant's average score deviates from the grand mean. This provides us with a measure of participant variance.

3. How much error variance is there? We can work this out by looking at the extent to which each score is not what we would predict from the row and column means. You can also think of this as the variance resulting from different participants responding differently to the change in the factor.

For example, with regard to the score for participant 1 in list A – we know that their mean time is 47 seconds. Participant 1 is, on average, 7.33 seconds faster compared with the overall grand mean of 54.33 seconds. The mean for the list A column is 36.75 seconds, so participants are, on average, 17.58 seconds faster at learning list A than the overall grand mean of 54.33 seconds. So, altogether, we would expect participant 1 to be 17.58 + 7.33 seconds faster than the grand mean of 54.33 seconds at learning list A, giving an expected time of 29.42 seconds. The observed score is 35 seconds, which is slower than we would expect. (Looking at participant 1's scores, we can see that they are relatively faster with lists B and C compared with list A.)

With regard to participant 2's score in list A condition – we know that their row mean is 66 seconds, which is 11.67 seconds slower than the grand mean of 54.33 seconds. So, we would expect participant 2 to be 17.58 seconds faster at learning list A, but 11.67 seconds slower because this participant is slower on average. Thus, we expect a time of 54.33 − 17.58 + 11.67 = 48.42 seconds. The observed score is 48 seconds – close to what we would expect.

The extent to which the observed scores vary from the expected scores reflects the extent to which participants are inconsistent and, as illustrated above, provides us with a measure of error variance.

Using SPSS to calculate the *F*-ratio

The calculation of the *F*-ratio for a within-subjects factor is tricky and, as you will see, the SPSS output is rather more complex for a within-subjects factor compared to a between-subjects factor. Furthermore, because SPSS uses a procedure called the General Linear Model, it will give you much more information than just the *F*-ratio statistic. You will see both ANOVA and multiple regression statistics in the SPSS output, as ANOVA can be considered to be a special case of multiple linear regression (see Chapter 9), which itself is a special case of the General Linear Model.

Effect size and ANOVA

We mentioned in Chapter 1 that it is usual to report effect size alongside the statement of whether the result is significant. This provides information about the magnitude of the finding and also may draw attention to the influence of sample size. For example, if our results show a marginal, but non-significant result and a moderate or large effect size, power may be an issue and it may be appropriate to consider a follow-up study with a larger sample. In Chapter 5, where we covered tests of differences for two samples, we introduced you to one measure of effect size, namely Cohen's *d*, which was calculated from the descriptive statistics provided by SPSS. You may remember that this involved calculating the size of the difference between the means relative to the standard deviation of the scores. The effect size estimates that are calculated for ANOVA are different, in that they tend to describe the proportion of the variability accounted for by each factor (or combination of factors) included in the ANOVA design (in that sense, they are similar to r^2 described in Chapter 6, which also is a measure of the proportion of variance accounted for). They include eta squared, partial eta squared, generalized eta squared, associated omega square measures and also correlational measures. Fritz, Morris and Richler (2012) explain that one can distinguish between:

1. Estimates that describe the effect size in the observed sample but do not consider the population from which the sample was drawn, and this is the case with eta squared and partial eta squared.

2. Estimates of effect size, such as omega squared measures, which try to estimate the variability in the sampled population rather than just in the observed sample, and these are therefore less likely to be inflated by chance factors.

We recommend that you consult your statistics text, or Fritz et al. (2012), for advice on how to calculate these different estimates of effect size. Field (2005) demonstrates how to calculate an omega square measure (which involves a different equation depending on whether between-subjects or within-subjects ANOVA). Mulhern and Greer (2011) explain how to calculate eta squared and recommend against using partial eta squared, which is the only measure of effect size that SPSS will calculate for you. They explain that partial eta squared is not easy to interpret as it is an adjusted measure: the variance explained by one factor *after* taking into account the variance explained by the other factor(s). Fritz et al. (2012) suggest that partial eta squared is limited in terms of its usefulness and may only be helpful if making cross-study comparison with identical designs. Eta squared, on the other hand, is relatively straightforward to calculate by hand and will tell you the proportion of the total variability accounted for by each factor in your design. We will demonstrate how to do this in Section 3.

Whichever effect size measure you decide on, do report this for significant and non-significant effects, and identify which statistic is used.

Planned and unplanned comparisons

Imagine you have a design involving one factor with three conditions: A, B and C. If ANOVA reveals a significant effect of this factor, this suggests a difference between the conditions. However, to find out exactly where this difference is, we need to carry out further tests that compare the pairs of conditions. There are three possibilities:

1. All three possible comparisons are significant, so conditions A and B are significantly different from each other, as are conditions B and C, and conditions A and C.

2. Only two of the three comparisons are significant, for example only conditions A and C and conditions B and C differ significantly.

3. Only one of the three comparisons is significant, for example only conditions A and C are significantly different.

There are two types of comparisons that we can conduct:

1. Planned (*a priori*) comparisons. These are decided on before the data were collected. The researcher has predicted which means will differ significantly from each other.

2. Unplanned (*a posteriori* or *post-hoc*) comparisons. Here, differences among means are explored after the data have been collected.

Why should this matter? We need to use different tests for these two kinds of comparison because the probability of a Type I error is smaller when the comparisons are planned in advance. Type I error involves incorrectly rejecting a null hypothesis, thus concluding that there is a real effect when, in fact, the means differ due to chance. When making multiple comparisons, there is an increased risk of Type I errors. Howell (1987) gives the following example: assume that we give a group of males and a group of females 50 words and ask them to give us as many associations to these words as possible in one minute. For each word, we then test whether there is a significant difference in the number of associations given by male and female participants. We could run 50 more or less independent *t* tests, but we would run the risk that 2.5 of these (50*.05) will be declared 'significant' by chance.

Why is there a greater risk of making a Type I error when carrying out unplanned comparisons? Consider the following. Imagine an experiment to look at the effect of five different levels of noise on memory that employed a one-way ANOVA design. You will have five means (one for each condition) and could do a total of ten comparisons (you could compare mean 1 to mean 2; mean 1 to mean 3; mean 1 to mean 4 etc.). Assume that the null hypothesis is true, and that noise does not affect memory, but that, by chance, two of the means are far enough apart to lead us erroneously to reject the null hypothesis; thus giving rise to a Type I error. If you had planned your single comparison in advance, you would have a probability of 0.1 of hitting on the one comparison out of 10 that involves the Type I error. But if you first look at the data, you are certain to make a Type I error, since you are likely to test the largest difference you can observe.

As you will see, it is possible to ask SPSS to carry out planned and unplanned comparisons. Unplanned or *post-hoc* comparisons are easy to perform using SPSS. However, there is no need to perform these if the factor has only two levels (the main effect is sufficient) or if the main effect is not significant. Planned comparisons, on the other hand, are less easy to perform. We demonstrate how to perform both types of comparisons in Sections 2 and 4.

Section 2: ONE-WAY BETWEEN-SUBJECTS ANOVA, PLANNED AND UNPLANNED COMPARISONS, AND NONPARAMETRIC EQUIVALENT

Example study: the effects of witness masking

To practise the use of the one-way between-subjects ANOVA, we shall consider an applied experiment, which looked at the effects of masking the face of a witness. There is growing awareness that the identity of witnesses in sensitive cases should be protected, especially in light of the move towards televising live court cases. The technology to mask a witness's face is available and has been used in America. Towell, Kemp and Pike (1996) reported the results of a study investigating the effect that masking might have on jurors' memory for a witness's testimony and on jurors' perceptions of the witness's credibility. The testimony of an alleged victim of rape presented in a televised trial in America was shown to participants.

The design employed was a one-way between-subjects ANOVA design. The between-subjects factor, presentation condition, had four levels: unmasked, grey blob, pixelation and negation. These were operationalised by showing some participants the witness unmasked, so that her face was fully visible; some with her face masked by a grey blob, some with her face masked by pixelation and some with her face negated (white and black were reversed). One of the dependent variables was the percentage of facts from the testimony correctly remembered by the participants. The hypothesis was that there would be a negative effect of masking on memory. Results revealed that participants' memory for the victim's testimony was affected by presentation condition; while negating the face did not lower memory compared to the unmasked condition, masking with a grey blob and pixelation both impaired memory. For the purposes of this book, we have created a data file that will reproduce some of these findings. (These data are available from he.palgrave.com/psychology/brace.)

SPSS provides two ways of carrying out a one-way, between-subjects ANOVA, one using the **General Linear Model** command and one using the **One-Way ANOVA** command. The first command can also be used to perform a multi-between-subjects ANOVA, as you will see in Section 3, and also has the option of including in the output the measure of effect size called partial eta squared. In Section 1, we indicated that this particular measure is not that useful; however, when the design involves just one factor, there is no difference between partial eta squared and eta squared. The second command will only permit analysis of a one-way ANOVA design, but has the advantage of a much simpler output and of providing alternative *F*s should the assumption of homogeneity of variance be violated. Both ways allow you to do planned and unplanned comparisons to evaluate the differences between pairs of group means. See Section 1 for general guidance on these comparisons.

We will first describe the **General Linear Model** command, followed by the **One-Way ANOVA** command. We will then demonstrate how to carry out planned and unplanned comparisons and finish this section by describing a nonparametric equivalent test.

How to do it: using General Linear Model command

1. Click on the word **Analyze**.

2. Click on **General Linear Model.**

3. Click on **Univariate.** The **Univariate** dialogue box will appear (see below).

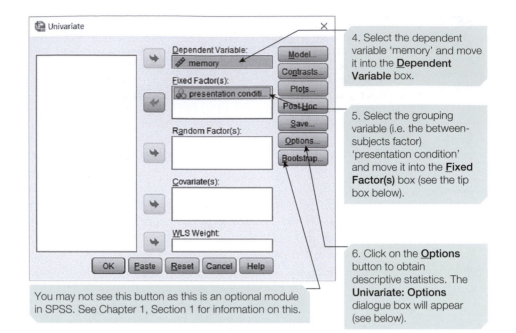

4. Select the dependent variable 'memory' and move it into the **Dependent Variable** box.

5. Select the grouping variable (i.e. the between-subjects factor) 'presentation condition' and move it into the **Fixed Factor(s)** box (see the tip box below).

You may not see this button as this is an optional module in SPSS. See Chapter 1, Section 1 for information on this.

6. Click on the **Options** button to obtain descriptive statistics. The **Univariate: Options** dialogue box will appear (see below).

With a fixed factor, data has been collected from all the levels of the factor that are of interest to the researcher. An alternative is to choose the levels by a random procedure but this rarely happens in psychological research.

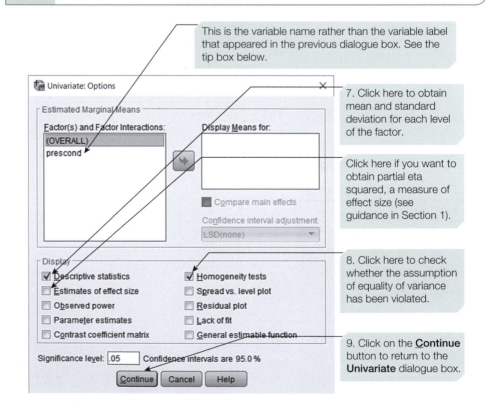

This is the variable name rather than the variable label that appeared in the previous dialogue box. See the tip box below.

7. Click here to obtain mean and standard deviation for each level of the factor.

Click here if you want to obtain partial eta squared, a measure of effect size (see guidance in Section 1).

8. Click here to check whether the assumption of equality of variance has been violated.

9. Click on the **Continue** button to return to the **Univariate** dialogue box.

Means, standard errors and 95% confidence intervals for each level of a factor can be obtained by clicking on the factor/variable name in the **Factor(s) and Factor Interactions** box in the **Univariate: Options** dialogue box, and then clicking on ⬇ to move it into the **Display Means for** box. This is useful when you have more than one factor in your design as you can also ask for the descriptive statistics for the main effects and interactions.

Finally, click on the ⬜ OK ⬜ button and SPSS will calculate the test for you. See below for an example of the output using the **Univariate** command via **General Linear Model**, which includes the means, standard deviations and *N* (number of scores) obtained by clicking on **Descriptive statistics** in the **Univariate: Options** dialogue box.

SPSS output for one-way between-subjects ANOVA

Obtained using menu items: General Linear Model > Univariate

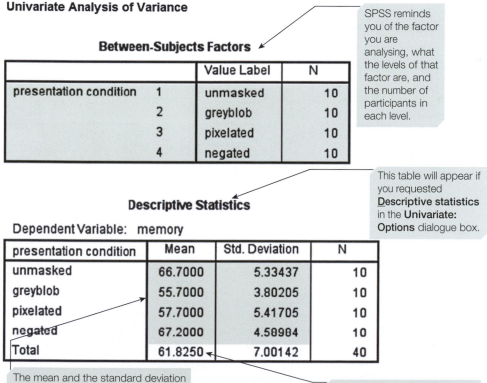

Univariate Analysis of Variance

Between-Subjects Factors

		Value Label	N
presentation condition	1	unmasked	10
	2	greyblob	10
	3	pixelated	10
	4	negated	10

SPSS reminds you of the factor you are analysing, what the levels of that factor are, and the number of participants in each level.

Descriptive Statistics

This table will appear if you requested **Descriptive statistics** in the **Univariate: Options** dialogue box.

Dependent Variable: memory

presentation condition	Mean	Std. Deviation	N
unmasked	66.7000	5.33437	10
greyblob	55.7000	3.80205	10
pixelated	57.7000	5.41705	10
negated	67.2000	4.58984	10
Total	61.8250	7.00142	40

The mean and the standard deviation (SD) for each level of the factor.

The total mean and SD; that is, for all participants regardless of which condition they were in.

CHAPTER 8

Levene's Test of Equality of Error Variancesa

Dependent Variable: memory

F	df1	df2	Sig.
.490	3	36	.692

Tests the null hypothesis that the error
variance of the dependent variable is equal
across groups.

If Levene's test is significant, this would
indicate that the assumption of homogeneity
of variance has been violated. Here, it is not
significant.

Each row shows information
for each source of variance
which are listed underneath
this heading.

The degrees of freedom
for each source of
variance.

The *F*-ratio for each
explained source of
variance.

The *p* value for each
explained source of
variance.

The Sum of Squares
for each source of
variance.

The Mean Square for
each source of
variance.

Tests of Between-Subjects Effects

Dependent Variable: memory

Source	Type III Sum of Squares	df	Mean Square	F	Sig.
Corrected Model	1071.875a	3	357.292	15.314	.000
Intercept	152893.225	1	152893.225	6553.347	.000
prescond	1071.875	3	357.292	15.314	.000
Error	839.900	36	23.331		
Total	154805.000	40			
Corrected Total	1911.775	39			

a. R Squared = .561 (Adjusted R Squared = .524)

This row contains the values of *F*, df,
and *p* for the factor 'prescond' that you
will report.

You also need the df value
from the Error row.

 **Reporting the results**

In a report you might write:

A one-way between-subjects ANOVA was conducted to examine the effect of
presentation condition on participants' recall of the witness testimony. This
revealed a significant effect of presentation condition: $F(3,36) = 15.31, p < .001$.

You would also want to report in your results section a measure of effect
size (see Section 1) and information regarding the confidence intervals
for each condition. See also Chapter 5, Section 2 for guidance on how to
obtain an error bar chart. To identify which pair(s) of conditions significantly
differed, you would carry out planned or unplanned comparisons as
appropriate and these are demonstrated later on in this section.

CHAPTER 8

How to do it: using One-Way ANOVA command

As stated earlier, one-way between-subjects ANOVA can be carried out in two different ways in SPSS. This is the second way, which provides a simpler output and also offers alternative *F*s should the variances in the groups not be equal.

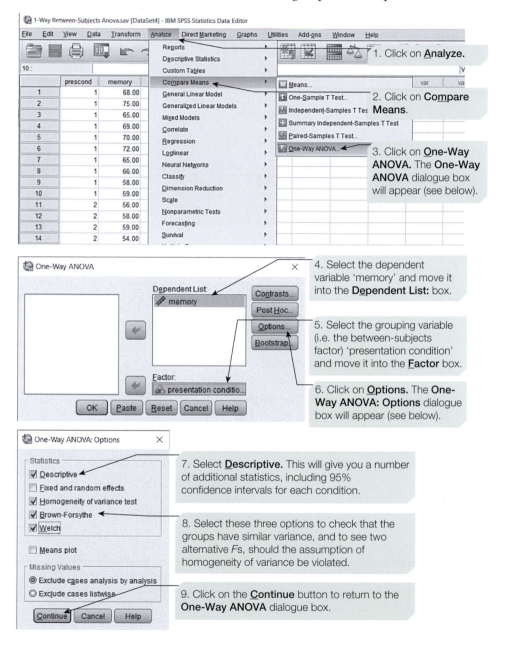

1. Click on **Analyze**.

2. Click on **Compare Means**.

3. Click on **One-Way ANOVA**. The **One-Way ANOVA** dialogue box will appear (see below).

4. Select the dependent variable 'memory' and move it into the **Dependent List:** box.

5. Select the grouping variable (i.e. the between-subjects factor) 'presentation condition' and move it into the **Factor** box.

6. Click on **Options**. The **One-Way ANOVA: Options** dialogue box will appear (see below).

7. Select **Descriptive.** This will give you a number of additional statistics, including 95% confidence intervals for each condition.

8. Select these three options to check that the groups have similar variance, and to see two alternative *F*s, should the assumption of homogeneity of variance be violated.

9. Click on the **Continue** button to return to the **One-Way ANOVA** dialogue box.

Finally, click on the ⬚ OK ⬚ button. See below for annotated output.

SPSS output for one-way between-subjects ANOVA

Obtained using menu items: Compare Means > One-Way ANOVA

Oneway

This table is produced by selecting **Descriptive** in the **One-Way ANOVA: Options** dialogue box.

Descriptives

memory

	N	Mean	Std. Deviation	Std. Error	95% Confidence Interval for Mean Lower Bound	95% Confidence Interval for Mean Upper Bound	Minimum	Maximum
unmasked	10	66.7000	5.33437	1.68688	62.8840	70.5160	58.00	75.00
greyblob	10	55.7000	3.80205	1.20231	52.9802	58.4198	48.00	61.00
pixelated	10	57.7000	5.41705	1.71302	53.8249	61.5751	51.00	68.00
negated	10	67.2000	4.58984	1.45144	63.9166	70.4834	58.00	74.00
Total	40	61.8250	7.00142	1.10702	59.5858	64.0642	48.00	75.00

This table is produced by selecting **Homogeneity of variance test** in the **One-Way ANOVA: Options** dialogue box. If Levene's test is significant, this would indicate that the assumption of homogeneity of variance has been violated. Here, it is not significant.

Test of Homogeneity of Variances

memory

Levene Statistic	df1	df2	Sig.
.490	3	36	.692

This table shows the outcome of the analysis of variance. Each row shows information for a source of variance.

ANOVA

memory

	Sum of Squares	df	Mean Square	F	Sig.
Between Groups	1071.875	3	357.292	15.314	.000
Within Groups	839.900	36	23.331		
Total	1911.775	39			

This row contains the values of *F*, df, and *p* for the factor 'prescond', that you will report.

You also need the df value from the **Within Groups** row (the Error variance row).

This table is produced by selecting **Brown-Forsythe** and **Welch** in the **One-Way ANOVA: Options** dialogue box. These are alternative *F*s, which can be used should Levene's test be significant and hence the assumption of homogeneity of variance violated.

Robust Tests of Equality of Means

memory

	Statistic[a]	df1	df2	Sig.
Welch	16.488	3	19.797	.000
Brown-Forsythe	15.314	3	33.733	.000

a. Asymptotically F distributed.

Reporting the results

In a report you might write:

A one-way between-subjects ANOVA was conducted to examine the effect of presentation condition on participants' recall of the witness testimony. This revealed a significant effect of presentation condition: $F(3,36) = 15.31$, $p < .001$.

You would also want to report in your results section a measure of effect size (see Section 1) and information regarding the confidence intervals for each condition. See also Chapter 5, Section 2 for guidance on how to obtain an error bar chart. To identify which pair(s) of conditions significantly differed, you would carry out planned or unplanned comparisons as appropriate and these are demonstrated next.

Planned and unplanned comparisons

The one-way between-subjects ANOVA identified a significant effect of presentation condition, but we need to carry out further analysis to compare the pairs of conditions to pinpoint the source of this effect. In Section 1 we explained that there are two main types of comparisons, planned and unplanned. For demonstration purposes, we carry out both of these on the same data set; however, normally you would only perform one type.

Unplanned (post-hoc) comparisons in SPSS

There is a range of post-hoc tests to choose from and you will need to consult your statistics text to select the one most suitable for your data. For example, some are more suitable than others depending on whether you have equal sample sizes or whether the population variances are equal (Field, 2013). We demonstrate how to select these tests in the respective SPSS dialogue boxes of both ways of performing a one-way between-subjects ANOVA. The output is the same and is shown on page 207.

Using General Linear Model command

Click on <u>A</u>nalyze ⇒ <u>G</u>eneral Linear Model ⇒ <u>U</u>nivariate.

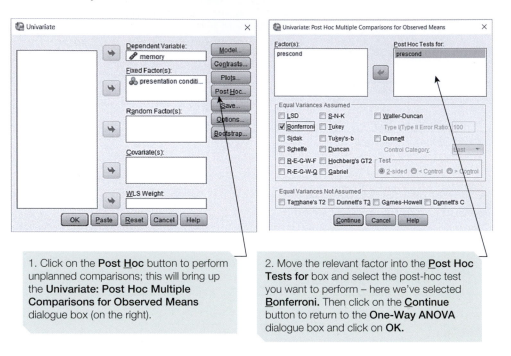

1. Click on the **Post Hoc** button to perform unplanned comparisons; this will bring up the **Univariate: Post Hoc Multiple Comparisons for Observed Means** dialogue box (on the right).

2. Move the relevant factor into the **Post Hoc Tests for** box and select the post-hoc test you want to perform – here we've selected **Bonferroni**. Then click on the **Continue** button to return to the **One-Way ANOVA** dialogue box and click on **OK**.

Using One-Way ANOVA command

Click on <u>A</u>nalyze ⇒ Compare <u>M</u>eans ⇒ <u>O</u>ne-Way ANOVA.

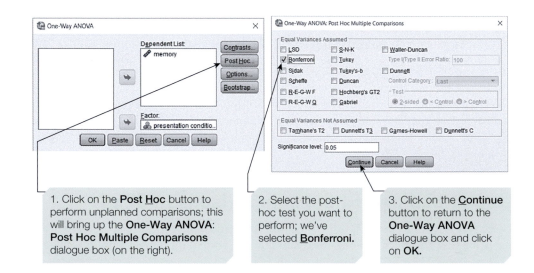

1. Click on the **Post Hoc** button to perform unplanned comparisons; this will bring up the **One-Way ANOVA: Post Hoc Multiple Comparisons** dialogue box (on the right).

2. Select the post-hoc test you want to perform; we've selected **Bonferroni**.

3. Click on the **Continue** button to return to the **One-Way ANOVA** dialogue box and click on **OK**.

SPSS output for post-hoc tests

Post Hoc Tests ◄━━━━━━━━━━━━━━━━━━━━━

This heading and the **Multiple Comparisons** table will appear after all the other tables in the ANOVA output.

presentation condition

Multiple Comparisons

Dependent Variable: memory

Bonferroni

(I) presentation condition	(J) presentation condition	Mean Difference (I-J)	Std. Error	Sig.	95% Confidence Interval	
					Lower Bound	Upper Bound
unmasked	greyblob	11.0000*	2.16012	.000	4.9690	17.0310
	pixelated	9.0000*	2.16012	.001	2.9690	15.0310
	negated	-.5000	2.16012	1.000	-6.5310	5.5310
greyblob	unmasked	-11.0000*	2.16012	.000	-17.0310	-4.9690
	pixelated	-2.0000	2.16012	1.000	-8.0310	4.0310
	negated	-11.5000*	2.16012	.000	-17.5310	-5.4690
pixelated	unmasked	-9.0000*	2.16012	.001	-15.0310	-2.9690
	greyblob	2.0000	2.16012	1.000	-4.0310	8.0310
	negated	-9.5000*	2.16012	.001	-15.5310	-3.4690
negated	unmasked	.5000	2.16012	1.000	-5.5310	6.5310
	greyblob	11.5000*	2.16012	.000	5.4690	17.5310
	pixelated	9.5000*	2.16012	.001	3.4690	15.5310

Based on observed means.

The error term is Mean Square(Error) = 23.331.

*. The mean difference is significant at the .05 level.

SPSS prints a complete matrix (as it does for correlations). You have to pick out the comparisons required, and ignore the repetitions.

As our factor had four levels, there are six possible comparisons. Their p values are highlighted here.

Reporting the results

In a report you might write:

Employing the Bonferroni post-hoc test, significant differences were found between the unmasked and greyblob conditions ($p < .001$), between the unmasked and pixelated conditions ($p = .001$), between the greyblob and negated conditions ($p < .001$), and between the pixelated and negated conditions ($p = .001$). There was no significant difference between the unmasked and negated conditions ($p = 1$), or between the greyblob and pixelated conditions ($p = 1$).

Or, to abbreviate:

There was no significant difference between the unmasked and negated conditions, or between the greyblob and pixelated conditions (for both, $p = 1$). The greyblob and pixelated conditions were each significantly different from each of the unmasked and negated conditions ($p \leq .001$).

Planned comparisons in SPSS

Generally, for planned comparisons, the technique of linear contrasts is used, which allows us to compare one level, or set of levels, with another level or set of levels. The simplest way of doing this is to assign weights to each. These weights are known as 'coefficients'. This technique is available on SPSS, which uses the t-statistic to test specific contrasts. Indeed, the printout will give you two t-values, one for 'assume equal variances' and one for 'does not assume equal variances'. Since the variances of the groups being compared should be broadly similar (otherwise you should not be using ANOVA), you can 'assume equal variances', but check both values and their significance. A point to note here is that the overall main effect does not have to be significant for you to test for specific differences using planned comparisons.

By assigning weights (or coefficients), we can make three sorts of comparison:

1. We can compare one condition with one other condition.

2. We can compare one condition with the mean of two or more other conditions.

3. We can compare the mean of one set of conditions with the mean of another set of conditions.

In all three cases, we assign a weight of zero to a condition (or conditions) that we do not want to be included in the comparison. Conditions (or groups of conditions) that are to be compared with each other are assigned opposite signs (positive or negative). In all cases, the sum of the weights must be zero.

So, suppose you had four conditions, C1, C2, C3 and C4:

- If you wanted to compare only conditions 1 and 3, you could assign the weights: 1, 0, −1, 0.

- If you wanted to compare the average of the first two conditions with the third condition, you could assign the weights: 1, 1, −2, 0.

- If you wanted to compare the mean of the first two groups with the mean of the last two groups, you could use the weights: 1, 1, −1, −1.

If you wish to perform more than one planned comparison on the same data set, you need to check that the comparisons are independent of one another, that they are non-overlapping – these are called *orthogonal* comparisons. You can do this by taking each pair of comparisons and checking that the products of the coefficients assigned to each level sum to zero (see any good statistics text, for example Howell, 2013).

If you perform a planned comparison using the **One-Way ANOVA** command, then you can design your own contrasts (as shown above), and enter the weights (coefficients) into a dialogue box. We show you how to do this next.

Using One-Way ANOVA command

Click on <u>A</u>nalyze ⇒ Compare <u>M</u>eans ⇒ <u>O</u>ne-Way ANOVA.

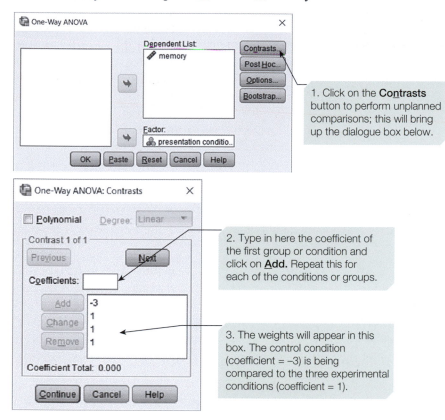

1. Click on the **Contrasts** button to perform unplanned comparisons; this will bring up the dialogue box below.

2. Type in here the coefficient of the first group or condition and click on **Add**. Repeat this for each of the conditions or groups.

3. The weights will appear in this box. The control condition (coefficient = –3) is being compared to the three experimental conditions (coefficient = 1).

The dialogue box above shows a planned comparison, where the control group (who were shown the witness giving evidence with her face visible) is compared with the three experimental groups (who were all shown the witness giving evidence with her face masked). A linear contrast is requested and the coefficients have been entered, first for group 1, then groups 2, 3 and 4. The output below shows that this comparison is significant.

SPSS output for contrasts

Obtained using menu items: Compare Means > One-Way ANOVA

Oneway

ANOVA

memory

	Sum of Squares	df	Mean Square	F	Sig.
Between Groups	1071.875	3	357.292	15.314	.000
Within Groups	839.900	36	23.331		
Total	1911.775	39			

Contrast Coefficients

Contrast	presentation condition			
	unmasked	greyblob	pixelated	negated
1	-3	1	1	1

Contrast Tests

		Contrast	Value of Contrast	Std. Error	t	df	Sig. (2-tailed)
memory	Assume equal variances	1	-19.5000	5.29119	-3.685	36	.001
	Does not assume equal variances	1	-19.5000	5.66539	-3.442	13.818	.004

This row contains the values of *t*, df, and *p* for the contrast that you requested, and assuming equal variance.

Reporting the results

In a report you might write:

A planned comparison revealed that participants who saw the witness's face unmasked remembered significantly more of her testimony than the participants in the three masking conditions ($t = 3.69$, df $= 36$, $p = .001$).

Note that the contrast test can tell you whether the conditions you compared are significantly different or not, but nothing about the *direction* of the difference(s). In order to fully interpret the result, you will need to inspect the descriptive statistics for the conditions or groups being compared.

Using General Linear Model command

For the other way of performing the one-way ANOVA, you have the option of choosing between a range of preset contrasts.

Click on **Analyze** ⇒ **General Linear Model** ⇒ **Univariate**.

1. Click on the **Contrasts** button to obtain the **Univariate: Contrasts** dialogue box (overlaid here).

2. Click on the arrow to view the list of contrasts available. Select the one appropriate for your planned comparison (these are described on the next page). This will then appear in the SPSS output.

For some contrasts, you can decide whether the **Reference Category** is set to **Last** or **First**.

1. A **Deviation** contrast compares the effect for each level of the factor, except the reference category, to the overall effect. Thus, if there are three levels of the factor, two comparisons will be carried out. If the reference category is set to last, then levels 1 and 2 will be compared to the overall effect (of levels 1, 2 and 3 combined). If you select the reference category to be the first, then levels 2 and 3 will be compared to the overall effect of all three.

2. In a **Simple** contrast, each level of the factor is compared to the reference level, which can be set to either the first or last level. For example, if there are three levels and the reference category is set to the first level, then the second and the third levels will each be compared to the first level.

3. In a **Difference** contrast, each level of the factor except the first is compared to the mean effect of all previous levels. Thus, if there are three levels, level 3 is compared to the combined effects of level 2 and level 1, and level 2 is compared to level 1.

4. A **Helmert** contrast is the reverse of the **Difference** contrast, and the effect of each level of the factor except the last is compared to the mean effect of subsequent levels. If there are three levels, level 1 is compared to levels 2 and 3 combined, and level 2 is compared to level 3.

5. In a **Repeated** contrast, each level is compared to the previous level, so if there are three levels, level 2 is compared to level 1 and level 3 to level 2.

6. The **Polynomial** contrast should be used to look for trends in the data; for example, it can be used to look for a linear trend.

The Kruskal–Wallis test

To end this section, we introduce you to the nonparametric equivalent of the one-way between-subjects ANOVA, which can be used if your data fail to meet the assumptions for the ANOVA. For demonstration purposes, we perform the Kruskal–Wallis test on the same data used throughout the section.

How to do it

1. Click on the word **Analyze**.

2. Click on **Nonparametric Tests**.

3. Click on **Legacy Dialogs**.

4. Click on **K Independent Samples**. The **Test for Several Independent Samples** dialogue box will appear (see below).

We are recommending you use **Legacy Dialogs** as this gives you more information in the output compared with the new alternative.

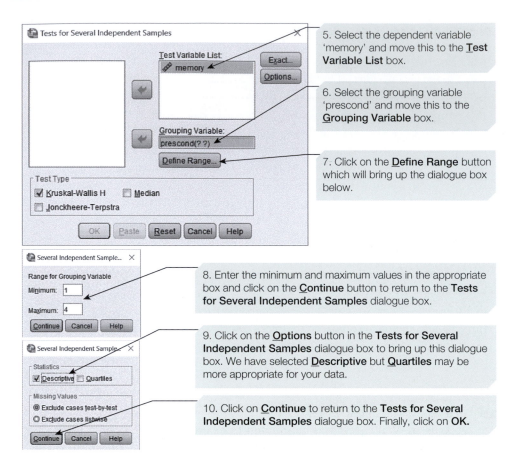

5. Select the dependent variable 'memory' and move this to the **Test Variable List** box.

6. Select the grouping variable 'prescond' and move this to the **Grouping Variable** box.

7. Click on the **Define Range** button which will bring up the dialogue box below.

8. Enter the minimum and maximum values in the appropriate box and click on the **Continue** button to return to the **Tests for Several Independent Samples** dialogue box.

9. Click on the **Options** button in the **Tests for Several Independent Samples** dialogue box to bring up this dialogue box. We have selected **Descriptive** but **Quartiles** may be more appropriate for your data.

10. Click on **Continue** to return to the **Tests for Several Independent Samples** dialogue box. Finally, click on **OK**.

SPSS output for Kruskal–Wallis test

Obtained by using menu items: Nonparametric Tests > K Independent Samples

NPar Tests

This table was obtained via the **Options** button. The first row shows the amount participants correctly recalled of the witness testimony; however, it is for all 40 participants, regardless of the between-subjects condition they were in. For a report, descriptives for each group separately, obtained using **Explore**, would be much more useful (see Chapter 3, Section 4).

Descriptive Statistics

	N	Mean	Std. Deviation	Minimum	Maximum
memory	40	61.8250	7.00142	48.00	75.00
presentation condition	40	2.50	1.132	1	4

Kruskal–Wallis Test

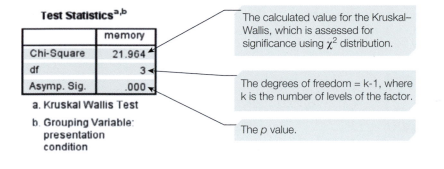

Ranks

	presentation condition	N	Mean Rank
memory	unmasked	10	28.70
	greyblob	10	10.40
	pixelated	10	13.45
	negated	10	29.45
	Total	40	

This table provides information about the calculations for the Kruskal–Wallis, which can be considered as an extension of the Mann–Whitney U test. Therefore, you might like to refer to the annotated output of that test for an explanation (Chapter 5, Section 5).

Test Statistics[a,b]

	memory
Chi-Square	21.964
df	3
Asymp. Sig.	.000

a. Kruskal Wallis Test

b. Grouping Variable: presentation condition

The calculated value for the Kruskal–Wallis, which is assessed for significance using χ^2 distribution.

The degrees of freedom = k-1, where k is the number of levels of the factor.

The p value.

 Reporting the results

In a report you might write:

A Kruskal–Wallis test was conducted to examine the effect of presentation condition on participants' recall of the witness testimony. This revealed a significant effect of presentation condition: $\chi^2(3, N = 40) = 21.96, p < .001$.

Section 3: TWO-WAY BETWEEN-SUBJECTS ANOVA

Example study: the effect of defendant's attractiveness and sex on sentencing

To practise how to analyse data from the two-way between-subjects ANOVA design, we will consider the possible effects of attractiveness and also the gender of the defendant in a mock trial. In the study described here, conducted by one of our past students, the testimony of a hypothetical defendant describing a murder and admitting guilt was presented as written text to 60 participants: 20 participants simply received the written text with no photo attached, 20 participants received the text and a photo of an attractive defendant, and 20 participants received the text and a photo of an unattractive defendant. The photo was of either a man or a woman. Participants were asked to indicate how many years in jail the defendant should receive as punishment.

CHAPTER 8

The design employed was a 3*2 between-subjects ANOVA design. The first between-subjects factor was the knowledge about attractiveness, which had three levels; the factor is operationalised as showing: no photo of the defendant (so no knowledge about attractiveness is provided, a control condition), a photo of an attractive defendant, or a photo of an unattractive defendant. The second between-subjects factor was same or different sex, operationalised by showing a photo of the defendant of the same or opposite sex as the participant. Sex of the defendant was stated in the written text, for the participants who received no photo. The dependent variable was the sentence given, operationalised as how many years the defendant should spend in prison, ranging from a minimum of 3 to a maximum of 25. The hypothesis tested was that the unattractive defendant would be sentenced more harshly and that the length of sentence given might also depend on the sex of the participant. (These data are available from he.palgrave.com/psychology/brace.)

How to do it

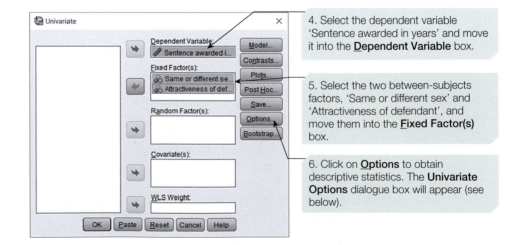

7. We have moved 'attract' into the **Display Means for** box and in doing so the **Compare main effects** tick box became active. If you click in this box, the **Confidence interval adjustment** option becomes active. Click on the arrow to see three tests; select **Bonferroni**. This is one way of obtaining post-hoc comparisons (see the tip box below).

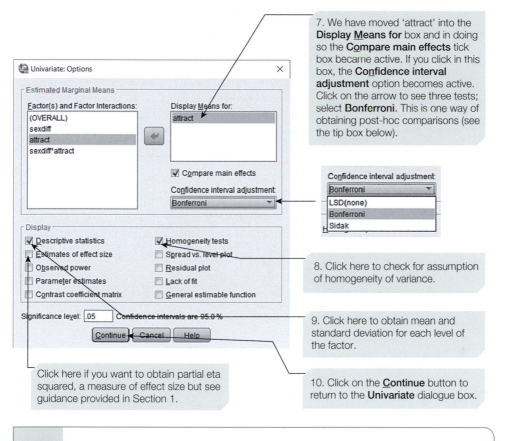

8. Click here to check for assumption of homogeneity of variance.

9. Click here to obtain mean and standard deviation for each level of the factor.

Click here if you want to obtain partial eta squared, a measure of effect size but see guidance provided in Section 1.

10. Click on the **Continue** button to return to the **Univariate** dialogue box.

You can perform post-hoc comparisons by clicking on the **Plots** button in the **Univariate** dialogue box and if you do so, you will have a variety of post-hoc tests to choose from (see Section 2). Here, we demonstrate how to select from a smaller selection of post-hoc tests in the **Univariate: Options** dialogue box. These vary in terms of how conservative (cautious) they are: the default, LSD(none), is not recommended, and of the other two, the Sidak is less conservative than the Bonferroni (Field, 2005).

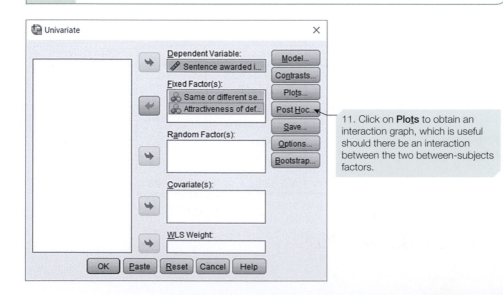

11. Click on **Plots** to obtain an interaction graph, which is useful should there be an interaction between the two between-subjects factors.

> 12. Select each between-subjects factor, moving 'attract' into the **Horizontal Axis** box and 'sexdiff' into the **Separate Lines** box. The **Add** button will become active and click on this so that 'attract*sexdiff' appears in the **Plots** box (shown on the right).

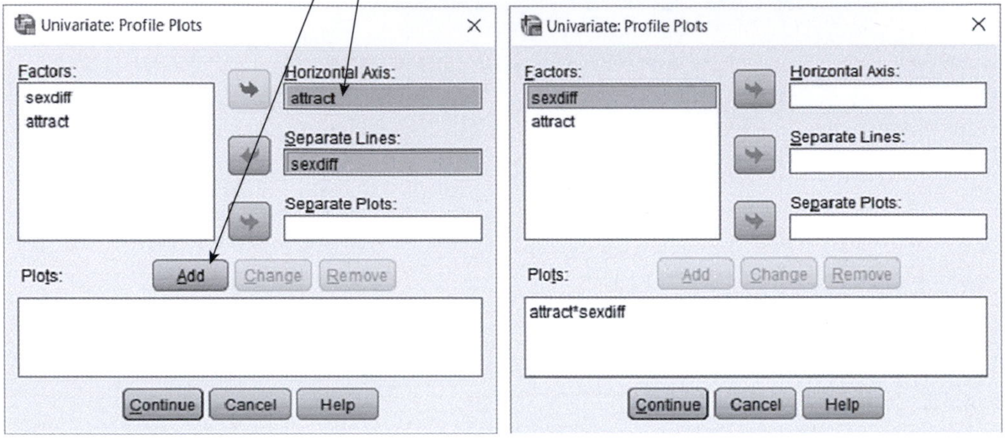

Finally, click on the **OK** button. The annotated output is shown below.

SPSS output for two-way between-subjects ANOVA

Obtained using menu items: General Linear Model > Univariate

Univariate Analysis of Variance

Between-Subjects Factors

		Value Label	N
Same or different sex	1	Same sex as defendant	30
	2	Opposite sex to defendant	30
Attractiveness of defendant	1	Attractive	20
	2	Unattractive	20
	3	No picture	20

> SPSS reminds you of the factors that you are analysing, what the levels of each factor are, and the number of participants in each level.

This table was produced by requesting **Descriptive statistics** in the **Univariate: Options** dialogue box.

Descriptive Statistics

Dependent Variable: Sentence awarded in years

Same or different sex	Attractiveness of defendant	Mean	Std. Deviation	N
Same sex as defendant	Attractive	7.50	1.780	10
	Unattractive	11.20	2.300	10
	No picture	14.50	1.269	10
	Total	11.07	3.403	30
Opposite sex to defendant	Attractive	7.50	2.415	10
	Unattractive	10.30	2.058	10
	No picture	13.50	1.650	10
	Total	10.43	3.191	30
Total	Attractive	7.50	2.065	20
	Unattractive	10.75	2.173	20
	No picture	14.00	1.522	20
	Total	10.75	3.286	60

These three rows show descriptives for each level of the factor 'attract', collapsing across the levels of the other factor, 'sexdiff'.

Each of these six rows shows the descriptives for one of the conditions of the study. Thus, the first row is for participants who were given a photo of an attractive defendant and were the same sex as that defendant.

These two Total rows show descriptives for each level of the factor 'sexdiff', collapsing across the levels of the other factor, 'attract'.

Levene's Test of Equality of Error Variances[a]

Dependent Variable: Sentence awarded in years

F	df1	df2	Sig.
1.509	5	54	.202

Tests the null hypothesis that the error variance of the dependent variable is equal across groups.

a. Design: Intercept + sexdiff + attract + sexdiff * attract

To check that the assumption of equality of variance was not violated, we clicked on **Homogeneity tests** in the **Univariate: Options** dialogue box. A significance level greater than .05, as here, suggests that the data do not violate the assumption of equality of error variances.

This table shows the outcome of the analysis of variance. Each row shows information for a source of variance.

Tests of Between-Subjects Effects

Dependent Variable: Sentence awarded in years

Source	Type III Sum of Squares	df	Mean Square	F	Sig.
Corrected Model	431.550[a]	5	86.310	22.658	.000
Intercept	6933.750	1	6933.750	1820.236	.000
sexdiff	6.017	1	6.017	1.579	.214
attract	422.500	2	211.250	55.457	.000
sexdiff * attract	3.033	2	1.517	.398	.674
Error	205.700	54	3.809		
Total	7571.000	60			
Corrected Total	637.250	59			

a. R Squared = .677 (Adjusted R Squared = .647)

This row shows information about the main effect of the factor 'sexdiff'.

This row shows information about the main effect of the factor 'attract'.

This row shows information about the interaction between the factors 'sexdiff' and 'attract'.

Estimates

Dependent Variable: Sentence awarded in years

Attractiveness of defendant	Mean	Std. Error	95% Confidence Interval	
			Lower Bound	Upper Bound
Attractive	7.500	.436	6.625	8.375
Unattractive	10.750	.436	9.875	11.625
No picture	14.000	.436	13.125	14.875

This table gives the descriptives for 'attract', because in the **Univariate: Options** dialogue box, we moved 'attract' into the box labelled **Display Means for**.

However, the main reason for doing so was to obtain the **Pairwise Comparisons** table (below), which shows the output from the Bonferroni post-hoc test.

Pairwise Comparisons

Dependent Variable: Sentence awarded in years

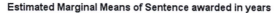

(I) Attractiveness of defendant	(J) Attractiveness of defendant	Mean Difference (I-J)	Std. Error	Sig.b	95% Confidence Interval for Differenceb	
					Lower Bound	Upper Bound
Attractive	Unattractive	-3.250*	.617	.000	-4.775	-1.725
	No picture	-6.500*	.617	.000	-8.025	-4.975
Unattractive	Attractive	3.250*	.617	.000	1.725	4.775
	No picture	-3.250*	.617	.000	-4.775	-1.725
No picture	Attractive	6.500*	.617	.000	4.975	8.025
	Unattractive	3.250*	.617	.000	1.725	4.775

Based on estimated marginal means

*. The mean difference is significant at the .05 level.

b. Adjustment for multiple comparisons: Bonferroni.

SPSS prints out a matrix (as it does for correlations) and you have to pick out the three possible comparisons.

As our factor 'attract' had three levels, there are three possible comparisons. Their *p* values are highlighted here.

Profile Plots

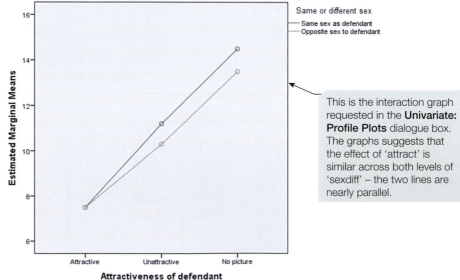

This is the interaction graph requested in the **Univariate: Profile Plots** dialogue box. The graphs suggests that the effect of 'attract' is similar across both levels of 'sexdiff' – the two lines are nearly parallel.

Calculating eta squared: one measure of effect size

In Section 1 we provided guidance on reporting effect size when carrying out ANOVAs. Although SPSS will calculate partial eta squared, this is not easy to interpret as it is an adjusted measure: the variance explained by one factor *after* taking into account the variance explained by the other factor(s). Instead, Mulhern and Greer (2011) recommend eta squared, which is relatively straightforward to calculate by hand and will tell you the proportion of the total variability accounted for by each factor and interaction in your design. We will demonstrate how to do this now. Note, however, that there are alternative measures which are preferable, as they attempt to estimate the effect size in the population rather than just in the sample (see Fritz, Morris and Richler, 2012 for a review and guidance on how to calculate these, and/or consult your statistics text). Eta squared (η^2) can be calculated from the ANOVA output. It is the sum of squares for the factor or interaction divided by the corrected total sum of squares, and these values can be found in the **Tests of Between-Subjects Effects** table.

Tests of Between-Subjects Effects

Dependent Variable: Sentence awarded in years

Source	Type III Sum of Squares	df	Mean Square	F	Sig.
Corrected Model	431.550[a]	5	86.310	22.658	.000
Intercept	6933.750	1	6933.750	1820.236	.000
sexdiff	6.017	1	6.017	1.579	.214
attract	422.500	2	211.250	55.457	.000
sexdiff * attract	3.033	2	1.517	.398	.674
Error	205.700	54	3.809		
Total	7571.000	60			
Corrected Total	637.250	59			

a. R Squared = .677 (Adjusted R Squared = .647)

- For the factor 'sexdiff' (η^2) = 6.02 / 637.25 = .009
- For the factor 'attract' (η^2) = 422.50 / 637.25 = .663
- For the interaction 'sexdiff*attract' (η^2) = 3.03 / 637.25 = .005

The factor 'attract' accounts for approximately 66% of the variance in the dependent variable, whereas the other factor 'sexdiff', and the interaction, account for only a tiny proportion. The remainder of the variance is accounted for by error (205.7 / 637.25 = .32).

Reporting the results

In a report you might write:

A two-way between-subjects ANOVA was conducted on sentencing judgements. Whether the sex of the defendant was the same as, or different from, the sex of the participant did not affect the length of sentence given ($F(1,54) = 1.58$, $p = .214$, $\eta^2 = .009$). However, information about the attractiveness of the defendant did influence sentencing judgements ($F(2,54) = 55.46$, $p < .001$. $\eta^2 = .663$), see graph below. There was no significant interaction between these two factors ($F(2,54) = 0.40$, $p = .674$, $\eta^2 = .005$). Bonferroni post-hoc comparisons showed significant differences between no picture and attractive conditions ($p < .001$), no picture and unattractive conditions ($p < .001$), and attractive and unattractive conditions ($p < .001$).

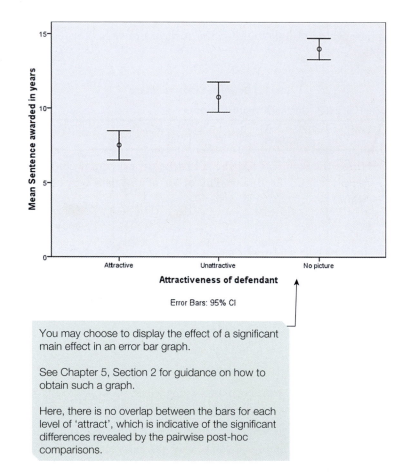

Error Bars: 95% CI

You may choose to display the effect of a significant main effect in an error bar graph.

See Chapter 5, Section 2 for guidance on how to obtain such a graph.

Here, there is no overlap between the bars for each level of 'attract', which is indicative of the significant differences revealed by the pairwise post-hoc comparisons.

Section 4: ONE-WAY WITHIN-SUBJECTS ANOVA, PLANNED AND UNPLANNED COMPARISONS, AND NONPARAMETRIC EQUIVALENT

Example study: the Stroop effect

Many experiments have been conducted to investigate the Stroop effect (Stroop, 1935). The most common way of demonstrating this effect is to show participants the names of colours printed in an incongruous colour (e.g. the word 'red' written in green ink) and ask them to name the colour of the ink. Results show that this is not an easy task because of our tendency to read the word, which then interferes with the task of naming the colour of the ink. In one experiment conducted with undergraduate students, we devised three lists. One list was incongruent and contained four words with strong colour associations (grass, coal, blood, sky) repeated three times in a random order, each time in a different incongruent colour ink (e.g. 'grass' printed in black, red and blue ink). The second list was congruent and contained the same four words repeated three times in a random order, each time in their congruent colour ink (e.g. 'grass' printed in green ink). The third list was neutral and contained four new words, matched in word length to the original words, and repeated three times. These words were not associated with any particular colour and were printed in one of the four different colour inks (e.g. 'table' written in green). These three lists constituted the different experimental conditions, and all participants completed all three lists. The order of the lists was counterbalanced across participants.

The design employed was a one-way within-subjects ANOVA design. The within-subjects factor, the type of list, had three levels: incongruent, congruent and neutral. The dependent variable was the total time taken in seconds to name the colour of the ink of the 12 words in the list. The hypothesis was that there would be an effect of type of list on performance, with the shortest naming time for the congruent list and the longest naming time for the incongruent list. (These data are available from he.palgrave.com/psychology/brace.)

Understanding the output

The within-subjects ANOVA output contains several additional sections not seen previously in the between-subjects output. We describe these here and draw attention to them again when working through the output:

1. **Mauchly's test of Sphericity**: this is important. If you have two or more levels of a within-subjects factor, SPSS will print a test called the Mauchly's test of Sphericity. The Mauchly's test of Sphericity is a statistical test to determine whether the data entered into the within-subjects ANOVA meet certain assumptions, rather like the Levene's equality of variance test. The assumption of sphericity is that the variances of the differences between all possible pairs of levels of the

factor are equal. Because the same participants are performing in each level of the within-subjects factor, you would assume that the correlations between all possible combinations of levels are roughly the same. If there are only two levels, there will be only one correlation so this test is valuable when there are three or more levels. A chi value is estimated to test the significance of the Mauchly's test of Sphericity procedure (hence the output reports 'Approx. Chi-square'). The significance of this value of chi is reported. If it is significant (i.e. less than .05), then the assumption of sphericity has been violated. When this occurs there are two things you can do: corrections using Epsilon, or multivariate tests, described next.

2. **Corrections using Epsilon**: SPSS provides three estimates of a statistic called **Epsilon** that can be used to correct for a violation revealed by Mauchly's test of Sphericity. The greater the violation, the smaller the value of Epsilon. All you need to do is decide which of the three estimates of Epsilon to use. Greenhouse–Geisser Epsilon is probably the most appropriate value to use, but if you have relatively few participants, this can be rather too conservative (i.e. its use will decrease the chances of finding a significant result) – in these cases the Huynh–Feldt Epsilon may be preferable. The third estimate, the Lower-bound Epsilon, is a minimum value for Epsilon that will give the most conservative correction. SPSS gives corrected values in the table. When reporting any result, make it clear which you have used.

3. **Multivariate tests**: these make fewer assumptions about the data and hence are more appropriate when the Mauchly's test of Sphericity is significant. In the Multivariate Tests table, SPSS reports four different multivariate statistics: Pilliai's Trace, Wilks' Lambda, Hotelling's Trace and Roy's Largest Root. Each of these tests reports a value of F with associated degrees of freedom and a significance value. You will probably find that there is little difference between the significance of F reported by these four procedures, so we suggest you pick one of them and report it. The multivariate values of F are always lower than the univariate values; hence, if a result is not significant by the univariate method, it cannot be significant for the multivariate method. For this reason, SPSS does not report the multivariate estimates when the univariate test is non-significant.

4. Finally, it is worth mentioning the **Test of between-subjects effects** table that appears towards the end of the output even when your design does not include a between-subjects factor. This can be ignored when you only have within-subjects factors in your design, as is the case here with the one-way within-subjects ANOVA. What SPSS is doing is assuming that 'participant' is an additional, between-subjects factor in the analysis. One way to think of this is to say that the part of the output reporting the between-subjects effects is asking 'Did all participants perform the same?' It is in the nature of psychology that participants are variable in almost all tasks and hence you will find that the F-ratio is invariably very high and highly significant. As we are not normally interested in this question of whether the participants are all performing in the same way (we usually want to know about general trends across groups of participants), we can ignore this section of the output. Indeed, you will rarely see this result reported in psychology papers.

How to do it

1-Way Within-Subjects Anova.sav [DataSet6] – IBM SPSS Statistics Data Editor

File	Edit	View	Data	Transform	Analyze	Direct Marketing	Graphs	Utilities	Add-ons

Reports
Descriptive Statistics
Custom Tables
Compare Means
General Linear Model
Generalized Linear Models
Mixed Models
Correlate
Regression
Loglinear
Neural Networks
Classify
Dimension Reduction
Scale
Nonparametric Tests
Forecasting
Survival
Multiple Response
Missing Value Analysis...
Multiple Imputation
Complex Samples
Simulation...
Quality Control

Univariate...
Multivariate...
Repeated Measures...
Variance Components...

	incong	cong
1	13.00	9.00
2	13.00	10.00
3	16.00	9.00
4	13.00	8.00
5	14.00	9.00
6	15.00	10.00
7	14.00	8.00
8	13.00	9.00
9	16.00	8.00
10	17.00	9.00
11		
12		
13		
14		
15		
16		
17		
18		
19		
20		

1. Click on **Analyze**.

2. Click on **General Linear Model.**

3. Click on **Repeated Measures**. The **Repeated Measures Define Factor(s)** dialogue box will appear (see below).

CHAPTER 8

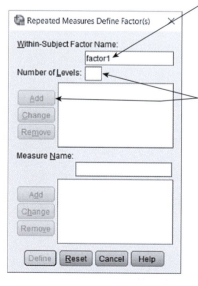

Repeated Measures Define Factor(s)

Within-Subject Factor Name:
factor1
Number of Levels:

Add
Change
Remove

Measure Name:

Add
Change
Remove

Define   Reset   Cancel   Help

4. Replace the factor name suggested by SPSS by highlighting factor 1 and typing the word 'list'.

'list' represents the type of list, the factor manipulated in this Stroop study, which was the lists of words in different colour inks.

5. There were three different lists in the study, so type the number '3' in the **Number of Levels** box and click on the **Add** button. The dialogue box will now show **list(3)** (see below).

Repeated Measures Define Factor(s)

Within-Subject Factor Name:

Number of Levels:

list(3)

Add
Change
Remove

Measure Name:

Add
Change
Remove

Define   Reset   Cancel   Help

6. Click on the **Define** button; the **Repeated Measures** dialogue box will appear (see below).

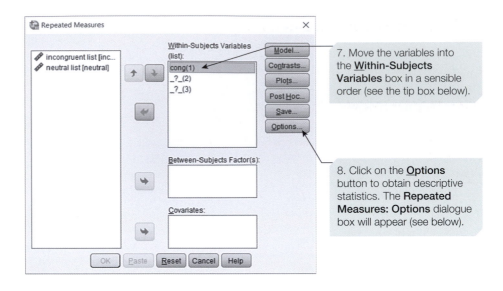

7. Move the variables into the **Within-Subjects Variables** box in a sensible order (see the tip box below).

8. Click on the **Options** button to obtain descriptive statistics. The **Repeated Measures: Options** dialogue box will appear (see below).

As SPSS does a trend test, we entered the variables in line with the hypothesis: first, congruent list, then neutral list and then incongruent list. We hypothesised that the time taken to name the ink colour would be shortest for the congruent list, longer for the neutral list and longest for the incongruent list.

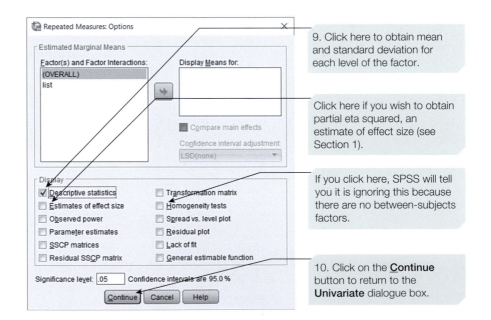

9. Click here to obtain mean and standard deviation for each level of the factor.

Click here if you wish to obtain partial eta squared, an estimate of effect size (see Section 1).

If you click here, SPSS will tell you it is ignoring this because there are no between-subjects factors.

10. Click on the **Continue** button to return to the **Univariate** dialogue box.

Click on ⎡ OK ⎤ to obtain the SPSS output shown below. You will find that there is a significant effect of type of list, and you may wish to include in your results section a table displaying the mean for each condition and the 95% confidence intervals (see Chapter 3, Section 5).

SPSS output for one-way within-subjects ANOVA
Obtained using menu items: General Linear Model > Repeated Measures

General Linear Model

Within-Subjects Factors

Measure: MEASURE_1

list	Dependent Variable
1	cong
2	neutral
3	incong

These are the names for each level of the factor 'list'. If these were entered into the **Repeated Measures** dialogue box in a meaningful order, they will be displayed here in that order, and the table **Tests of Within-Subjects Contrasts** (shown below) will also be relevant.

Descriptive Statistics

	Mean	Std. Deviation	N
congruent list	8.9000	.73786	10
neutral list	11.1000	1.19722	10
incongruent list	14.4000	1.50555	10

Useful descriptives that you can incorporate into your report, obtained by ticking **Descriptive statistics** in the **Repeated Measures: Options** dialogue box.

Multivariate Tests[a]

Effect		Value	F	Hypothesis df	Error df	Sig.
list	Pillai's Trace	.920	45.993[b]	2.000	8.000	.000
	Wilks' Lambda	.080	45.993[b]	2.000	8.000	.000
	Hotelling's Trace	11.498	45.993[b]	2.000	8.000	.000
	Roy's Largest Root	11.498	45.993[b]	2.000	8.000	.000

a. Design: Intercept
   Within Subjects Design: list

b. Exact statistic

If **Mauchly's test of Sphericity** (shown below) is significant, you might consider using one of the four multivariate statistics shown in this table, as these make fewer assumptions about the data. Guidance on these statistics was given towards the start of this section.

Remember that should Mauchly's test be significant, there are two options: either adopt a multivariate approach and report one of the four statistics given in the **Multivariate Tests** table above, or use the values for your chosen Epsilon from the **Tests of Within-Subjects Effects** table (shown below).

Mauchly's Test of Sphericity determines whether the data meet the assumption that the correlations between all the levels of the factor 'list' are roughly the same. Here, it is not significant, so this assumption has not been violated.

Measure: MEASURE_1

Within Subjects Effect	Mauchly's W	Approx. Chi-Square	df	Sig.	Epsilon[b]		
					Greenhouse-Geisser	Huynh-Feldt	Lower-bound
list	.892	.914	2	.633	.903	1.000	.500

Tests the null hypothesis that the error covariance matrix of the orthonormalized transformed dependent variables is proportional to an identity matrix.

a. Design: Intercept
   Within Subjects Design: list

b. May be used to adjust the degrees of freedom for the averaged tests of significance. Corrected tests are displayed in the Tests of Within-Subjects Effects table.

Tests of Within-Subjects Effects

Measure: MEASURE_1

Source		Type III Sum of Squares	df	Mean Square	F	Sig.
list	Sphericity Assumed	153.267	2	76.633	68.741	.000
	Greenhouse-Geisser	153.267	1.805	84.906	68.741	.000
	Huynh-Feldt	153.267	2.000	76.633	68.741	.000
	Lower-bound	153.267	1.000	153.267	68.741	.000
Error(list)	Sphericity Assumed	20.067	18	1.115		
	Greenhouse-Geisser	20.067	16.246	1.235		
	Huynh-Feldt	20.067	18.000	1.115		
	Lower-bound	20.067	9.000	2.230		

This row is the one you use when Mauchly's test is not significant. It gives the values for the within-subjects factor 'list' that has three levels (the three types of list). Underneath are the three estimates of Epsilon. Because Mauchly's test was not significant, no correction is needed and the four different entries for F in this table are identical. For more information, see the start of this section.

You also need the df for the Error term.

Tests of Within-Subjects Contrasts

This table shows the outcome of two trend tests: Linear and Quadratic.

Measure: MEASURE_1

Source	list	Type III Sum of Squares	df	Mean Square	F	Sig.
list	Linear	151.250	1	151.250	102.736	.000
	Quadratic	2.017	1	2.017	2.663	.137
Error(list)	Linear	13.250	9	1.472		
	Quadratic	6.817	9	.757		

This row is for the Linear trend test.

Tests of Between-Subjects Effects

Measure: MEASURE_1
Transformed Variable: Average

Source	Type III Sum of Squares	df	Mean Square	F	Sig.
Intercept	3944.533	1	3944.533	1957.765	.000
Error	18.133	9	2.015		

As mentioned earlier, you can ignore this table.

For these data, as we predicted, there is a significant linear trend, $F(1,9) = 102.74$, $p < .001$. The means suggest that participants took the shortest time to name the ink colour for the congruent list, and took the longest time to name the colour of the ink in the incongruent list, with the mean for the neutral list falling between these two values.

Furthermore, for these data, there is no significant quadratic trend, $F(1,9) =$ 2.66, $p = .137$. A linear trend test is used to see if the points tend to fall onto a straight line (as here). A quadratic trend test looks for a U-shaped or inverted U-shaped trend. If you entered the three levels in the order 'cong', 'incong' and 'neutral', then the quadratic trend would be significant. You might like to try this.

Reporting the results

In a report you might write:

A one-way within-subjects ANOVA was conducted on response times to a Stroop task. There was a significant effect of the type of list: $F(2,18) = 68.74$, $p < .001$. A significant linear trend emerged, $F(1,9) = 102.74$, $p < .001$, with naming times increasing across congruent, neutral and incongruent lists.

> You would also want to report in your results section a measure of effect size (see Section 1) and information regarding the confidence intervals for each condition.

Note that the **Tests of Within-Subjects Contrasts** table shows only whether a trend is significant or not. It is not a test of whether the individual conditions significantly differ from one another. However, ANOVA commands via the **General Linear Model** allow you to choose between a range of preset contrasts, described in Section 2. It is also possible to carry out some unplanned (post-hoc) comparisons. We illustrate how to do each of these next for a within-subjects factor, using the data analysed above. Consult Section 1 for general guidance on planned versus unplanned comparisons.

Planned comparisons: more contrasts for within-subjects factor

Click on **Analyze** ⇒ **General Linear Model** ⇒ **Repeated Measures**

Repeated Measures

Within-Subjects Variables (list):

cong(1)

Model...
Contrasts...
Plots...
Post Hoc...
Save...
Options...

Click on the **Contrasts** button in the **Repeated Measures** dialogue box.

Repeated Measures: Contrasts

Factors:
list(Polynomial)

Change Contrast

Contrast: Polynomial
Deviation
Simple
Difference
Helmert
Repeated
Polynomial

Change

○ First

Reference

OK   Paste   Reset   Cancel   Help

Click on the arrow to view the list of contrasts available. The default is Polynomial contrasts, which we saw in the output described above, showing the linear and quadratic trends.

CHAPTER 8

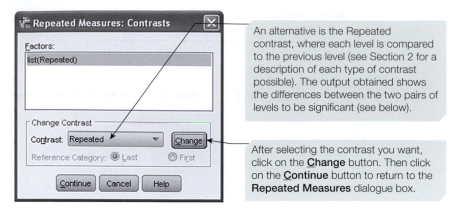

An alternative is the Repeated contrast, where each level is compared to the previous level (see Section 2 for a description of each type of contrast possible). The output obtained shows the differences between the two pairs of levels to be significant (see below).

After selecting the contrast you want, click on the **Change** button. Then click on the **Continue** button to return to the **Repeated Measures** dialogue box.

Tests of Within-Subjects Contrasts

Measure: MEASURE_1

Source	list	Type III Sum of Squares	df	Mean Square	F	Sig.
list	Level 1 vs. Level 2	48.400	1	48.400	27.923	.001
	Level 2 vs. Level 3	108.900	1	108.900	54.149	.000
Error(list)	Level 1 vs. Level 2	15.600	9	1.733		
	Level 2 vs. Level 3	18.100	9	2.011		

Unplanned comparisons for within-subjects factor ANOVA

In terms of unplanned (post-hoc) comparisons, the choice for a within-subjects factor is more limited than for a between-subjects factor. If you click on the **Post Hoc** button in the **Repeated Measures** dialogue box, you will not see the within-subjects factor listed. However, a smaller selection of post-hoc tests are available in the **Repeated Measures: Options** dialogue box.

We have moved 'list' into the **Display Means for:** box and in doing so the **Compare main effects** box became active.

If you click here, then the **Confidence interval adjustment** box becomes active. Click on the arrow to view all three options. These vary in terms of how conservative (cautious) they are. The default, LSD(none), is not recommended, and Sidak is less conservative than Bonferroni (Field, 2005).

Click on the **Continue** button to return to the **Repeated Measures** dialogue box.

Pairwise Comparisons

Measure: MEASURE_1

(I) list	(J) list	Mean Difference (I-J)	Std. Error	Sig.^{b}	95% Confidence Interval for Difference^b	
					Lower Bound	Upper Bound
1	2	3.300*	.448	.000	2.286	4.314
	3	5.500*	.543	.000	4.272	6.728
2	1	-3.300*	.448	.000	-4.314	-2.286
	3	2.200*	.416	.001	1.258	3.142
3	1	-5.500*	.543	.000	-6.728	-4.272
	2	-2.200*	.416	.001	-3.142	-1.258

Based on estimated marginal means

*. The mean difference is significant at the .05 level.

b. Adjustment for multiple comparisons: Least Significant Difference (equivalent to no adjustments).

> The **Pairwise Comparisons** table will appear in the output. This shows the differences between all of the pairs to be significant.

Finally, it is worth noting that as with the one-way between-subjects ANOVA, there is a nonparametric version of the one-way within-subjects ANOVA, and this is described in the last part of this section.

The Friedman test

The Friedman test is the nonparametric equivalent of the one-way within-subjects analysis of variance. Confusingly, the Friedman test is sometimes referred to as the 'Friedman two-way ANOVA' (this is because for a within-subjects analysis of variance, the participants are also considered to be a factor). For demonstration purposes, we perform this test using the same data as for the one-way within-subjects ANOVA.

How to do it

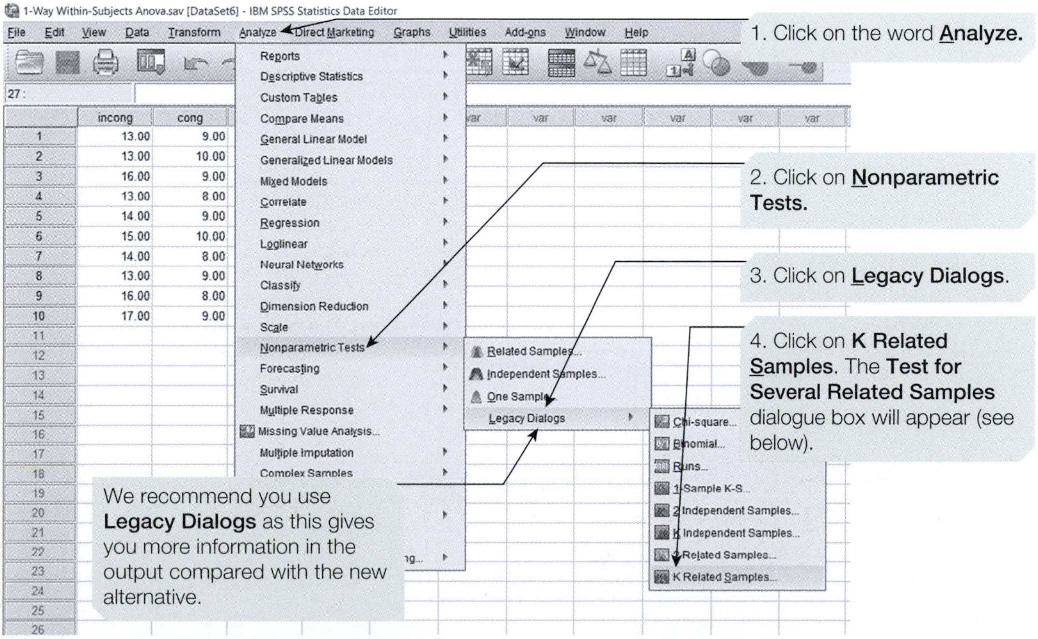

1. Click on the word **Analyze**.

2. Click on **Nonparametric Tests**.

3. Click on **Legacy Dialogs**.

4. Click on **K Related Samples**. The **Test for Several Related Samples** dialogue box will appear (see below).

> We recommend you use **Legacy Dialogs** as this gives you more information in the output compared with the new alternative.

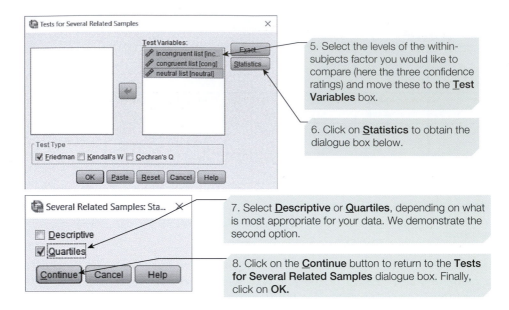

5. Select the levels of the within-subjects factor you would like to compare (here the three confidence ratings) and move these to the **Test Variables** box.

6. Click on **Statistics** to obtain the dialogue box below.

7. Select **Descriptive** or **Quartiles**, depending on what is most appropriate for your data. We demonstrate the second option.

8. Click on the **Continue** button to return to the **Tests for Several Related Samples** dialogue box. Finally, click on **OK**.

SPSS output for Friedman test

Obtained by using menu items: Nonparametric Tests > K Related Samples

NPar Tests

Descriptives for each level of the within-subjects factor, here in the form of quartiles, were obtained via the **Statistics** button in the dialogue box.

Descriptive Statistics

		Percentiles		
	N	25th	50th (Median)	75th
incongruent list	10	13.0000	14.0000	16.0000
congruent list	10	8.0000	9.0000	9.2500
neutral list	10	10.0000	11.0000	12.0000

Friedman Test

Ranks

	Mean Rank
incongruent list	3.00
congruent list	1.00
neutral list	2.00

In the Friedman test, for each participant, the scores for each level of the factor are put into rank order, with the faster (smaller) response times allocated lower (smaller) ranks. SPSS has calculated the mean rank for each level of the within-subjects factor. (Here, the three mean ranks are integers; this is unlikely to be the case in most studies, and occurred here because all participants were fastest with the congruent list and slowest with the incongruent list.)

CHAPTER 8

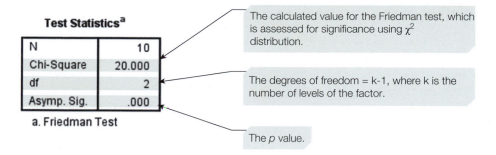

Test Statistics[a]

N	10
Chi-Square	20.000
df	2
Asymp. Sig.	.000

a. Friedman Test

The calculated value for the Friedman test, which is assessed for significance using χ^2 distribution.

The degrees of freedom = k-1, where k is the number of levels of the factor.

The p value.

 Reporting the results

In a report you might write:

A Friedman test revealed that response times to a Stroop task varied significantly for incongruent, congruent and neutral lists: $\chi^2(2, N = 10) = 20.00, p < .001$.

Section 5: TWO-WAY WITHIN-SUBJECTS ANOVA

Example study: the effects of two memory tasks on finger tapping performance

To practise a two-way within-subjects ANOVA, we shall look at an experiment carried out to examine the effects of two memory tasks on tapping performance. Research has identified that right index finger tapping is largely controlled by the left hemisphere, and left index finger tapping by the right hemisphere. If a cognitive task is performed at the same time as this finger tapping task, then the way in which the cognitive task interferes with such tapping could reflect the extent to which either hemisphere is involved in controlling the cognitive task. Many studies that required participants to tap as fast as possible with their index finger while also performing a verbal task found that right-hand tapping was disrupted more than left-hand tapping. This result is compatible with the notion that the left side of the brain, more so than the right side, is involved in controlling both right-hand tapping and many verbal tasks. In a study by Towell, Burton and Burton (1994), participants were asked to tap with each hand while memorising either the words presented to them on a screen (a verbal memory task) or the position of the words on the screen (a visuospatial memory task). Memorising the words should disrupt right-hand tapping more than left-hand tapping, whereas, because of the right side of the brain involvement in many visuospatial tasks, memorising the positions of words should disrupt left-hand tapping more than right-hand tapping.

The design employed was a 2*2 within-subjects ANOVA. Each factor had two levels; the first was tapping hand (left or right hand) and the second was the memory task (memorising the words or memorising the positions). All participants were tested under each possible combination of the two factors. The dependent variable was a percentage change score, showing the extent to which tapping is slowed down by the concurrent performance of the memory task. The hypothesis tested was that there would be an interaction between tapping hand and memory task. This hypothesis was supported and for the purposes of this book, we have created a data file that will reproduce some of the findings reported by Towell et al. (1994). (These data are available from he.palgrave.com/psychology/brace.)

CHAPTER 8

Labelling within-subjects factors

Consider the factors and levels in this example; they could be set out as in Table 8.4. As each factor has two levels, there are four conditions, each with one level of one factor and one level of the other factor. The name that was given in the SPSS data file to each column containing the data for each condition incorporates a number for each level of each factor, as shown in the bottom row of Table 8.4. In these column names:

- 'h1s1' means tapping hand 1 (right) and stimulus for task 1 (memorising words)

- 'h2s2' means tapping hand 2 (left) and stimulus for task 2 (memorising positions).

Table 8.4 The numbering system for the within-subjects factors

Factor 1	Tapping hand			
Levels	Right		Left	
Factor 2	Memory task		Memory task	
Levels	Words	Position	Words	Position
Column name, SPSS data file, for conditions	h1s1	h1s2	h2s1	h2s2

You should jot down a rough table such as this before entering the data for any design with two or more within-subjects factors. This will help you when you define the within-subjects factors, because you will find that the numbers you have used for the column names will match with the numbers that SPSS uses when requesting variable selection.

How to do it

1. Click on the word Analyze.

2. Click on General Linear Model.

3. Click on Repeated Measures. The Repeated Measures Define Factor(s) dialogue box will appear (see below).

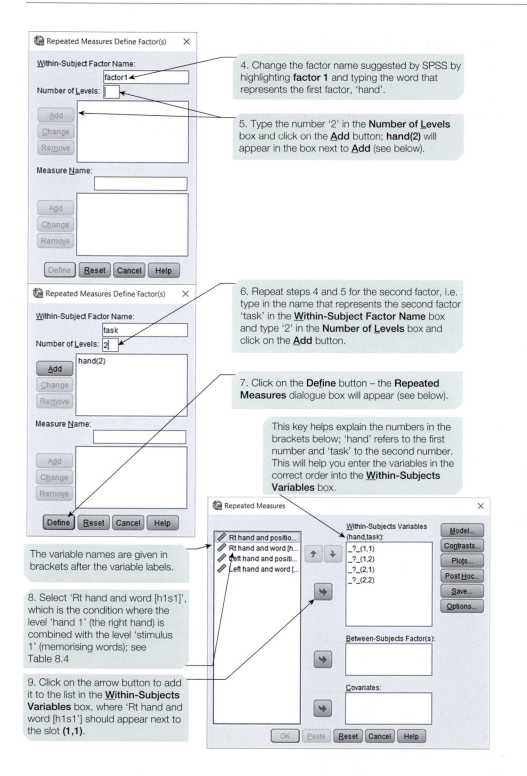

4. Change the factor name suggested by SPSS by highlighting **factor 1** and typing the word that represents the first factor, 'hand'.

5. Type the number '2' in the **Number of Levels** box and click on the **Add** button; **hand(2)** will appear in the box next to **Add** (see below).

6. Repeat steps 4 and 5 for the second factor, i.e. type in the name that represents the second factor 'task' in the **Within-Subject Factor Name** box and type '2' in the **Number of Levels** box and click on the **Add** button.

7. Click on the **Define** button – the **Repeated Measures** dialogue box will appear (see below).

This key helps explain the numbers in the brackets below; 'hand' refers to the first number and 'task' to the second number. This will help you enter the variables in the correct order into the **Within-Subjects Variables** box.

The variable names are given in brackets after the variable labels.

8. Select 'Rt hand and word [h1s1]', which is the condition where the level 'hand 1' (the right hand) is combined with the level 'stimulus 1' (memorising words); see Table 8.4

9. Click on the arrow button to add it to the list in the **Within-Subjects Variables** box, where 'Rt hand and word [h1s1]' should appear next to the slot **(1,1)**.

CHAPTER 8

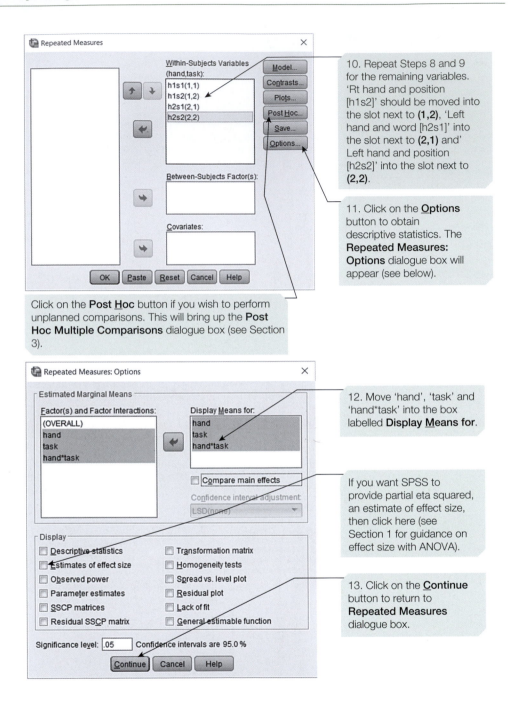

10. Repeat Steps 8 and 9 for the remaining variables. 'Rt hand and position [h1s2]' should be moved into the slot next to **(1,2)**, 'Left hand and word [h2s1]' into the slot next to **(2,1)** and' Left hand and position [h2s2]' into the slot next to **(2,2)**.

11. Click on the **Options** button to obtain descriptive statistics. The **Repeated Measures: Options** dialogue box will appear (see below).

Click on the **Post Hoc** button if you wish to perform unplanned comparisons. This will bring up the **Post Hoc Multiple Comparisons** dialogue box (see Section 3).

12. Move 'hand', 'task' and 'hand*task' into the box labelled **Display Means for**.

If you want SPSS to provide partial eta squared, an estimate of effect size, then click here (see Section 1 for guidance on effect size with ANOVA).

13. Click on the **Continue** button to return to **Repeated Measures** dialogue box.

Click on ⬜ OK ⬜. SPSS will perform the calculations. You may wish to obtain an interaction graph should the analysis reveal a significant interaction – this is an option available on the **Repeated Measures** dialogue box – see the steps outlined below.

How to obtain an interaction graph

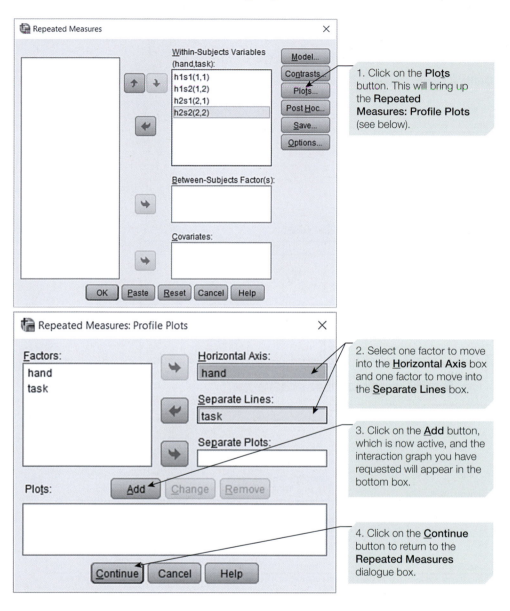

Repeated Measures

Within-Subjects Variables
(hand,task):
h1s1(1,1)
h1s2(1,2)
h2s1(2,1)
h2s2(2,2)

Model...
Contrasts...
Plots...
Post Hoc...
Save...
Options...

Between-Subjects Factor(s):

Covariates:

OK Paste Reset Cancel Help

1. Click on the **Plots** button. This will bring up the **Repeated Measures: Profile Plots** (see below).

Repeated Measures: Profile Plots

Factors:
hand
task

Horizontal Axis:
hand

Separate Lines:
task

Separate Plots:

Plots: Add Change Remove

Continue Cancel Help

2. Select one factor to move into the **Horizontal Axis** box and one factor to move into the **Separate Lines** box.

3. Click on the **Add** button, which is now active, and the interaction graph you have requested will appear in the bottom box.

4. Click on the **Continue** button to return to the **Repeated Measures** dialogue box.

Click on ⟨ OK ⟩ to obtain the ANOVA output, shown below, with the interaction graph at the end of the output.

> The output for a within-subjects ANOVA is lengthier than that for a between-subjects ANOVA and we explain the purpose of some of the tables at the start of Section 4. If you have not read this already, now would be a good time to do so.

CHAPTER 8

SPSS output for two-way within-subjects ANOVA
Obtained using menu items: General Linear Model > Repeated Measures

General Linear Model

Within-Subjects Factors

Measure: MEASURE_1

hand	task	Dependent Variable
1	1	h1s1
	2	h1s2
2	1	h2s1
	2	h2s2

> This table is important when there are more than two levels of a within-subjects factor and when **Mauchly's Test of Sphericity** (see the next table) is significant. See guidance provided at the start of Section 4 on understanding the output of within-subjects ANOVAs.

Multivariate Tests[a]

Effect		Value	F	Hypothesis df	Error df	Sig.
hand	Pillai's Trace	.006	.133[b]	1.000	23.000	.719
	Wilks' Lambda	.994	.133[b]	1.000	23.000	.719
	Hotelling's Trace	.006	.133[b]	1.000	23.000	.719
	Roy's Largest Root	.006	.133[b]	1.000	23.000	.719
task	Pillai's Trace	.078	1.955[b]	1.000	23.000	.175
	Wilks' Lambda	.922	1.955[b]	1.000	23.000	.175
	Hotelling's Trace	.085	1.955[b]	1.000	23.000	.175
	Roy's Largest Root	.085	1.955[b]	1.000	23.000	.175
hand * task	Pillai's Trace	.173	4.807[b]	1.000	23.000	.039
	Wilks' Lambda	.827	4.807[b]	1.000	23.000	.039
	Hotelling's Trace	.209	4.807[b]	1.000	23.000	.039
	Roy's Largest Root	.209	4.807[b]	1.000	23.000	.039

a. Design: Intercept
   Within Subjects Design: hand + task + hand * task

b. Exact statistic

> This table is important when there are more than two levels; here, each of the within-subjects factors have only two levels.

Mauchly's Test of Sphericity[a]

Measure: MEASURE_1

Within Subjects Effect	Mauchly's W	Approx. Chi-Square	df	Sig.	Epsilon[b] Greenhouse-Geisser	Huynh-Feldt	Lower-bound
hand	1.000	.000	0	.	1.000	1.000	1.000
task	1.000	.000	0	.	1.000	1.000	1.000
hand * task	1.000	.000	0	.	1.000	1.000	1.000

Tests the null hypothesis that the error covariance matrix of the orthonormalized transformed dependent variables is proportional to an identity matrix.

a. Design: Intercept
   Within Subjects Design: hand + task + hand * task

b. May be used to adjust the degrees of freedom for the averaged tests of significance. Corrected tests are displayed in the Tests of Within-Subjects Effects table.

This row gives the values for the factor 'hand', the within-subjects factor with two levels (right and left).

This table shows the outcome of the analysis of variance. For information about the non-highlighted rows, see the start of Section 4.

Tests of Within-Subjects Effects

Measure: MEASURE_1

Source		Type III Sum of Squares	df	Mean Square	F	Sig.
hand	Sphericity Assumed	2.295	1	2.295	.133	.719
	Greenhouse-Geisser	2.295	1.000	2.295	.133	.719
	Huynh-Feldt	2.295	1.000	2.295	.133	.719
	Lower-bound	2.295	1.000	2.295	.133	.719
Error(hand)	Sphericity Assumed	398.267	23	17.316		
	Greenhouse-Geisser	398.267	23.000	17.316		
	Huynh-Feldt	398.267	23.000	17.316		
	Lower-bound	398.267	23.000	17.316		
task	Sphericity Assumed	70.906	1	70.906	1.955	.175
	Greenhouse-Geisser	70.906	1.000	70.906	1.955	.175
	Huynh-Feldt	70.906	1.000	70.906	1.955	.175
	Lower-bound	70.906	1.000	70.906	1.955	.175
Error(task)	Sphericity Assumed	834.213	23	36.270		
	Greenhouse-Geisser	834.213	23.000	36.270		
	Huynh-Feldt	834.213	23.000	36.270		
	Lower-bound	834.213	23.000	36.270		
hand * task	Sphericity Assumed	21.441	1	21.441	4.807	.039
	Greenhouse-Geisser	21.441	1.000	21.441	4.807	.039
	Huynh-Feldt	21.441	1.000	21.441	4.807	.039
	Lower-bound	21.441	1.000	21.441	4.807	.039
Error(hand*task)	Sphericity Assumed	102.585	23	4.460		
	Greenhouse-Geisser	102.585	23.000	4.460		
	Huynh-Feldt	102.585	23.000	4.460		
	Lower-bound	102.585	23.000	4.460		

This row gives the values for the factor 'task', the within-subjects factor with two levels (memorising the word or memorising its position).

This row gives the values for the interaction between the factor 'hand' and the factor 'task'.

You also need the degrees of freedom for the error associated with each main effect or interaction. In this example, the error df is the same for all three. This is not always the case.

CHAPTER 8

This table shows the outcome of trend tests. Each factor only has two levels, and so:
1. Only linear tests can be carried out, and not quadratic.
2. The values are simply those for the analysis of variance.
If, however, you have at least one factor with three or more levels, this table would be useful, as shown in the one-way within-subjects ANOVA example. The trend test is the default contrast carried out and in Section 4 we show you how to select alternative contrasts.

Tests of Within-Subjects Contrasts

Measure: MEASURE_1

Source	hand	task	Type III Sum of Squares	df	Mean Square	F	Sig.
hand	Linear		2.295	1	2.295	.133	.719
Error(hand)	Linear		398.267	23	17.316		
task		Linear	70.906	1	70.906	1.955	.175
Error(task)		Linear	834.213	23	36.270		
hand * task	Linear	Linear	21.441	1	21.441	4.807	.039
Error(hand*task)	Linear	Linear	102.585	23	4.460		

Tests of Between-Subjects Effects

Measure: MEASURE_1
Transformed Variable: Average

Source	Type III Sum of Squares	df	Mean Square	F	Sig.
Intercept	2544.862	1	2544.862	33.553	.000
Error	1744.438	23	75.845		

You can ignore this table; see guidance provided at start of Section 4.

These three tables give the descriptives requested in the **Repeated Measures: Options** dialogue box: 'hand', 'task', and 'hand*task' were moved into the box labelled **Display Means for**.

Estimated Marginal Means

1. hand

Measure: MEASURE_1

hand	Mean	Std. Error	95% Confidence Interval	
			Lower Bound	Upper Bound
1	4.994	1.017	2.890	7.098
2	5.303	.952	3.334	7.273

This table shows descriptives for each level of the factor 'hand', collapsed across the other factor 'task'. We used the code 1 = right and 2 = left, so the first row is for the right hand, and the second row is for the left hand.

2. task

Measure: MEASURE_1

task	Mean	Std. Error	95% Confidence Interval	
			Lower Bound	Upper Bound
1	6.008	1.137	3.655	8.361
2	4.289	1.021	2.178	6.401

This table shows descriptives for each level of the factor 'task' collapsed across the two levels of the factor 'hand'.

3. hand * task

Measure: MEASURE_1

hand	task	Mean	Std. Error	95% Confidence Interval	
				Lower Bound	Upper Bound
1	1	6.326	1.352	3.530	9.123
	2	3.662	.967	1.662	5.662
2	1	5.690	1.122	3.369	8.011
	2	4.916	1.248	2.334	7.499

This table shows descriptives for each of the conditions of the study. Thus, the first row gives details of performance when participants were tapping with their right hand while memorising words. The bottom row gives details of performance when participants were tapping with their left hand while memorising the positions of the words.

The interaction graph shown below was obtained by clicking on the **Plots** button at the bottom of the **Repeated Measures** dialogue box.
The labels and title are not helpful, so double-click on the graph in the SPSS output to go into the **Chart Editor** dialogue box. Double-click on the labels and title to change them.

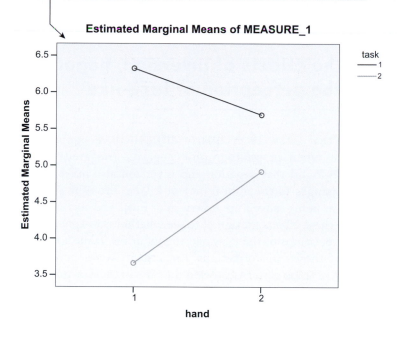

Reporting the results

In a report you might write:

A two-way within-subjects ANOVA was conducted on decrement of finger tapping speed. The main effect of tapping hand was not significant: $F(1,23) = 0.13$, $p = .719$. The main effect of type of task was not significant: $F(1,23) = 1.96$, $p = .175$. There was a significant interaction between tapping hand and type of task: $F(1,23) = 4.81$, $p = .039$. This interaction is displayed in the graph above, which suggests that type of task has a different effect on right- and left-hand tapping.

You would also want to report in your results section a measure of effect size (see Section 1) and information regarding the confidence intervals for each condition.

Section 6: MIXED ANOVA

Here, we show you how to perform an ANOVA that involves between- and within-subjects factors in the same experiment. We shall do so by referring to a study employing a three-way mixed design.

Example study: the effects of inversion, negation and priming on the perception of face-like patterns

It has been demonstrated that faces are peculiarly difficult to recognise when inverted (upside-down) or when in photographic negative (negated). Kemp, McManus and Pigott (1990) found that negation and inversion also make it more difficult to detect minor changes to the appearance of a face, brought about by moving the features (the eyes being moved up, down, in or out). The current study is a further investigation of these effects, designed to see whether non-face patterns (three dots arranged in the positions of the eyes and the mouth to make a face-like pattern) are also affected by these transformations. Participants were shown three such patterns at a time. One of these patterns showed the dots in their original location. The participants were required to decide which of the other two patterns had been modified.

The design employed was a 2*2*2 mixed ANOVA design. The first factor was the within-subjects factor of negation, with two levels, operationalised by showing face-like dot patterns as normal images or in photographic negative. The second factor was the within-subjects factor of orientation, with two levels, operationalised by showing the face-like dot patterns upright or inverted. The third factor was the between-subjects factor of priming, where some participants were primed by being asked to perform this task on faces before taking part in the experiment whereas others were not.

The dependent variable was the percentage of correct judgements made by the participants. The hypothesis tested was that the effects of negation and inversion would only be apparent in the group that was primed.

For the purposes of this book, we have created a data file that will reproduce some of the findings of this study. In the data file, the columns holding the data for the combination of levels of the two within-subjects factors have been named using the numbering systems described in Section 5. (These data are available from he.palgrave.com/psychology/brace.)

How to do it

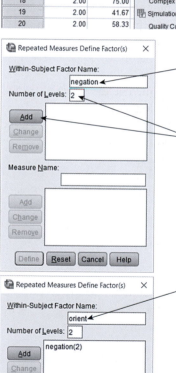

1. Click on the word **Analyze**.

2. Click on **General Linear Model.**

3. Click on **Repeated Measures**. The **Repeated Measures Define Factor(s)** dialogue box will appear (see below).

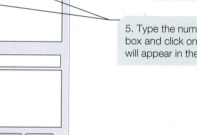

4. Change the factor name suggested by SPSS by highlighting **factor 1** and typing the word that represents the first within-subjects factor, 'negation'.

5. Type the number '2' in the **Number of Levels** box and click on the **Add** button, **negation(2)** will appear in the box next to **Add** (see below).

6. Repeat steps 4 and 5 for the second within-subjects factor, i.e. type in the name that represents the second factor 'orient' in the **Within-Subject Factor Name** box and type '2' in the **Number of Levels** box and click on the **Add** button.

7. Click the **Define** button, the **Repeated Measures** dialogue box will appear (see below).

If, when following Step 8, you put one of the levels in the wrong place, you can move it by highlighting it and then clicking on the up or down arrow as appropriate.

This key helps explain the numbers in the brackets below; 'negation' refers to the first number and 'orient' to the second number. This will help you enter the variables in the correct order into the **Within-Subjects Variables** box.

Repeated Measures   ✕

Within-Subjects Variables
(negation,orient):

↑ ↓

n1o1(1,1)
n1o2(1,2)
n2o1(2,1)
n2o2(2,2)

Model...
Contrasts...
Plots...
Post Hoc...
Save...
Options...

↩

Between-Subjects Factor(s):

↩   group

Covariates:

↪

OK   Paste   Reset   Cancel   Help

8. Select the levels of the within-subject factors in the correct order and enter these into the **Within-Subjects Variables** box. They were labelled in such a way to make the correct order obvious. 'n1o1' refers to the combination of the first level of the factor 'negation' (normal) with the first level of the face 'orient' (upright).

9. Select **group** and move it to the **Between-Subjects Factor(s)** box.

10. Click on the **Options** button to obtain descriptive statistics. The **Repeated Measures: Options** dialogue box will appear (see below).

Repeated Measures: Options   ✕

Estimated Marginal Means

Factor(s) and Factor Interactions:

(OVERALL)
group
negation
orient
group*negation
group*orient
negation*orient
group*negation*orient

↩

Display Means for:

group*negation
group*orient
negation*orient
group*negation*orient

☐ Compare main effects

Confidence interval adjustment

LSD(none)

11. Move the factors and interactions into **Display Means for** box.

12. Select **Homogeneity** tests.

Display

☐ Descriptive statistics   ☐ Transformation matrix
☐ Estimates of effect size   ☑ Homogeneity tests
☐ Observed power   ☐ Spread vs. level plot
☐ Parameter estimates   ☐ Residual plot
☐ SSCP matrices   ☐ Lack of fit
☐ Residual SSCP matrix   ☐ General estimable function

Significance level: .05   Confidence intervals are 95.0 %

Continue   Cancel   Help

If you want partial eta square, a measure of effect size, select **Estimates of effect size**.

13. Click on **Continue** button to return to **Repeated Measures** dialogue box.

Click on   OK . SPSS will calculate the ANOVA and produce the output that is explained below.

SPSS output for three-way mixed ANOVA
Obtained using menu items: General Linear Model > Repeated Measures

General Linear Model

Within-Subjects Factors

Measure:MEASURE_1

negation	orient	Dependent Variable
1	1	n1o1
	2	n1o2
2	1	n2o1
	2	n2o2

If you requested **Descriptive statistics** in the **Repeated Measures: Options** dialogue box, the Descriptive Statistics table would appear after these first two tables. Instead, we moved all factors and interactions into the box labelled **Display Means for** in the **Repeated Measures Options** dialogue box, which produces tables that appear at the end of the output.

Between-Subjects Factors

		Value Label	N
group	1.00	unprimed	38
	2.00	primed	23

Box's Test of Equality of Covariance Matrices[a]

Box's M	10.298
F	.947
df1	10
df2	10064.509
Sig.	.488

Tests the null hypothesis that the observed covariance matrices of the dependent variables are equal across groups.

a. Design: Intercept +
   group
   Within Subjects
   Design: negation +
   orient + negation *
   orient

This table appears because we selected **Homogeneity tests** in the **Repeated Measures Options** dialogue box. This is checking that for each level of the between-subjects factor, the pattern of correlations among the levels of the within-subjects factor are the same. Check that this is not significant.

Multivariate Tests[a]

Effect		Value	F	Hypothesis df	Error df	Sig.
negation	Pillai's Trace	.002	.137[b]	1.000	59.000	.713
	Wilks' Lambda	.998	.137[b]	1.000	59.000	.713
	Hotelling's Trace	.002	.137[b]	1.000	59.000	.713
	Roy's Largest Root	.002	.137[b]	1.000	59.000	.713
negation * group	Pillai's Trace	.006	.384[b]	1.000	59.000	.538
	Wilks' Lambda	.994	.384[b]	1.000	59.000	.538
	Hotelling's Trace	.007	.384[b]	1.000	59.000	.538
	Roy's Largest Root	.007	.384[b]	1.000	59.000	.538
orient	Pillai's Trace	.009	.539[b]	1.000	59.000	.466
	Wilks' Lambda	.991	.539[b]	1.000	59.000	.466
	Hotelling's Trace	.009	.539[b]	1.000	59.000	.466
	Roy's Largest Root	.009	.539[b]	1.000	59.000	.466
orient * group	Pillai's Trace	.038	2.319[b]	1.000	59.000	.133
	Wilks' Lambda	.962	2.319[b]	1.000	59.000	.133
	Hotelling's Trace	.039	2.319[b]	1.000	59.000	.133
	Roy's Largest Root	.039	2.319[b]	1.000	59.000	.133
negation * orient	Pillai's Trace	.048	3.006[b]	1.000	59.000	.088
	Wilks' Lambda	.952	3.006[b]	1.000	59.000	.088
	Hotelling's Trace	.051	3.006[b]	1.000	59.000	.088
	Roy's Largest Root	.051	3.006[b]	1.000	59.000	.088
negation * orient * group	Pillai's Trace	.051	3.185[b]	1.000	59.000	.079
	Wilks' Lambda	.949	3.185[b]	1.000	59.000	.079
	Hotelling's Trace	.054	3.185[b]	1.000	59.000	.079
	Roy's Largest Root	.054	3.185[b]	1.000	59.000	.079

a. Design: Intercept + group
   Within Subjects Design: negation + orient + negation * orient

b. Exact statistic

For information about these two tables, see the start of Section 4. The **Mauchly's Test of Sphericity** is important if there are more than two levels of either within-subjects factors. If this is not significant, the assumption of sphericity has not been violated.

Mauchly's Test of Sphericity[a]

Measure: MEASURE_1

Within Subjects Effect	Mauchly's W	Approx. Chi-Square	df	Sig.	Epsilon[b]		
					Greenhouse-Geisser	Huynh-Feldt	Lower-bound
negation	1.000	.000	0	.	1.000	1.000	1.000
orient	1.000	.000	0	.	1.000	1.000	1.000
negation * orient	1.000	.000	0	.	1.000	1.000	1.000

Tests the null hypothesis that the error covariance matrix of the orthonormalized transformed dependent variables is proportional to an identity matrix.

a. Design: Intercept + group
   Within Subjects Design: negation + orient + negation * orient

b. May be used to adjust the degrees of freedom for the averaged tests of significance. Corrected tests are displayed in the Tests of Within-Subjects Effects table.

This table shows the outcome of any part of the mixed ANOVA that incorporates a within-subjects factor. See the start of Section 4 for an explanation of the 2nd–4th rows of each cell.

Tests of Within-Subjects Effects

Measure: MEASURE_1

Source		Type III Sum of Squares	df	Mean Square	F
negation	Sphericity Assumed	9.470	1	9.470	.137
	Greenhouse-Geisser	9.470	1.000	9.470	.137
	Huynh-Feldt	9.470	1.000	9.470	.137
	Lower-bound	9.470	1.000	9.470	.137
negation * group	Sphericity Assumed	26.587	1	26.587	.384
	Greenhouse-Geisser	26.587	1.000	26.587	.384
	Huynh-Feldt	26.587	1.000	26.587	.384
	Lower-bound	26.587	1.000	26.587	.384
Error(negation)	Sphericity Assumed	4079.831	59	69.150	
	Greenhouse-Geisser	4079.831	59.000	69.150	
	Huynh-Feldt	4079.831	59.000	69.150	
	Lower-bound	4079.831	59.000	69.150	
orient	Sphericity Assumed	33.631	1	33.631	.539
	Greenhouse-Geisser	33.631	1.000	33.631	.539
	Huynh-Feldt	33.631	1.000	33.631	.539
	Lower-bound	33.631	1.000	33.631	.539
orient * group	Sphericity Assumed	144.622	1	144.622	2.319
	Greenhouse-Geisser	144.622	1.000	144.622	2.319
	Huynh-Feldt	144.622	1.000	144.622	2.319
	Lower-bound	144.622	1.000	144.622	2.319
Error(orient)	Sphericity Assumed	3678.712	59	62.351	
	Greenhouse-Geisser	3678.712	59.000	62.351	
	Huynh-Feldt	3678.712	59.000	62.351	
	Lower-bound	3678.712	59.000	62.351	
negation * orient	Sphericity Assumed	201.313	1	201.313	3.006
	Greenhouse-Geisser	201.313	1.000	201.313	3.006
	Huynh-Feldt	201.313	1.000	201.313	3.006
	Lower-bound	201.313	1.000	201.313	3.006
negation * orient * group	Sphericity Assumed	213.273	1	213.273	3.185
	Greenhouse-Geisser	213.273	1.000	213.273	3.185
	Huynh-Feldt	213.273	1.000	213.273	3.185
	Lower-bound	213.273	1.000	213.273	3.185
Error(negation*orient)	Sphericity Assumed	3950.946	59	66.965	
	Greenhouse-Geisser	3950.946	59.000	66.965	
	Huynh-Feldt	3950.946	59.000	66.965	
	Lower-bound	3950.946	59.000	66.965	

This table shows the outcome of trend tests. Each factor only has two levels, and so:
1. Only linear tests can be carried out, and not quadratic.
2. The values are simply those for the analysis of variance.
If, however, you have at least one factor with three or more levels, this table would be useful, as shown in the one-way within-subjects ANOVA example. The trend test is the default contrast carried out and in Sections 2 and 4 we show you how to select alternative contrasts.

Tests of Within-Subjects Contrasts

Measure: MEASURE_1

Source	negation	orient	Type III Sum of Squares	df	Mean Square	F	Sig.
negation	Linear		9.470	1	9.470	.137	.713
negation * group	Linear		26.587	1	26.587	.384	.538
Error(negation)	Linear		4079.831	59	69.150		
orient		Linear	33.631	1	33.631	.539	.466
orient * group		Linear	144.622	1	144.622	2.319	.133
Error(orient)		Linear	3678.712	59	62.351		
negation * orient	Linear	Linear	201.313	1	201.313	3.006	.088
negation * orient * group	Linear	Linear	213.273	1	213.273	3.185	.079
Error(negation*orient)	Linear	Linear	3950.946	59	66.965		

Levene's Test of Equality of Error Variances[a]

	F	df1	df2	Sig.
normal upright	.932	1	59	.338
normal inverted	.146	1	59	.704
negative upright	1.422	1	59	.238
negative inverted	2.472	1	59	.121

Tests the null hypothesis that the error variance of the dependent variable is equal across groups.

a. Design: Intercept + group
   Within Subjects Design: negation + orient + negation * orient

This table appears because we selected **Homogeneity tests** in the **Repeated Measures Options** dialogue box. If not significant for all levels of the within-subjects factors, the assumption of homogeneity has not been violated. If any were significant, this has implications for the accuracy of F for the between-subjects factor.

This last table shows the outcome of any part of the mixed ANOVA that incorporates only between-subjects factor(s). In our example, there was only one between-subjects factor: priming group, which is called 'group', and the results for this are shown in the highlighted parts.

Tests of Between-Subjects Effects

Measure: MEASURE_1

Transformed Variable: Average

Source	Type III Sum of Squares	df	Mean Square	F	Sig.
Intercept	990995.857	1	990995.857	5833.883	.000
group	193.383	1	193.383	1.138	.290
Error	10022.271	59	169.869		

Estimated Marginal Means

1. group

Measure: MEASURE_1

group	Mean	Std. Error	95% Confidence Interval	
			Lower Bound	Upper Bound
unprimed	64.830	1.057	62.715	66.945
primed	66.667	1.359	63.948	69.386

2. negation

Measure: MEASURE_1

negation	Mean	Std. Error	95% Confidence Interval	
			Lower Bound	Upper Bound
1	65.545	1.119	63.305	67.785
2	65.952	.912	64.126	67.777

3. orient

Measure: MEASURE_1

orient	Mean	Std. Error	95% Confidence Interval	
			Lower Bound	Upper Bound
1	66.131	.958	64.215	68.048
2	65.365	1.053	63.258	67.473

4. group * negation

Measure: MEASURE_1

group	negation	Mean	Std. Error	95% Confidence Interval	
				Lower Bound	Upper Bound
unprimed	1	64.967	1.375	62.217	67.718
	2	64.693	1.120	62.451	66.934
primed	1	66.123	1.767	62.587	69.659
	2	67.211	1.440	64.329	70.092

5. group * orient

Measure: MEASURE_1

group	orient	Mean	Std. Error	95% Confidence Interval	
				Lower Bound	Upper Bound
unprimed	1	64.419	1.176	62.065	66.772
	2	65.241	1.293	62.653	67.829
primed	1	67.844	1.512	64.819	70.869
	2	65.490	1.662	62.163	68.816

6. negation * orient

Measure: MEASURE_1

negation	orient	Mean	Std. Error	95% Confidence Interval	
				Lower Bound	Upper Bound
1	1	64.991	1.187	62.616	67.366
	2	66.099	1.508	63.081	69.118
2	1	67.272	1.203	64.864	69.679
	2	64.632	1.138	62.354	66.909

7. group * negation * orient

Measure: MEASURE_1

group	negation	orient	Mean	Std. Error	95% Confidence Interval	
					Lower Bound	Upper Bound
unprimed	1	1	64.583	1.458	61.667	67.500
		2	65.351	1.852	61.644	69.058
	2	1	64.254	1.477	61.297	67.210
		2	65.131	1.398	62.334	67.928
primed	1	1	65.399	1.874	61.650	69.148
		2	66.847	2.381	62.083	71.612
	2	1	70.290	1.899	66.489	74.090
		2	64.132	1.797	60.536	67.727

These tables appear because we moved all factors and interactions into the box labelled **Display Means for** in the **Repeated Measures Options** dialogue box.

The descriptives in the first three tables are for each level of each factor: 'group', 'negation' and 'orient'.

The next three tables show descriptives for each level of each two-way interaction, i.e. for each combination of levels of two of the factors (ignoring the third factor).

The final table provides descriptives for each level of the three-way interaction and hence for each of the eight conditions.

Should any main effect or interaction be significant, you would look here at the relevant table to interpret the results.

CHAPTER 8

Reporting the results
In a report you might write:

A three-way mixed ANOVA was performed on the percentage of correct judge-ments made by participants to non-face patterns. The main effect of the within-subjects factor negation was not significant: $F(1,59) = 0.14$, $p = .713$. The main effect of the within-subjects factor orientation was also not significant: $F(1,59) = 0.54$, $p = .466$, nor was the main effect of the between-subjects fac-tor priming group: $F(1,59) = 1.14$, $p = .290$. The priming group by negation interaction was not significant: $F(1,59) = 0.39$, $p = .538$, nor were the other two-way interactions: priming group by orientation: $F(1,59) = 2.32$, $p = .133$, and negation by orientation: $F(1,59 = 3.01$, $p = .088$. Finally, the three-way interaction between negation, orientation and priming group was also not sig-nificant: $F(1,59) = 3.19$, $p = .079$.

 You would also want to report in your results section a measure of effect size (see Section 1) and information regarding the confidence intervals for each condition. If your factors have more than two levels and you want to follow up significant results with planned or unplanned comparisons, then see Sections 2 and 4 for guidance on how to perform these.

Summary

- This chapter introduced you to one-way and multi-way ANOVA, planned and unplanned comparisons, and nonparametric equivalents of the one-way ANOVA.

- These tests of differences are used for experimental designs involving more than two groups or conditions, or for more than one IV.

- Appropriate descriptive statistics, the mean and standard deviation, can be obtained either by following the advice in Chapter 3 or by selecting the appropri-ate options on the ANOVA Options dialogue box.

- Error bar charts and interaction graphs are often used to display the statistically significant findings.

- If your dependent variable is a total score from several raw scores, which have already been entered into your data file, then see Chapter 4 for guidance on how to create such a total score in SPSS.

- For guidance on incorporating SPSS output into a report, or on printing the output, see Chapter 13.

9 Multiple regression

SPSS for Psychologists online
Visit he.palgrave.com/psychology/brace for data sets, online tutorials and exercises.

Section 1: AN INTRODUCTION TO MULTIPLE REGRESSION

- Regression was first introduced in Chapter 6, Sections 6 and 7, and we advise you to reread those sections before starting this chapter.

- Bivariate regression, also covered in Chapter 6, involves one dependent variable, which we term the *criterion variable*, and only one independent variable, which we refer to as the *predictor variable*.

- Multiple regression involves a criterion variable and two or more predictor variables.

- The predictor variables can be measured using a range of scales (although ideally at interval or ratio level), but the criterion variable should be measured using a ratio or interval scale.

- Although it is not possible to produce totally accurate predictions, multiple regression allows us to identify which set of the predictor variables together provides the best prediction of the score on the criterion variable.

- As with bivariate correlation and regression, multiple regression does not imply causal relationships unless variables have been manipulated.

- As we stated in Chapter 6, Section 7, regression can be used as a model to explain and simplify data we have measured, in a way that allows prediction of future cases.

From bivariate to multiple

Bivariate correlation measures the strength of association between two variables, and bivariate regression allows one variable to be predicted by one other variable. We can extend this. Multiple correlation measures the strength of association between one variable and a set of other variables, and multiple regression allows prediction of one variable (the criterion variable) from the set of other variables (the predictor variables). In practice, the term *multiple regression* usually includes multiple correlation.

In multiple regression, the criterion variable is still represented by Y, and the predictor variables by X. Now that there are two or more predictors, we use subscripts to identify them: X_1, X_2, X_3, etc., up to X_k, where k = number of predictors.

Having more than one predictor variable is useful when predicting human behaviour, as our actions, thoughts and emotions are all likely to be influenced by some combination of several variables. The advantage of applying multiple regression instead of several bivariate correlations (between the criterion variable and each of the predictor variables) is that multiple regression corrects for the correlations among the predictor variables. The bivariate correlation between a particular variable (X_1) and the criterion variable may be partly, or only, due to the correlation between X_1 and another predictor variable (X_2) (see ice cream and temperature example in Chapter 6, Section 1). Using multiple regression we can test theories (or models) about precisely which set of variables allows us to predict behaviour. There are a few different methods for conducting multiple regression, which can be used to apply different models. We will discuss these methods below.

An excellent text is that by Miles and Shevlin (2001).

An example

Consider our example in Chapter 6, Section 6, of predicting how confident in using IBM SPSS Statistics software (SPSS) students are after completing a module (we shall refer to this as 'SPSS confidence'). For bivariate regression, we suggested that time spent practising could be a predictor. Other variables can also be considered; attendance at lectures, attendance at practical sessions, time spent reading SPSS books, anxiety about using computers before the module, and total study time might all contribute towards SPSS confidence. We can propose a model that suggests that this set of predictor variables will predict SPSS confidence. Next, we collect data, perhaps by surveying a module with 200 or 300 students, in order to test the model in terms of how many and which variables give rise to the most accurate prediction of SPSS confidence. We might find that SPSS confidence is most accurately predicted by time spent practising, attendance at practical sessions, time spent reading SPSS books, and computer anxiety before the module, with the other variables we measured not helping us to predict SPSS confidence. Note that we would predict a positive effect for most of those variables, but a negative effect for computer anxiety before the module.

How does multiple regression relate to analysis of variance?

What we are doing in both ANOVA and multiple regression is seeking to account for the variance in the scores we observe. Thus, in the example above, people might vary greatly in their levels of SPSS confidence. Some of this variance will be accounted for by the variables we have identified. For example, we might be able to say that time spent practising accounts for a fairly large percentage of the variance in SPSS confidence; hence, it is useful to know how much time a student spends practising when trying to predict their SPSS confidence. The concepts are rather similar to those underlying ANOVA. In ANOVA, we determine how much of the variance is accounted for by the IVs (relative to the percentage of the variance we cannot account for). In multiple regression, we are not restricted to a few levels of the IVs; instead we measure the variables and test how well they predict the score on the dependent variable (or criterion variable). Thus, ANOVA is actually a rather specific and restricted example of the general approach adopted in multiple regression.

Another way in which ANOVA is more restricted than multiple regression relates to whether the predictors/IVs are *orthogonal* or not. Two variables are orthogonal if the relationship between them is zero. ANOVA designs are orthogonal if IVs 'are completely crossed with equal sample sizes in each combination of levels' (Tabachnick and Fidell, 2014, 40). If combined with good experimental control and design, this has the great advantage of allowing clear causal statements about effects on the DV. It cannot, however, be achieved with many variables of interest in psychology. Multiple regression allows for the common, *non-orthogonal*, situation, in which predictors/IVs are correlated with each other. We return to this issue below, when discussing the various multiple regression methods.

The similarities between multiple regression and ANOVA (and also between bivariate correlation and the *t*-test) are because these statistical techniques are basically seeking to do the same thing – estimate how much of the variance in one variable is explained by one or more other variables. These other variables might be manipulated directly in the case of controlled experiments (allowing causal relationships to be tested), or be naturally occurring in non-experimental studies, but the underlying principle is the same. Each of these procedures is usually treated separately but they are fundamentally all the same procedure. This underlying single approach is called the General Linear Model, a term we first introduced when undertaking ANOVA in Chapter 8, Section 1.

Causation

Whether we can draw conclusions about cause-and-effect relationships depends on whether variables were manipulated or simply measured, and whether there was random allocation of participants to conditions. In ANOVA, we often directly manipulate the factors, meaning that random allocation is possible, and then we measure the resulting change in the dependent variable. Sometimes, however, the levels of the factors are chosen from existing groups (such as educated to degree level or not), and so random allocation is not feasible and causal relationships cannot be assumed. In multiple regression, we normally measure the naturally occurring scores on a number of predictor variables and try to establish which set of the observed variables gives rise to the best prediction of the criterion variable. In such studies, a significant outcome does not imply causation. If one can, however, manipulate a predictor variable used in a multiple regression, then conclusions about causation could be drawn (provided all the normal controls for experimental research are applied). Alternatively, if no variable is manipulated, then one could argue for causal relationships and perhaps design future studies that would test those hypotheses.

When should I use multiple regression?

1. You can use this statistical technique when exploring linear (straight line) relationships between the predictor and criterion variables. If any relationship is nonlinear, transforming one or more variables may be required. If a relationship remains nonlinear, other techniques may be possible. Nonlinear relationships include U-shaped and inverted U-shaped relationships (mentioned in Chapter 6, Section 1, and Chapter 8.)

2. The criterion variable should be measured on a scale at either interval or ratio level. There are separate statistical procedures for predicting values on a criterion variable that is nominal (see Chapter 11).

3. The predictor variables you select should be measured on a ratio, interval or ordinal scale. A nominal predictor variable is legitimate, but only if it is dichotomous (see Chapter 7, Section 1). For example, if we are interested in whether people live in a city or not, then that variable has two values and is acceptable. If, however, we classify their environment as city, town or village, then that could not be entered into multiple regression as a single variable. Instead, you would create three different variables, each with two categories (city/not city; town/not town and village/not village). The term 'dummy variable' is used to describe this type of dichotomous variable.

4. Multiple regression requires a large number of observations. The estimate of R (the multiple correlation, see below) depends on the number of predictor variables and the number of participants (N). One rule of thumb is to have at least ten times as many participants as predictor variables. Tabachnick and Fidell (2014) suggest that, to test both overall correlation and the effect of individual predictors, N should equal the greater of the following: either the number of predictors times 8, plus 50; or the number of predictors plus 104. Of course, you could instead calculate N for the power you require.

5. You should screen your data for outliers, normality, and homoscedasticity of residuals. (See Tabachnick and Fidell (2014) for guidelines.) SPSS provides you with a means of checking residuals, which we describe below. Note that we show you how to check for homoscedasticity but check your statistics book for an explanation of it.

6. You should check for multicollinearity. When choosing a predictor variable, you should select one that might be correlated with the criterion variable, but that is

not strongly correlated with the other predictor variables. Non-orthogonality, with correlations among the predictor variables, is not unusual. The term 'multi-collinearity' (or collinearity) is used to describe the situation when a high correlation is detected between two or more predictor variables. Such high correlations cause problems when trying to draw inferences about the relative contribution of each predictor variable to the success of the model. SPSS provides you with means of checking for collinearity, which we describe below.

The multiple regression equation

This equation allows us to predict the criterion variable Y from the set of predictor variables X_1, X_2, X_3, X_4, etc. It is an extension of the bivariate regression equation:

$$Y' = A + B_1 X_1 + B_2 X_2 + B_3 X_3 + ... + B_k X_k$$

where:

- Y' is again the predicted value of the criterion variable.

- A is the Y intercept for multiple regression, the value predicted for Y when all Xs equal 0.

- B is the regression weight, or regression coefficient, for each predictor variable; as with b in the bivariate equation, a B indicates how much Y' will change if that X changes by one unit. We return to regression coefficients below.

- k is the number of predictors, so the equation above is the general form.

   When solving the equation, values of A and B are set that achieve:

1. The least squares criterion; as with bivariate regression, this means that $\Sigma(Y-Y')^2$ is at a minimum.

2. The correlation of Y with Y' is maximised; the multiple correlation, R, is the Pearson's correlation coefficient for Y with Y'. This is explained further below.

Regression coefficients: *B* (unstandardised) and beta (standardised)

Regression coefficients (or regression weights) are measures of how strongly each predictor variable influences the criterion variable, if all the other predictor variables were held constant. B indicates the change in the measured units of the criterion variable for a change in one unit in the predictor variable (if all other predictors are held constant). With two or more predictors, we will be interested in which of them has most effect on the criterion variable; that is, which is the strongest predictor. As B is *unstandardised* (measured in the original units of its X), it can be difficult to interpret. For example, the effect on Y' from a change of one unit in 'course anxiety' cannot be directly compared with the effect of a change of one unit in 'time spent practising'. In addition, the variability of each variable will differ and this will also affect the coefficients. A useful alternative is beta (β), the *standardised* regression coefficient, which is measured in units of standard deviation allowing us to more easily compare the influence of several predictors. For example, if $\beta = 2.5$ for one of the predictor variables, a change of one standard deviation in that variable will result in a change of 2.5 standard deviations in the criterion variable. Thus, a higher β value for one predictor variable indicates a greater impact of that predictor variable on the criterion variable; the β values for the different predictor variables are directly comparable.

A regression coefficient is either negative or positive, indicating whether an increase in the predictor will result in a decrease or increase in the criterion variable.

With only one predictor variable in the model, β is equivalent to the correlation coefficient between the predictor and the criterion variable. This equivalence makes sense, as this situation is a correlation between two variables. When you have more than one predictor variable, however, you cannot compare the contribution of each predictor variable by simply comparing the bivariate correlation coefficients. Each bivariate relationship may be affected by one or more of the other predictor variables. Multiple regression takes account of all the relationships, and β allows you to compare the strength of the relationships between predictor variables and the criterion variable.

The significance of each predictor in explaining the variance in the criterion variable is assessed using t, and we will highlight this in the annotated output in Section 2.

R, R-squared and adjusted R-squared

R is a measure of the correlation between the observed values of the criterion variable and its predicted values. In our example, this would be the correlation between the observed SPSS confidence score (reported by participants) and the SPSS confidence score predicted for them from the predictor variables. Unlike r or r_s for bivariate correlation, R can only take positive values even if all the individual correlations or βs are negative; this is because R is *not* the relationship between the criterion variable and predictor variables – instead R is the relationship between the observed and the predicted scores for the criterion variable.

R-squared (R^2) indicates the proportion of the variance in the criterion variable that is accounted for by the model; in our example, the proportion of the variance in the SPSS confidence accounted for by the set of predictor variables (time spent practising etc.). In essence, this is a measure of how well we can predict the criterion variable by knowing the predictor variables.

However, R and R^2 tend to somewhat overestimate the success of the model. One reason for this is that R, unlike r, can never be negative (because it is the correlation of Y and Y'), and as all chance variations will be positive, they tend to increase R. Such random chance variations are greater in small samples. Thus, an adjusted R^2 value is calculated, which takes into account the number of predictor variables in the model and the number of observations (participants) that the model is based on. This adjusted R^2 value gives the most useful measure of the success of the model. If, for example, we have an adjusted R^2 value of .75, we can say that our model has accounted for 75% of the variance in the criterion variable. (This would be considered a large proportion of variance explained.) If there are few participants, then adjusted R^2 can be quite a bit smaller than R^2 (as chance variations are greater in small samples), and even negative. Note, though, that a negative value is an artefact, and the convention is to report a negative adjusted R^2 as 0.

Whether R^2 is significant or not is assessed using F, and we will highlight this in the annotated output in Section 2.

Regression methods

The relative contribution of each predictor variable to explaining the variance in Y can be assessed by different methods that give rise to different models. For each method, the success of the model/s in predicting the criterion variable is assessed. The methods vary in the following ways:

1. Shared variance is treated in different ways; shared variance is an issue in non-orthogonal situations in which predictors share variance with each other as well as with the criterion variable.

2. Predictors can be entered as a single block or separately.

3. When predictors are entered separately, the order in which they are entered into the regression equation can be specified in advance by selecting a specific method.

Unique and shared variance

Venn diagrams are commonly used in statistics textbooks to illustrate unique and shared variance:

- Figure 9.1(a) shows the situation in a bivariate correlation; the overlapping area represents the proportion of variance in Y explained by X; this is a simple situation, but adding even one more predictor often complicates the issue.

- Figure 9.1(b) illustrates a multiple correlation, in which each X explains some variance in Y, but does not share variance with the other. Thus, each X explains unique variance, and there will be no problem whichever regression method is used.

- Figure 9.1(c) illustrates a multiple correlation, in which each X explains some unique variance, but also shares some of the variance explained in Y with the other X. This is the non-orthogonal situation. See figure legend for further explanation.

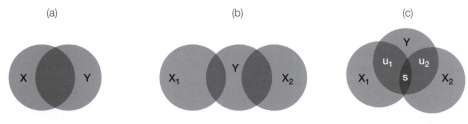

Figure 9.1 Venn diagrams

Notes: The overlapping areas illustrate:

(a) proportion of variance in Y explained by X in a bivariate correlation.
(b) proportion of variance in Y explained, in a multiple correlation, by each of two Xs, which are orthogonal with each other. All the explained variance is unique to either X_1 or X_2.
(c) proportion of variance in Y explained, in a multiple correlation, by each of two Xs, which are non-orthogonal; 'u' indicates the variance explained in Y that is unique to each X and 's' indicates the variance explained in Y that is shared by X_1 and X_2.

The way in which the different regression methods treat shared variance is explained next.

Simultaneous or standard method

In the simultaneous or standard method, the researcher specifies the set of predictor variables in the model, and they are all entered into the model at the same time. This method is performed in SPSS by selecting all the predictor variables in one single block and using the option **Enter**. Each predictor is assessed on the variance it explains that is additional to the variance explained by all the other predictors combined. It is probably the safest method to use if you have no theoretical rationale that certain predictor/s may be more important than others. It has the drawback, however, that when the regression coefficients are calculated, only unique variance is attributed to each predictor variable. Shared variance, indicated by 's' in Fig. 9.1(c), is not attributed to any predictor when the regression coefficients are calculated. Thus, a predictor that is, in fact, important may appear to account for only a small proportion of the variance because it shares a fair amount of variance with other predictors. All the variance explained in the criterion variable does, however, contribute to R and other statistics that summarise the whole model. So, the model as a whole may be quite strong even if some or all the predictor variables appear quite weak.

Sequential or hierarchical method

In the sequential or hierarchical method, the researcher enters predictor variables in a particular sequence determined by theoretical or empirical considerations. Thus, the researcher assigns a 'hierarchy' to the predictors, leading to its alternative name. If you have no rationale for an order of entry, then you should not use this method. Each predictor can be entered singly, or as part of a set of predictors, which means entering in several blocks. Note that SPSS calls each entry a 'block' whether it contains only one or more than one predictor. Each block specifies a different model, which is assessed for how well it predicts the criterion variable. First, let us consider single predictors. The first predictor to be entered is assigned all the variance that it explains in the criterion variable. Each subsequent predictor is only assigned its additional, unique variance. Any shared variance remains with predictors higher up the hierarchy. As each predictor is entered into the model, its contribution is assessed. If the predictive power of the model is not significantly increased over the previous model, then that predictor is dropped. The process moves on to the next predictor and so on until all have been considered. The models can then be compared.

Whether SPSS assigns shared variance as we have just outlined depends on which SPSS option you use when entering each predictor. Indeed, one option is to use **Enter** so that as each predictor is added, the set of predictors in each successive model is analysed using the standard method; as described previously, shared variance will not be attributed to any predictor. This is explained further in Section 3.

In addition to entering predictors singly, we can enter two or more predictors at the same stage. The variance assigned to each block should follow the same hierarchical principle outlined above for predictors entered one at a time, and again this will depend on the SPSS option that you use. Within a block, if it contains more than one predictor, the variance assigned to each of those predictors will follow the rules of the SPSS option that you choose for that block. That may be the **Enter** option (which follows the standard 'rules' explained above), but could be one of the statistical options we explain below. Using the **Forward** option seems to treat individually entered predictors in a way closest to the spirit of the sequential method, as it leaves shared variance with a predictor you entered earlier in the hierarchy. Alternatively, with the **Remove** option, you first **Enter** all the predictors and then **Remove** them from the model in blocks according to your rationale; the use of this option will not be further described here.

Statistical methods

There are several statistical regression methods, sometimes called 'stepwise' after the name of one of them. In all of them, the researcher specifies the set of predictor variables, but then the order in which they are entered into (or taken out of) the model is determined according to their strength and not according to any theoretical rationale. Thus, these methods are considered controversial (Tabachnick and Fidell, 2014, 174) and 'unwise regression' (see Howell, 2013, 540), although they may be useful in exploratory research. Guidance on validating results from these methods is given below. SPSS offers the following statistical options. The description here is for the situation when you include all the predictors in a single block:

1. In **Forward** selection, SPSS enters the predictors into the model one at a time in an order determined by the strength of their correlation with the criterion variable (the strongest is entered first). As each predictor is added, its effect is assessed, and if it does not significantly add to the success of the model, it is excluded.

2. In **Backward** selection, SPSS first enters all the predictors into the model. The weakest predictor (based on partial correlation with the criterion variable) is then removed and the regression recalculated. If the model was significantly weakened, then the predictor is re-entered – otherwise it is deleted. This procedure is repeated until only useful predictors remain in the model.

3. **Stepwise** is the most sophisticated of the statistical methods. SPSS enters the predictors into the model one at a time in an order determined by the strength of their correlation with the criterion variable, and the strength of the predictor in adding to the predictive power is assessed. If adding the predictor contributes to the model, it is retained. So far, this is like the **Forward** option, but then all other predictors in the model are retested for their contribution to the success of the model. Any predictor that no longer contributes significantly is removed. Thus, with this method, you end up with the smallest possible set of predictors included in your model.

Validating results from statistical regression methods

Statistical methods for multiple regression should be used with caution and only when you have a large number of cases. This is because minor variations in the data due to sampling error can have a large effect on the order in which variables are entered and therefore the likelihood of them being retained. If you decide to select a statistical method, then you should really validate your results with a second independent set of data. This can be done either by conducting a second study, or, if you have sufficient data, by first randomly splitting your data set into two halves. Use **Select Cases** with **Random sample of cases** method (see Chapter 4, Section 4) and set sample size at 50%. A variable called 'filter_$' will be added to your data file. To ensure that you run a separate analysis on each randomly selected half, proceed as follows:

1. Reset **Select Cases** to **All** cases.

2. Use **Select Cases** with **If condition is satisfied** method to select those cases for which filter_$ = 0, and run your analysis on the selected cases.

3. Use **Select Cases** with **If condition is satisfied** method to select those cases for which filter_$ = 1, and run your analysis on those cases. Only results that are common to both analyses should be reported.

Section 2: STANDARD OR SIMULTANEOUS METHOD OF MULTIPLE REGRESSION

Example study: state anxiety

Rosemary Snelgar and colleagues Alan Porter and Tina Cartwright were concerned about the fairly common phenomenon that students are anxious both about statistics and about tests, which might affect their performance on modules in which research methods and statistics are taught. We carried out a project (Snelgar, Porter and Cartwright, in preparation) and used structural equation modelling (a statistical procedure not covered in this book) to test an explanatory model of state anxiety (Hong and Karstensson, 2002). We used a subset of the data to illustrate three methods of conducting a multiple regression: standard, sequential and stepwise. We measured both trait and state anxiety for two components of anxiety. The worry component includes such things as concern about the consequences of doing badly in the statistics course. The emotionality component of anxiety includes physiological responses, such as feeling 'jittery'. We also measured or recorded other variables suggested to be related to statistics and test anxiety. Trait test worry ('tw'), trait test emotionality ('te'), perceived statistics course difficulty ('pcd'), and statistics course anxiety ('ca') were measured early in the module. Later, perceived test difficulty ('ptd') was measured just before a test, and state test worry ('sw') and state test emotionality ('se') were measured just after the test. Other variables included were whether or not students had psychology as one of their 'A' levels ('psycha') because students without this often assume that they will struggle, age and gender. State test emotionality is the criterion variable. These data are available from he.palgrave.com/psychology/brace.

We first checked whether data were skewed; age was positively skewed, as would be expected with a student population; 'ca' just failed the skewness test (see Tabachnick and Fidell, 2014, 113); other variables were not skewed. We also obtained correlation coefficients between state test emotionality and the other variables. The relationships of 'se' with gender, age, maths experience, and perceived statistics course difficulty were all low and not significant; for our current purpose, these variables were omitted from the multiple regression.

How to perform multiple regression using the standard method

The standard method should also be used to check assumptions about residuals and collinearity. Normally, you would inspect that output first and decide whether you can continue or need to rethink. We describe the relevant output where it appears in the whole output.

Click on **Analyze⇒Regression⇒Linear**. You will be presented with the **Linear Regression** dialogue box (shown below). You now select the criterion variable, state test emotionality ('se'), and the predictor variables, Psychology 'A' level ('psycha'), trait test worry ('tw'), trait test emotionality ('te'), statistics course anxiety ('ca'), perceived test difficulty ('ptd') and state test worry ('sw'). Note that 'psycha' is a nominal variable, but is dichotomous (completed or not completed) and so it is a suitable predictor for multiple regression.

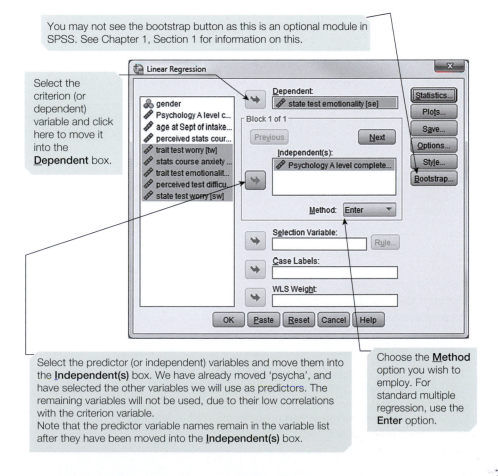

You may not see the bootstrap button as this is an optional module in SPSS. See Chapter 1, Section 1 for information on this.

Select the criterion (or dependent) variable and click here to move it into the **Dependent** box.

Select the predictor (or independent) variables and move them into the **Independent(s)** box. We have already moved 'psycha', and have selected the other variables we will use as predictors. The remaining variables will not be used, due to their low correlations with the criterion variable.
Note that the predictor variable names remain in the variable list after they have been moved into the **Independent(s)** box.

Choose the **Method** option you wish to employ. For standard multiple regression, use the **Enter** option.

CHAPTER 9

Now click on the ⬚Statistics⬚ button for the **Linear Regression: Statistics** dialogue box (shown below).

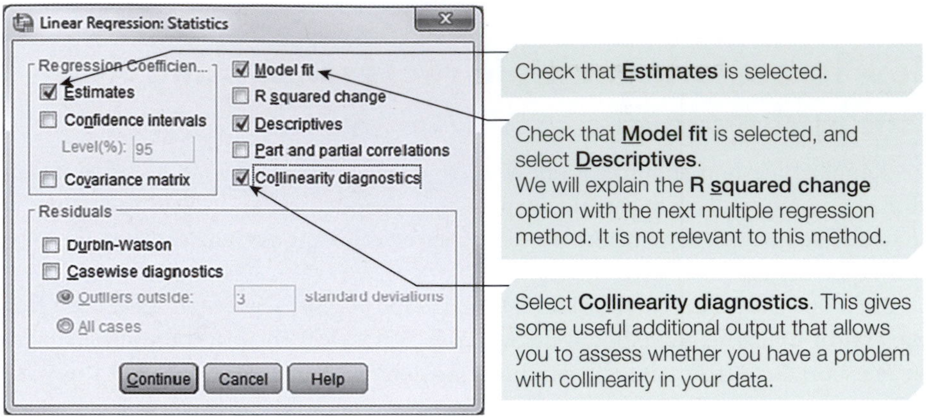

Linear Regression: Statistics

Regression Coefficien...
- ☑ Estimates
- ☐ Confidence intervals
  - Level(%): 95
- ☐ Covariance matrix

- ☑ Model fit
- ☐ R squared change
- ☑ Descriptives
- ☐ Part and partial correlations
- ☑ Collinearity diagnostics

Residuals
- ☐ Durbin-Watson
- ☐ Casewise diagnostics
  - ◉ Outliers outside: 3 standard deviations
  - ◉ All cases

Continue   Cancel   Help

Check that **Estimates** is selected.

Check that **Model fit** is selected, and select **Descriptives**.
We will explain the **R squared change** option with the next multiple regression method. It is not relevant to this method.

Select **Collinearity diagnostics**. This gives some useful additional output that allows you to assess whether you have a problem with collinearity in your data.

When you have selected the statistics options you require, click on the **Continue** button. This will return you to the **Linear Regression** dialogue box.

Now click on the **Plots** button, for the **Linear Regression: Plots** dialogue box to select useful graphs for checking residuals.

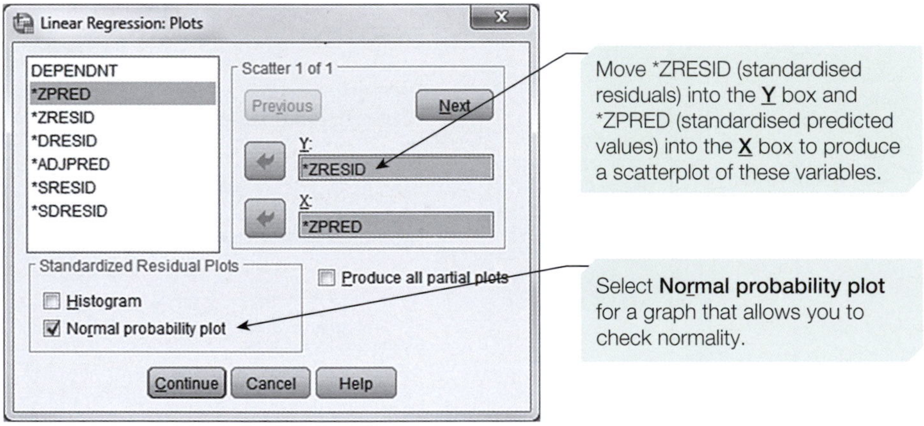

Linear Regression: Plots

DEPENDNT
*ZPRED
*ZRESID
*DRESID
*ADJPRED
*SRESID
*SDRESID

Scatter 1 of 1
Previous   Next
Y: *ZRESID
X: *ZPRED

Standardized Residual Plots
- ☐ Histogram
- ☑ Normal probability plot

☐ Produce all partial plots

Continue   Cancel   Help

Move *ZRESID (standardised residuals) into the **Y** box and *ZPRED (standardised predicted values) into the **X** box to produce a scatterplot of these variables.

Select **Normal probability plot** for a graph that allows you to check normality.

Click on the **Continue** button, and then on the ⬚OK⬚ button. The output that will be produced is illustrated below.

The SPSS multiple regression default (under Options button) is to **Exclude cases listwise**. Unless you change this, SPSS will only analyse data from participants who have no missing values. The alternatives are pairwise or replace with the mean, but the latter should be used with caution. This data set has complete data for all participants.

SPSS output for standard multiple regression

Obtained using menu items: Regression > Linear (method = enter)

Descriptive Statistics

	Mean	Std. Deviation	N
state test emotionality	2.5556	1.03775	90
Psychology A level completed	1.5333	.50168	90
trait test worry	2.3139	.78572	90
stats course anxiety	2.1889	.63744	90
trait test emotionality	2.5722	.87510	90
perceived test difficulty	2.8611	.71118	90
state test worry	2.7639	.75174	90

This first table is produced by the **Descriptives** option, and is useful for reporting your results.

Remember that for any nominal variables ('psycha' here), you should not report mean and SD, but counts instead.

This second table gives details of the correlation between each pair of variables. We do not want strong correlations between the predictor variables. The values here are acceptable.

Correlations

		state test emotionality	Psychology A level completed	trait test worry	stats course anxiety	trait test emotionality	perceived test difficulty	state test worry
Pearson Correlation	state test emotionality	1.000	.212	.493	.500	.609	.562	.705
	Psychology A level completed	.212	1.000	.148	.173	.218	.155	.129
	trait test worry	.493	.148	1.000	.504	.644	.201	.403
	stats course anxiety	.500	.173	.504	1.000	.532	.387	.406
	trait test emotionality	.609	.218	.644	.532	1.000	.267	.346
	perceived test difficulty	.562	.155	.201	.387	.267	1.000	.529
	state test worry	.705	.129	.403	.406	.346	.529	1.000
Sig. (1-tailed)	state test emotionality	.	.022	.000	.000	.000	.000	.000
	Psychology A level completed	.022	.	.082	.051	.019	.073	.113
	trait test worry	.000	.082	.	.000	.000	.029	.000
	stats course anxiety	.000	.051	.000	.	.000	.000	.000
	trait test emotionality	.000	.019	.000	.000	.	.006	.000
	perceived test difficulty	.000	.073	.029	.000	.006	.	.000
	state test worry	.000	.113	.000	.000	.000	.000	.
N	state test emotionality	90	90	90	90	90	90	90
	Psychology A level completed	90	90	90	90	90	90	90
	trait test worry	90	90	90	90	90	90	90
	stats course anxiety	90	90	90	90	90	90	90
	trait test emotionality	90	90	90	90	90	90	90
	perceived test difficulty	90	90	90	90	90	90	90
	state test worry	90	90	90	90	90	90	90

Variables Entered/Removed[a]

Model	Variables Entered	Variables Removed	Method
1	state test worry, Psychology A level completed, trait test emotionality, perceived test difficulty, stats course anxiety, trait test worry[b]		Enter

a. Dependent Variable: state test emotionality

b. All requested variables entered.

This third table tells us about the predictor variables and the method used. Here we can see that all our predictor variables were entered simultaneously; that is because we used the **Enter** option.

This table and the next are important. R^2 indicates the overall explanatory power of the model. The Adjusted R Square value tells us that our model accounts for 66.0% of variance in the 'se' scores.

Model Summary[b]

Model	R	R Square	Adjusted R Square	Std. Error of the Estimate
1	.827[a]	.683	.660	.60492

a. Predictors: (Constant), state test worry, Psychology A level completed, trait test emotionality, perceived test difficulty, stats course anxiety, trait test worry

b. Dependent Variable: state test emotionality

This table reports an ANOVA that assesses significance of R^2. The first df is the number of predictors (m); the residual df is N-m-1 (here 90-6-1). As $p < .001$, the model is significant.

ANOVA[a]

Model		Sum of Squares	df	Mean Square	F	Sig.
1	Regression	65.475	6	10.913	29.822	.000[b]
	Residual	30.372	83	.366		
	Total	95.847	89			

a. Dependent Variable: state test emotionality

b. Predictors: (Constant), state test worry, Psychology A level completed, trait test emotionality, perceived test difficulty, stats course anxiety, trait test worry

B (the unstandardised coefficient) for each predictor variable shows the predicted increase in the value of the criterion variable for a 1 unit increase in that predictor (while controlling for the other predictors). The next column gives the standard error of B.

Coefficients[a]

Model		Unstandardized Coefficients		Standardized Coefficients		
		B	Std. Error	Beta	t	Sig.
1	(Constant)	-1.394	.344		-4.050	.000
	Psychology A level completed	.073	.132	.035	.553	.582
	trait test worry	.021	.113	.016	.190	.850
	stats course anxiety	.049	.129	.030	.381	.704
	trait test emotionality	.433	.102	.365	4.239	.000
	perceived test difficulty	.304	.110	.208	2.757	.007
	state test worry	.614	.108	.445	5.671	.000

a. Dependent Variable: state test emotionality

The standardised coefficient, Beta (β), gives a measure of the contribution of the variable to the model in terms of standard deviations. β is the predicted change in SD of the criterion variable, for a change of 1 SD in the predictor (while controlling for the other predictors). Thus, if trait test emotionality increased by 1 SD, we can predict that state test emotionality would increase by .37 SD; and if state test worry increased by 1SD, we can predict that state test emotionality would increase by .45 SD.

The t-test values indicate whether the predictor's regression coefficient is significant. For the standard method, however, it only tests the unique variance explained by the predictor. Thus, a predictor that is correlated with the criterion variable but shares variance explained with another predictor may have a non-significant β.

If you request **Collinearity diagnostics** (in the **Linear Regression: Statistics** dialogue box), two additional columns appear on the right of the Coefficients table. These extra columns are usually sufficient to check whether your data meet this assumption.

The tolerance values are a measure of the correlation between the predictor variables and can vary between 0 and 1. The closer to zero the tolerance value is for a variable, the stronger the relationship between this and the other predictor variables. You should worry about variables that have a very low tolerance. SPSS will not include a predictor variable in a model if it has a tolerance of less than .0001. However, you may want to set your own criteria rather higher, perhaps excluding any variable that has a tolerance level of less than .01.

		Collinearity Statistics	
t	Sig.	Tolerance	VIF
-4.050	.000		
.553	.582	.941	1.063
.190	.850	.518	1.931
.381	.704	.605	1.654
4.239	.000	.516	1.940
2.757	.007	.668	1.498
5.671	.000	.621	1.610

VIF is an alternative measure of collinearity (in fact, it is the reciprocal of tolerance); a large value indicates a strong relationship between predictor variables.

The extra columns shown above are normally sufficient, but this table also appears if you request **Collinearity diagnostics** from the **Linear Regression: Statistics** dialogue box. You can read up about this output if you want to understand it.

Collinearity Diagnostics[a]

				Variance Proportions						
Model	Dimension	Eigenvalue	Condition Index	(Constant)	Psychology A level completed	trait test worry	stats course anxiety	trait test emotionality	perceived test difficulty	state test worry
1	1	6.686	1.000	.00	.00		.00	.00	.00	.00
	2	.104	8.025	.02	.37	.13	.01	.10	.02	.00
	3	.078	9.251	.01	.42	.04	.01	.07	.11	.11
	4	.042	12.622	.00	.01	.32	.56	.06	.01	.18
	5	.036	13.610	.00	.01	.24	.34	.72	.08	.00
	6	.030	14.930	.60	.15	.05	.07	.00	.03	.47
	7	.024	16.663	.38	.04	.22	.01	.05	.74	.23

a. Dependent Variable: state test emotionality

Residuals Statistics[a]

	Minimum	Maximum	Mean	Std. Deviation	N
Predicted Value	1.0614	4.3618	2.5556	.85772	90
Residual	-1.27640	1.35944	.00000	.58417	90
Std. Predicted Value	-1.742	2.106	.000	1.000	90
Std. Residual	-2.110	2.247	.000	.966	90

a. Dependent Variable: state test emotionality

The **Residuals Statistics** table is produced if you request any Plots.

Charts

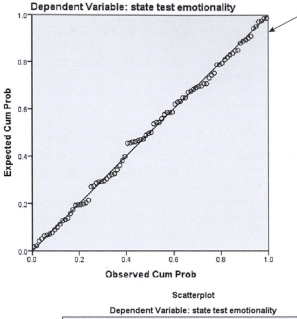

Normal P-P Plot of Regression Standardized Residual

Dependent Variable: state test emotionality

This graph is produced by the **Normal probability plot** option. If the points, which represent the cumulative expected and observed probabilities, are reasonably close to the straight line, then you can assume normality of the residuals.

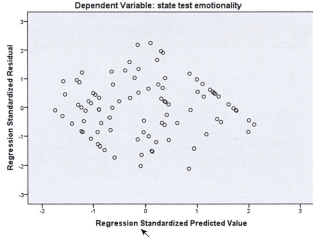

Scatterplot

Dependent Variable: state test emotionality

In the scatterplot of *ZRESID (standardised residuals) and *ZPRED (standardised predicted values), if the points form a rectangle across the middle of the graph, you can assume that your data meet assumptions about normality, linearity, and homoscedasticity of residuals. This spread of points is not rectangular but the distribution is not too bad.

For more guidance on these issues, see Tabachnick and Fidell (2014).

Next, we give some guidance on reporting a multiple regression.

> We haven't shown this here, but you can save various new variables produced by the multiple regression as we showed you for bivariate regression (Chapter 6, Section 7). Click on **Save** in the **Linear Regression** dialogue box, to get the **Linear Regression: Save** dialogue box. You could explore the new variables that are available through the options there.

Reporting the results

When you describe your data analysis, in a methods subsection or in the results section, you should report on assumption checks that you carried out, whether the data met them, and any transformations you made as a consequence (for example, for badly skewed data).

When reporting the results of a multiple regression analysis, you should inform the reader about the proportion of variance accounted for by the model, the significance of the model, and the significance of the predictor variables. In addition, if the regression coefficient of any predictor is negative (unlike in this example), you must point out that direction of impact on the criterion variable. Note that some psychological constructs are scored in opposite directions; for example, a high score on a self-esteem questionnaire may indicate either high self-esteem or low self-esteem. In addition to being clear in your methods subsection what a high score indicates for each of your constructs, you also need to think carefully about the direction of relationship between each predictor and the criterion variable in order to describe these correctly in the results section. You would also include other information, such as summary descriptives for all variables, and the correlation matrix for all the variables you included in the multiple regression analysis.

For the multiple regression itself, in a report you might write:
Those variables that were significantly correlated with the criterion variable, state test emotionality, were entered as predictors into a multiple regression using the standard method. A significant model emerged: $F(6,83) = 29.82$, $p < .001$. The model explains 66.0% of the variance in state test emotionality (adjusted $R^2 = .660$). Table 9.1 gives information about regression coefficients for the predictor variables entered into the model. Trait test emotionality, perceived test difficulty, and state test worry were significant predictors, with a positive relationship to state test emotionality. Psychology 'A' level, trait test worry, and statistics course anxiety were not significant predictors.

Table 9.1 The unstandardised and standardised regression coefficients for the variables entered into the model

Variable	B	SE B	β	p
state test worry	.61	.11	.45	<.001
trait test emotionality	.43	.10	.37	<.001
perceived test difficulty	.30	.11	.21	.007
Psychology A level completed	.07	.13	.04	.582
stats course anxiety	.05	.13	.03	.704
trait test worry	.02	.11	.02	.850

Section 3: SEQUENTIAL OR HIERARCHICAL METHOD OF MULTIPLE REGRESSION

Only use the sequential or hierarchical method if you have a rationale for entering predictors in a particular sequence, as described in Section 1. Remember that first you should run a standard multiple regression, requesting collinearity diagnostics and residual plots in order to check those assumptions.

How to perform it on SPSS

Click on **Analyze⇒Regression⇒Linear**. In the **Linear Regression** dialogue box, we enter predictors in blocks (as shown below).

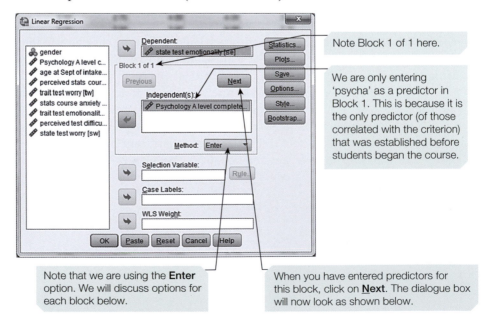

Note Block 1 of 1 here.

We are only entering 'psycha' as a predictor in Block 1. This is because it is the only predictor (of those correlated with the criterion) that was established before students began the course.

Note that we are using the **Enter** option. We will discuss options for each block below.

When you have entered predictors for this block, click on **Next**. The dialogue box will now look as shown below.

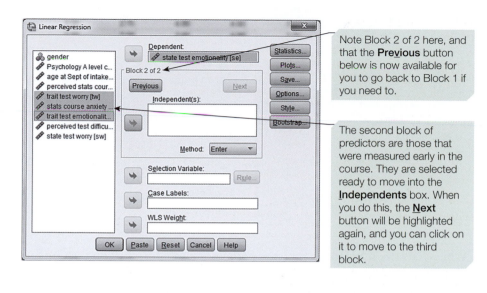

Note Block 2 of 2 here, and that the **Previous** button below is now available for you to go back to Block 1 if you need to.

The second block of predictors are those that were measured early in the course. They are selected ready to move into the **Independents** box. When you do this, the **Next** button will be highlighted again, and you can click on it to move to the third block.

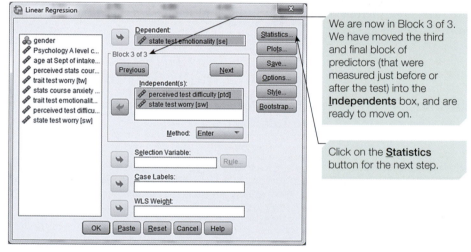

We are now in Block 3 of 3. We have moved the third and final block of predictors (that were measured just before or after the test) into the **Independents** box, and are ready to move on.

Click on the **Statistics** button for the next step.

CHAPTER 9

When you have entered two or more blocks of predictors, you can use the **Next** and **Previous** buttons to check that you have entered the predictors that you intended to in each block.

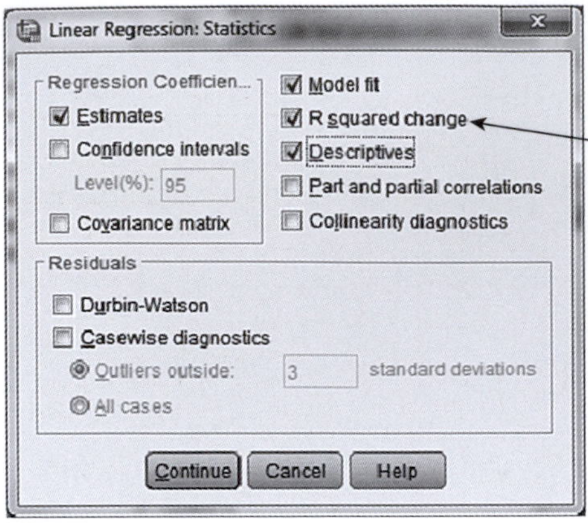

When blocks are entered, SPSS will produce output for different models. Selecting **R squared change** will test for significant difference between successive models.

We have not selected **Collinearity diagnostics**, because we will have done this in a previous standard multiple regression, as we advised above, to give us this and other assumption checks that SPSS provides.

When you have selected the statistics options you require, click on the **Continue** button. This will return you to the **Linear Regression** dialogue box. Now click on the **OK** button. The output that will be produced is illustrated below, for those tables that are different from the output for the standard or simultaneous method shown in Section 2.

SPSS output for sequential multiple regression

Obtained using menu items: Regression > Linear (method = enter; three blocks have been entered)

Variables Entered/Removed[a]

Model	Variables Entered	Variables Removed	Method
1	Psychology A level completed[b]	.	Enter
2	trait test worry, stats course anxiety, trait test emotionality[b]	.	Enter
3	perceived test difficulty, state test worry[b]	.	Enter

a. Dependent Variable: state test emotionality

b. All requested variables entered.

This is the first table that is different from using the standard method. Each time a block is introduced, a new model is formed, and a multiple regression is conducted on each successive model. Thus, with three blocks, there are three models.

SPSS shows here which variables were entered in each block. None were removed, because we used **Enter** for each block.

Model Summary

Model	R	R Square	Adjusted R Square	Std. Error of the Estimate	R Square Change	F Change	df1	df2	Sig. F Change
						Change Statistics			
1	.212[a]	.045	.034	1.01986	.045	4.150	1	88	.045
2	.652[b]	.425	.398	.80509	.380	18.738	3	85	.000
3	.827[c]	.683	.660	.60492	.258	33.781	2	83	.000

a. Predictors: (Constant), Psychology A level completed

b. Predictors: (Constant), Psychology A level completed, trait test worry, stats course anxiety, trait test emotionality

c. Predictors: (Constant), Psychology A level completed, trait test worry, stats course anxiety, trait test emotionality, perceived test difficulty, state test worry

We can see that Model 1, which included only 'psycha', accounted for just 3.4% of the variance (Adjusted R^2 = .034). The inclusion of the second block of predictors into Model 2 resulted in an additional 38% of the variance being explained (R^2 change = .380). Model 3 resulted in an additional 26% of variance explained (R^2 change = .258), accounting for 66% of the variance (Adjusted R^2 = .660).

SPSS provides a test of whether each model is significantly different from the preceding model in terms of proportion of variance explained in the criterion variable.

For Model 1, this comparison is against a 'model' with no predictors (that is, when R^2 = 0) and the F and p values are therefore the same as for the model alone (shown in the next table).

The next row indicates that Model 2 explains significantly more variance than Model 1 (F (3,85) = 18.74, p< .001), and the third row indicates that Model 3 explains significantly more variance than Model 2 (F (2,83) = 33.78, p< .001).

The degrees of freedom here are: first, the number of predictors entered in that block; and second, $N - m - 1$ where m is the total number of predictors in that model.

ANOVA[a]

Model		Sum of Squares	df	Mean Square	F	Sig.
1	Regression	4.317	1	4.317	4.150	.045[b]
	Residual	91.531	88	1.040		
	Total	95.847	89			
2	Regression	40.753	4	10.188	15.718	.000[c]
	Residual	55.095	85	.648		
	Total	95.847	89			
3	Regression	65.475	6	10.913	29.822	.000[d]
	Residual	30.372	83	.366		
	Total	95.847	89			

This table reports the ANOVA result for the three models. They are all significant, although Model 1 (with 'psycha' as the sole predictor) only just reaches significance.

a. Dependent Variable: state test emotionality

b. Predictors: (Constant), Psychology A level completed

c. Predictors: (Constant), Psychology A level completed, trait test worry, stats course anxiety, trait test emotionality

d. Predictors: (Constant), Psychology A level completed, trait test worry, stats course anxiety, trait test emotionality, perceived test difficulty, state test worry

CHAPTER 9

In the Coefficients table, SPSS reports B, β, t and p values (and the Collinearity Statistics if you requested them) for each of the models. These were explained in the output from the sequential method.

Note that, for predictors in more than one model, the regression coefficients change in successive models (see text below).

Coefficients[a]

Model		Unstandardized Coefficients B	Unstandardized Coefficients Std. Error	Standardized Coefficients Beta	t	Sig.
1	(Constant)	1.882	.347		5.418	.000
	Psychology A level completed	.439	.215	.212	2.037	.045
2	(Constant)	-.015	.388		-.038	.970
	Psychology A level completed	.144	.175	.069	.823	.413
	trait test worry	.147	.147	.112	1.005	.318
	stats course anxiety	.350	.164	.215	2.138	.035
	trait test emotionality	.483	.135	.407	3.568	.001
3	(Constant)	-1.394	.344		-4.050	.000
	Psychology A level completed	.073	.132	.035	.553	.582
	trait test worry	.021	.113	.016	.190	.850
	stats course anxiety	.049	.129	.030	.381	.704
	trait test emotionality	.433	.102	.365	4.239	.000
	perceived test difficulty	.304	.110	.208	2.757	.007
	state test worry	.614	.108	.445	5.671	.000

a. Dependent Variable: state test emotionality

For the predictor 'psycha' in Model 1, β is identical to its correlation coefficient with 'se'; as explained in Section 1, with one predictor, the regression coefficient and correlation coefficient are the same.

Here, SPSS gives some information for the predictors that were excluded from each model. When the **Enter** option is used in the **Linear Regression** dialogue box, the variables excluded for each model are simply the predictors that were entered in later blocks.

Excluded Variables[a]

Model		Beta In	t	Sig.	Partial Correlation	Collinearity Statistics Tolerance
1	trait test worry	.471[b]	5.064	.000	.477	.978
	stats course anxiety	.477[b]	5.120	.000	.481	.970
	trait test emotionality	.591[b]	6.811	.000	.590	.952
	perceived test difficulty	.542[b]	6.104	.000	.548	.976
	state test worry	.689[b]	9.117	.000	.699	.983
2	perceived test difficulty	.402[c]	5.082	.000	.485	.838
	state test worry	.542[c]	7.456	.000	.631	.779

a. Dependent Variable: state test emotionality

b. Predictors in the Model: (Constant), Psychology A level completed

c. Predictors in the Model: (Constant), Psychology A level completed, trait test worry, stats course anxiety, trait test emotionality

A note on sequential method and regression coefficients

As we explained earlier, in the sequential or hierarchical method, the researcher uses a theoretical or empirical rationale to decide the order in which predictors are entered into the model. This contrasts with the standard or simultaneous method, in which all predictors are entered at once. As we demonstrated above, in SPSS we use successive blocks to enter predictors in the sequence we decided on and we are given information about whether each additional block of predictors significantly improves the explanatory power (that is, whether R^2 is significantly increased).

However, the regression coefficients above do not follow the sequential 'rule' that shared variance remains with predictors entered earlier. This is because, for each block, we used the SPSS **Enter** option; thus, for each model all the predictors in that model are analysed with the standard method. For the predictor 'psycha', in Model 1, its β is .21, whereas in Model 2, its β is much lower at .06. This reduction demonstrates that 'psycha' shares explained variance with at least one of the predictors added in Model 2, because the standard method excludes shared variance when calculating regression coefficients (although it is taken into account for R^2).

You may be specifically interested in the regression coefficients for predictors entered according to your rationale, and wish the predictors higher up the hierarchy to 'keep' the variance they explain in the criterion variable, with variables further down the hierarchy only given any additional variance they explain. Instead of using the **Enter** option for each predictor when you add it as a block, you would use another SPSS option such as **Forward** (see Section 1). Note, however, that if you enter two or more predictors in a block (as we did above), they will all be treated in that block by the **Forward** statistical criterion, and you might not want that.

Reporting the results

When reporting the results of a sequential multiple regression analysis, you should inform the reader about the proportion of the variance accounted for by each model, the significance of each model, and whether a later model explained significantly more variance than an earlier model. In addition, you can report on the significance of the predictor variables for one or more of the models, as appropriate for the purpose of your report. (See also the general guidance on reporting the results provided in Section 2.)

In a report you might write:
Model 1, with Psychology 'A' level as the only predictor, explained 3.4% of variance and was just significant ($F(1,88) = 4.15, p < .045$). Model 2, in which stats course anxiety, trait test worry, and trait test emotionality were added, explained significantly more variance (R^2change $= .38, F(3,85) = 18.74, p < .001$). The model explains 40% of the variance in state test emotionality (adjusted $R^2 = .398$) and was significant ($F(4,85) = 15.72, p < .001$). Model 3, in which perceived test difficulty and state test worry were added, explained yet more variance and this increase was also significant (R^2change $= .26, F(2,83) = 33.78, p < .001$). Model 3 explains 66.0% of the variance in state

test emotionality (adjusted $R^2 = .660$) and was significant ($F(6,83) = 29.82$, $p < .001$). The significant predictors in Model 3 were trait test emotionality, perceived test difficulty, and state test worry.

Section 4: STATISTICAL METHODS OF MULTIPLE REGRESSION

Stepwise is one of the statistical methods that should be used with caution, as described in Section 1; results must be validated by cross-checking on two separate samples. Stepwise checks all predictors as it enters each one, and removes any that no longer meet its statistical criterion. Thus, it results in a model with the smallest number of predictors. See Regression methods in Section 1 for more explanation.

How to perform multiple regression using the stepwise method

Remember to run a standard multiple regression first, requesting collinearity diagnostics and residual plots to check those assumptions.

Click on **Analyze⇒Regression⇒Linear**.

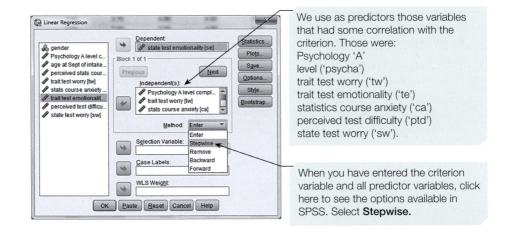

We use as predictors those variables that had some correlation with the criterion. Those were:
Psychology 'A'
level ('psycha')
trait test worry ('tw')
trait test emotionality ('te')
statistics course anxiety ('ca')
perceived test difficulty ('ptd')
state test worry ('sw').

When you have entered the criterion variable and all predictor variables, click here to see the options available in SPSS. Select **Stepwise.**

Next, click on the **Statistics** button and select for **R squared change**, to assess the different models that the stepwise method produces. Relevant output is shown below. The output tables are similar to those produced for the sequential method, and certain tables have been omitted if we do not need to make a point about them.

SPSS output for a statistical multiple regression
Obtained using menu items: Regression > Linear (method = stepwise)

Variables Entered/Removed[a]

Model	Variables Entered	Variables Removed	Method
1	state test worry	.	Stepwise (Criteria: Probability-of-F-to-enter <= .050, Probability-of-F-to-remove >= .100).
2	trait test emotionality	.	Stepwise (Criteria: Probability-of-F-to-enter <= .050, Probability-of-F-to-remove >= .100).
3	perceived test difficulty	.	Stepwise (Criteria: Probability-of-F-to-enter <= .050, Probability-of-F-to-remove >= .100).

a. Dependent Variable: state test emotionality

This table shows us the order in which predictors were entered and removed. In this run, three predictors were added in successive models and none were removed.

In stepwise, predictors are considered in order of magnitude of their correlation with the criterion variable. They are all reconsidered whenever the next predictor is entered, on the basis of a significant contribution to R^2, and may be removed if they do not meet that statistical criterion.
The criteria for entry and removal are shown in the right-hand column of this table. They can be amended, if you wish, in the **Linear Regression: Options** dialogue box.

Model Summary

Model	R	R Square	Adjusted R Square	Std. Error of the Estimate	R Square Change	F Change	df1	df2	Sig. F Change
1	.705[a]	.497	.491	.74043	.497	86.830	1	88	.000
2	.805[b]	.648	.640	.62299	.151	37.303	1	87	.000
3	.825[c]	.681	.670	.59623	.033	8.985	1	86	.004

a. Predictors: (Constant), state test worry
b. Predictors: (Constant), state test worry, trait test emotionality
c. Predictors: (Constant), state test worry, trait test emotionality, perceived test difficulty

ANOVA[a]

Model		Sum of Squares	df	Mean Square	F	Sig.
1	Regression	47.603	1	47.603	86.830	.000[b]
	Residual	48.244	88	.548		
	Total	95.847	89			
2	Regression	62.081	2	31.040	79.977	.000[c]
	Residual	33.766	87	.388		
	Total	95.847	89			
3	Regression	65.275	3	21.758	61.206	.000[d]
	Residual	30.572	86	.355		
	Total	95.847	89			

a. Dependent Variable: state test emotionality

b. Predictors: (Constant), state test worry

c. Predictors: (Constant), state test worry, trait test emotionality

d. Predictors: (Constant), state test worry, trait test emotionality, perceived test difficulty

The Model Summary table shows Adj. R^2 and R^2 .change, and whether the change is significant for each model.

The ANOVA table shows the test of significance for each model considered independently.

You will extract values from these two tables for your report; see detailed annotations on the sequential multiple regression above.

As for the sequential multiple regression, the Coefficients table shows the regression coefficients and whether they are significant, for each model. See annotations on the previous two multiple regressions for detailed comments.

Coefficients[a]

Model		Unstandardized Coefficients		Standardized Coefficients		
		B	Std. Error	Beta	t	Sig.
1	(Constant)	-.133	.299		-.446	.657
	state test worry	.973	.104	.705	9.318	.000
2	(Constant)	-.849	.278		-3.061	.003
	state test worry	.775	.094	.561	8.273	.000
	trait test emotionality	.491	.080	.414	6.108	.000
3	(Constant)	-1.280	.302		-4.240	.000
	state test worry	.627	.102	.454	6.121	.000
	trait test emotionality	.467	.077	.394	6.032	.000
	perceived test difficulty	.316	.105	.216	2.997	.004

a. Dependent Variable: state test emotionality

Reporting the results

See the general guidance on reporting the results provided for the standard method in Section 2. Results for the models from a statistical method can be reported in a similar way to that shown for the sequential method, and with a table showing coefficient information for the final model. If you use a statistical method, however, you should validate your results in the way described at the end of Section 1 and report both multiple regressions. Only results that are common to both analyses should be relied on.

In a report you might write:

State test worry, in Model 1, explained 49% of variance and was significant ($F(1,88) = 86.83$, $p < .001$). Model 2, in which trait test emotionality was added, explained significantly more variance (R^2 change = .15, $F(1,87) = 37.30$, $p < .001$). The model explains 64% of the variance in state test emotionality (adjusted $R^2 = .640$) and was significant ($F(2,87) = 79.98$, $p < .001$). Model 3, in which perceived test difficulty was added, explained another 3.3% of variance and this increase was significant (R^2 change = .033, $F(1,86) = 8.96$, $p = .004$). Model 3 explains 67.0% of the variance in state test emotionality (adjusted $R^2 = .670$) and was significant ($F(3,86) = 61.21$, $p < .001$).

Summary

- This chapter introduced you to multiple regression, a statistical technique that allows us to predict someone's score on one variable (the criterion variable) on the basis of their scores on other variables (the predictor variables).

- Remember that multiple regression requires a large number of observations.

- There are different ways that the predictor variables can be assessed and unless you have a theoretical model in mind, it is safest to use the Enter option, which applies the simultaneous method.

- Multiple regression makes certain assumptions about the data; if your criterion variable is measured at nominal level, see Chapter 11.

- For guidance on recoding values, see Chapter 4, Section 5.

- For guidance on incorporating SPSS output into a report, or on printing the output, see Chapter 13.

10 Analysis of covariance and multivariate analysis of variance

In this chapter

- An introduction to analysis of covariance
- Performing analysis of covariance on SPSS
- An introduction to multivariate analysis of variance
- Performing multivariate analysis of variance on SPSS

SPSS for Psychologists online
Visit he.palgrave.com/psychology/brace for data sets, online tutorials and exercises.

Section 1: AN INTRODUCTION TO ANALYSIS OF COVARIANCE

- Analysis of covariance (ANCOVA) is a statistical procedure that allows us to look at the effect of one or more factors on a dependent variable, while partialling out or removing the effect of another variable.

- ANCOVA can be considered as a cross between ANOVA and multiple regression.

- With ANCOVA, we look at the effect of one or more factors on a dependent variable (as does ANOVA) but, in addition, we acknowledge the influence of another variable – a covariate.

- ANCOVA partials out (or removes) the effect of the covariate by using the regression equation to measure its influence (as in multiple regression).

- In this chapter we cover the one-factor ANCOVA analysis, looking at how one factor, the independent variable, affects the dependent variable once the variance of the covariate is removed.

An example

ANCOVA is commonly used when there is a pretest–posttest design, where a test is given before participants are allocated to the experimental condition and then the same test is given after the experimental condition. The scores on the pretest reveal any pre-existing differences between the groups allocated to the different conditions, and by including these scores as a covariate, these differences can be partialled out.

Alternatively, sometimes it is not possible to randomly assign participants to conditions. Imagine, for example, that you were interested in the speed with which students could learn how to use different computerised statistical packages (the IBM SPSS Statistics software referred to here as SPSS is not the only one available). You might choose three different packages and give these to three different classes of first-year students who have no prior knowledge of any statistical package. However, the three classes might differ in terms of certain attributes, such as familiarity with computer software, which could affect the dependent variable speed of learning. If you measured familiarity with computer software before exposing students to one of the statistical packages, you could then control for and remove its effect on the dependent variable so that you can obtain a clearer insight into the differences in learning speed for the different packages.

What does ANCOVA do?

Remember, we described how ANOVA compares the amount of variance brought about by our manipulation of the IV against the amount of error variance, that is, the variance brought about by other 'nuisance variables' such as individual differences. By getting rid of the effects due to a covariate, ANCOVA allows us to reduce the error variance, which in turn leads to a larger F-value. The inclusion of covariates can therefore increase statistical power.

You will realise from your own experience of conducting research that it is not always possible to control for all possible confounding variables, and where you can identify and measure a variable that you know will influence the dependent variable, then ANCOVA will allow you to get rid of the effects of this variable. If we return to our example of looking at the influence of type of statistical package on speed of learning, we may expect the group that was given SPSS to learn to be the fastest (as this package is very user-friendly). However, we would also expect to see variability in the performance of students within each group, and because speed of learning is also related to familiarity with computer software, some of this variability will be directly attributable to differences in this familiarity. If we ran a test of correlation, we would probably find that there is a positive correlation, so that as familiarity increases, so does speed of learning. ANCOVA examines the association between familiarity and speed and removes the variance due to this association.

You might be thinking that had we randomly assigned our participants to the three groups, probably there would be no systematic differences in familiarity across the three groups. Therefore, the means on this covariate would not differ too much. This is the ideal situation in which to use ANCOVA, because it will get rid of the effects of the covariate in each of the groups and in doing so reduce error variance and hence result in a larger F-value. However, it is also possible to use ANCOVA when the means on the covariate differ significantly. For example, imagine that in one group, either due to bad luck or poor experimental control, there were more individuals with greater familiarity with computer software. ANCOVA is now useful because it will adjust the means on our dependent variable, speed of learning, to an estimate of what they would have been if the groups had not differed in level of familiarity. In other words, these adjusted means are our best guess as to what the means would have been had our three groups not differed on the covariate.

So, by performing an ANCOVA, we may:

1. Reduce error variance.
2. Reduce error variance *and* adjust the means on the dependent variable.

When should I use ANCOVA?

ANCOVA can be used when you have one between-subjects factor (IV) – and this is what we will demonstrate in this chapter – or it can also be used when you have more than one between-subjects factor. It is also possible to have more than one covariate, although interpreting the output from such an analysis would be difficult. We have already said that it is best to use ANCOVA when participants are randomly assigned to one of the levels of the independent variable and, ideally, the covariate should be measured beforehand rather than afterwards, as exposure to the independent variable may affect the covariate.

As mentioned previously, there are two types of situation when ANCOVA is used. The first is when there is a pretest–posttest design, where a test is given before participants are allocated to the experimental condition and then the same test is given after the experimental condition. Here, the pretest scores are used as the covariate. One of our colleagues, Helen Paterson from Sydney University, used such a design to study witness memory for a crime scenario (Paterson, Kemp and Forgas, 2009). She was interested in the effect on a participant's memory of information obtained through discussion with fellow witnesses. She showed participants a video and then gave them a pretest questionnaire. Participants were allocated to one of three groups: a discussion and misinformation group, a discussion and no misinformation group, and a control group where there was no discussion. The participants were then given a posttest questionnaire. Performance on the pretest recognition questionnaire was the covariate in her analysis.

You might be wondering why Helen did not work out the difference between the pretest and posttest scores (that is, the extent to which performance changed) and then perform a one-way ANOVA. However, calculating difference scores does not eliminate the variation present in the pretest scores – these scores vary because participants differ in their ability to remember the information from the video, caused by such things as differences in attention directed to the video. This variation will not be removed by calculating difference scores (the pretest scores will normally be correlated with the difference scores). Helen was not interested in this variation and by partialling out or removing it, she could focus on the effect of participating in one of the three groups.

The second situation is when it has not been possible to randomly assign your participants to the different conditions, and it was not possible to control for a confounding variable and so you want to remove the effects of this variable. This was the case in a study involving Nicola's colleague Gini Harrison (Mackenzie Ross, Brewin, Curran, Furlong, Abraham-Smith and Harrison, 2010). Here, the performance of two groups of participants was compared on a number of different psychometric tasks designed to measure neuropsychological functioning, and the two groups differed in terms of their exposure to particular chemicals. The groups were chosen according to their occupation, and participants were either farmers who had been exposed to the chemicals as they are used for agricultural purposes, or rural police officers who had not been exposed to the chemicals and so formed the control group. The researchers also measured other factors known to affect performance on the psychometric tests, such as mood and years in education. This allowed the researchers to compare the performance of the two groups on these tests after removing the effects of the potentially confounding variables.

Checklist for choosing one or more covariates

1. A covariate should be chosen on the basis of existing theory and research.

2. A covariate should ideally be measured using a scale at ratio, interval or ordinal level. According to Howell (2013), it can even be nominal but, like the predictor variables in multiple regression, if nominal, it has to be a dichotomous variable.

3. Ideally, a covariate should be measured before the experimental manipulation takes place, as it is assumed that the covariate is independent from the experimental manipulation.

4. A covariate should be measured reliably, that is, if it were measured several times across a time period, there would be a high correlation between the scores.

5. The relationship between a covariate and the dependent variable must be linear (straight line). You can check this by looking at the scatterplots for each group and if there is more than one covariate, then they should not be strongly correlated with each other.

6. There should be *homogeneity of regression*. The relationship between the dependent variable and the covariate should be similar for all experimental groups, so that the regression lines are parallel. So, using our first example, the relationship between learning speed of statistical package and familiarity with computer software should be similar for each of the three groups tested.

7. In addition, ANCOVA makes the same assumptions as ANOVA (see Chapter 8, Section 1).

CHAPTER 10

Section 2: PERFORMING ANALYSIS OF COVARIANCE ON SPSS

Example study: exposure to low levels of organophosphates

Let us consider the study described previously that sought to examine the effects of exposure to certain chemicals on neuropsychological functioning (Mackenzie Ross et al., 2010). The chemicals under consideration were organophosphates, which had been found to cause neuropsychological or psychiatric impairment in previous studies. One particular finding that Mackenzie Ross et al. report is that the group of farmers exposed to low levels of organophosphate pesticides scored lower overall on the Wechsler Adult Intelligence Scale (WAIS) than the control group of police officers. Further analysis demonstrated that this was a result of poorer performance on certain WAIS subtests.

For the purposes of demonstrating ANCOVA here, the researchers have kindly provided us with part of their data set so that we can show you how to tease out the effects of a covariate, namely the number of years in education, from overall performance on the WAIS. Their data were carefully screened for outliers and transformed where necessary to ensure they met the requirements for parametric tests. (Many thanks to Gini Harrison for preparing the data file available from he.palgrave.com/psychology/brace.)

The analysis shown here involves one between-subjects factor called 'group', which had two levels. Group 1 involved 127 sheep famers (working and retired) who had been exposed to low levels of organophosphate pesticides. Group 2 involved 78 rural police officers (working and retired) who had not been exposed to these chemicals. The dependent variable we will look at here is overall performance on the WAIS ('wais_fsi' in the data file). The covariate consists of the number of years in education ('yrs_edu' in the data file). For the purposes of this demonstration, the hypothesis tested is that there will be a detrimental effect of low-level exposure to organophosphate pesticides on overall performance on the WAIS. Note that we are not replicating any analysis that Mackenzie Ross et al. undertook, but using a subset of their data to demonstrate how you would perform ANCOVA.

We have chosen to show you the ANCOVA procedure with a one-way between-subjects design, so that we can also show you how to check for homogeneity of regression statistically. It is much harder to check for this assumption statistically with more complex designs, so we shall also show you how you can look for this graphically and at the same time check that there is a linear relationship between your covariate and dependent variable. We do this first and after that we show you how to perform the ANCOVA test itself.

How to check for homogeneity of regression

If you have read Chapter 8 or performed ANOVA on SPSS, you will have already seen the dialogue boxes that appear next. This is because SPSS has incorporated ANCOVA as an option in the ANOVA dialogue box.

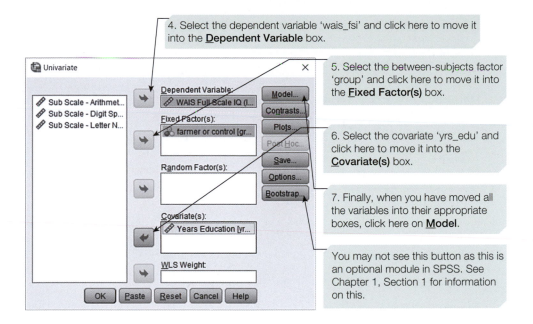

4. Select the dependent variable 'wais_fsi' and click here to move it into the **Dependent Variable** box.

5. Select the between-subjects factor 'group' and click here to move it into the **Fixed Factor(s)** box.

6. Select the covariate 'yrs_edu' and click here to move it into the **Covariate(s)** box.

7. Finally, when you have moved all the variables into their appropriate boxes, click here on **Model**.

You may not see this button as this is an optional module in SPSS. See Chapter 1, Section 1 for information on this.

When you click on the **Model** button, the following **Univariate: Model** dialogue box will appear.

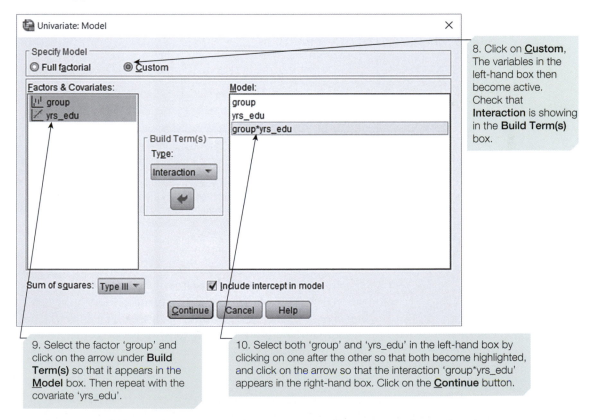

8. Click on **Custom**, The variables in the left-hand box then become active. Check that **Interaction** is showing in the **Build Term(s)** box.

CHAPTER 10

9. Select the factor 'group' and click on the arrow under **Build Term(s)** so that it appears in the **Model** box. Then repeat with the covariate 'yrs_edu'.

10. Select both 'group' and 'yrs_edu' in the left-hand box by clicking on one after the other so that both become highlighted, and click on the arrow so that the interaction 'group*yrs_edu' appears in the right-hand box. Click on the **Continue** button.

Once you click on the **Continue** button, you will return to the **Univariate** dialogue box. Now click on the ⬜ OK button. The output is shown below.

SPSS output from procedure to check for homogeneity of regression

Univariate Analysis of Variance

Between-Subjects Factors

		Value Label	N
farmer or control	1.00	farmer	122
	2.00	control	74

Note that N for each group is reduced, and this is because there are missing scores in the data file.

SPSS reminds you that 'WAIS Full Scale IQ' is the dependent variable. Here, you are interested in looking to see if there is an interaction between the covariate, 'yrs_edu' and the independent variable 'group'.

Tests of Between-Subjects Effects

Dependent Variable: WAIS Full Scale IQ (IQ indexed score)

Source	Type III Sum of Squares	df	Mean Square	F	Sig.
Corrected Model	5585.739[a]	3	1861.913	17.030	.000
Intercept	24315.619	1	24315.619	222.405	.000
group	54.513	1	54.513	.499	.481
yrs_edu	3199.170	1	3199.170	29.261	.000
group * yrs_edu	10.549	1	10.549	.096	.756
Error	20991.465	192	109.331		
Total	2260748.000	196			
Corrected Total	26577.204	195			

a. R Squared = .210 (Adjusted R Squared = .198)

This is the only row that you are interested in. If this interaction is significant, then the data violate the assumption of homogeneity of regression. Here, SPSS reports the interaction to be non-significant, so this assumption has *not* been violated.

Now that we have checked for homogeneity of regression, we can perform the ANCOVA test. First, however, we show you how to inspect the relationship between the covariate and the dependent variable graphically, using scatterplots. This procedure can be used to check that there is a linear relationship between the covariate and the dependent variable for both levels of the factor, and also that there is homogeneity of regression.

How to check for linear relationship between covariate and dependent variable

1. Click on <u>**Graphs**</u> and **Chart Builder** (see Chapter 3, Section 8 if you are unfamiliar with Chart Builder).

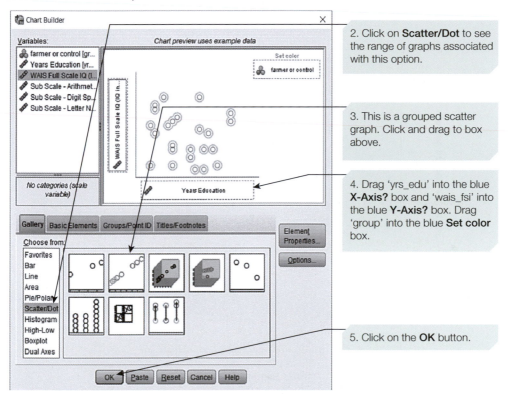

2. Click on **Scatter/Dot** to see the range of graphs associated with this option.

3. This is a grouped scatter graph. Click and drag to box above.

4. Drag 'yrs_edu' into the blue **X-Axis?** box and 'wais_fsi' into the blue **Y-Axis?** box. Drag 'group' into the blue **Set color** box.

5. Click on the **OK** button.

6. Double-click on the scattergram in the SPSS output to bring up the **Chart Editor** window (shown below on the left).

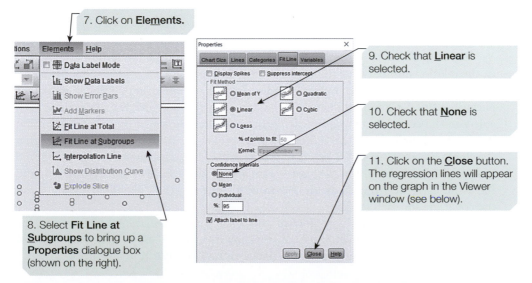

7. Click on **Elements**.

8. Select **Fit Line at Subgroups** to bring up a **Properties** dialogue box (shown on the right).

9. Check that **Linear** is selected.

10. Check that **None** is selected.

11. Click on the **Close** button. The regression lines will appear on the graph in the Viewer window (see below).

SPSS output for graph

To distinguish between 'farmer' and 'control' in the greyscale graph below, in the **Chart Editor** window we double-clicked on the dot next to 'control' in the legend, which opened a **Properties** dialogue box, showing the **Marker** option. There we changed the **Fill** option from transparent to black.

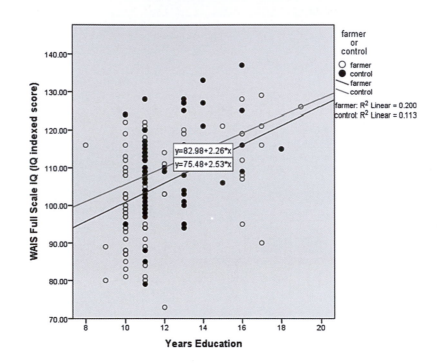

Inspect your graph to see if there is a linear relationship between the covariate and the dependent variable, one of the assumptions for ANCOVA. Here, the relationship for each group ('farmer' and 'control') may not be strictly linear but we will continue in order to demonstrate the procedure. In practice, you may need to transform your data or remove outliers (see Tabachnick and Fidell, 2014, Chapter 4, for details).

Remember that the slopes of the regression lines should be roughly parallel, that is, the relationship between the covariate and the dependent variable should be similar for all groups (the assumption of homogeneity of regression). This is important because ANCOVA assumes that the overall relationship between the dependent variable and the covariate is true for each group. We already know that this assumption has not been violated by our earlier check and this is confirmed here by the fact that the slopes are almost parallel. In Chapter 6, Section 2, we explained that the R-squared linear values to the right of the scattergram are the values of Pearson's r squared, and these indicate the strength of the relationship between the dependent variable and the covariate for each group.

We have shown you here how to check for a linear relationship between the covariate and the dependent variable, and how to check if there is homogeneity of regression. Next, we show you how to perform the ANCOVA test.

How to perform ANCOVA

1. Click on **<u>A</u>nalyze** ⇒ **<u>G</u>eneral Linear Model** ⇒ **<u>U</u>nivariate**. You will then see the **Univariate** dialogue box. You will find that you have already performed actions 2–4 shown for this dialogue box when checking for homogeneity of regression.

2. Select the dependent variable 'wais_fsi' and click here to move it into the **Dependent Variable** box.

3. Select the between-subjects factor 'group' and click here to move it into the **<u>F</u>ixed Factor(s)** box.

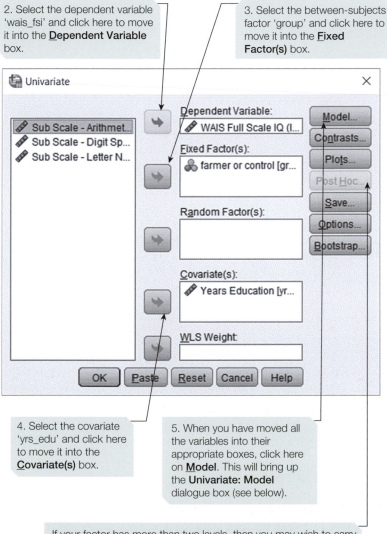

4. Select the covariate 'yrs_edu' and click here to move it into the **Covariate(s)** box.

5. When you have moved all the variables into their appropriate boxes, click here on **Model**. This will bring up the **Univariate: Model** dialogue box (see below).

If your factor has more than two levels, then you may wish to carry out planned or unplanned comparisons. The **Contrasts** button is clickable but the **Post <u>H</u>oc** button is deactivated. (See the tip box below for further guidance.)

You will return to the **Univariate** dialogue box. Click on the **Options** button to bring up the **Univariate: Options** dialogue box (shown below).

Click on [OK] and SPSS will calculate the ANCOVA. The output is shown next.

> If a covariate is selected, the **Post Hoc** button in the **Univariate** dialogue box is deactivated; however unplanned comparisons can be carried out by clicking in the box next to **Compare main effects** in the **Univariate: Options** dialogue box above (see Chapter 8, Section 4). Planned comparisons can be carried out by clicking the **Contrasts** button in the **Univariate** dialogue box (see Chapter 8, Section 2).

SPSS output for ANCOVA

Univariate Analysis of Variance

Between-Subjects Factors

		Value Label	N
farmer or control	1.00	farmer	122
	2.00	control	74

Levene's Test of Equality of Error Variances[a]

Dependent Variable: WAIS Full Scale IQ (IQ indexed score)

F	df1	df2	Sig.
.005	1	194	.943

Tests the null hypothesis that the error variance of the dependent variable is equal across groups.

a. Design: Intercept + yrs_edu + group

> To check that the assumption of equality of variance was not violated, we clicked on **Homogeneity tests** in the **Univariate: Options** dialogue box. If this is not significant, as here, then this assumption has not been violated.

> The first line highlighted shows that the covariate is significantly related to the dependent variable. The next line shows the main effect of group is significant when the effects of the covariate 'yrs_edu' are partialled out.

Tests of Between-Subjects Effects

Dependent Variable: WAIS Full Scale IQ (IQ indexed score)

Source	Type III Sum of Squares	df	Mean Square	F	Sig.
Corrected Model	5575.190[a]	2	2787.595	25.617	.000
Intercept	30770.937	1	30770.937	282.772	.000
yrs_edu	4310.391	1	4310.391	39.611	.000
group	818.381	1	818.381	7.521	.007
Error	21002.014	193	108.819		
Total	2260748.000	196			
Corrected Total	26577.204	195			

a. R Squared = .210 (Adjusted R Squared = .202)

Estimated Marginal Means

> These are the adjusted means, i.e. the effect of the covariate has been statistically removed. To obtain these, we clicked on **Display Means for** in the **Univariate: Options** dialogue box.

farmer or control

Dependent Variable: WAIS Full Scale IQ (IQ indexed score)

farmer or control	Mean	Std. Error	95% Confidence Interval	
			Lower Bound	Upper Bound
farmer	105.165[a]	.946	103.299	107.032
control	109.403[a]	1.217	107.003	111.803

a. Covariates appearing in the model are evaluated at the following values: Years Education = 11.72.

CHAPTER 10

Reporting the results

In a report you might write:

A one-way between-subjects analysis of covariance was carried out to assess the impact of exposure to low levels to organophosphate pesticides on overall performance on the WAIS. Checks were carried out to confirm homogeneity of regression and linear relationship between covariate and dependent variable. The between-subjects factor comprised two groups: farmers who had been exposed to the pesticides and a control group of rural police officers. The covariate comprised number of years in education, and this was significantly related to the overall WAIS scores: $F(1,193) = 39.61$, $p < .001$. Adjusting for this covariate resulted in a significant effect of the between-subjects factor group: $F(1,193) = 7.52$, $p = .007$. The adjusted mean WAIS score for those exposed to the chemicals was 105.17 compared to 109.40 for the control group.

 You would also want to report in your results section a measure of effect size (see Chapter 8, Section 1) and information regarding the confidence intervals for each condition.

Section 3: AN INTRODUCTION TO MULTIVARIATE ANALYSIS OF VARIANCE

- Multivariate analysis of variance (MANOVA) is a statistical procedure similar to ANOVA and is used when the design of the experiment involves more than one dependent variable.

- Like ANOVA, MANOVA can be used to explore the effects of one or more independent variables and interactions between independent variables. However, whereas ANOVA can only be used when there is one dependent variable (hence it is described as a 'univariate' test), MANOVA can handle several dependent variables all together (hence it is described as a 'multivariate' test).

- This type of design is quite common in clinical research when evaluating the impact of an intervention programme, as several different outcome measures would be explored, for example cognitive and behavioural measures.

- MANOVA is useful when seeking to measure a variable that is complex to operationalize, and when a single dependent variable fails to capture all the elements of this complex variable. Instead, several different dependent variables could be measured, each of which represents a different element.

An example

Imagine you wanted to investigate whether being exposed to certain chemicals, for example those used to spray crops, has a detrimental effect on human health. You could select different groups of people who had different levels of exposure to such chemicals and compare them to a control group of people who had no or minimal exposure. You might then measure a number of different aspects of health, including cognitive processes. For example, you might choose to use different subtests of the Wechsler Adult Intelligence Scale (WAIS) that have been found to be reliable and valid measures of working memory. You could perform one-way ANOVAs on the scores from each different measure of working memory but, as you may remember from Chapter 8, Section 1, by performing multiple tests, you would run an increased risk of making a Type I error (that is, incorrectly rejecting a null hypothesis). To avoid this, you could use MANOVA.

What does MANOVA do?

MANOVA allows you to not only look at the effect of different independent variables and see if these interact, it also tells you if there is any relationship between the different dependent variables. Because all these are analysed simultaneously, MANOVA can check whether the different levels of the factors not only differ from one another on one dependent variable but whether they differ along a combination of several dependent variables. It does this by creating a new dependent variable, which is the linear combination of each of the original dependent variables. MANOVA will tell you if the mean differences among groups on the combined dependent variable are larger than expected by chance.

There are other tests that also combine variables. In Chapter 9, a model containing a combination of predictor variables sought to predict the scores on a criterion variable. In Chapter 11 you will read about how variables are combined together to predict category membership in a type of analysis called 'discriminant analysis'.

You may remember that for ANOVA the statistic calculated is the *F*-ratio, which is the ratio of the variance due to the manipulation of the IV and the error variance. Conceptually, MANOVA does something similar, but this is statistically far more complicated and it will provide you with a choice of four different statistics to choose from, all of which indicate whether there are significant differences among the levels of the independent variable on the linear combination of the dependent variables. They are:

Pillai's Trace
Hotelling's Trace
Wilks' Lambda
Roy's Largest Root.

SPSS will report a value for each of these, along with the *F* tests for each. If your factor has only two levels, then the *F* tests reported will be identical. This is because when the factor has only two levels, and hence one degree of freedom, there is only one way of combining the different dependent variables to separate the levels or the groups. However, when your factor has more than two levels, then the *F* tests reported for the four test statistics are usually different and it is possible that some may be significant and some not. Most researchers report the values for the Wilks' Lambda, so we suggest you report these too. However, Pillai's is considered to be the most robust (although all four are reasonably robust), so you might consider reporting the values for Pillai's when your sample size is small.

Following up a significant result

If you find a significant result, you will then want to follow it up. One possibility is to look at the univariate ANOVAs that are included in the SPSS printout, after the section that presents the MANOVA test statistics. This will tell you which of the individual dependent variables are contributing to the significant overall result. If you do this, you need to consider something we mentioned earlier, the possibility of committing a Type I error. The analyses you carry out following a significant MANOVA are considered to be 'protected', because if the multivariate test is non-significant, then any subsequent tests are ignored. However, this notion of 'protection' is a little misleading because a significant MANOVA often reflects a significant difference for one rather than all dependent variables. Therefore, it is probably best to ensure against a Type I error and there are several ways of doing so. One conservative way is to apply the Bonferroni correction. Normally, a result is regarded as 'significant' if the p value is less than .05. If our design involves two dependent variables and we want to look at the two ANOVAs performed on these, we apply the following correction: $.05 \div 2 = .025$, and for our result to be significant, p now has to be less than .025. If our design involves three dependent variables and we want to look at the three ANOVAs performed on these, we apply the following correction: $.05 \div 3 = .017$, and for our result to be significant, p now has to be less than .017. So, .05 is divided by the number of dependent variables in the study.

Another possibility is to explore a significant MANOVA result by conducting discriminant analysis (described in Chapter 11); more guidance on this is provided below.

When should I use MANOVA?

MANOVA can be used when your design is a simple one-way design – as demonstrated in this chapter – or with more complex designs where you have more than one independent variable or factor. There should be some conceptual reason for considering several dependent variables together in the same analysis. Adding dependent variables may decrease the power of the test, so MANOVA should only be used when there is a reason to measure several dependent variables.

There is some controversy over the extent to which the dependent variables can or should be correlated (see Cole, Maxwell, Arvey and Salas, 1994). Multicollinearity should be avoided (see Chapter 9, Section 1), so check that the correlation coefficients for any pair of dependent variables do not exceed .9, and correlations around .8 are also cause for concern. Tabachnick and Fidell (2014, 291) suggest that in terms of the research design, one should avoid selecting dependent variables that are correlated because they essentially measure the same thing, albeit in a slightly different way. They write: 'MANOVA works best with highly negatively correlated DVs and acceptably well with moderately correlated DVs in either direction (about |.6|)' (p. 310). Certainly, if the dependent variables are highly positively correlated, and MANOVA shows a significant result, it is difficult to tease apart the contribution of each of the individual dependent variables to this overall effect. Rather than looking at the univariate ANOVAs, you would need to explore your data using discriminant analysis, as this will allow you to explore the relationship between the dependent variables. We recommend that you perform tests of correlation to check the strength of the correlations between your dependent variables to help you decide whether or not to use MANOVA or how best to follow up any significant MANOVA result.

Checklist for using MANOVA

1. There should be a theoretical or empirical basis underpinning your choice of dependent variables.

2. The dependent variables should be measured using an interval or ratio scale and any relationship between them should be linear (straight line). You can check this by looking at the scatterplots between pairs of dependent variables for each level of your factor. (If you are not sure how to generate scatterplots on SPSS, see Chapter 6, Section 2.)

3. You must ensure that the number of cases in each cell is greater than the number of dependent variables.

4. There should be *homogeneity of variance–covariance matrices,* and this is similar to the assumption of homogeneity of variance, mentioned previously in relation to parametric tests. SPSS can check this assumption for you and we will show you how to do this in Section 4.

5. There should be univariate and multivariate *normality of distributions.* Assessment of multivariate normality is difficult in practice, and cannot be checked using SPSS; however, you should at least check that each dependent variable is normally distributed, that is, that univariate normality holds, as this is likely to reflect multivariate normality. Giles (2002) points to two ways in which normality may be violated. The first is *platykurtosis* and this is evident when the distribution curve looks like a low plateau. You can check for this by generating histograms of each dependent variable. The second is the presence of *outliers;* these are data points far outside the area covered by the normal distribution. (See Chapter 3, Section 6; and/or Tabachnick and Fidell, 2014, Chapter 4, for advice on screening for outliers.)

Generally, if you have equal sample sizes and a reasonable number of participants in each group, and you've checked for outliers before conducting your analysis, MANOVA will still be a valid test even with modest violations of these assumptions.

Section 4: PERFORMING MULTIVARIATE ANALYSIS OF VARIANCE ON SPSS

Example study: exposure to low levels of organophosphates

Let us return to the example from Section 2 and the study by Mackenzie Ross et al. (2010), which looked at whether low-level exposure to organophosphate pesticides brought about neuropsychological or psychiatric impairment. The researchers had asked working and retired sheep farmers to complete a range of cognitive and mood tests, and compared their performance to that of a matched control group, and to published test norms.

Their study examined two groups. Group 1 involved 127 sheep famers (working and retired) who had been exposed to low levels of organophosphate pesticides. Group 2 involved 78 rural police officers (working and retired) who had not been exposed to these chemicals. The dependent variables we will look at here are scores on three subtests of the WAIS designed to measure working memory: the arithmetic test, the digit span test and the letter number substitution test.

The hypothesis we shall be testing is that there will be a difference between the groups in terms of their working memory. Analysis conducted by Mackenzie Ross et al. (2010) revealed that farmers were significantly impaired on measures of memory, including working memory, visual memory and auditory memory. Note that we are not replicating any analysis that Mackenzie Ross et al. undertook, and their data were carefully screened for outliers and transformed where necessary to ensure they met the requirements for parametric tests. Instead, we are using a subset of their data kindly provided by the researchers to demonstrate how you would perform MANOVA. (Many thanks to Gini Harrison for preparing the data file available from he.palgrave.com/psychology/brace.)

Before conducting the MANOVA procedure, we first check the correlations among the dependent variables. To obtain such correlations, click on **Analyze** $\Rightarrow$ **Correlate** $\Rightarrow$ **Bivariate** and then select your dependent variables (see Chapter 4 for more detail on obtaining correlations). Below is the SPSS output. Scatterplots would confirm that the relationships between the dependent variables are linear.

Correlations

		Sub Scale - Arithmetic	Sub Scale - Digit Span	Sub Scale - Letter Number Substitution
Sub Scale - Arithmetic	Pearson Correlation	1	.356**	.374**
	Sig. (2-tailed)		.000	.000
	N	197	197	197
Sub Scale - Digit Span	Pearson Correlation	.356**	1	.577**
	Sig. (2-tailed)	.000		.000
	N	197	201	201
Sub Scale - Letter Number Substitution	Pearson Correlation	.374**	.577**	1
	Sig. (2-tailed)	.000	.000	
	N	197	201	205

**. Correlation is significant at the 0.01 level (2-tailed).

> This correlation matrix suggests that there are moderate correlations between the different dependent variables.

How to perform MANOVA

ANCOVA MANOVA new data file.sav [DataSet2] - IBM SPSS Statistics Data Editor

File	Edit	View	Data	Transform	Analyze	Direct Marketing	Graphs	Utilities	Add-ons	Window

5:

	group	yrs_edu		
1	1	10		
2	1	14		
3	2	18		
4	2	11		
5	2	13		
6	2	11	11.00	
7	2	11	14.00	
8	2	11	12.00	
9	2	11	10.00	
10	2	11	11.00	
11	2	11	10.00	
12	1	11	6.00	
13	2	11	11.00	
14	2	11	14.00	
15	2	13	11.00	

Menu items: Reports, Descriptive Statistics, Custom Tables, Compare Means, General Linear Model, Generalized Linear Models, Mixed Models, Correlate, Regression, Loglinear, Neural Networks, Classify, Dimension Reduction, Scale, Nonparametric Tests, Forecasting, Survival, Multiple Response

Submenu: Univariate..., Multivariate..., Repeated Measures..., Variance Components...

1. Click on **Analyze.**

2. Select **General Linear Model.**

3. Select **Multivariate.** You will then see the **Multivariate** dialogue box.

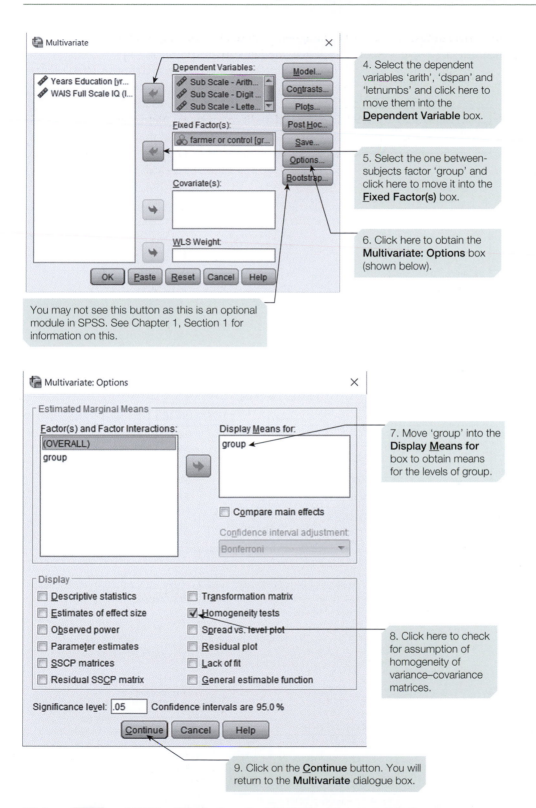

4. Select the dependent variables 'arith', 'dspan' and 'letnumbs' and click here to move them into the **Dependent Variable** box.

5. Select the one between-subjects factor 'group' and click here to move it into the **Fixed Factor(s)** box.

6. Click here to obtain the **Multivariate: Options** box (shown below).

You may not see this button as this is an optional module in SPSS. See Chapter 1, Section 1 for information on this.

7. Move 'group' into the **Display Means for** box to obtain means for the levels of group.

8. Click here to check for assumption of homogeneity of variance–covariance matrices.

9. Click on the **Continue** button. You will return to the **Multivariate** dialogue box.

Click on ⬚ OK ⬚ and SPSS will calculate the MANOVA. The output is shown next.

SPSS output for MANOVA

General Linear Model

Between-Subjects Factors

		Value Label	N
farmer or control	1.00	farmer	122
	2.00	control	75

Box's Test of Equality of Covariance Matrices[a]

Box's M	8.416
F	1.377
df1	6
df2	163196.327
Sig.	.219

Tests the null hypothesis that the observed covariance matrices of the dependent variables are equal across groups.

a. Design: Intercept + group

> Box's test checks whether your data violate the assumption of homogeneity of variance–covariance matrices and was obtained by clicking on **Homogeneity tests** in the **Multivariate: Options** dialogue box. If this is significant, you have violated this assumption. As this test is very sensitive, it is most useful when your sample size is small and unequal. Here, p (sig. value) = .219, so we have not violated this assumption.

Multivariate Tests[a]

Effect		Value	F	Hypothesis df	Error df	Sig.
Intercept	Pillai's Trace	.985	4162.385[b]	3.000	193.000	.000
	Wilks' Lambda	.015	4162.385[b]	3.000	193.000	.000
	Hotelling's Trace	64.700	4162.385[b]	3.000	193.000	.000
	Roy's Largest Root	64.700	4162.385[b]	3.000	193.000	.000
group	Pillai's Trace	.204	16.469[b]	3.000	193.000	.000
	Wilks' Lambda	.796	16.469[b]	3.000	193.000	.000
	Hotelling's Trace	.256	16.469[b]	3.000	193.000	.000
	Roy's Largest Root	.256	16.469[b]	3.000	193.000	.000

a. Design: Intercept + group

b. Exact statistic

> In this table, we are only interested in the results for the variable 'group', and we ignore those reported for the Intercept. SPSS reports the four MANOVA test statistics that tell us whether the new combined dependent variable, 'working memory', is different across the two groups of participants. Here, p is smaller than .05 for each test statistic, so all are significant. We are going to report the values for Wilks' Lambda, the row highlighted, citing the F value, the two sets of degrees of freedom, and p.

Levene's Test of Equality of Error Variances[a]

	F	df1	df2	Sig.
Sub Scale - Arithmetic	.030	1	195	.862
Sub Scale - Digit Span	.005	1	195	.943
Sub Scale - Letter Number Substitution	.553	1	195	.458

Tests the null hypothesis that the error variance of the dependent variable is equal across groups.

a. Design: Intercept + group

> These statistics were obtained by clicking on **Homogeneity tests** in the **Multivariate: Options** dialogue box. If Levene's p > .05, as here, then there is equality of variance. This is important in terms of the reliability of the results below and in supporting the robustness of the multivariate statistics.

Tests of Between-Subjects Effects

Source	Dependent Variable	Type III Sum of Squares	df	Mean Square	F	Sig.
Corrected Model	Sub Scale - Arithmetic	.096[a]	1	.096	.012	.913
	Sub Scale - Digit Span	3.853[b]	1	3.853	25.349	.000
	Sub Scale - Letter Number Substitution	223.241[c]	1	223.241	34.855	.000
Intercept	Sub Scale - Arithmetic	24387.812	1	24387.812	3058.878	.000
	Sub Scale - Digit Span	1884.565	1	1884.565	12397.739	.000
	Sub Scale - Letter Number Substitution	21021.617	1	21021.617	3282.098	.000
group	Sub Scale - Arithmetic	.096	1	.096	.012	.913
	Sub Scale - Digit Span	3.853	1	3.853	25.349	.000
	Sub Scale - Letter Number Substitution	223.241	1	223.241	34.855	.000
Error	Sub Scale - Arithmetic	1554.695	195	7.973		
	Sub Scale - Digit Span	29.642	195	.152		
	Sub Scale - Letter Number Substitution	1248.962	195	6.405		
Total	Sub Scale - Arithmetic	27390.000	197			
	Sub Scale - Digit Span	1988.921	197			
	Sub Scale - Letter Number Substitution	22680.000	197			
Corrected Total	Sub Scale - Arithmetic	1554.792	196			
	Sub Scale - Digit Span	33.495	196			
	Sub Scale - Letter Number Substitution	1472.203	196			

a. R Squared = .000 (Adjusted R Squared = -.005)

b. R Squared = .115 (Adjusted R Squared = .111)

c. R Squared = .152 (Adjusted R Squared = .147)

The rows labelled 'group' provide values for each of your dependent variables. These are the univariate ANOVAs and you interpret these as you would for a one-way ANOVA. As there are three dependent variables, we apply Bonferroni correction by dividing 0.05 by 3, so sig. values need to be smaller than 0.017 for results to be significant. This is the case for two of the three dependent variables, digit span and letter number substitution.

Estimated Marginal Means

farmer or control

Dependent Variable	farmer or control	Mean	Std. Error	95% Confidence Interval	
				Lower Bound	Upper Bound
Sub Scale - Arithmetic	farmer	11.434	.256	10.930	11.939
	control	11.480	.326	10.837	12.123
Sub Scale - Digit Span	farmer	3.041	.035	2.971	3.111
	control	3.329	.045	3.240	3.418
Sub Scale - Letter Number Substitution	farmer	9.541	.229	9.089	9.993
	control	11.733	.292	11.157	12.310

These descriptive statistics were obtained by clicking on **Display Means for** in the **Multivariate: Options** dialogue box.

CHAPTER 10

Reporting the results

In a report you might write:

A one-way between-subjects multivariate analysis of variance was carried out to assess the impact of exposure to low levels of organophosphate pesticides on working memory. The between-subjects factor comprised two groups: farmers who had been exposed to the pesticides and a control group of rural police officers. The dependent variables comprised scores on three different measures of working memory, all of which were subtests of the WAIS. Assumptions of homogeneity of variance-covariance matrices and equality of variance were confirmed, and moderate correlations were found among the dependent variables. There was a significant difference between the two groups on the combined dependent variable 'working memory', $F(3,193) = 16.47$, $p < .001$; Wilks' Lambda = .8. Analysis of each individual dependent variable, using a Bonferroni adjusted alpha level of .017, showed that there was no significant contribution of the subtest arithmetic, $F(1,195) = 0.01$, $p = .913$. The two groups differed significantly on the other two subtests: digit span, $F(1,195) = 25.35$, $p < .001$ and letter number substitution, $F(1,195) = 34.86$, $p < .001$. The mean scores for those exposed to the chemicals were lower for both these subtests ($M = 3.04$ and $M = 9.54$ respectively) compared to those of the control group ($M = 3.33$ and $M = 11.73$ respectively).

 You would also want to report in your results section a measure of effect size (see Chapter 8, Section 1) and information regarding the confidence intervals for each condition. Furthermore, the example shown here involved a between-subjects factor that involved only two levels. If your design involves a factor with more than two levels, and significant differences emerge, you will need to follow these up to find out where the significant differences lie. The easiest way would be to conduct one-way between-subjects ANOVAs on any dependent variable that emerges as significant in the MANOVA, and conduct unplanned (or planned) comparisons, as shown in Chapter 8, Section 2 for one-way between-subjects design and Chapter 8, Section 4 for a one-way within-subjects design.

Next, we finish this section by looking at how to perform MANOVA with one within-subjects factor.

A note on within subjects designs

As mentioned previously, MANOVA can be used when your design is a simple one-way design or with more complex designs where you have more than one independent variable or factor. We have shown you how to perform this test when the design involves one between-subjects factor and we will end this chapter by providing a note on how to conduct this test when the design involves one within-subjects factor.

Imagine our design involved a within-subjects factor, before and after being exposed to chemicals and three dependent variables each measuring working memory.

Our data file would contain six SPSS variables representing the three 'before' scores and the three 'after' scores. In the dialogue box shown below, we name the variables as follows: 'befaft' for the within-subjects factor (before and after exposure to chemicals), and the three dependent variables are 'arith', 'dspan' and 'letnumbs' (the arithmetic test, the digit span test and the letter number substitution test).

We would start analysing the data in the following way. Click on **Analyze** ⇒ **General Linear Model** ⇒ **Repeated Measures**.

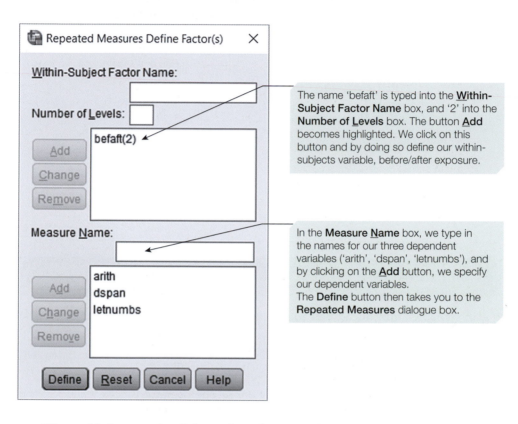

The name 'befaft' is typed into the **Within-Subject Factor Name** box, and '2' into the **Number of Levels** box. The button **Add** becomes highlighted. We click on this button and by doing so define our within-subjects variable, before/after exposure.

In the **Measure Name** box, we type in the names for our three dependent variables ('arith', 'dspan', 'letnumbs'), and by clicking on the **Add** button, we specify our dependent variables.
The **Define** button then takes you to the **Repeated Measures** dialogue box.

We would then get the dialogue box shown in Chapter 8, Section 4, for the one-way within-subjects ANOVA.

The output will look similar to that shown previously, and will provide values for the combined dependent variable followed by univariate ANOVA test statistics.

Summary

- This chapter introduced you to two different statistical procedures related to ANOVA.

- ANCOVA allows you to look at the effect of one or more factors on a dependent variable, while removing the effect of a covariate.

- MANOVA allows you to look at the effect of one or more factors when there is more than one dependent variable.

- We have shown you how to conduct both tests using SPSS when there is one between-subjects factor.

- Both make certain assumptions about the data, listed here, and we have shown you how to check for these.

- If your dependent variable is a total score from several raw scores that have already been entered into your data file, see Chapter 4 for guidance on how to create such a total score in SPSS.

- For guidance on incorporating SPSS output into a report, or on printing the output, see Chapter 13.

11 Discriminant analysis and logistic regression

In this chapter

- Discriminant analysis and logistic regression
- An introduction to discriminant analysis
- Performing discriminant analysis using SPSS
- An introduction to logistic regression
- Performing logistic regression on SPSS

SPSS for Psychologists online
Visit he.palgrave.com/psychology/brace for data sets, online tutorials and exercises.

Section 1: DISCRIMINANT ANALYSIS AND LOGISTIC REGRESSION

- Discriminant analysis and logistic regression are statistical procedures that can be used to predict category membership from a number of predictor variables.

- Like multiple regression, these procedures predict an outcome. In multiple regression, the outcome variable is a continuous variable, such as score on a test. In contrast, discriminant analysis and logistic regression procedures can be employed when the outcome variable is categorical, for example pass vs fail on a test.

- The two procedures are designed for use when we want to predict a categorical outcome on the basis of several other variables. For example, we might try to predict whether someone is going to pass or fail their driving test on the basis of a number of predictor variables, such as their age, sex, educational achievement and employment history.

- Discriminant analysis makes various assumptions about the predictor variables, including that they should be normally distributed. Logistic regression makes no such assumptions about the distribution of the predictor variables.

An example

Consider a forensic psychologist working with prison inmates. The psychologist might be interested in identifying factors that predict whether or not a particular inmate will be reconvicted after release from prison. To undertake this analysis, the psychologist would first collect data from the records of past prisoners. This data would include the outcome (whether or not the prisoner was reconvicted after release) in addition to a number of other variables that the psychologist thinks may influence the chances of reconviction. These predictor variables might include the length of the sentence served, a measure of the behaviour of the prisoner when in custody (such as the number of days 'on report'), a measure of the level of drug use and a measure of social support (such as number of hours of prison visits per month). The psychologist could use either discriminant analysis or logistic regression to analyse these data. Although these two procedures are technically very different, their outcomes are similar, in that each allows the psychologist to identify which combination of these variables (if any) is useful in predicting reconviction. The psychologist could then apply this knowledge to all new prisoners entering the jail in order to identify those who are most likely to be reconvicted after their release and to target resources towards these high-risk prisoners in an attempt to reduce recidivism.

Similarities and differences between discriminant analysis and logistic regression

Both discriminant analysis and logistic regression allow us to predict a categorical dependent variable on the basis of a number of predictor or independent variables. These independent variables are normally continuous variables, but logistic regression can also handle categorical independent variables. In general, logistic regression can be used in a wider range of situations than discriminant analysis. For example, discriminant analysis makes various assumptions about the predictor variables, including that they should be normally distributed. Logistic regression makes no such assumptions about the distribution of the predictor variables.

Both logistic regression and discriminant analysis can be used in situations where the outcome variable has more than two categories. However, in cases with more than two categories, the output becomes more difficult to interpret. For the purpose of this book, we are only going to consider cases with dichotomous outcome variables.

An important distinction lies in the interpretation of the output. The output of discriminant analysis is rather more difficult to interpret than that of logistic regression. Discriminant analysis results in the calculation of a discriminant function – a formula that combines the predictor variables to calculate a value that is then used to predict category membership. The value of the discriminant function is somewhat arbitrary and tells us relatively little about the basis on which the prediction is being made. Although logistic regression is a more complex procedure, the output is rather easier to interpret. Logistic regression computes the probability (actually the log odds – see Section 4 for more details) that a case will belong to a particular category.

As a result of these advantages, many researchers now recommend the use of logistic regression over discriminant analysis. However, we describe discriminant analysis because it is still commonly employed in some fields of psychology.

Section 2: AN INTRODUCTION TO DISCRIMINANT ANALYSIS

Tabachnick and Fidell (2014) note that discriminant analysis is rather like reverse MANOVA. Indeed, discriminant analysis could be described as a cross between backwards analysis of variance and multiple regression. In ANOVA designs, we manipulate membership of some group or category (the levels of the IV or factor) and investigate the effect on the DV. If we find a significant effect of one of our IVs, then we could say that we can partially predict a participant's DV score if we know which category they belong to. A similar attempt to predict category membership is at the heart of discriminant analysis.

Discriminant analysis is similar to multiple regression in that both techniques allow us to make predictions on the basis of several predictor variables. The difference is that, while multiple regression is used to predict a participant's score on the DV, discriminant analysis is used to predict which of a number of categories or groups the participant will belong to.

In discriminant analysis, the dependent variable is sometimes also referred to as the 'category variable', the 'criterion variable', or the 'grouping variable'. The other variables are independent variables or predictor variables.

An example

Let us return to our earlier example of a forensic psychologist working with prison inmates. It would be useful to predict which of these individuals are at the greatest risk of being reconvicted following release. This would allow you to target treatment towards these high-risk individuals and produce a cost-effective programme to reduce reconviction rates. First, you will need to collect data from each of the prisoners on a number of likely variables such as age at release, number of previous convictions, and the level of drug use. You can now investigate whether some weighted combination of these variables reliably discriminates between the group of prisoners who are reconvicted following release, and those who are not reconvicted. This combination of the predictor variables is called a *discriminant function* (it is a mathematical function that discriminates between the categories). Having calculated this discriminant function, you could apply it to all new inmates entering the prison, and, based on their score on each of the predictor variables, make a prediction regarding their chances of reconviction following release. You might then go on to develop a treatment programme that seeks to reduce reconviction by directly tackling some of the variables you have shown to significantly predict reconviction. For example, if drug use was a variable that predicted reconviction, you might consider including an intensive drug and alcohol module as part of the programme.

Two steps in discriminant analysis

As the above example shows, there are often two distinct steps involved in discriminant analysis:

1. Use cases where category membership is already known to develop a discriminant function that can reliably predict category membership in these cases.

2. Use this discriminant function to predict category membership for a new group of cases for whom category membership is not known.

A discriminant function is a mathematical formula that combines a set of predictor variables to predict the value of a categorical variable. For example, in the output shown in Section 3, the discriminant function (the variable named 'Dis1_1') has a high positive value for prisoners who we predict will be reconvicted and a high negative value for prisoners who we predict will not be reconvicted. The higher the value, the stronger the prediction. Once derived, the function can be applied to new prisoners, allowing us to make an informed prediction of their behaviour at the end of their sentence.

Assumptions

The category variable can have two or more distinct levels. Category membership must be mutually exclusive (each case must be classified into no more than one category) and collectively exhaustive (every case must be a member of a category). The requirements for predictor or independent variables are similar to those for dependent variables in MANOVA, but some violation of the rules regarding the distribution of these variables may be acceptable, especially if the analysis results in accurate classification. If the rate of prediction of classification is not acceptable, this might be due to the violation of some of these assumptions, especially those regarding outliers and homogeneity of variance (see Tabachnick and Fidell, 2014).

Methods in discriminant analysis

As in multiple regression, there are different methods that can be adopted. SPSS allows you to choose between the 'enter' method (also known as the 'simultaneous' method) and the stepwise method (also called 'statistical').

Choosing a method to adopt

1. Unless you have some very good reason to do otherwise, you should use the enter (simultaneous) method.

2. The stepwise (statistical) method can be used to produce a discriminant function that includes the minimum number of predictor variables.

What does each method tell us?

Suppose we were seeking to predict reconviction based on age, previous convictions and drug use. The two types of analysis would give us slightly different information about the data. The enter (simultaneous) method would tell us how good a prediction we can make on the basis of all three predictor variables together. In addition, we would be able to see how much each of the predictor variables contributes to the discriminant function (and hence the accuracy of our prediction). Stepwise or statistical methods would allow us to identify the best combination of predictor variables to use to predict category membership.

How does each method work?

1. **Enter (simultaneous)**: All the variables are entered simultaneously and the predictive power of the combination of all the variables is considered.

2. **Stepwise (statistical)**: If there are no theoretical grounds for predicting the relative importance of the variables, then stepwise can be used to determine the smallest useful set of predictor variables. In stepwise, the variables are entered and/or removed based on statistical assessments of their importance. However, just like stepwise multiple regression, this approach can be dangerous. The variables adopted, and hence the predictions made, can be influenced by minor variation in the predictor variables. Just as with multiple regression, if you choose to adopt a statistical method in discriminant analysis, then you should double-check the validity of your discriminant function by using cross-validation procedures. Discriminant analysis (especially when you use statistical methods) tends to overestimate the success of the discriminant function. Cross-validation reduces this overestimation by checking the validity of the discriminant function derived. There are two basic approaches to cross-validation:

   a. We can calculate a discriminant function based on one-half of our data and test it out on the other half (a little like split-half reliability).

   b. We can test the ability of the discriminant function to classify the same cases measured at some second time interval. This is a little like test-retest reliability.

Within the statistical methods, there are a variety of statistical criteria to adopt. These are the criteria by which SPSS decides which predictor variables to enter and/or remove from the discriminant function. This is a complex subject area that is covered in some detail by Tabachnick and Fidell (2014). If in doubt, we would advise you to use the default settings in SPSS.

Section 3: PERFORMING DISCRIMINANT ANALYSIS USING SPSS

Example study: reconviction among offenders

Hollin, Palmer and Clark (2003) collected data from 221 prison inmates in an attempt to identify the variables that predict reconviction among offenders. The data file contains just a few of the variables they measured. The variable 'age' records the prisoner's age in years, and 'precons' the number of previous convictions. The variable 'recon' is a categorical variable that records whether the prisoner was reconvicted after release. The value 1 indicates reconviction, while 0 indicates that the prisoner was not reconvicted. The variables 'crimhist2' and 'educemp2' are derived from a scale called the LSI-R (Level of Service Inventory – Revised), which is used by psychologists working in prisons. The LSI-R measures several aspects of an offender's life, including previous offending, drug use, behaviour in prison, family history, and education and employment. In the data file we will be using here, we have only included the measures of criminal history (crimhist2) and education and employment history (educemp2). We will use discriminant analysis to determine whether age, previous convictions, criminal history, and education and employment history can be used to predict reconviction. These data are available from he.palgrave.com/psychology/brace.

To perform a simultaneous (enter method) discriminant analysis

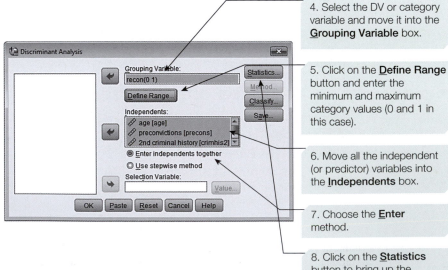

1. Click on **Analyze**.

2. Select **Classify**.

3. Select **Discriminant**. The **Discriminant Analysis** dialogue box will appear (see below).

4. Select the DV or category variable and move it into the **Grouping Variable** box.

5. Click on the **Define Range** button and enter the minimum and maximum category values (0 and 1 in this case).

6. Move all the independent (or predictor) variables into the **Independents** box.

7. Choose the **Enter** method.

8. Click on the **Statistics** button to bring up the dialogue box (shown below).

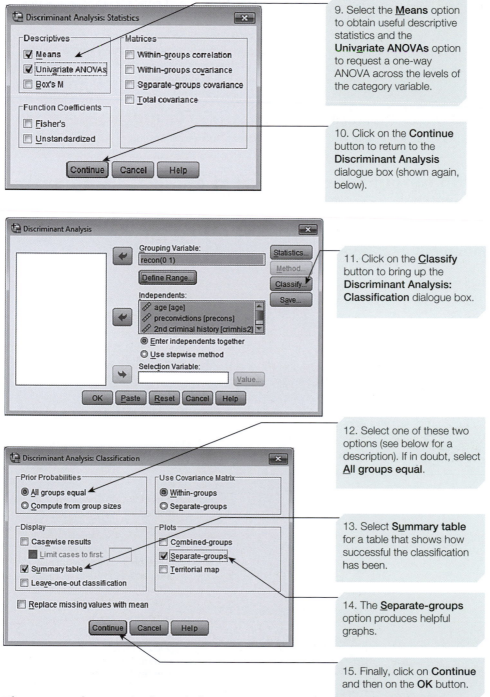

9. Select the **Means** option to obtain useful descriptive statistics and the **Univariate ANOVAs** option to request a one-way ANOVA across the levels of the category variable.

10. Click on the **Continue** button to return to the **Discriminant Analysis** dialogue box (shown again, below).

11. Click on the **Classify** button to bring up the **Discriminant Analysis: Classification** dialogue box.

12. Select one of these two options (see below for a description). If in doubt, select **All groups equal**.

13. Select **Summary table** for a table that shows how successful the classification has been.

14. The **Separate-groups** option produces helpful graphs.

15. Finally, click on **Continue** and then on the **OK** button.

CHAPTER 11

The annotated output is shown below.

In the **Discriminant Analysis: Classification** dialogue box, you can set the **Prior Probabilities** to either **All groups equal** or **Compute from group sizes**. The default setting is **All groups equal**. In this case, the analysis assumes that, all other things being equal, the probability of a case falling into one particular category is equal. Thus, if you have two groups, it assumes that the prior probability is 0.5. For three groups, it would be 0.333 and so on. There may be occasions when the probability of each outcome might not be the same. For example, you might decide that it is rather more likely that a patient will live rather than die regardless of the treatment you offer. In cases like this, it might be more appropriate to ask SPSS to compute the prior probabilities on the basis of the number of cases that fall into each outcome category. Thus, if you have 100 cases with 60 falling into one category and 40 into another, then the prior probabilities would be set at 0.6 and 0.4 respectively. If in doubt, it is safer to leave this option at the default setting of **All groups equal**.

SPSS output for discriminant analysis using enter method

Obtained using menu items: Classify > Discriminant (enter independents together)

Discriminant

Analysis Case Processing Summary

Unweighted Cases		N	Percent
Valid		221	100.0
Excluded	Missing or out-of-range group codes	0	.0
	At least one missing discriminating variable	0	.0
	Both missing or out-of-range group codes and at least one missing discriminating variable	0	.0
	Total	0	.0
Total		221	100.0

This table tells you that 100% of the 221 cases in the data file have been included in the analysis.

If any case had a missing value for one of the IVs (the predictor variables), the case would have been dropped from the analysis and this would have been reported in this table.

This is the table of means we requested in the **Discriminant Analysis: Statistics** dialogue box. It gives the mean and SD for each of our IVs broken down by category membership.

Group Statistics

reconvicted		Mean	Std. Deviation	Valid N (listwise) Unweighted	Valid N (listwise) Weighted
no	age	31.9873	12.86966	157	157.000
	preconvictions	4.9809	6.44451	157	157.000
	2nd criminal history	5.5796	3.17063	157	157.000
	2nd education and employment	4.6115	2.86144	157	157.000
yes	age	26.0000	8.32285	64	64.000
	preconvictions	7.7656	6.55802	64	64.000
	2nd criminal history	7.5313	2.88383	64	64.000
	2nd education and employment	6.0938	2.58026	64	64.000
Total	age	30.2534	12.02872	221	221.000
	preconvictions	5.7873	6.58545	221	221.000
	2nd criminal history	6.1448	3.20891	221	221.000
	2nd education and employment	5.0407	2.85771	221	221.000

For example, in this case we can see that while the overall mean age was 30.25, the individuals who were reconvicted had a mean age of only 26.0 compared to a mean of 31.99 for those who were not reconvicted.

Tests of Equality of Group Means

	Wilks' Lambda	F	df1	df2	Sig.
age	.949	11.818	1	219	.001
preconvictions	.963	8.403	1	219	.004
2nd criminal history	.924	18.127	1	219	.000
2nd education and employment	.944	12.894	1	219	.000

This table was produced because we requested Univariate ANOVAs in the **Discriminant Analysis: Statistics** dialogue box. It shows whether there is a significant effect of category for each of the predictor variables. For example, here we can see that there is a significant difference in the age of those reconvicted and not reconvicted ($F = 11.818$; df = 1,219; $p = 0.001$). In addition, SPSS gives Wilks' Lambda, a multivariate test of significance, which varies between 0 and 1. Values *very* close to 1 indicate that the differences are not significant.

Analysis 1
Summary of Canonical Discriminant Functions

Canonical functions are used to discriminate between pairs of categories, or groups. For each possible orthogonal (independent) contrast, a discriminant function is calculated that best discriminates between the categories. The number of canonical functions is either one less than the number of categories, or equal to the number of predictor variables, whichever is the smaller. The following tables give details of each of the discriminant functions calculated. In this example, there are only two categories, so only one function is calculated.

Eigenvalues

Function	Eigenvalue	% of Variance	Cumulative %	Canonical Correlation
1	.150ᵃ	100.0	100.0	.362

a. First 1 canonical discriminant functions were used in the analysis.

The eigenvalue is a measure of how well the discriminant function discriminates between the categories (the larger the value, the better the discrimination).

The % of Variance column allows you to compare the relative success of the functions. When there is only 1 function (as here), this column and the Cumulative % column tell us nothing useful. Where there are several functions, you will probably find that only the first few usefully discriminate among groups.

Wilks' Lambda

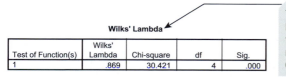

Test of Function(s)	Wilks' Lambda	Chi-square	df	Sig.
1	.869	30.421	4	.000

This table provides a test of the null hypothesis that the value of the discriminant function is the same for the reconvicted and non-reconvicted cases. As p is less than 0.05, we can reject the null hypothesis.

Standardized Canonical Discriminant Function Coefficients

	Function 1
age	-.601
preconvictions	.249
2nd criminal history	.547
2nd education and employment	.174

This table allows you to see the extent to which each of the predictor variables is contributing to the ability to discriminate between the categories. The coefficients have been standardised so that you can compare the contribution of each regardless of the units in which it was measured. Rather like correlation coefficients, the values range from –1 to +1. In this case, 'age' and '2nd criminal history' are making a larger contribution than the other predictor variables.

Structure Matrix

	Function 1
2nd criminal history	.742
2nd education and employment	.625
age	-.599
preconvictions	.505

Pooled within-groups correlations between discriminating variables and standardized canonical discriminant functions
Variables ordered by absolute size of correlation within function.

The Structure Matrix table gives a different measure of the contribution that each variable is making to the discriminant function. Here the variables are ordered by the magnitude of their contribution. The negative value for the variable 'age' tells us that age correlates negatively with the value of the function, whereas '2nd criminal history' correlates positively. This is because older prisoners are less likely to be reconvicted, whereas prisoners with a higher criminal history score are more likely to be reconvicted.

If you have more than 2 categories, and hence more than 1 Function calculated, this table also allows you to see which of the functions each variable is contributing most to (for example, is a particular variable helping you predict between membership of category a and b or between b and c?).

Functions at Group Centroids

reconvicted	Function 1
no	-.247
yes	.605

Unstandardized canonical discriminant functions evaluated at group means

This table gives the mean value of the discriminant function for each of the categories. Note that here the mean value of the function is positive for reconvicted prisoners but negative for non-reconvicted prisoners. In this way, the function is discriminating between the two categories of prisoners.

Classification Statistics

Classification Processing Summary

Processed		221
Excluded	Missing or out-of-range group codes	0
	At least one missing discriminating variable	0
Used in Output		221

This table informs you of the total number of cases processed, the number excluded and the number used in the output.

Prior Probabilities for Groups

reconvicted	Prior	Cases Used in Analysis Unweighted	Weighted
no	.500	157	157.000
yes	.500	64	64.000
Total	1.000	221	221.000

Prior Probability is the assumed probability that a particular case will belong to a particular category. In this case, in the **Discriminant Analysis: Classification** dialogue box (see page 305), under **Prior Probabilities**, we selected 'All groups equal', so the probability is equal for all groups – i.e. 0.5 or 50%.

Separate - Groups Graphs

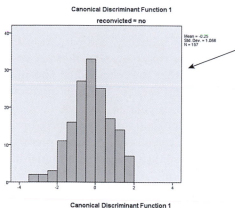

Canonical Discriminant Function 1
reconvicted = no

Mean = -0.25
Std. Dev. = 1.056
N = 157

These are the Separate-Groups Plots we requested in the **Discriminant Analysis: Classification** dialogue box (see above). Note we have edited the plots so that the x-axis is drawn to the same scale on both.

If the discriminate function is discriminating between the two groups of inmates, then the distribution will be different in these two plots. It is apparent that the distribution for those who were reconvicted is slightly shifted to the right, relative to those who were not reconvicted, but there is a lot of overlap between the two groups, indicating the discrimination is far from perfect.

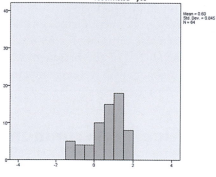

Canonical Discriminant Function 1
reconvicted = yes

Mean = 0.60
Std. Dev. = 0.845
N = 64

Classification Results[a]

			Predicted Group Membership		
		reconvicted	no	yes	Total
Original	Count	no	104	53	157
		yes	16	48	64
	%	no	66.2	33.8	100.0
		yes	25.0	75.0	100.0

a. 68.8% of original grouped cases correctly classified.

This is the Summary table we requested in the **Discriminant Analysis: Classification** dialogue box (see above). It provides a particularly useful summary of the success (or otherwise) of our discriminant function. It shows a cross-tabulation of the category membership (reconvicted or not) against what we would have predicted using our discriminant function.

We can see that in 104 cases the discriminant function correctly predicted that the offender would not be reconvicted, and in 48 cases it correctly predicted that they would be reconvicted. Thus, 152 (104 + 48) of our 221 cases were correctly classified – a success rate of 68.8% (as noted in the footnote to the table). However, the table also shows us that 25% of the prisoners we predicted would not be reconvicted were reconvicted, and that 33.8% of the cases we predicted would be reconvicted were not. It is up to you to interpret these failures of prediction; in some cases it may be more important to avoid one type of error than another. For example, here you may feel that it is more important to avoid erroneously predicting that someone will not be reconvicted than erroneously predicting that they will.

CHAPTER 11

Reporting the results

In a report you might write:

A discriminant analysis was performed with reconviction as the DV and age, number of previous convictions, and the criminal history, and education and employment, subscales of the LSI-R as predictor variables. A total of 221 cases were analysed. Univariate ANOVAs revealed that the reconvicted and non-reconvicted prisoners differed significantly on each of the four predictor variables. A single discriminant function was calculated. The value of this function was significantly different for reconvicted and non-reconvicted prisoners (chi-square = 30.42, df = 4, $p < .001$). The correlations between predictor variables and the discriminant function suggested that age and criminal history were the best predictors of future convictions. Age was negatively correlated with the discriminant function value, suggesting that older prisoners were less likely to be reconvicted. Criminal history was positively correlated with the discriminant function value, suggesting that prisoners with higher numbers of previous convictions were more likely to be reconvicted. Overall, the discriminant function successfully predicted the outcome for 68.8% of cases, with accurate predictions being made for 66.2% of the prisoners who did not go on to be reconvicted and 75% of the prisoners who were reconvicted.

To perform a stepwise (or statistical) discriminant analysis

To perform a stepwise discriminant analysis, follow the procedure outlined for the enter method except that, at step 7 (see above, page 304), select **Use stepwise method**, then click on the **Method** button to bring up the **Discriminant Analysis: Stepwise Method** dialogue box (see below).

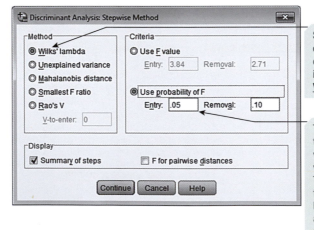

Select one of these methods. These control the statistical rules used to determine when a variable is entered into the equation. If in doubt, select **Wilks' lambda**, the default setting.

The criteria for entry and removal from the equation can be based on either *F* values or probability values and the values for both can be adjusted. Tabachnick and Fidell (2014) suggest that the **Entry** probability value could be changed from .05 to .15. This is a more liberal rule that will ensure that any important variable gets entered into the equation.

If in doubt, leave the Method set to **Wilks' lambda**, and the Criteria set to **Use F Value**, with the <u>E</u>ntry and Rem<u>o</u>val values set to 3.84 and 2.71 respectively (see above). Then click on the **Continue** button and complete steps 8–15 (see above, pages 304–5).

The output produced by the stepwise discriminant analysis is similar to that for the simultaneous discriminant analysis, and so only tables that differ are shown below. This output was produced using the default settings.

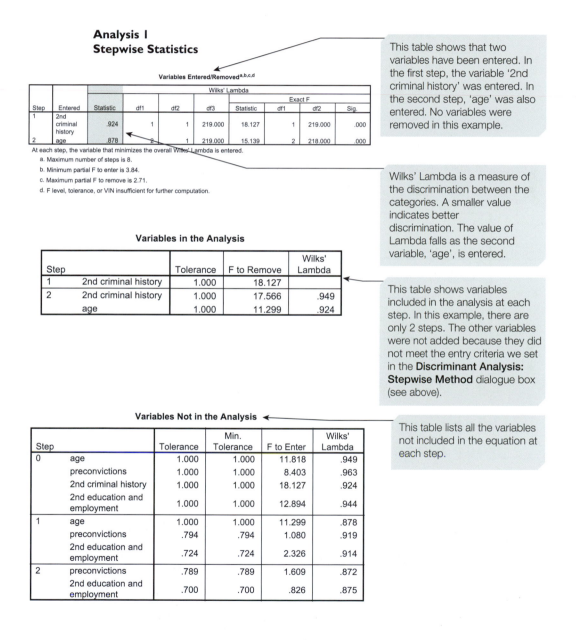

Analysis 1
Stepwise Statistics

Variables Entered/Removed [a,b,c,d]

Step	Entered	Statistic	df1	df2	df3	Statistic	df1	df2	Sig.
						Wilks' Lambda		**Exact F**	
1	2nd criminal history	.924	1	1	219.000	18.127	1	219.000	.000
2	age	.878	2	1	219.000	15.139	2	218.000	.000

At each step, the variable that minimizes the overall Wilks' Lambda is entered.

a. Maximum number of steps is 8.

b. Minimum partial F to enter is 3.84.

c. Maximum partial F to remove is 2.71.

d. F level, tolerance, or VIN insufficient for further computation.

This table shows that two variables have been entered. In the first step, the variable '2nd criminal history' was entered. In the second step, 'age' was also entered. No variables were removed in this example.

Wilks' Lambda is a measure of the discrimination between the categories. A smaller value indicates better discrimination. The value of Lambda falls as the second variable, 'age', is entered.

Variables in the Analysis

Step		Tolerance	F to Remove	Wilks' Lambda
1	2nd criminal history	1.000	18.127	
2	2nd criminal history	1.000	17.566	.949
	age	1.000	11.299	.924

This table shows variables included in the analysis at each step. In this example, there are only 2 steps. The other variables were not added because they did not meet the entry criteria we set in the **Discriminant Analysis: Stepwise Method** dialogue box (see above).

Variables Not in the Analysis

Step		Tolerance	Min. Tolerance	F to Enter	Wilks' Lambda
0	age	1.000	1.000	11.818	.949
	preconvictions	1.000	1.000	8.403	.963
	2nd criminal history	1.000	1.000	18.127	.924
	2nd education and employment	1.000	1.000	12.894	.944
1	age	1.000	1.000	11.299	.878
	preconvictions	.794	.794	1.080	.919
	2nd education and employment	.724	.724	2.326	.914
2	preconvictions	.789	.789	1.609	.872
	2nd education and employment	.700	.700	.826	.875

This table lists all the variables not included in the equation at each step.

CHAPTER 11

This table indicates how successful the discriminant function is at each step. A smaller value of Lambda indicates a better discrimination between categories. Here, the function significantly distinguishes between the two categories at both steps 1 and 2.

Wilks' Lambda

Step	Number of Variables	Lambda	df1	df2	df3	Exact F Statistic	df1	df2	Sig.
1	1	.924	1	1	219	18.127	1	219.000	.000
2	2	.878	2	1	219	15.139	2	218.000	.000

This is the Classification Results table for the stepwise discriminant analysis. It is interesting to compare this to the equivalent table produced using the enter method (see above). Which method results in the most successful prediction?

Classification Results[a]

		reconvicted	Predicted Group Membership		
			no	yes	Total
Original	Count	no	102	55	157
		yes	19	45	64
	%	no	65.0	35.0	100.0
		yes	29.7	70.3	100.0

a. 66.5% of original grouped cases correctly classified.

Using discriminant function analysis to predict group membership

So far we have been trying to develop discriminant functions that can predict category membership with a reasonable level of accuracy. Having produced these functions, the next step is to use them to try to make real predictions. For example, if we collect data from another group of prisoners before they are released, we can apply our discriminant function to predict which of these prisoners will be reconvicted following release.

To do this we need to compute the discriminant function for the new cases. The easiest way to do this is to add the new cases to the existing data file. Because we do not know whether these individuals will be reconvicted, we will have to enter a missing value for the variable 'recon'. As a result, these new cases will not be included when the discriminant function is calculated and, therefore, the result will be identical to that found before these cases were added.

Follow steps 1–15 listed above (pages 304–5), selecting **Use stepwise method** at step 7, but then click on the **Save** button in the **Discriminant Analysis** dialogue box. The **Discriminant Analysis: Save** dialogue box will be revealed (see below).

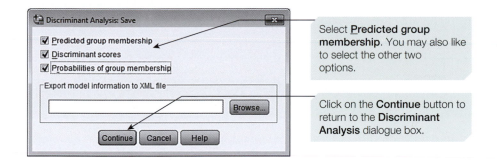

Select **Predicted group membership**. You may also like to select the other two options.

Click on the **Continue** button to return to the **Discriminant Analysis** dialogue box.

Now click on the OK button. In addition to the output described above, several new variables will be computed and added to your data file (see below).

This new variable gives the predicted category membership.

This new variable gives the value of the computed discriminant function. Notice that the value is higher for prisoners who are predicted to be reconvicted.

*Chapter11Dataset.sav [DataSet2] - IBM SPSS Statistics Data Editor

File Edit View Data Transform Analyze Direct Marketing Graphs Utilities Add-ons Window Help

	age	precons	recon	crimhis2	educemp2	Dis_1	Dis1_1	Dis1_2	Dis2_2
1	15.00	4	0	8.00	8.00	1	1.29516	.28525	.71475
2	17.00	6	0	2.00	4.00	0	-.33125	.60150	.39850
3	17.00	9	1	4.00	7.00	1	.17479	.49945	.50055
4	17.00	2	1	10.00	10.00	1	1.69294	.22375	.77625
5	18.00	0	0	4.00	1.00	0	.12066	.51052	.48948
6	18.00	8	1	4.00	9.00	0	.12066	.51052	.48948
7	18.00	0	0	11.00	10.00	1	1.89183	.19677	.80323
8	18.00	1	1	4.00	8.00	0	.12066	.51052	.48948
9	18.00	0	0	1.00	2.00	0	-.63841	.65992	.34008
10	18.00	9	1	4.00	3.00	0	.12066	.51052	.48948
11	19.00	9	1	10.00	9.00	1	1.58467	.23951	.76049
12	19.00	4	1	6.00	9.00	1	.57257	.41883	.58117
13	19.00	4	1	10.00	6.00	1	1.58467	.23951	.76049
14	19.00	1	1	1.00	3.00	0	-.69255	.66979	.33021
15	19.00	6	1	9.00	5.00	1	1.33164	.27920	.72080
16	19.00	1	0	3.00	3.00	0	-.18650	.57281	.42719
17	19.00	2	0	6.00	6.00	1	.57257	.41883	.58117
18	19.00	1	0	4.00	3.00	0	.06652	.52158	.47842
19	19.00	4	0	8.00	6.00	1	1.07862	.32268	.67732

This new variable is the predicted probability of being in group 1 (not reconvicted).

This new variable gives the predicted probability of being in group 2 (reconvicted).

In this way, we can first compute the best discriminant function and then use this to make real predictions. For example, we can predict that participant 1 will be reconvicted on release, and that our estimate of the probability of reconviction is 71.4%. Based on this relatively high risk of reconviction, we might decide to target some extra resources at this individual prior to their release in the hope of reducing their likelihood of reconviction.

Section 4: AN INTRODUCTION TO LOGISTIC REGRESSION

Logistic regression differs from discriminant analysis in that whereas discriminant analysis computes a function that best discriminates between two categories, logistic regression computes the log odds that a particular outcome will occur. For example, we can use logistic regression to compute the odds that a particular prisoner will be reconvicted after release.

The odds of an event occurring are given by the ratio of the probability of it occurring to the probability of it not occurring. For example, if four horses are running in a race and we pick one of them at random, the odds of our horse winning will be 0.25 / (1 − 0.25) = 0.333. The odds for any event lie between the values of 0 and +infinity. This is problematic for the mathematics involved in logistic regression, and to overcome this problem, the log of the odds is calculated (natural log or $\log_e$). The log odds of an event will vary between −infinity and +infinity, with a high value indicating an increased probability of occurrence. A positive value indicates that the event is more likely to occur than not (odds are in favour), while a negative value indicates that the event is more likely not to occur (odds are against). To illustrate the difference between odds and log odds, consider the example of the four-horse race. We have already seen that the odds of us picking the correct horse are 0.333. The odds of us picking the wrong horse are given by 0.75/(1 − 0.75) = 3. If we now take the log of each of these values, we will see that the log odds of us picking the correct horse are $\log_e (0.333) = -1.1$ and the log odds of us picking the wrong horse are $\log_e (3) = 1.1$. The advantage of log odds over odds is clear from this example: unlike odds, log odds are symmetric about zero. The term 'logistic' in the name logistic regression derives from this use of log odds.

It is possible to use logistic regression in situations when there are two or more categories of the grouping variable. In cases where there are just two categories of the grouping variable, the SPSS binary logistic regression command should be employed. Where there are more than two categories, the multinomial logistic regression command should be used. The multinomial command is not described here, but is similar to the binary logistic regression command.

As for discriminant analysis, we will show how the analysis can be used to predict category membership for cases where it is not known.

Section 5: PERFORMING LOGISTIC REGRESSION ON SPSS

Example study: reconviction among offenders

We will demonstrate binary logistic regression using the prisoner data set used to demonstrate discriminant analysis (see Section 3). This will allow us to compare the output of these two commands.

To perform a binary logistic regression

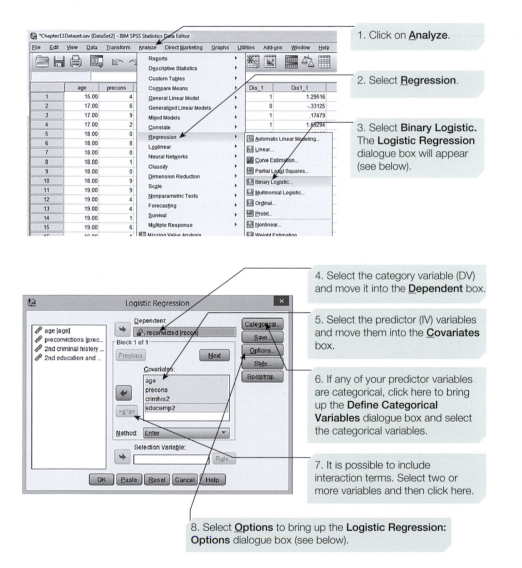

1. Click on **Analyze**.

2. Select **Regression**.

3. Select **Binary Logistic**. The **Logistic Regression** dialogue box will appear (see below).

4. Select the category variable (DV) and move it into the **Dependent** box.

5. Select the predictor (IV) variables and move them into the **Covariates** box.

6. If any of your predictor variables are categorical, click here to bring up the **Define Categorical Variables** dialogue box and select the categorical variables.

7. It is possible to include interaction terms. Select two or more variables and then click here.

8. Select **Options** to bring up the **Logistic Regression: Options** dialogue box (see below).

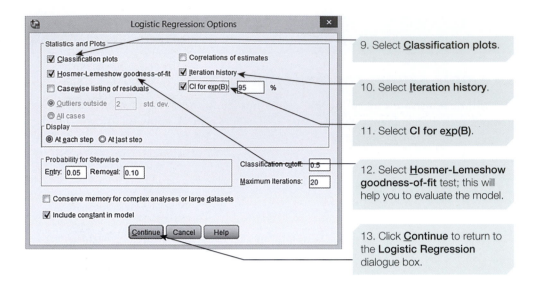

Finally, click on the ☐ OK ☐ button. The annotated output is shown below.

SPSS output for logistic regression using Enter method

Obtained using menu items: Regression > Binary Logistic

Logistic Regression

Case Processing Summary

Unweighted Cases[a]		N	Percent
Selected Cases	Included in Analysis	221	100.0
	Missing Cases	0	.0
	Total	221	100.0
Unselected Cases		0	.0
Total		221	100.0

a. If weight is in effect, see classification table for the total number of cases.

This table tells you that 100% of the 221 cases have been processed.

Dependent Variable Encoding

Original Value	Internal Value
no	0
yes	1

This table tells you how the two outcomes (reconvicted and not reconvicted) have been coded; this is important when interpreting the output.

Block 0: Beginning Block

This section of the output headed Block 0: Beginning Block reports the results of the most basic attempt to predict outcome; one in which all cases are predicted to result in the most common outcome.

Iteration History[a,b,c]

Iteration		-2 Log likelihood	Coefficients Constant
Step 0	1	266.132	-.842
	2	265.990	-.897
	3	265.990	-.897

a. Constant is included in the model.

b. Initial -2 Log Likelihood: 265.990

c. Estimation terminated at iteration number 3 because parameter estimates changed by less than .001.

This shows the iteration history.

This table reports the results of this simple prediction. As most of our prisoners are not reconvicted after release, the predicted outcome for all has been set to 'not reconvicted'. This crude method results in an accurate prediction for 71% of cases. Hopefully, our logistic regression will do better than this.

Classification Table[a,b]

			Predicted		
			reconvicted		Percentage
Observed			no	yes	Correct
Step 0	reconvicted	no	157	0	100.0
		yes	64	0	.0
	Overall Percentage				71.0

a. Constant is included in the model.

b. The cut value is .500

Variables in the Equation

		B	S.E.	Wald	df	Sig.	Exp(B)
Step 0	Constant	-.897	.148	36.612	1	.000	.408

Variables not in the Equation

			Score	df	Sig.
Step 0	Variables	AGE	11.316	1	.001
		PRECONS	8.167	1	.004
		CRIMHIS2	16.894	1	.000
		EDUCEMP2	12.288	1	.000
	Overall Statistics		28.909	4	.000

These two tables tell us that so far no variables have been entered into the equation.

We can ignore both these tables.

CHAPTER 11

Block I: Method = Enter ◄

This block of output reports the results of the logistic regression analysis. This analysis should result in a more accurate prediction than that reported in Block 0.

Iteration History[a,b,c,d]

Iteration		-2 Log likelihood	Coefficients				
			Constant	age	precons	crimhis2	educemp2
Step 1	1	237.530	-.888	-.031	.024	.109	.038
	2	233.181	-.797	-.052	.033	.155	.033
	3	233.002	-.727	-.058	.036	.165	.029
	4	233.001	-.722	-.058	.036	.166	.029
	5	233.001	-.722	-.058	.036	.166	.029

a. Method: Enter

b. Constant is included in the model.

c. Initial -2 Log Likelihood: 265.990

d. Estimation terminated at iteration number 5 because parameter estimates changed by less than .001.

Logistic regression employs a process known as *iteration*. In an iterative process, we attempt to arrive at the best answer to a problem through a series of approximations. Each iteration results in a slightly more accurate approximation than the previous iteration. This table reports this iterative process. The statistic −2 log likelihood is used in logistic regression to measure the success of the model. A high value indicates that the model poorly predicts the outcome. With each iteration we can see the value falling; however, the benefit derived at each iteration decreases until after 4 iterations there is no change in the value and SPSS terminates this process. You can also see how the coefficients of each of the predictor variables are adjusted at each iteration.

Omnibus Tests of Model Coefficients

		Chi-square	df	Sig.
Step 1	Step	32.988	4	.000
	Block	32.988	4	.000
	Model	32.988	4	.000

Omnibus tests are general tests of how well the model performs. In a report, we can use either this or the Hosmer-Lemeshow test (shown below). When the Enter method has been employed (as here), there is only 1 step and so the Step, Block and Model rows in this table will be identical.

Model Summary ◄

Step	-2 Log likelihood	Cox & Snell R Square	Nagelkerke R Square
1	233.001[a]	.139	.198

a. Estimation terminated at iteration number 5 because parameter estimates changed by less than .001.

This table give useful statistics that are equivalent to R^2 in multiple regression. It is not possible to compute an exact R^2 in logistic regression, but these two statistics are useful approximations. Here, we can see that our model accounts for between 13.9% and 19.8% of the variance.

Hosmer and Lemeshow Test ◄

Step	Chi-square	df	Sig.
1	5.876	8	.661

This table gives the results of the Hosmer-Lemeshow test we requested. It gives a measure of the agreement between the observed outcomes and the predicted outcomes. This statistic is a test of the null hypothesis that the model is good, hence a good model is indicated by a high p value, as in this example, where $p = .661$. If the p value is less than .05, then the model does not adequately fit the data.

Contingency Table for Hosmer and Lemeshow Test

		reconvicted = no		reconvicted = yes		
		Observed	Expected	Observed	Expected	Total
Step 1	1	21	20.940	1	1.060	22
	2	18	19.824	4	2.176	22
	3	20	18.573	2	3.427	22
	4	19	17.698	3	4.302	22
	5	18	16.845	4	5.155	22
	6	17	15.747	5	6.253	22
	7	12	14.333	10	7.667	22
	8	12	12.867	10	9.133	22
	9	9	10.798	13	11.202	22
	10	11	9.376	12	13.624	23

This table is used in the calculation of the Hosmer-Lemeshow statistic reported in the previous table. The cases are ranked by estimated probability on the criterion variable and then divided into 10 'deciles of risk'. Within each decile, the numbers of observed and expected positive (reconviction) and negative (no reconviction) outcomes are calculated. The Hosmer-Lemeshow statistic (above) is then calculated from this 10*2 contingency table. Note that a high proportion of the participants in decile 1 are not reconvicted, whereas the majority of those in decile 10 are reconvicted. This pattern indicates that our model is good.

Classification Table[a]

			Predicted		
			reconvicted		Percentage Correct
Observed			no	yes	
Step 1	reconvicted	no	138	19	87.9
		yes	44	20	31.3
Overall Percentage					71.5

a. The cut value is .500

This table summarises the results of our prediction and should be compared to the equivalent table in Block 0. Our model correctly predicts the outcome for 71.5% of cases. Although, overall, this is not much better than the situation reported in Block 0, in this new classification table we correctly predict reconviction in 31.3% of prisoners who are reconvicted. Compare this to the outcome of the discriminant analysis reported previously in this chapter.

Variables in the Equation

		B	S.E.	Wald	df	Sig.	Exp(B)	95.0% C.I.for EXP(B)	
								Lower	Upper
Step 1[a]	age	-.058	.018	10.221	1	.001	.944	.911	.978
	precons	.036	.026	1.871	1	.171	1.037	.984	1.092
	crimhis2	.166	.068	5.860	1	.015	1.180	1.032	1.349
	educemp2	.029	.070	.166	1	.684	1.029	.897	1.181
	Constant	-.722	.642	1.267	1	.260	.486		

a. Variable(s) entered on step 1: age, precons, crimhis2, educemp2.

This table contains some of the most critical information.

The first column gives the coefficients for each predictor variable in the model. The negative coefficient for 'age' indicates that the odds of reconviction declines with increasing age.

The Wald statistic and associated Sig. values indicate how useful each predictor variable is. In this case, only 'age' and 'crimhis2' are significant; the analysis could be rerun with only these variables included.

The Exp(B) column gives an indication of the change in the predicted odds of reconviction for each unit change in the predictor variable. Values less than 1 indicate that an increase in the value of the predictor variable is associated with a decrease in the odds of the event. Thus, for every extra year of age, the odds of the prisoner being reconvicted on release decrease by a factor of 0.944. The 95% CI values indicate that the magnitude of this decrease is likely to be in the range .911 to .978.

CHAPTER 11

Reporting the results

In a report you might write:

A logistic regression analysis was performed with reconviction as the DV, and age, number of previous convictions, and the LSI-R criminal history, education and employment subscales as predictor variables. A total of 221 cases were analysed and the full model significantly predicted reconviction status (omnibus chi-square = 32.99, df = 4, $p < .001$). The model accounted for between 13.9% and 19.8% of the variance in reconviction status, with 87.9% of the non-reconvicted prisoners successfully predicted. However, only 31.3% of predictions for the reconvicted group were accurate. Overall, 71.5% of predictions were accurate. Table 11.1 (not included here) gives coefficients and the Wald statistic and associated degrees of freedom and probability values for each of the predictor variables. This shows that only age and criminal history reliably predicted reconviction. The values of the coefficients reveal that an increase of one year of age is associated with a decrease in the odds of conviction by a factor of 0.94 (95% CI 0.91 and 0.98), and that each unit increase in criminal history score is associated with an increase in the odds of reconviction by a factor of 1.18 (95% CI 1.03–1.35).

Using logistic regression to predict group membership

We can now use the results of our logistic regression analysis to calculate the level of risk of reconviction for each new inmate who enters the prison. To do this, we need to add to the data file the data from each new prisoner as they arrive to start their sentence. For each of these new cases, enter a missing value for the category variable ('recon'). Now repeat the analysis as before, but in the **Logistic Regression** dialogue box, click on the **Save** button. This will bring up the **Logistic Regression: Save** dialogue box (see below).

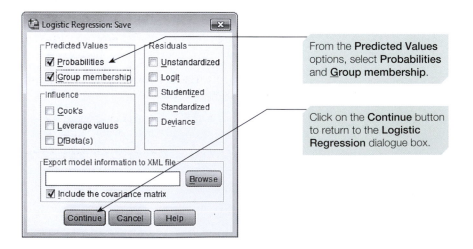

From the **Predicted Values** options, select **Probabilities** and **Group membership**.

Click on the **Continue** button to return to the **Logistic Regression** dialogue box.

Now click on the OK button. In addition to the output described above, two new variables will be added to the data file. The first of these gives the predicted probability of reconviction for each case, and the second gives the predicted group (reconvicted or not). We could use these predicted probabilities to make decisions about treatment or early release. However, in doing so, it would be important to remember the classification table (see output above), which showed that when we predict reconviction, we will be wrong on about 50% of occasions.

*Chapter11Dataset.sav [DataSet2] - IBM SPSS Statistics Data Editor

File   Edit   View   Data   Transform   Analyze   Direct Marketing   Graphs   Utilities   Add-ons   Window   Help

9 :

	age	precons	recon	crimhis2	educemp2	PRE_1	PGR_1
1	15.00	4	0	8.00	8.00	.52662	1
2	17.00	6	0	2.00	4.00	.26018	0
3	17.00	9	1	4.00	7.00	.37297	0
4	17.00	2	1	10.00	10.00	.57609	1
5	18.00	0	0	4.00	1.00	.25450	0
6	18.00	8	1	4.00	9.00	.36440	0
7	18.00	0	0	11.00	10.00	.58469	1
8	18.00	1	1	4.00	8.00	.30193	0
9	18.00	0	0	1.00	2.00	.17612	0
10	18.00	9	1	4.00	3.00	.33359	0
11	19.00	9	1	10.00	9.00	.60237	1
12	19.00	4	1	6.00	9.00	.39465	0
13	19.00	4	1	10.00	6.00	.53708	1
14	19.00	1	1	1.00	3.00	.17712	0
15	19.00	6	1	9.00	5.00	.50668	1
16	19.00	1	0	3.00	3.00	.23062	0
17	19.00	2	0	6.00	6.00	.35755	0
18	19.00	1	0	4.00	3.00	.26129	0

This new variable gives the predicted probability of reconviction. Note participant 1 is predicted to be at higher risk of reconviction than participant 2.

This new variable gives the predicted outcome with regards to reconviction. It is predicted that participant 1 will be reconvicted but that participant 2 will not.

Summary

- This chapter introduced two statistical procedures, discriminant analysis and logistic regression, which can be used to make a prediction about category membership. See Chapter 9 for a test that makes a prediction about an outcome variable that is a score.

- Logistic regression and discriminant analysis differ in the assumptions they make about the predictor variables.

- If you need to recode any of your predictor variables, see Chapter 4 for guidance on recoding values or computing new variables.

- For guidance on incorporating SPSS output into a report, or on printing the output, see Chapter 13.

CHAPTER 11

12 Factor analysis, and reliability and dimensionality of scales

> ## In this chapter
> - An introduction to factor analysis
> - Performing a basic factor analysis using SPSS
> - Other aspects of factor analysis
> - Reliability analysis for scales and questionnaires
> - Dimensionality of scales and questionnaires

SPSS for Psychologists online
Visit he.palgrave.com/psychology/brace for data sets, online tutorials and exercises.

Section 1: AN INTRODUCTION TO FACTOR ANALYSIS

- Exploratory factor analysis, usually just called factor analysis, enables us to investigate whether there is an underlying structure in the pattern of correlations between a number of variables.

- An example is the factor structure underlying human abilities and aptitudes (e.g. Kline, 1994). If people undertake a large number of ability and aptitude tests, it is likely that each test will be correlated with at least some of the other tests. There are likely to be groups of tests and, within each group, all tests will be correlated with each other; whereas, for tests from two different groups, the correlation will be lower or absent. It is well established for human abilities that different dimensions, such as verbal ability and spatial ability, underlie these groups of tests.

- To generalise, if we measure a large number of variables, we can investigate whether those variables represent a smaller number of dimensions.

- If these dimensions are psychological, they can be called *psychological constructs*, but the more general term is *factors*.

- Factor analysis can establish whether one or more factors do underlie a large number of variables; if so, the analysis identifies the number of factors and it also identifies which of the variables make up which factor.

- Factor analysis is sometimes called a 'data reduction technique', because you could use the outcome to choose a smaller set of variables than those initially measured, for use in future analysis or studies.

- Exploratory factor analysis does not test hypotheses (except for the number of factors, see below). Instead, it explores the possibility of a factor structure underlying the variables. The analysis provides a large amount of information, from which the researcher can make informal inferences about factors.

- Hypotheses about the number of factors can be tested in IBM SPSS Statistics software (SPSS); this will be briefly mentioned in Section 3.

- For hypothesis testing about structure and relationships, a somewhat different analysis, confirmatory factor analysis, has been developed. For this, instead of SPSS, use a structural equation modelling package such as AMOS (now available from IBM and known as IBM SPSS Amos) or LISREL.

How this chapter is organised

This chapter is organised somewhat differently from other chapters, in that later in this section we will be using tables produced by SPSS to explain some aspects of factor analysis. We will not at that point explain how to produce those tables; instead, we just use them to talk about factor analysis. We will also explain how these tables can give an indication of whether a factor analysis is likely to be useful with the variables you have measured. For this section, the tables are *not* derived from data suitable for a real factor analysis. Instead, the data are simply convenient for the purpose of this demonstration. If you are already familiar with factor analysis, you could omit this section. If you are going to use factor analysis in real research, then you should understand more about factor analysis than can be explained in any book on how to use SPSS. We recommend the following: Cooper (2010, Chapters 16 and 17); Giles (2002); Kline (1994, who introduces the calculations for factor analysis in detail); and Tabachnick and Fidell (2014).

Section 2 returns to our normal style, showing how to perform a basic factor analysis and then how to interpret the output. Section 3 discusses some other aspects of factor analysis. Finally, in Sections 4 and 5, we provide some guidelines on using SPSS to check the reliability and dimensionality of scales/questionnaires. First, we continue this section with an introduction to factor analysis.

How factor analysis relates to other statistical tests

Correlation and covariance

Bivariate correlation identifies the level of linear relationship between two variables. The covariance of two variables, the extent to which they vary together, is the unstandardised equivalent. Factor analysis identifies variables that all relate to a single factor by exploring the relationships between the variables. It does so by carrying out calculations based on the matrix of correlation coefficients, or the matrix of covariances, between each variable with each of the other variables. As a default, SPSS uses the correlation matrix in factor analysis.

Multiple regression

In multiple regression, we are interested in which of a number of predictor variables may be useful in predicting scores on another variable, the criterion variable. Factor analysis could be used in predicting what score someone might get on a variable; for example, if you find out that a new test can be accounted for by the factor verbal ability, then someone who scores highly on other tests that tap verbal ability should also score highly on the new test.

In multiple regression, correlations between the predictor variables should not be too high; if they are, then those predictor variables may actually be measuring the same thing and so do not add to our understanding of what predicts the criterion variable. By contrast, in factor analysis, we are interested in relatively high correlations, because we want to investigate which variables are measuring aspects of the same thing (the same dimension, factor, or psychological construct). See Tabachnick and Fidell (2014), however, for limitations on multicollinearity in factor analysis.

Analysis of variance

It is important that you recognise the difference between the meaning of the term *factor* in ANOVA and its meaning in factor analysis. In a true experimental ANOVA design, the experimenter manipulates the levels of each factor in order to explore cause-and-effect relationships between the factors and the dependent variable. In an ANOVA design incorporating any factor with levels from a natural group variable, the levels are not manipulated but instead they are chosen from existing groups, such as male and female, or high extroversion and low extroversion, so causal relationships cannot be assumed. In either case, in ANOVA terminology, the word 'factor' is simply a more convenient name for an independent variable, whereas in factor analysis, it means a dimension (or a psychological construct) that underlies several measured variables. So, in factor analysis, the term has a more profound but less concrete meaning than it does in ANOVA. Of course, in any specific study in which an ANOVA design is used, one or more of the factors may represent a psychological construct.

Discriminant analysis and logistic regression

Discriminant analysis and logistic regression are methods for determining which variables will predict membership of, or discriminate between, different categories of another variable. The example given in Chapter 11 was an investigation of which variables would discriminate between those offenders who had been reconvicted and those who had not. In factor analysis, by contrast, we are usually not interested in the scores of any individual participant. Instead, we want to explain the pattern of correlations between variables, and identify factors (dimensions) underlying those variables.

Correlation matrix and other matrices in factor analysis

Here, we consider certain aspects of factor analysis, including how it makes use of the matrix of correlations. For our explanations, we will use the data previously used for Spearman's r_s correlation coefficient (Chapter 6, Section 4). Those data were for only three variables, and thus are *not* appropriate for factor analysis. Three variables, however, give rise to small matrices that will be much more useful for illustration than the large matrices produced by the number of variables typically entered into a real factor analysis.

One point to note is that factor analysis in SPSS makes use of Pearson's, not Spearman's, correlation coefficients. This is acceptable for our data because factor analysis can be used with continuous and discrete data. For a continuous scale the data points can have fractional values, whereas for a discrete scale the data points have to be integers (whole numbers). Both continuous and discrete, however, can be of ratio, interval or ordinal level of measurement. For the study on the relationships between attractiveness, believability and confidence, the three variables, 'confdt' (confidence in the woman's testimony), 'believ' (how believable the woman was) and 'attrct' (how attractive the woman was), were all entered into a Pearson's *r* analysis. The table below is from the SPSS output. Details of the study are in Chapter 6, Section 4, and how to obtain and interpret the output for Pearson's correlation coefficient is described in Chapter 6, Section 3.

We show the Pearson's *r* output itself for comparison purposes. Next, we will show various matrices that can be produced by means of the factor analysis command. Details of how to obtain these tables are given in Section 2 of this chapter; for now we simply use them to explain aspects of factor analysis. They can also help to indicate whether our variables have *factorability*; that is, whether it is likely that there are any factors underlying the variables we measured (Tabachnick and Fidell, 2014, 667).

Pearson's *r* output

Correlations

		confdt	believ	attrct
confdt	Pearson Correlation	1	.278**	.073
	Sig. (2-tailed)		.008	.498
	N	89	89	89
believ	Pearson Correlation	.278**	1	.429**
	Sig. (2-tailed)	.008		.000
	N	89	89	89
attrct	Pearson Correlation	.073	.429**	1
	Sig. (2-tailed)	.498	.000	
	N	89	89	89

**. Correlation is significant at the 0.01 level (2-tailed).

In Pearson's *r* output, each cell of the matrix contains the values of *r*, *p* and *N*, allowing a quick assessment of the strength and significance of each individual bivariate correlation. In the equivalent table produced by factor analysis, shown next, the matrix of coefficients is in the upper part of the table, and the matrix of *p* values, if you request it, is in the lower part of the table. This separation reflects the fact that the coefficients are used in factor analysis calculations, whereas the p values are just for information. These coefficient values are also known as the *observed correlations*. In a matrix, there is usually a distinction between the on-diagonal values and the off-diagonal values: see annotations below.

Correlation matrix from factor analysis output

1(a). The upper part of this table is a complete matrix of the correlation coefficients for each variable with each of the other variables and with itself.

1(b). The diagonal of a matrix is usually worth noting in factor analysis. The diagonal in this matrix holds the correlation coefficient for each variable with itself (and therefore these on-diagonal values are all equal to 1.0).

Correlation Matrix

		confdt	believ	attrct
Correlation	confdt	1.000	.278	.073
	believ	.278	1.000	.429
	attrct	.073	.429	1.000
Sig. (1-tailed)	confdt		.004	.249
	believ	.004		.000
	attrct	.249	.000	

1(c). These off-diagonal values are the three possible correlation coefficients between the different pairs of variables. These values are called the *observed correlations*. They are mirrored below left of the diagonal (see 1(a)).

2. The lower half of the table is a matrix of the p values corresponding to the correlation coefficients. The diagonal is left blank in this matrix.

For an indication of factorability, look at the sizes of the correlation coefficients between the different variables. If the coefficients are mostly small (less than .3), there is little likelihood that a factor structure underlies the variables.

Partial correlations from factor analysis output

The anti-image table (shown below) contains two matrices. The upper matrix is automatically printed if you request the anti-image matrices, but for now we are most interested in the lower matrix.

In the lower matrix, the off-diagonal values are the *partial correlations* with the signs reversed, known as the *negative partial correlations*. (This term does not mean that the value has to be negative; simply that the original sign is reversed.) A partial correlation is the correlation between two variables when the effects of any other variables are controlled for or 'partialled out'. Thus, in Chapter 6, we said that if there is a correlation between the number of ice creams sold and the number of drownings that occur, then it is likely that the relationship is explained by a third variable, temperature. To investigate this possibility, one could partial out the effect of temperature from both variables and then find the partial correlation between them; it is likely to be small in that example.

Anti-image Matrices

		confdt	believ	attrct
Anti-image Covariance	confdt	.920	-.228	.046
	believ	-.228	.755	-.335
	attrct	.046	-.335	.813
Anti-image Correlation	confdt	.515[a]	-.273	.053
	believ	-.273	.504[a]	-.427
	attrct	.053	-.427	.506[a]

a. Measures of Sampling Adequacy(MSA)

The diagonal holds the values of the Kaiser-Meyer-Olkin (KMO) measure of sampling adequacy for each variable. The KMO will be discussed in Section 2.

The off-diagonal values are the *negative partial correlations* (see above): these values indicate whether there is a factor structure underlying the variables (see below).

As stated above, if the correlation coefficients are mostly small, then the variables are unlikely to have factorability. However, if the correlation coefficients are mostly large, then we cannot conclude that the variables definitely do have factorability. The partial correlations provide the next check, as explained here. If there is a factor structure underlying a number of variables, then they should all be fairly well correlated with each other. So, we would expect the correlation between any two variables to become weaker once the effects of the other variables have been partialled out. If the partial correlation between two variables is not weaker than the correlation between them, then those two variables have a strong relationship to each other and little relationship to any of the other variables we measured.

> Use of the partial correlations as an indication of factorability depends on their absolute size; thus, the fact that SPSS reverses their sign and prints the negative partial correlations is irrelevant. If the partial correlations are mostly large, then there is little likelihood of a factor structure underlying the variables.

Reproduced correlations and residuals from factor analysis output

The *reproduced correlations* (the off-diagonal values in the upper matrix of the table below) are the values predicted for the correlations between the variables under the assumption that the factor analysis is correct. So, if the solution to the factor analysis represents the actual state of things, then these are the correlations that would be expected. Factor analysis then compares these predicted correlations with those that were actually obtained (the observed correlations); each *residual* value, in the lower matrix, is equal to the reproduced correlation subtracted from the observed correlation. If residuals are small, then the observed values are close to those predicted by the factors, which suggests a good factor fit (see the tip box on the next page).

The diagonal holds the reproduced communalities; these will be explained in Section 2.

These three values are the reproduced correlations between the different pairs of variables. They are mirrored below left of the diagonal.

Reproduced Correlations

		confdt	believ	attrct
Reproduced Correlation	confdt	.281[a]	.450	.391
	believ	.450	.721[a]	.627
	attrct	.391	.627	.545[a]
Residual[b]	confdt		-.172	-.318
	believ	-.172		-.197
	attrct	-.318	-.197	

Extraction Method: Principal Component Analysis.

a. Reproduced communalities
b. Residuals are computed between observed and reproduced correlations. There are 3 (100.0%) nonredundant residuals with absolute values greater than 0.05.

The observed correlation (see the first table in this section) minus the reproduced correlation equals the residual: .278 − .450 = −.172.

Factorability: the smaller the residuals are (unlike here), the more likely it is that the factor analysis gives a good explanation of the data. That is, the more likely it is that the identified factors do explain the actual state of things in the real world.

So far we have introduced you to some concepts that will be useful in understanding factor analysis. For that purpose, we used data that were simply convenient. In Section 2 we will show you how to carry out and interpret a real factor analysis. First, some issues about when factor analysis can be used and more terminology.

When should I use factor analysis?

The following criteria are usually suggested:

1. The variables should be of at least ordinal level of measurement.

2. The variables should be normally distributed: if they do not meet the criteria for normal distribution, you should consider a transformation (see Tabachnick and Fidell, 2014).

3. The relationships between variables should be reasonably linear.

4. It is usually considered that for a successful factor analysis, at least 100 participants should have provided data, and some say that 200 or more are required. Two pointers are:

   a. There should be more participants than variables. Kline (1994) suggests a minimum ratio of 2:1, but the more the better. Thus, if you wish to explore the factor structure underlying a questionnaire that contains 60 items, you should test a minimum of 120 participants.

b. There should be more participants than extracted factors. Kline suggests a minimum ratio of 20:1. In truly exploratory factor analysis, however, we do not know how many factors there will be.

In general, the more participants you test, the more likely it is that any factors that do underlie the measured variables will be revealed; thus, a sample size of 200 is a sensible minimum target.

Usefulness/validity of a factor analysis

Any data set containing a number of variables can be factor analysed, but the outcome may be invalid or simply useless. A number of methods for assessing whether the variables entered have factorability have already been described. Other pointers to factorability, and to whether the extracted factors are a good solution to explaining the variables, will be described below. These pointers should be inspected before considering the factors that may have been extracted. One should then consider whether the solution provided by the factor analysis makes sense.

Terminology

In addition to the terms introduced above, the following terms are required to follow the output from even a fairly basic factor analysis.

Component and factor

Kline (1994, 36) states: 'components are real factors because they are derived directly from the correlation matrix. Common factors of factor analysis are hypothetical because they are estimated from the data.' Common factors are therefore an example of what Skinner (1965) referred to as 'explanatory fictions'. This does not mean, however, that they are not useful, but it is important that you use caution when interpreting any factors you derive from a factor analysis. The simplest type of factor analysis, principal component analysis, extracts components as its name suggests, whereas other types extract common factors. Thus, principal component analysis and factor analysis are somewhat different things; we give more detail in Section 3.

In this book, in common with many others, the terms 'factor' and 'component' are used interchangeably when we discuss principal component analysis, but the distinction between them should be borne in mind throughout.

Extraction

Extraction is the name for the process by which the important factors are identified; those factors are then said to have been *extracted*. We illustrate the principal component method of extraction, and mention other methods in Section 3. Extraction is not an exact process, as should become clear as you work through Section 2.

Communality

Communality is a measure of how much variance in the data from a particular variable is explained by the analysis. The values can range from 0 to 1. Initially, all the factors (or components) in the analysis (equal to the number of variables entered) are used to calculate the communalities and all the variance is accounted for. Thus, in principal component analysis, the *initial* communalities are all equal to 1 (indicating that all the variance is explained). After the factor or component extraction, *extraction* communalities for each variable are calculated based on the extracted factors only. The higher the value of the extraction communality is for a particular variable, the more of its variance has been explained by the extracted factors. The communality is calculated from factor loadings (see below).

Eigenvalue

Eigenvalue is a measure of how much variance in the data is explained by a single factor. Remember that the analysis initially considers all the possible factors, and allocates the same number of possible factors as there are variables. The higher the value of the eigenvalue, the more of the variance in the data is explained by that factor. The magnitude of the eigenvalue can be used to determine whether a factor explains sufficient variance for it to be considered a useful factor. The default value for this in SPSS is 1.0 but it is possible to request SPSS to extract factors using a reference eigenvalue other than 1.0, as explained in Section 3.

Scree plot

The scree plot is a useful graph of the eigenvalues of all the factors initially considered. It can be used to decide on the number of factors that should be extracted. An annotated example is shown in Section 2.

Factor loadings

A factor loading is calculated for each combination of variable and extracted factor. These values are useful for seeing the pattern of which variables are likely to be explained by which factor. The factor loading can be thought of as the coefficient of the correlation between the component (or factor) and the variable; thus, the larger the number, the more likely it is that the component underlies that variable. Loadings may be positive or negative; this issue is considered further in Section 3.

The initial factor loadings can be inspected for patterns. Almost always, however, a rotation will be used (see below) and the rotation factor loadings are a more useful indicator of patterns. SPSS uses the before-rotation factor loadings to calculate the extraction communalities; we calculate an example in our annotations of the SPSS output in Section 2.

Rotation

A factor analysis prior to rotation provides an explanation of how many factors underlie the variables; for some purposes this is sufficient. In psychology, however, we normally wish to understand what it all means; so we want to establish whether any psychological constructs might underlie the variables. Rotation is a mathematical technique available in factor analysis that arrives at the simplest pattern of factor loadings.

There are different methods of rotation, with a broad distinction between orthogonal rotation methods and oblique rotation methods. Orthogonal methods do not allow correlations between the factors produced, whereas oblique methods produce factors that may have some intercorrelations. Kline (1994) points out that psychological constructs may well be correlated with one another, or non-orthogonal (see Chapter 9, Section 1, where we discuss this in relation to multiple regression). Kline recommends using the **Direct O̲blimin** method (one of the list of oblique rotation methods available in SPSS).

Section 2: PERFORMING A BASIC FACTOR ANALYSIS USING SPSS

Hypothetical study

To illustrate the use of this analysis, we shall suggest a hypothetical survey. Suppose that a psychologist who is interested in aesthetic values wanted to investigate people's appreciation of different types of plants. For example, they wished to study whether there were any underlying dimensions to a liking for plants typically found in different places, such as 'wild' English countryside, cottage gardens, and formal gardens. They might construct a questionnaire listing various plants to which people are asked to give a score from 1 (extreme dislike) to 7 (extreme liking). The plants could be wild flowers (e.g. celandine, primrose, bluebell, buttercup, daisy, speedwell), cottage garden-type flowers (such as cornflower, poppy, sweetpea, lavender, aster), and formal garden type plants (e.g. rose, wisteria, delphinium, hellebore). A data set of 50 cases only is used to illustrate factor analysis, but, as explained above, many more participants are required for the results of a factor analysis to be valid. The data are available from he.palgrave.com/psychology/brace. Note that these hypothetical data are skewed, which might be problematic for a real factor analysis (see Tabachnick and Fidell, 2014). The data file includes the sex of the participants, with 23 men and 27 women, so that you can try the option of selecting members of a group, if you wish. Remember that the survey described is hypothetical; we do not know what you would find if you tried this study yourself.

How to perform the analysis

Here, we show you how to carry out and interpret a principal component analysis; other extraction methods are described in Section 3.

> The first time we run a factor analysis, we can include all the variables (of ordinal, interval or ratio level of measurement) we have measured. We should then inspect the indicators of factorability in the factor analysis output and decide:
>
> 1. Whether there is any factor structure at all – if not, then give up.
> 2. Whether all the variables are useful – if any are not, then run a new factor analysis in which you only include the useful variables.

Click on <u>A</u>nalyze ⇒ <u>D</u>imension Reduction ⇒ <u>F</u>actor. In the **Factor Analysis** dialogue box (shown below), select all the variables you want to enter into the factor analysis, and move them across into the <u>V</u>ariables box.

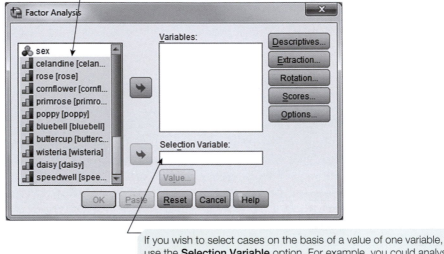

Select all the variables except 'sex' for the factor analysis and click on the arrow to move them into the <u>V</u>ariables box.

After an initial run through the analysis, you may want to deselect some of these (see tip box above).

If you wish to select cases on the basis of a value of one variable, use the **Sele<u>c</u>tion Variable** option. For example, you could analyse data from men only or from women only.

Next click on the <u>D</u>escriptives button, and the **Factor Analysis: Descriptives** dialogue box will appear (as shown below).

Factor Analysis: Descriptives

Statistics

☑ <u>U</u>nivariate descriptives

☑ <u>I</u>nitial solution

Correlation Matrix

☑ <u>C</u>oefficients ☐ In<u>v</u>erse

☑ <u>S</u>ignificance levels ☑ <u>R</u>eproduced

☐ <u>D</u>eterminant ☑ <u>A</u>nti-image

☑ <u>K</u>MO and Bartlett's test of sphericity

Continue Cancel Help

If you select **<u>U</u>nivariate descriptives**, SPSS will print the mean, standard deviation and number of cases for each of the variables you enter into the factor analysis.

The **<u>I</u>nitial solution** option is normally preselected.

Select the **Correlation Matrix** options as shown here. Don't select **In<u>v</u>erse** or **<u>D</u>eterminant** for now; we will explain those options in Section 3.

Output from some of the **Correlation Matrix** options were described in Section 1. All those we have selected here will be described below. We will cover the **Inverse** and **Determinant** options in Section 3. When you have selected all the options you require, click on the **Continue** button to return to the **Factor Analysis** dialogue box. Now click on the **Extraction** button; the **Factor Analysis: Extraction** dialogue box (shown below) will appear.

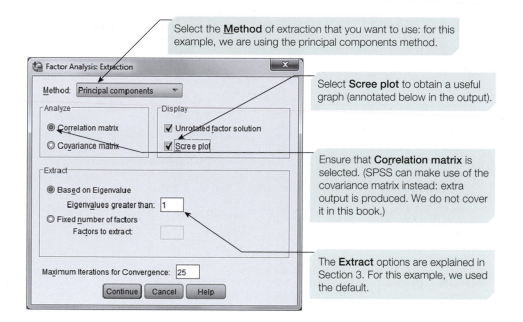

Select the **Method** of extraction that you want to use: for this example, we are using the principal components method.

Select **Scree plot** to obtain a useful graph (annotated below in the output).

Ensure that **Correlation matrix** is selected. (SPSS can make use of the covariance matrix instead: extra output is produced. We do not cover it in this book.)

The **Extract** options are explained in Section 3. For this example, we used the default.

Some of the other options in the **Factor Analysis: Extraction** dialogue box will be described in Section 3. When you have selected all the options you require, click on the **Continue** button to return to the **Factor Analysis** dialogue box. Now click on the **Rotation** button; the **Factor Analysis: Rotation** dialogue box will appear (see below).

Select the **Direct Oblimin** rotation method. The **Delta** option will become available; it affects how correlated the factors will be. The default value, zero, gives the most oblique solution.

Once you have selected a method, all the **Display** options will be highlighted. Normally, you will leave those settings at their default values, as shown.

Note that other rotation methods can be used: we mention them in Section 3.

Other options in the **Factor Analysis: Rotation** dialogue box will be described in Section 3. Click on the **Continue** button to return to the **Factor Analysis** dialogue box.

Clicking on **Options** brings up a dialogue box that allows you to specify how to treat missing values. It also allows you to control the appearance of part of the output; we will describe that in Section 3. Use of the dialogue box from **Scores** will not be described until Section 3. Finally, click on **OK**. The annotated output is shown below.

Output from factor analysis using principal component extraction and direct oblimin rotation

Obtained using menu items: Analyze > Dimension Reduction > Factor

Descriptive Statistics

	Mean	Std. Deviation	Analysis N
celandine	5.2200	1.56870	50
rose	5.2200	1.51577	50
cornflower	5.4600	1.66856	50
primrose	5.3800	1.39810	50
poppy	6.1200	1.25584	50
bluebell	5.7200	1.29426	50
buttercup	5.3400	1.63645	50
wisteria	5.3200	1.42055	50
daisy	5.6200	1.29189	50
speedwell	5.9600	1.21151	50
sweetpea	5.2800	1.57843	50
delphinium	4.3800	1.71298	50
aster	5.4000	1.55183	50
lavender	5.9400	1.50387	50
hellebore	3.9000	1.85439	50

This table is produced by the **Univariate Descriptives** option in the **Factor Analysis: Descriptives** dialogue box.

Remember that in a real factor analysis, you should aim to test a minimum of 200 participants.

The descriptives table above is the only part of the output with a note of the number of participants you entered into the factor analysis, so we recommend that you always request this table, for reference purposes.

The contents of this table are produced by the **Coefficients** and **Significance levels** options in the **Factor Analysis: Descriptives** dialogue box. Here, the whole table is shown shrunk to fit. Next, there is an annotated section of the upper matrix.

Correlation Matrix

		celandine	rose	cornflower	primrose	poppy	bluebell	buttercup	wisteria	daisy	speedwell	sweetpea	delphinium	aster	lavender	hellebore
Correlation	celandine	1.000	.099	.194	.566	.111	.785	.519	.206	.697	.660	.205	.014	.072	.110	-.126
	rose	.099	1.000	.355	.104	.672	.136	.027	.744	.398	.272	.554	.525	.743	.543	.516
	cornflower	.194	.355	1.000	.378	.694	.344	.188	.531	.405	.393	.725	.145	.440	.735	.279
	primrose	.566	.104	.378	1.000	.206	.782	.656	.164	.692	.612	.256	.015	.070	.186	-.142
	poppy	.111	.672	.694	.206	1.000	.235	.019	.699	.406	.379	.724	.453	.572	.868	.461
	bluebell	.785	.136	.344	.782	.235	1.000	.653	.227	.667	.722	.319	-.015	.189	.243	-.122
	buttercup	.519	.027	.188	.656	.019	.653	1.000	.154	.468	.511	.089	.048	.106	.025	-.204
	wisteria	.206	.744	.531	.164	.699	.227	.154	1.000	.524	.458	.687	.603	.811	.678	.562
	daisy	.697	.398	.405	.692	.406	.667	.468	.524	1.000	.851	.584	.334	.352	.366	.214
	speedwell	.660	.272	.393	.612	.379	.722	.511	.458	.851	1.000	.582	.253	.323	.301	.180
	sweetpea	.205	.554	.725	.256	.724	.319	.089	.687	.584	.582	1.000	.458	.620	.721	.512
	delphinium	.014	.525	.145	.015	.453	-.015	.048	.603	.334	.253	.458	1.000	.556	.397	.719
	aster	.072	.743	.440	.070	.572	.189	.106	.811	.352	.323	.620	.556	1.000	.649	.532
	lavender	.110	.735	.735	.186	.868	.243	.025	.678	.366	.301	.721	.397	.649	1.000	.444
	hellebore	-.126	.516	.279	-.142	.461	-.122	-.204	.562	.214	.180	.512	.719	.532	.444	1.000
Sig. (1-tailed)	celandine		.246	.088	.000	.222	.000	.000	.076	.000	.000	.076	.462	.309	.224	.192
	rose	.246		.006	.236	.000	.173	.427	.000	.002	.028	.000	.000	.000	.000	.000
	cornflower	.088	.006		.003	.000	.007	.095	.000	.002	.002	.000	.158	.001	.000	.025
	primrose	.000	.236	.003		.076	.000	.000	.128	.000	.000	.036	.458	.315	.098	.162
	poppy	.222	.000	.000	.076		.051	.447	.000	.002	.003	.000	.000	.000	.000	.000
	bluebell	.000	.173	.007	.000	.051		.000	.056	.000	.000	.012	.458	.094	.045	.198
	buttercup	.000	.427	.095	.000	.447	.000		.143	.000	.000	.270	.371	.232	.431	.078
	wisteria	.076	.000	.000	.128	.000	.056	.143		.000	.000	.000	.000	.000	.000	.000
	daisy	.000	.002	.002	.000	.002	.000	.000	.000		.000	.000	.009	.006	.004	.068
	speedwell	.000	.028	.002	.000	.003	.000	.000	.000	.000		.000	.038	.011	.017	.106
	sweetpea	.076	.000	.000	.036	.000	.012	.270	.000	.000	.000		.000	.000	.000	.000
	delphinium	.462	.000	.158	.458	.000	.458	.371	.000	.009	.038	.000		.000	.002	.000
	aster	.309	.000	.001	.315	.000	.094	.232	.000	.006	.011	.000	.000		.000	.000
	lavender	.224	.000	.000	.098	.000	.045	.431	.000	.004	.017	.000	.002	.000		.001
	hellebore	.192	.000	.025	.162	.000	.198	.078	.000	.068	.106	.000	.000	.000	.001	

A section of the matrix of correlation coefficients (from the table above): these are the observed correlations, which will later be compared with the reproduced correlations.

		celandine	rose	cornflower	primrose	poppy
Correlation	celandine	1.000	.099	.194	.566	.111
	rose	.099	1.000	.355	.104	.672
	cornflower	.194	.355	1.000	.378	.694
	primrose	.566	.104	.378	1.000	.206
	poppy	.111	.672	.694	.206	1.000
	bluebell	.785	.136	.344	.782	.235
	buttercup	.519	.027	.188	.656	.019
	wisteria	.206	.744	.531	.164	.699
	daisy	.697	.398	.405	.692	.406
	speedwell	.660	.272	.393	.612	.379
	sweetpea	.205	.554	.725	.256	.724
	delphinium	.014	.525	.145	.015	.453
	aster	.072	.743	.440	.070	.572
	lavender	.110	.543	.735	.186	.868
	hellebore	-.126	.516	.279	-.142	.461

Above the diagonal, and mirrored below it, are the observed correlations. Some of the correlations are quite large, indicating that the variables have factorability (.3 is normally considered to be the lower cut-off).
If you do the analysis, you will be able to see all correlation coefficients in the complete matrix.

If you selected the **Inverse** option in the **Factor Analysis: Descriptives** dialogue box, then that table would appear here. It is not required for principal components analysis, so we will show it in Section 3.

This table is produced by the **KMO and Bartlett's Test of Sphericity** option in the **Factor Analysis: Descriptives** dialogue box. These tests give some information about the factorability of your data, in addition to the information from the various matrices as described in Section 1.

KMO and Bartlett's Test

Kaiser-Meyer-Olkin Measure of Sampling Adequacy.		.754
Bartlett's Test of Sphericity	Approx. Chi-Square	659.906
	df	105
	Sig.	.000

The KMO measure of sampling adequacy is a test of the amount of variance within the data that could be explained by factors. As a measure of factorability: a KMO value of .5 is poor; .6 is acceptable; a value closer to 1 is better.

The KMO value here is the mean of individual values shown in the next table.

Bartlett's test indicates that the data are probably factorable if $p < .05$; however, it is considered to be a sensitive test, so it is better to use it in reverse: if $p > .05$, do not continue; but if $p < .05$, check other indicators of factorability before proceeding.

This table is produced by the **Anti-image** option in the **Factor Analysis: Descriptives** dialogue box. The upper matrix contains negative partial covariances and the lower matrix contains negative partial correlations. This is the whole table shrunk to fit. Below is an annotated section of the lower matrix.

Anti-image Matrices

		celandine	rose	cornflower	primrose	poppy	bluebell	buttercup	wisteria	daisy	speedwell	sweetpea	delphinium	aster	lavender	hellebore
Anti-image Covariance	celandine	.210	-.019	-.043	.091	.021	-.110	.004	-.017	-.076	.005	.055	-.033	.043	-.008	.044
	rose	-.019	.214	.050	-.012	-.096	.005	-.008	-.026	-.036	.068	.047	-.106	.076	.076	-.049
	cornflower	-.043	.050	.225	-.074	-.036	.036	-.056	-.030	.029	.020	-.106	.112	-.011	-.025	-.061
	primrose	.091	-.012	-.074	.174	.001	-.091	-.058	.022	-.083	.028	.050	-.037	.025	.007	.037
	poppy	.021	-.096	-.036	.001	.112	-.008	.033	-.023	.023	-.047	.004	-.049	.073	-.087	.035
	bluebell	-.110	.005	.036	-.091	-.008	.133	-.041	.021	.044	-.045	-.025	.046	-.035	-.014	-.016
	buttercup	.004	-.008	-.056	-.058	.033	-.041	.398	-.036	.024	-.049	.050	-.098	-.007	.004	.098
	wisteria	-.017	-.026	-.030	.022	-.023	.021	-.036	.190	-.025	-.009	.012	-.027	-.080	.001	-.011
	daisy	-.076	-.036	.029	-.083	.023	.044	.024	-.025	.112	-.071	-.039	-.011	.021	-.024	-.003
	speedwell	.005	.068	.020	.028	-.047	-.045	-.049	-.009	-.071	.152	-.047	.030	-.029	.055	-.035
	sweetpea	.055	.047	-.106	.050	.004	-.025	.050	.012	-.039	-.047	.187	-.044	-.009	-.017	.005
	delphinium	-.033	-.106	.112	-.037	-.049	.046	-.098	-.027	-.011	.030	-.044	.296	-.046	.018	-.187
	aster	.043	-.106	-.011	.025	.073	-.035	-.007	-.080	.021	-.029	-.009	-.046	.179	-.071	.020
	lavender	-.008	.076	-.025	.007	-.087	-.014	.004	.001	-.024	.055	-.017	.018	-.071	.129	-.019
	hellebore	.044	-.049	-.061	.037	.035	-.016	.098	-.011	-.003	-.035	.005	-.187	.020	-.019	.329
Anti-image Correlation	celandine	.667a	-.090	-.200	.473	.138	-.654	.013	-.085	-.497	.029	.278	-.133	.222	-.050	.168
	rose	-.090	.714a	.226	-.062	-.618	.028	-.028	-.127	-.234	.379	-.093	.186	-.543	.454	-.184
	cornflower	-.200	.226	.752a	-.373	-.225	.210	-.187	-.146	.184	.109	-.517	.434	-.057	-.145	-.226
	primrose	.473	-.062	-.373	.660a	.007	-.597	-.222	.122	-.593	.170	.279	-.162	.142	.044	.156
	poppy	.138	-.618	-.225	.007	.712a	-.062	.156	-.156	.208	-.358	.027	-.269	.513	-.720	.183
	bluebell	-.654	.028	.210	-.597	-.062	.710a	-.179	.132	.361	-.313	-.157	.229	-.224	-.105	-.078
	buttercup	.013	-.028	-.187	-.222	.156	-.179	.812a	-.130	.115	-.198	.184	-.285	-.026	.019	.270
	wisteria	-.085	-.127	-.146	.122	-.156	.132	-.130	.922a	-.175	-.053	.061	-.114	-.432	.007	-.045
	daisy	-.497	-.234	.184	-.593	.208	.361	.115	-.175	.743a	-.542	-.267	-.061	.151	-.196	-.017
	speedwell	.029	.379	.109	.170	-.358	-.313	-.198	-.053	-.542	.770a	-.279	.143	-.174	.395	-.156
	sweetpea	.278	-.093	-.517	.279	.027	-.157	.184	.061	-.267	-.279	.855a	-.187	-.050	-.111	.019
	delphinium	-.133	.186	.434	-.162	-.269	.229	-.285	-.114	-.061	.143	-.187	.702a	-.199	-.465	.082
	aster	.222	-.543	-.057	.142	.513	-.224	-.026	-.432	.151	-.174	-.050	-.199	.742a	-.465	.082
	lavender	-.050	.454	-.145	.044	-.720	-.105	.019	.007	-.196	.395	-.111	.090	-.465	.754a	-.094
	hellebore	.168	-.184	-.226	.156	.183	-.078	.270	-.045	-.017	-.156	.019	-.598	.082	-.094	.780a

a. Measures of Sampling Adequacy(MSA)

A section of anti-image correlation matrix.

Anti-image Correlation	celandine	.667a	-.090	-.200	.473
	rose	-.090	.714a	.226	-.062
	cornflower	-.200	.226	.752a	-.373
	primrose	.473	-.062	-.373	.660a
	poppy	.138	-.618	-.225	.007
	bluebell	-.654	.028	.210	-.597
	buttercup	.013	-.028	-.187	-.222
	wisteria	-.085	-.127	-.146	.122
	daisy	-.497	-.234	.184	-.593
	speedwell	.029	.379	.109	.170
	sweetpea	.278	-.093	-.517	.279
	delphinium	-.133	.186	.434	-.162
	aster	.222	-.543	-.057	.142
	lavender	-.050	.454	-.145	.044
	hellebore	.168	-.184	-.226	.156

a. Measures of Sampling Adequacy(MSA)

Above the diagonal, and mirrored below it, are the negative partial correlations. Many of these partial correlation values are small, indicative of a factor structure underlying the variables.

The on-diagonal values are the KMO values for each variable, indicating the factorability. Thus, for the variable 'primrose', KMO = .660. If any variable has a KMO value of less than .5, consider dropping it from the analysis. If you carry out the analysis, you will see that the KMO for 'primrose' is the smallest, so none of the variables need be dropped. The single KMO value, in the KMO and Bartlett's Test table above, is the mean of all these KMO values.

The matrices above were all described in Section 1. The remaining tables in this factor analysis output are mostly new to you.

Communalities

	Initial	Extraction
celandine	1.000	.721
rose	1.000	.668
cornflower	1.000	.848
primrose	1.000	.752
poppy	1.000	.837
bluebell	1.000	.850
buttercup	1.000	.606
wisteria	1.000	.814
daisy	1.000	.832
speedwell	1.000	.786
sweetpea	1.000	.779
delphinium	1.000	.788
aster	1.000	.710
lavender	1.000	.862
hellebore	1.000	.723

Extraction Method: Principal Component Analysis.

The communalities indicate how much variance in each variable is explained by the analysis.

In a principal component analysis, the initial communalities are calculated using all possible components, and always = 1.

The extraction communalities are calculated using the extracted factors only, so these are the useful values. For 'bluebell', 85% of the variance is explained by the extracted factors. If a particular variable has a low communality, then consider dropping it from the analysis.

We give a note on the calculation of extraction communalities on the Component Matrix table, further down.

SPSS reminds you of the extraction method you used, under all the tables whose values differ depending on the method.

This table summarises the total variance explained by the solution to the factor analysis. Here, it is shrunk to fit; each third of it is reproduced below, and annotated.

This is the first part of the output that gives a clear indication of the solution, in terms of how many factors explain how much variance. The previous tables and matrices are important, though, for indicating whether the solution is likely to be a good one.

Total Variance Explained

Component	Initial Eigenvalues			Extraction Sums of Squared Loadings			Rotation Sums of Squared Loadings[a]
	Total	% of Variance	Cumulative %	Total	% of Variance	Cumulative %	Total
1	6.810	45.403	45.403	6.810	45.403	45.403	4.663
2	3.540	23.602	69.004	3.540	23.602	69.004	4.785
3	1.226	8.176	77.180	1.226	8.176	77.180	5.152
4	.716	4.773	81.953				
5	.591	3.937	85.890				
6	.419	2.793	88.683				
7	.381	2.538	91.221				
8	.299	1.995	93.216				
9	.252	1.683	94.899				
10	.233	1.555	96.454				
11	.189	1.261	97.716				
12	.139	.924	98.639				
13	.108	.717	99.356				
14	.052	.347	99.703				
15	.045	.297	100.000				

Extraction Method: Principal Component Analysis.

a. When components are correlated, sums of squared loadings cannot be added to obtain a total variance.

In this type of table, the rows relate not to variables but to factors/components.

Below are the three sections of the Total Variance Explained table.

Component	Initial Eigenvalues		
	Total	% of Variance	Cumulative %
1	6.810	45.403	45.403
2	3.540	23.602	69.004
3	1.226	8.176	77.180
4	.716	4.773	81.953
5	.591	3.937	85.890
6	.419	2.793	88.683
7	.381	2.538	91.221
8	.299	1.995	93.216
9	.252	1.683	94.899
10	.233	1.555	96.454
11	.189	1.261	97.716
12	.139	.924	98.639
13	.108	.717	99.356
14	.052	.347	99.703
15	.045	.297	100.000

Extraction Method: Principal Component Analysis.

a. When components are correlated, sums of squared loa

The left section contains initial eigenvalues: the eigenvalues for all possible components, ranked in order of how much variance each accounts for.

There are 15 possible components: the same as the number of variables entered into the analysis, but that does not mean that each variable is a component.

For each component, the total variance that it explains on its own (its eigenvalue) is followed by the variance that it explains expressed as a percentage of all the variance, then by the cumulative percentage.

Extraction Sums of Squared Loadings		
Total	% of Variance	Cumulative %
6.810	45.403	45.403
3.540	23.602	69.004
1.226	8.176	77.180

The three extracted components together explain 77.2% of variance.

The middle section contains information for those components with eigenvalue > 1.0: in this example there are three such components.

These values are called extraction values, because they are calculated after extraction of components. Note that in principal component analysis, these values are the initial values (the first three rows above).

Rotation Sums of Squared Loadings[a]
Total
4.663
4.785
5.152

a. When components are correlated, sums of squared loadings cannot be added to obtain a total variance.

The right section shows the values for the extracted components after rotation has been carried out. (This section only appears if you request rotation, and may differ depending on the rotation method.)

Note that the eigenvalues have changed. Relative percentages and cumulative percentage of variance explained are not given for this rotation method.

The fact that three components have been extracted is neat; to that extent, the factor analysis might support our hypothetical aesthete's view. We do not yet know, however, what the factors represent. For example, they could represent not the type of flower but the colour of the flowers (pink, blue and yellow). Nor do we yet know which variables will be associated with which of the factors. So, rejoicing should be postponed.

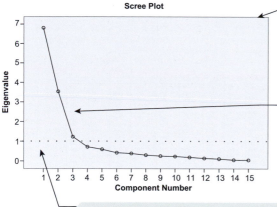

Scree Plot

This graph is produced by the **Scree plot** option in the **Factor Analysis**: **Extraction** dialogue box. It can be used as an alternative to eigenvalues > 1.0, to decide on which components should be extracted.

In the scree plot, the eigenvalues are plotted in decreasing order. It is called a scree plot because the shape of the curve is reminiscent of the profile of rock scree that accumulates at the foot of steep hills.

This dotted line, which we have superimposed, indicates the approximate point at which the scree plot 'breaks' between the steep and shallow parts of the slope: components above that point would be chosen. In this example, three factors are indicated, which concurs with the choice made on the basis of selecting factors with eigenvalues greater than 1.

Some authors suggest that the next factor should also be included (giving four in this example): see Cooper (2010, 287–8) for discussion.

Component Matrix[a]

	Component		
	1	2	3
celandine	.455	.701	.149
rose	.706	-.375	.170
cornflower	.709	-.044	-.587
primrose	.498	.706	-.074
poppy	.798	-.315	-.319
bluebell	.561	.731	-.034
buttercup	.353	.679	.142
wisteria	.842	-.300	.126
daisy	.772	.443	.197
speedwell	.724	.487	.158
sweetpea	.844	-.183	-.182
delphinium	.565	-.415	.544
aster	.741	-.377	.134
lavender	.774	-.316	-.403
hellebore	.517	-.585	.336

Extraction Method: Prncipal Component Analysis.
a. 3 components extracted.

This is a table of the factor loadings *before* the rotation is carried out.

Each column shows the loading of each variable on that component. The loading can be thought of as the correlation between the component and the variable: thus, the larger the number, the more likely it is that the component underlies that variable.

Note that some loadings are positive and some negative: we will mention this in Section 3.

The variable 'poppy' has:
quite a strong loading (.798) on component 1
a medium loading (-.315) on component 2
a medium loading (-.319) on component 3.

These loadings may be useful for seeing the pattern of which variables load most strongly onto which factors: almost always a rotation will be used, however, and then the pattern becomes clearer. In particular, the negative loadings here may be an artefact of the method of calculation (Kline, 1994, 39).

The extraction communalities, in the Communalities table above, are calculated using the formula Σx^2, where x is the factor loadings in this table. Thus, for 'lavender':

$$(.774)^2 + (-.316)^2 + (-.403)^2 = .862$$

As stated above, the size of the communality indicates how much of that variable's variance is explained by the solution to the factor analysis.

CHAPTER 12

This table is produced by the **Reproduced** option in the **Factor Analysis: Descriptives** dialogue box. The upper matrix contains the reproduced correlations and the lower matrix contains the residuals. This is the whole table shrunk to fit. Underneath is an annotated section of each matrix.

Reproduced Correlations

		celandine	rose	cornflower	primrose	poppy	bluebell	buttercup	wisteria	daisy	speedwell	sweetpea	delphinium	aster	lavender	hellebore
Reproduced Correlation	celandine	.721[a]	.084	.205	.711	.095	.763	.658	.192	.692	.694	.229	.048	.093	.071	-.125
	rose	.084	.668[a]	.417	.074	.627	.116	.019	.728	.412	.355	.634	.647	.688	.597	.642
	cornflower	.205	.417	.848[a]	.366	.766	.386	.137	.536	.412	.399	.713	.099	.463	.799	.195
	primrose	.711	.074	.366	.752[a]	.199	.798	.645	.198	.683	.693	.305	-.052	.093	.193	-.180
	poppy	.095	.627	.766	.199	.837[a]	.228	.023	.726	.414	.374	.789	.408	.667	.846	.490
	bluebell	.763	.116	.386	.798	.228	.950[a]	.690	.249	.750	.756	.346	-.005	.136	.217	-.149
	buttercup	.658	.019	.137	.645	.023	.690	.606[a]	.112	.602	.609	.148	-.005	.025	.002	-.167
	wisteria	.192	.728	.536	.198	.726	.249	.112	.814[a]	.542	.483	.743	.669	.754	.696	.653
	daisy	.692	.412	.412	.683	.414	.750	.602	.542	.832[a]	.806	.535	.360	.432	.378	.207
	speedwell	.694	.355	.399	.693	.374	.756	.609	.483	.806	.786[a]	.494	.293	.374	.343	.143
	sweetpea	.229	.634	.713	.305	.789	.346	.148	.743	.535	.494	.779[a]	.454	.671	.785	.483
	delphinium	.048	.647	.099	-.052	.408	-.005	-.005	.669	.360	.293	.454	.788[a]	.648	.349	.718
	aster	.093	.688	.463	.093	.667	.136	.025	.754	.432	.374	.671	.648	.710[a]	.639	.649
	lavender	.071	.597	.799	.193	.846	.217	.002	.696	.378	.343	.785	.349	.639	.862[a]	.450
	hellebore	-.125	.642	.195	-.180	.490	-.149	-.167	.653	.207	.143	.483	.718	.649	.450	.723[a]
Residual[b]	celandine		.016	-.010	-.145	.016	.022	-.139	.014	.005	-.035	-.024	-.034	-.021	.039	-.001
	rose	.016		-.063	.030	.045	.020	.008	.016	-.015	-.084	-.080	-.122	.055	-.054	-.126
	cornflower	-.010	-.063		.012	-.072	-.041	.051	-.005	-.007	-.006	.012	.045	-.024	-.064	.084
	primrose	-.145	.030	.012		.007	-.016	.011	-.035	.009	-.081	-.049	.067	-.024	-.007	.038
	poppy	.016	.045	-.072	.007		.006	-.003	-.027	-.007	.005	-.065	.045	-.096	.022	-.029
	bluebell	.022	.020	-.041	-.016	.006		-.037	-.021	-.083	-.035	-.027	-.011	.053	.026	.026
	buttercup	-.139	.008	.051	.011	-.003	-.037		.042	-.134	-.097	-.060	.052	.081	.023	-.037
	wisteria	.014	.016	-.005	-.035	-.027	-.021	.042		-.018	-.025	-.055	-.065	.057	-.018	-.091
	daisy	.005	-.015	-.007	.009	-.007	-.083	-.134	-.018		.045	.049	.049	-.026	-.079	.007
	speedwell	-.035	-.084	-.006	-.081	.005	-.035	-.097	-.025	.045		.089	-.040	-.051	-.042	.037
	sweetpea	-.024	-.080	.012	-.049	-.065	-.027	-.060	-.055	.049	.089		.004	-.051	-.064	.029
	delphinium	-.034	-.122	.045	.067	.045	-.011	.052	-.065	-.026	-.040	.004		-.092	.048	.001
	aster	-.021	.055	-.024	-.024	-.096	.053	.081	.057	-.079	-.051	-.051	-.092		.010	-.117
	lavender	.039	-.054	-.064	-.007	.022	.026	.023	-.018	-.012	-.042	-.064	.048	.010		-.006
	hellebore	-.001	-.126	.084	.038	-.029	.026	-.037	-.091	.007	.037	.029	.001	-.117	-.006	

Extraction Method: Principal Component Analysis.

a. Reproduced communalities

b. Residuals are computed between observed and reproduced correlations. There are 35 (33.0%) nonredundant residuals with absolute values greater than 0.05.

	celandine	rose	cornflower	primrose
celandine	.721[a]	.084	.205	.711
rose	.084	.668[a]	.417	.074
cornflower	.205	.417	.848[a]	.366
primrose	.711	.074	.366	.752[a]
poppy	.095	.627	.766	.199
bluebell	.763	.116	.386	.798
buttercup	.658	.019	.137	.645

This is part of the reproduced correlations matrix. Compare this value, of .711 for 'primrose' with 'celandine', with the *observed* correlation of .566 between those two variables (see the Correlation Matrix table above). The values are not very similar. Another point to note is that the factor analysis gives a stronger relationship between the two.

The diagonal holds the reproduced communalities. They are the same values as the extraction communalities in the Communalities table above.

	celandine	rose	cornflower	primrose
celandine		.016	-.010	-.145
rose	.016		-.063	.030
cornflower	-.010	-.063		.012
primrose	-.145	.030	.012	
poppy	.016	.045	-.072	.007
bluebell	.022	.020	-.041	-.016
buttercup	-.139	.008	.051	.011

Rather than do the comparison suggested above, one can simply inspect the residuals. The residual for 'primrose' with 'celandine' is –.145 (the negative sign indicates that the reproduced correlation is the stronger as mentioned above.) This is a fairly large residual, but inspect the whole matrix on your own screen to see that the other residuals are mostly small. That most of residuals are small is another indication of factorability, and it is also an indication of a good factor analysis solution.

Note that the contents of the Reproduced Correlations table are calculated after the factor extraction has been carried out, so the values will vary depending on how many factors were extracted.

CHAPTER 12

This is the Pattern Matrix table of factor loadings *after* the rotation is carried out. (The pattern matrix is easier to interpret than the structure matrix, shown below.) If you compare these values with those in the Component Matrix table above, you will see that the factor loading values have changed.

At the foot of the table, SPSS notes the number of iterations required for the rotation.

Pattern Matrix[a]

	Component		
	1	2	3
celandine	-.006	.873	.104
rose	.651	.039	-.269
cornflower	-.203	.083	-.968
primrose	-.194	.823	-.147
poppy	.214	-.028	-.804
bluebell	-.141	.886	-.130
buttercup	-.046	.806	.141
wisteria	.633	.152	-.363
daisy	.304	.802	-.069
speedwell	.226	.806	-.074
sweetpea	.296	.155	-.652
delphinium	.950	.065	.177
aster	.634	.041	-.324
lavender	.128	-.068	-.879
hellebore	.822	-.176	-.056

Extraction Method: Principal Component Analysis.
Rotation Method: Oblimin with Kaiser Normalization.

a. Rotation converged in 17 iterations.

The variable 'poppy' now has a strong loading (-.804) on component 3 and low loadings on components 1 (.214) and 2 (-.028). Whether a value is negative or positive is not relevant to the strength of the loading (as with r in correlation). However, if the loadings on one factor are not all in the same direction, there may be a problem; for example, if scores for reversed items were not corrected before the analysis.

Note that components 1, 2 and 3 after rotation need not necessarily be the same as components 1, 2 and 3 before rotation; they are just listed in a convenient order in each table.

For each variable, we have highlighted its strongest loading: thus, the highlights indicate which variables load most strongly on which component, as specified in the annotations below.

The variables 'cornflower', 'poppy', 'sweetpea' and 'lavender' load most strongly onto component 3.

The variables 'celandine', 'primrose', 'bluebell', 'buttercup', 'daisy' and 'speedwell' load most strongly onto component 2.

The variables 'rose', 'wisteria', 'delphinium', 'aster' and 'hellebore' load most strongly onto component 1.

We have shown you the Pattern Matrix table in the layout above to demonstrate all the factor loadings. SPSS will, however, display output in a more easily interpretable layout. See the description of the **Options** dialogue box in Section 3.

Structure Matrix

	Component		
	1	2	3
celandine	.019	.843	-.143
rose	.778	.170	-.579
cornflower	.249	.343	-.899
primrose	-.058	.849	-.293
poppy	.581	.219	-.894
bluebell	-.008	.911	-.318
buttercup	-.044	.762	-.067
wisteria	.813	.308	-.697
daisy	.403	.847	-.437
speedwell	.327	.846	-.408
sweetpea	.608	.365	-.832
delphinium	.874	.093	-.278
aster	.786	.186	-.627
lavender	.526	.194	-.919
hellebore	.834	-.092	-.384

Extraction Method: Principal Component Analysis.
Rotation Method: Oblimin with Kaiser Normalization.

The Structure Matrix table gives the correlations between factors and variables; whereas the Pattern Matrix table (above) gives the unique relationship between each factor and each variable excluding the overlap between factors. The Pattern Matrix table is easier to interpret in terms of which variables load onto which factors.

Component Correlation Matrix

Component	1	2	3
1	1.000	.083	-.459
2	.083	1.000	-.285
3	-.459	-.285	1.000

Extraction Method: Principal Component Analysis.
Rotation Method: Oblimin with Kaiser Normalization.

This table gives the factor transformation matrix that was used to carry out the rotation used to derive the rotated factors. See the texts recommended in Section 1.

Under this and the two previous tables, SPSS reminds you of the rotation method that you used.

Considering the results

Once you have inspected the Pattern Matrix table (above) to see which variables load on which factors, you can decide on a suitable name to describe each factor. The extracted factors may, or may not, be the same as the factors you suggested before you started the survey. If we now compare the pattern of loadings in the table with the aesthete's initial suggestion, we can see that there is close agreement, with just one variable on a different factor. Use caution, however; the dimensions that were suggested (liking for *types* of flower) may not be the true factors. To be more certain, you should carefully check the characteristics of the questions/items that measure your variables, and consider all possibilities and alternative explanations. In the results section of a report, you could write about the outcome of the analysis as shown below. You could incorporate more tables (e.g. the pattern matrix) or values (e.g. the factor loadings; KMO) to illustrate your points as necessary. If you have used principal component analysis, then do ensure that you refer to that and not factor analysis in your report.

 Reporting the results

In a report you might write:

The data were analysed by means of a principal component analysis, with direct oblimin rotation. The various indicators of factorability were good, and the residuals indicate that the solution was a good one. Three components with an eigenvalue of greater than 1.0 were found; the scree plot also indicated three components. The components can be thought of as representing liking for different types of flowers: component 1 – formal garden flowers; component 2 – wild flowers; component 3 – cottage garden flowers. The component loadings are shown in Table 12.1.

Table 12.1 The components found by principal component analysis, and the variables that load on them

Component 1		Component 2		Component 3	
delphinium	.95	bluebell	.89	cornflower	−.97
hellebore	.82	celandine	.87	lavender	−.88
rose	.65	primrose	.82	poppy	−.80
aster	.63	speedwell	.81	sweetpea	−.65
wisteria	.63	buttercup	.81		
		daisy	.80		

Remember that the survey we used to illustrate factor analysis is fictitious, and we do not know what you would find if you carried out this study.

Section 3: OTHER ASPECTS OF FACTOR ANALYSIS

Other options from the Factor Analysis: Descriptives dialogue box

Determinant

The **Determinant** option is in the **Correlation Matrix** section of the **Factor Analysis: Descriptives** dialogue box. If you select it, the value of the determinant will be printed underneath the Correlation Matrix table (as shown below). Its value is an indication of whether factor analysis methods other than principal component analysis can be used. Its value must not be zero. If it is zero, the correlation matrix cannot be inverted (see below).

delphinium	.462	.000
aster	.309	.000
lavender	.224	.000
hellebore	.192	.000

a. Determinant = 2.29E-007 ◄

> The determinant will be printed at the bottom left of the Correlation Matrix table. NB: The determinant may be printed to three decimal places, instead of in exponential format. If so, this determinant would appear as .000 (see the tip box).

> 💡 Whether the determinant is printed to three decimal places or in exponential format depends on a setting on the **Edit**, **Options**, **General** tab. On that tab, in the Output area, the **No scientific notation for small numbers in tables** allows you to select this; however, for numbers with three or more zeros following the decimal point, exponential format is more useful.

Inverse

The **Inverse** option produces the Inverse of Correlation Matrix, a complete matrix for all the variables. A section of it is shown below.

Inverse of Correlation Matrix

	celandine	rose	cornflower	primrose	poppy	bluebell	buttercup	wisteria
celandine	4.755	-.425	-.918	2.469	.897	-3.904	.046	-.425
rose	-.425	4.672	1.030	-.323	-3.984	.165	-.097	-.627
cornflower	-.918	1.030	4.	-1.	-1.	1.	-(	-.
primrose	2.469	-.323						
poppy	.897	-3.984						
bluebell	-3.904	.165						
buttercup	.046	-.097						
wisteria	-.425	-.627						
daisy	-3.244	-1.513	1.					
speedwell	.162	2.102	.588	1.044	-2.737	-2.198	-.805	-.313

> The values in this table (obtained by inverting the correlation matrix) are used in the calculations of many methods of factor extraction other than principal component analysis. If this table cannot be obtained (see above), then those methods cannot be applied.

The details of matrix determinants and inverses are not covered in this book. See Tabachnick and Fidell (2014, 23–32).

Other options from the Factor Analysis: Extraction dialogue box

Method

You can choose from the various methods of extracting factors that SPSS allows. To make a sensible choice, you will need to read up about each of the methods. Here we make just a few points.

Principal component analysis, shown in Section 2, tends to be the most robust method. Remember, though, that components are distinct from factors (Kline, 1994) and that principal component analysis and factor analysis are somewhat different things. Nonetheless, with large matrices, there is little difference between the solutions from different methods (Kline, 1994). Furthermore, if a factor analysis solution is stable, then you should obtain similar results regardless of the extraction method used (Tabachnick and Fidell, 2014). Cooper (2010), however, stresses that because principal component analysis always gives larger loadings than other methods, some rules of thumb may be misleading with this method.

The SPSS output from each of the other methods looks similar to the output from principal component analysis. The values in the particular tables that show the results of the factor extraction will, of course, differ at least slightly between methods. Some other differences and similarities are:

1. The word 'component' is replaced by the word 'factor' for all other methods.

2. The same tables are produced, except that for both generalised least squares and maximum likelihood methods, SPSS prints a Goodness-of-fit Test table that can be used to test hypotheses about the number of factors. See Kline (1994) for information about this use of the goodness of fit test. If you change the number of factors to be extracted, you may also need to increase the **Maximum Iterations for Convergence** in the **Factor Analysis: Extraction** dialogue box to allow the Goodness-of-fit Test table to be produced.

3. Communalities table:

   a. Initial communalities have a value of 1.0 in principal component analysis. In all other methods they are less than 1.0, because those methods explain the variance that is shared between all the variables (common variance) and attempt to eliminate other variance (error variance and unique variance).

   b. Extraction communalities are calculated from the factor matrix in the same way as they are from the component matrix, except for generalised least squares.

4. Total Variance Explained table:

   a. The **Initial Eigenvalues** part of the table will hold the same values for all methods of extraction because it shows how all the variance could be explained.

   b. In the **Extraction Sums of Squared Loadings** part of the table, for principal component analysis the row values are identical to the **Initial Eigenvalues** row values for each component because that method explains all the variance for the extracted factors. For the other methods, the row values here differ from the **Initial Eigenvalues** row values because these methods explain common variance and eliminate other variance.

Extract options

Two mutually exclusive options, described next, by which you can affect how many factors will be extracted are presented in the lower half of the **Factor Analysis: Extraction** dialogue box. Either of these options may be useful for your final analysis or for obtaining information on more of the initial factors. You will need to use one of those options if you wish to inspect 'extracted factor' information (e.g. the factor loadings) for more factors than may be extracted using the default values. That information may also be useful if you want to compare factors from your data with those obtained in previous research on the same variables. In any report, you should comment on how the number of factors to be extracted was decided upon.

The first option is to change the minimum eigenvalue, normally set at 1. The eigenvalue varies according to the number of variables entered, so it is not a robust guide for the number of factors to extract. The second option is to set the number of factors (you could do that after inspecting the scree plot).

Other options from the Factor Analysis: Rotation dialogue box

Method

The default setting is **None**, for no rotation. The technique of rotation, however, was devised in order to simplify the solution to the factor analysis. Thus, you would normally select one of the rotation methods that SPSS allows, from the **Factor Analysis: Rotation** dialogue box. SPSS provides orthogonal rotation methods (**Varimax**, **Eqamax** and **Quartimax**) and oblique rotation methods (**Direct Oblimin** and **Promax**). As Kline (1994) pointed out, psychological constructs are likely to be correlated with one another. Of the oblique rotation methods, he recommends using **Direct Oblimin** and we used this for the analysis described in Section 2.

If you require an orthogonal method, **Varimax** is normally thought to give rotated factors that are the most easy to interpret. The **Varimax** output differs somewhat from that for **Direct Oblimin**, in the following ways:

1. In the Total Variance Explained table, the Rotation section has three columns as percent and cumulative percent of variance are included.
2. There is a single Rotated Component Matrix table in place of the Pattern Matrix and the Structure Matrix tables.

Display

If you select a rotation method, then **Rotated solution** is also selected; don't unselect it, as it provides the tables that contain the solution.

If you select **Loading plot(s)**, SPSS draws a graph of the variables on the factor axes (up to a maximum of three factors). If you have requested a rotation, then the axes represent the rotated factors.

Factor Analysis: Options dialogue box

As mentioned in Section 2, the **Factor Analysis: Options** dialogue box allows you to specify missing values, and control the appearance of part of the output, as described next.

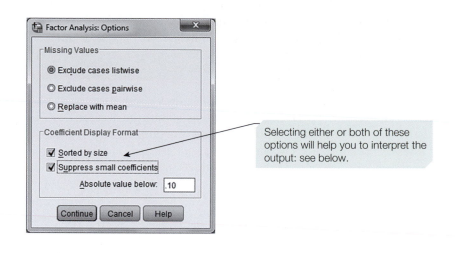

Selecting either or both of these options will help you to interpret the output: see below.

Coefficient Display Format

Two useful options here can make the output much easier to interpret. If you select **Sorted by size**, then, in the relevant tables (Component Matrix, Pattern and Structure Matrix), the variables will be sorted according to their factor loading size for each factor. If you select **Suppress absolute values less than**, then small factor loadings will be omitted from those tables. Once you have selected that option, the number can be changed, but the default of .10 seems sensible. You could try those options, and compare your output with the tables we have shown in Section 2.

Negative and positive factor loadings

Just as bivariate correlation coefficients can be positive or negative, so can factor loadings. A trivial example is when an item that taps a particular psychological construct is reversed (to avoid participant response bias). Such items should be reversed before analysis (see Chapter 4, Section 10). For factor loadings after rotation, you should note whether they are negative or positive. Negative loadings prior to rotation may be an artefact of the method of calculation used to extract factors (Kline, 1994, 39).

R factor analysis

R factor analysis is regular factor analysis, carried out on correlations between variables, as we have described in this chapter. There are other types of factor analysis in which other things are factored. For example, Q factor analysis uses correlations between participants (the rows and columns in the data file have to be reversed). More information on this and other types of factor analysis can be found in Kline (1994).

Section 4: RELIABILITY ANALYSIS FOR SCALES AND QUESTIONNAIRES

Anyone can produce a scale, and if the guidelines on writing items available in the literature are followed, then the individual items should be acceptable. There are many existing psychological scales, however, and it is unlikely that you cannot find one that assesses the construct/s in which you are interested. Moreover, it is considered better to use an existing scale than to produce another, as researchers can then compare findings from different samples and situations. For many existing scales, reliability information has been published. Nonetheless, cultural differences, or changes in language over time, or simply sample and situation differences, may affect a scale. Thus, whether you are constructing a scale or using an existing one, it is good practice to analyse the data for reliability and dimensionality. Many issues surrounding the use of scales are beyond the scope of this book. We recommend: Cooper (2010, particularly Chapters 15 and 18); Fife-Schaw (2012); Rust (2012); and John and Benet-Martinez (2014). Here, we only consider reliability, and dimensionality (Section 5).

Test-retest reliability involves testing the same participants with the same scale on two separate occasions, and calculating the correlation between the two sets of scores. It assesses the stability of a scale across time. Parallel forms, or parallel tests, describe the situation in which more than one version of a scale is available, designed to measure the same construct. To assess how similar they are, one would administer them to the same participants at the same time and correlate the scores. Internal consistency is the type of reliability we are concerned with here.

Internal consistency

If items within a scale are intended to measure aspects of the same construct, then they should all be fairly strongly correlated with each other. One way of assessing this is to correlate every item with each of the other items and inspect the matrix. Measures of internal consistency have been developed, however, which greatly simplify this process. *Split-half reliability* is an early measure, in which responses for two halves of the items are summed and then the correlation between them is calculated. Which items should go in which half, however, is a matter of debate. *Cronbach's alpha*, also called 'coefficient alpha', became easy to obtain with increasing computer power. It is related to the mean correlation between each pair of items and the number of items in the scale. It is the most commonly reported measure, with a rule of thumb that a scale should have a minimum Cronbach's alpha value of .7. It does have drawbacks, however. For example, even if a scale does have a high alpha, some individual items may be poorly correlated with the others. Thus, we should also inspect other information in the SPSS output. In the annotations below, we describe how to use three particular values, which are provided for each item:

1. The *part-whole correlation* (or *item-total correlation*), which is the correlation between each item and the sum of the other items.

2. The *squared multiple correlation* for each item; that is, the R^2 obtained if the item is entered into a multiple regression as the criterion variable with all the other items as predictor variables.

3. The value of Cronbach's alpha for the scale if a particular item is deleted.

   In addition to reliability, we should also assess whether a scale is unidimensional (see Section 5).

How to perform a reliability analysis

Before you start on this section, you should run through Chapter 4, Section 10. You will need data file 'ScaleV3.sav', saved in the last exercise in that section. Remember that normally you would need many more cases. Below we demonstrate two of the ways of measuring reliability.

   Start by clicking on **Analyze** > **Scale** > **Reliability Analysis**. The **Reliability Analysis** dialogue box will appear (as shown below). Follow the instructions.

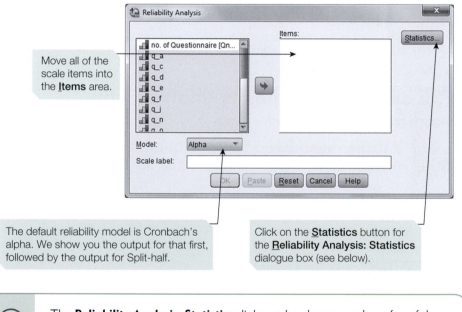

Move all of the scale items into the **Items** area.

The default reliability model is Cronbach's alpha. We show you the output for that first, followed by the output for Split-half.

Click on the **Statistics** button for the **Reliability Analysis: Statistics** dialogue box (see below).

The **Reliability Analysis: Statistics** dialogue box has a number of useful options for the purpose of checking scales. Otherwise, SPSS only gives output for the reliability measure that you request under **Model**.

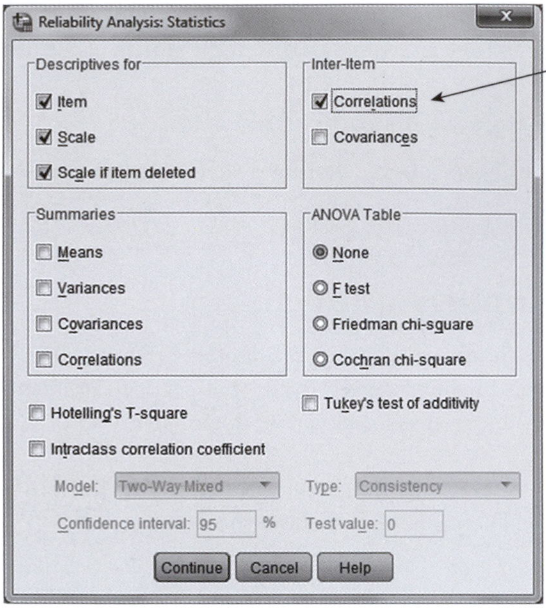

Select the options shown.

NB: From **Inter-Item**, we have selected **Correlations**, as this generates useful output in addition to the correlation matrix itself. We will not show the matrix.

Click on **Continue**, then on **OK**. The output is shown below.

SPSS output for reliability analysis with Cronbach's alpha

Obtained using menu item: Scale > Reliability Analysis (model = alpha)

Scale: ALL VARIABLES

Case Processing Summary

		N	%
Cases	Valid	48	96.0
	Excluded[a]	2	4.0
	Total	50	100.0

a. Listwise deletion based on all variables in the procedure.

This summary table shows the valid cases. Any cases with missing data are excluded listwise from the analysis.

Reliability Statistics

Cronbach's Alpha	Cronbach's Alpha Based on Standardized Items	N of Items
.899	.907	20

Cronbach's alpha for the scale is .899. This suggests that the scale has good reliability overall, but we still need to check individual items (see below).

This measure is based on the assumption that the variances of each item are equal; not necessarily a valid assumption. It is printed if you request any **Inter-Item** options in the **Reliability Analysis: Statistics** dialogue box.

The subsequent tables are obtained from options in the **Reliability Analysis: Statistics** dialogue box.

Item Statistics

	Mean	Std. Deviation	N
q_a	3.96	.849	48
q_c	3.90	1.036	48
q_d	4.27	.707	48
q_e	4.46	.651	48
q_f	4.02	1.062	48
q_j	4.33	.883	48
q_n	3.69	1.114	48
q_o	4.23	.778	48

This table (a section only is shown here) is from the **Item** option in the **Descriptives for** area.

We requested **Correlations** from the **Inter-Item** area in the **Reliability Analysis: Statistics** dialogue box above. A table called the Inter-Item Correlation Matrix is produced, and would normally appear here. We have omitted it, but you could inspect those correlations.

This table is from the **Scale if item deleted** option in the **Descriptives for** area, except for the Squared Multiple Correlation column, which is produced if you also select any **Inter-Item** option.

The part-whole correlation, or the correlation between each item and the sum of the rest of the items.

Item-Total Statistics

	Scale Mean if Item Deleted	Scale Variance if Item Deleted	Corrected Item-Total Correlation	Squared Multiple Correlation	Cronbach's Alpha if Item Deleted
q_a	72.85	107.106	.546	.726	.894
q_c	72.92	106.418	.465	.842	.897
q_d	72.54	108.041	.605	.783	.893
q_e	72.35	108.617	.618	.700	.894
q_f	72.79	101.147	.710	.751	.889
q_j	72.48	105.148	.635	.813	.892
q_n	73.13	114.707	.062	.380	.910
q_o	72.58	108.248	.530	.821	.895
q_s	73.46	112.466	.240	.378	.902
q_t	72.94	106.060	.467	.785	.897
q_bR	72.85	106.766	.515	.720	.895
q_gR	72.42	106.121	.710	.769	.891
q_hR	73.02	106.489	.678	.794	.892
q_iR	73.23	105.329	.550	.761	.894
q_kR	73.21	102.722	.590	.869	.893
q_lR	72.90	103.797	.600	.733	.892
q_mR	73.79	103.530	.555	.782	.894
q_pR	72.85	106.425	.630	.695	.892
q_qR	73.81	105.219	.554	.771	.894
q_rR	73.31	106.517	.601	.615	.893

The Squared Multiple Correlation is the R^2 which would be obtained by entering the item as the criterion variable in a multiple regression with all the other items as predictor variables.

Cronbach's alpha obtained if that item is omitted from the calculation.

For item 'q_n', there are strong indications that it is not a consistent part of the scale: the part-whole correlation is very low (.062), R^2 is also low (.38), and Cronbach's alpha is increased to .91 when this item is deleted. Thus, this item would be a strong candidate for either being deleted from the scale, or being rewritten.

NB: Cronbach's alpha including 'q_n' is .899 (shown in output above). That is well above the rule of thumb of .7 for a reliable scale. Thus, this example is a good illustration of the point that Cronbach's alpha alone may be insufficient to be sure of the reliability of all items in the scale.

Scale Statistics

Mean	Variance	Std. Deviation	N of Items
76.81	117.432	10.837	20

> This table of descriptives, for the sum of responses for the whole scale for each participant, is from the **Descriptives for: Scale** option.

Acting on the results

If this was the final scale, you could write: 'Cronbach's alpha for the ATR scale from the current sample was .90.' If you were assessing the scale, you would also describe other attributes from the SPSS output. For these results, however, you would consider deleting or rewriting item 'q_n', probably item 'q_s', and possibly others. If you delete items, you must repeat the reliability analyses on the remaining items. Additionally, you should consider dimensionality of the scale (Section 5).

SPSS output for reliability analysis with split-half

Obtained using menu item: Scale > Reliability Analysis (model = split-half)

In the **Reliability Analysis** dialogue box, select **Split-half** instead of **Alpha** from **Model**. Only those tables that differ from the output previously illustrated are shown here.

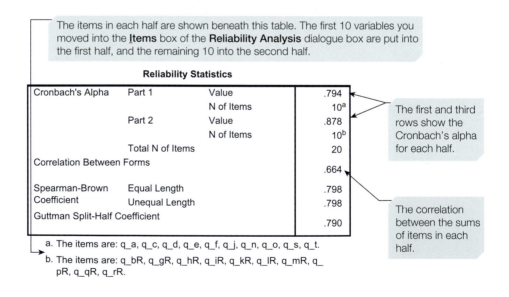

> The items in each half are shown beneath this table. The first 10 variables you moved into the **Items** box of the **Reliability Analysis** dialogue box are put into the first half, and the remaining 10 into the second half.

Reliability Statistics

Cronbach's Alpha	Part 1	Value	.794
		N of Items	10a
	Part 2	Value	.878
		N of Items	10b
	Total N of Items		20
Correlation Between Forms			.664
Spearman-Brown Coefficient	Equal Length		.798
	Unequal Length		.798
Guttman Split-Half Coefficient			.790

> The first and third rows show the Cronbach's alpha for each half.

> The correlation between the sums of items in each half.

a. The items are: q_a, q_c, q_d, q_e, q_f, q_j, q_n, q_o, q_s, q_t.

b. The items are: q_bR, q_gR, q_hR, q_iR, q_kR, q_lR, q_mR, q_pR, q_qR, q_rR.

> You can control which items go into which half by, in the **Reliability Analysis** dialogue box, moving the variable names across one at a time in the order you wish. This procedure can be useful if you wish to compare different combinations of items. When assessing scale reliability, however, Cronbach's alpha is more often used than split-half reliability.

Scale Statistics

	Mean	Variance	Std. Deviation	N of Items
Part 1	40.08	29.142	5.398	10[a]
Part 2	36.73	41.904	6.473	10[b]
Both Parts	76.81	117.432	10.837	20

a. The items are: q_a, q_c, q_d, q_e, q_f, q_j, q_n, q_o, q_s, q_t.

b. The items are: q_bR, q_gR, q_hR, q_iR, q_kR, q_lR, q_mR, q_pR, q_qR, q_rR.

The Scale Statistics table holds descriptives for the sum of responses from each half, in addition to those for the whole scale.

Section 5: DIMENSIONALITY OF SCALES AND QUESTIONNAIRES

We will describe two ways in which you can use an analysis of the dimensionality of a scale. Relevant references are given at the beginning of Section 4. First, if you want a scale in which all items assess a single construct, you can assess how strongly each item loads onto a single component. Weakly loading items would be discarded or rewritten. Second, to assess whether there is more than one construct underlying the scale, you can carry out a component or factor analysis to determine the structure. You could then use the items that load strongly on separate components as subscales. (You would need to assess the reliability of each subscale separately.) Ensuring that a scale is unidimensional, or that subscales are identified, is an aspect of construct validity.

Before you work through this section, you should be familiar with the content of Sections 1–3. Also, if you have not yet done so, you should run through Chapter 4, Section 10, as you will need data file 'ScaleV3.sav', from the last exercise in that section. We will show you the procedure with principal component analysis, but it may be more appropriate to use a factor analysis; for example, alpha factoring. Remember that normally you would need many more cases, and with the data file that we are using, alpha factoring does not converge (does not produce a solution) when one factor is requested.

To identify those items that load on a single component

Enter the items into a principal component analysis (Section 2). For this purpose, the only settings you need to make are as follows:

1. In the **Factor Analysis: Extraction** dialogue box, select the option **Fixed number of factors**, then type 1 in the **Factors to extract** field.

2. In the **Factor Analysis: Options** dialogue box, select for **Sorted by size**.

For this purpose, two tables are important. On the next page, we show an extract of one of those tables and the whole of the other.

Total Variance Explained

Component	Initial Eigenvalues			Extraction Sums of Squared Loadings		
	Total	% of Variance	Cumulative %	Total	% of Variance	Cumulative %
1	7.654	38.272	38.272	7.654	38.272	38.272
2	2.416	12.081	50.353			
3	1.463	7.313	57.666			

Note: the largest component explains only 38% of the variance.

Component Matrix[a]

	Component
	1
q_f	.777
q_gR	.765
q_hR	.721
q_j	.702
q_pR	.687
q_e	.684
q_kR	.663
q_d	.654
q_rR	.644
q_lR	.632
q_iR	.621
q_qR	.615
q_mR	.614
q_a	.605
q_bR	.597
q_o	.589
q_t	.518
q_c	.517
q_s	.280
q_n	.074

The rule of thumb is that items with loadings of less than .4 should be discarded.

Extraction Method:
Principal Component
Analysis.
a. 1 components extracted.

Acting on the results

From this analysis, we would either discard items 'q_s' and 'q_n', or rewrite them. Note that these items were also identified in the reliability analysis (Item-Total Statistics table above).

   If items are *discarded*, another analysis should be carried out on the data for the remaining items, as factor loadings will change somewhat. For these data, you will find that the variance explained by the largest component increases to 42%, and the loadings of the remaining 18 items are still all above .5. You could then use the scale data (for the 18 items) in other analyses, as long as you cite the reliability and dimensionality results in your report. You must be aware, however, that another sample may give different reliability and dimensionality results.

If you were constructing a scale, you might decide to *rewrite* items instead of just deleting them; then data from a new sample must be collected with the new version of the scale. Data from the new version must then be subjected to reliability and dimensionality analyses. Thus, scale construction/modification is an iterative process.

To assess the structure of items within a scale

Enter all 20 items into a principal component analysis or factor analysis. For this purpose, we carried out the analysis in the way described in Section 2, except that:

- In the **Factor Analysis: Options** dialogue box, we selected for **Sorted by size.**

- We selected **Promax** in the **Factor Analysis: Rotation** dialogue box, as the Direct Oblimin rotation failed to converge in 25 iterations. If you wish, you could try that.

Only some of the tables from this analysis are shown here; see Section 2 for a description of all the output. Check the indicators of factorability (described in Section 2). Some of them are reasonable. The KMO value, however, is only .59. Also, some of the individual KMO values, in the diagonal of the Anti-Image Correlation matrix, are well below the value of .5 that indicates poor performance of individual items.

The section of the Total Variance Explained table below shows that there were six components with eigenvalue greater than one.

Total Variance Explained

Component	Initial Eigenvalues			Extraction Sums of Squared Loadings			Rotation Sums of Squared Loadings[a]
	Total	% of Variance	Cumulative %	Total	% of Variance	Cumulative %	Total
1	7.654	38.272	38.272	7.654	38.272	38.272	5.631
2	2.416	12.081	50.353	2.416	12.081	50.353	5.544
3	1.463	7.313	57.666	1.463	7.313	57.666	4.515
4	1.185	5.924	63.590	1.185	5.924	63.590	2.199
5	1.099	5.495	69.085	1.099	5.495	69.085	2.100
6	1.059	5.297	74.381	1.059	5.297	74.381	1.290
7	.731	3.655	78.037				

The Scree Plot, however, shows just two components above the break between the steep and shallow parts of the curve.

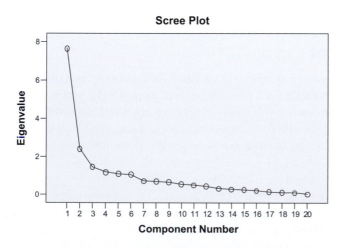

Scree Plot

In the Pattern Matrix table below, the heaviest loadings for each item are highlighted. Thirteen of the 20 items load most strongly on one of the first two components, with four items on the third. The last three components each have only one item with heaviest loading; note that items 'q_n' and 'q_s' are here.

Pattern Matrix[a]

	Component					
	1	2	3	4	5	6
q_hR	.907	-.074	.068	.264	-.223	.054
q_iR	.885	-.141	-.119	.267	.072	-.074
q_bR	.715	.210	-.044	-.174	-.070	-.239
q_mR	.669	.387	-.380	-.028	.082	.244
q_f	.668	.064	.282	.065	-.048	-.029
q_qR	.658	-.222	.334	-.141	.267	-.016
q_rR	-.025	.845	-.042	-.052	.044	.187
q_a	-.121	.640	.093	.422	-.078	-.109
q_pR	.029	.631	-.038	.093	.414	-.072
q_kR	.521	.617	-.109	-.191	-.265	-.076
q_d	-.097	.582	.135	.496	-.054	.086
q_j	.183	.560	.181	.082	-.096	-.208
q_lR	.047	.438	.263	-.027	.131	.333
q_o	.192	-.219	.876	.116	-.098	.067
q_c	-.177	.215	.839	-.150	-.140	.147
q_e	-.099	.400	.590	-.021	.148	-.210
q_gR	.397	.161	.400	-.083	.194	.094
q_t	.216	.025	-.090	.889	.162	.082
q_s	-.084	.054	-.116	.127	.944	-.110
q_n	-.108	.048	.113	.089	-.133	.881

Extraction Method: Principal Component Analysis.
Rotation Method: Promax with Kaiser Normalization.

a. Rotation converged in 17 iterations.

Acting on the results

If you obtained such results with a sufficient sample size, then you could check the content of those items loading on the first two components, and assess whether they may represent two distinct subscales. You should collect data from a new sample to assess whether the results are replicable. You could use exploratory factor analysis as described above, or you could use confirmatory factor analysis to test hypotheses about your measurement model. That is outside the scope of this book.

Important

As we have stated, a sample of 50 is small for reliability and dimensionality analyses. So if you collect data with the ATR scale (Larsen, 1995), you will probably get different results. Indeed, a different sample we analysed gave different reliability and dimensionality results to those shown above. Thus, in this and the previous section, we have shown you how to use these analyses; we have not given definitive results for the ATR scale.

Summary

- This chapter introduced you to factor analysis, and how to check the reliability and dimensionality of scales.

- Factor analysis allows you to investigate whether a factor structure underlies a set of variables.

- We have explained the output that SPSS generates for principal component analysis, which is the simplest type of factor analysis.

- Remember that, to be valid, factor analysis requires a large number of observations.

- When constructing a new scale, or using an existing scale in a new population, it is sensible to check its reliability and dimensionality.

- For guidance on incorporating SPSS output into a report, or on printing the output, see Chapter 13.

13 Using syntax and other useful features of SPSS

In this chapter

- The Syntax window
- Syntax examples
- Getting help in SPSS
- Option settings in SPSS
- Printing from SPSS
- Incorporating SPSS output into other documents
- SPSS and Excel: importing and exporting data files

SPSS for Psychologists online
Visit he.palgrave.com/psychology/brace for data sets, online tutorials and exercises.

Section 1: THE SYNTAX WINDOW

- The dialogue boxes you have been using to control SPSS form an interface that allows the user to specify the analysis they require. When you click on the [OK] button, this interface translates all your selections into a series of commands telling SPSS what to do. It is possible to control SPSS using these commands directly. The language in which these commands are expressed is called the SPSS syntax.

- Being able to use syntax commands will significantly increase your efficiency, allowing you to repeat complex series of analyses and to undertake analyses that would otherwise be impractical.

- A useful analogy is to think about how you record a TV programme at home. Most of the time you probably just select the programme you want from the electronic programme guide and accept all the default settings. Sometimes, however, you will want to do something a bit different, perhaps recording only the second half of a programme or deliberately overrunning the scheduled end of the programme to allow for delays in broadcast. In this situation, you will want to talk directly to the recorder and independently set the start and stop times. In the same way, using syntax commands allows you to be more flexible in your use of SPSS.

■ In this section, we describe how to control SPSS directly using syntax.

An example of a syntax command

You will already have seen some SPSS syntax. Unless you have opted to suppress it, the syntax required for each command is included at the top of the output for that command (to simplify things, we have not usually shown the syntax). For example, look back at the output we produced when using the **Descriptives** command in Chapter 3, Section 2 (reproduced below). You will see that the syntax for the command, including all the options you selected, appears at the start of the output. These commands have a precise structure, but it is not difficult to understand what each line does. The **Descriptives** syntax command is made up of two lines of text. The first specifies the **Descriptives** command and lists the variables to be included in the analysis. The second line specifies the options we have requested. The second line is indented and starts with a slash (/) to indicate it is still part of the same command. Critically, all SPSS syntax statements must end with a full stop.

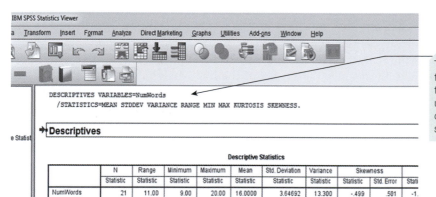

These two lines of text are the syntax commands that instruct SPSS to undertake the **Descriptives** command. The second line shows the options selected.

The Paste button and the Syntax window

You may have noticed that the dialogue boxes used to execute an analysis (those that include the OK button) also contain a button marked **Paste**, which looks like this Paste . If you click on the **Paste** button, the analysis is not executed, and no output is produced. Instead, control is switched to a new window called the Syntax Editor window (which we will call the Syntax window), and the command lines needed to execute your analysis are pasted into this window. You can now specify a second analysis and click on the Paste button again. The syntax for the new command will be pasted into the Syntax window below the first. In this way, you can build up a sequence of commands in the Syntax window, without executing any of them.

Finally, when you have selected all the analyses you require, you can execute or run the commands. This might seem like an odd thing to want to do, but there are at least four good reasons for working in this way.

1. Duplicating actions

You may choose to work in the Syntax Editor window because you need to repeat a complex command several times. For example, when analysing the data from the adoption survey described in Chapter 4, we might need to compute 10 new variables, each of which is the mean of 10 existing variables. This would be a tedious procedure using the dialogue boxes, but would be easy to perform using syntax commands. This example is demonstrated later in this section.

2. Keeping a record of your analysis and repeating an analysis

Sometimes, you may want to repeat a complex series of analyses after updating your data file. This is easy to do if you saved the lines of syntax needed to execute your analysis. Alternatively, if you are working with a large, complex data set, then it is common to make errors. For example, you might undertake the wrong analysis, or use the correct command but forget to select the options you need. As a result, the Output window will fill up with erroneous output. One solution is to use the Syntax window as a notepad in which to record the details of the successful analyses. When you have the analysis working the way you want, you can save the details to the Syntax window by clicking the `Paste` button. In this way, you can build up a permanent record of the analysis, which you can then run to produce a 'clean' set of output. Some researchers always save the syntax of the final analysis they undertake before submitting a report or paper for publication. This means that even months later they will be able to quickly repeat an analysis and make changes if these are requested by a reviewer.

3. Describing the analysis you have undertaken

Sometimes, you will want to be able to accurately and succinctly describe exactly how you analysed a data set; for example, when emailing a colleague or in an appendix to a publication or report. Syntax is perfect in this situation as it is easy to write and is concise and precise.

4. Tweaking the parameters of a command

Another reason for choosing to work in the Syntax window is that some of the options or parameters associated with certain commands can only be accessed using the syntax commands. In order to keep the number of buttons and options on the dialogue boxes manageable, the SPSS programmers have preset certain features of the commands. Occasionally, experienced users may want to alter one of these default settings. This can only be done using syntax. Details of the additional features of a command, which can be accessed only via syntax, are described in special help files available from the **Help** button on the dialogue box. See Section 3 for an example.

The Syntax window

The Syntax window is used to build up the syntax commands and execute them. In fact, syntax files are nothing more than simple text files, so you could use a text editor or word processing program to write these files, but the Syntax window incorporates several useful features to help you edit the syntax.

The **Edit** menu in the Syntax window provides access to all the normal text editing functions such as Copy, Cut, Paste, and Find & Replace. Using these functions, it is possible to copy a section of syntax produced by SPSS and edit it, for example changing variable names. In this way, we can quickly produce the syntax to undertake a long sequence of commands; something that would be tedious to do using the normal dialogue boxes. The toolbar across the top of the Syntax window includes a number of useful buttons to help us construct syntax files.

This button inserts an asterisk (*) to turn a line of text into a comment that will be ignored by SPSS. Comments can be used as notes, for example to remind you what the syntax does.

This is the **Run Selection** button, which runs (executes) any selected sections of syntax.

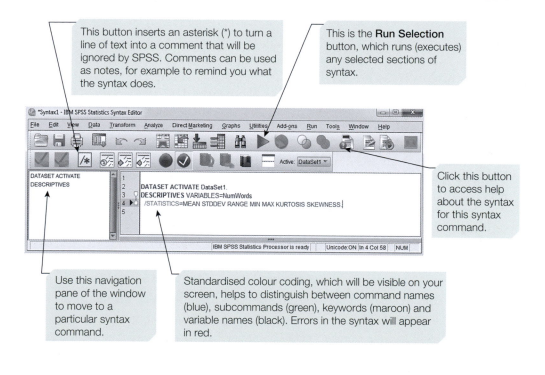

Click this button to access help about the syntax for this syntax command.

Use this navigation pane of the window to move to a particular syntax command.

Standardised colour coding, which will be visible on your screen, helps to distinguish between command names (blue), subcommands (green), keywords (maroon) and variable names (black). Errors in the syntax will appear in red.

> Once you have constructed a block of syntax commands, select the lines you want to execute then click on the **Run Selection** button (the large green arrow on the menu bar, labelled above).

Another useful feature available in the Syntax window is that it auto-completes the names of commands and offers you lists of options to choose from. To see this in operation, open a new Syntax window (**File** > **New** > **Syntax**). Now start typing the command **Oneway**. After you have typed the first few letters, SPSS offers you a list of commands to choose from. This is illustrated in the screenshot below.

CHAPTER 13

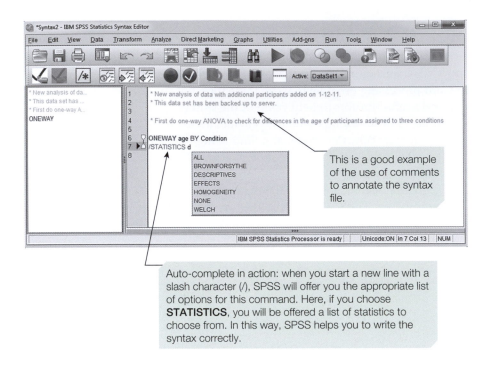

This is a good example of the use of comments to annotate the syntax file.

Auto-complete in action: when you start a new line with a slash character (/), SPSS will offer you the appropriate list of options for this command. Here, if you choose **STATISTICS**, you will be offered a list of statistics to choose from. In this way, SPSS helps you to write the syntax correctly.

Basic rules of syntax

There are some important characteristics of syntax to note:

1. Each new command must start on a new line. In practice, leaving several blank lines between commands makes the syntax easier to understand.

2. Each command must end with a full stop or period mark (.).

3. Subcommands or options are usually separated by the forward slash mark (/). It is a good idea (but not essential) to start each subcommand on a new line.

4. You can split a command over several lines; it is safest to break the line at the start of a new subcommand.

5. It is useful to include notes to help you remember what the syntax means. These notes are called 'comments'. A comment must start with an asterisk (*) and must end with a full stop. A comment can be split over more than one line of text. You can also use the comment button to mark text in this way. SPSS will not try to interpret comments.

6. Make sure that you spell your variable names correctly (i.e. exactly as they appear in the Data Editor window). Misspelling a variable name is one of the most common sources of errors when running syntax commands.

In practice, it is quite rare to write a piece of syntax 'from scratch'. It is more usual to use the dialogue boxes to select an analysis and set the options, and then to paste the syntax for this command into the Syntax window using the ⌗Paste⌗ button.

This syntax can then be copied and edited as required before being executed. Using this approach, you can be sure that the syntax and spelling will be correct. By careful use of the **F**ind and **R**eplace commands (available from the **E**dit menu), you can copy the syntax of a command, and change the variable(s) quickly and accurately to build up a series of analyses. An example is given below. In this example, we are seeking to compute 10 new variables. Each of these variables is the mean of a block of 10 questionnaire responses. The original variables were given names that reflect the block and question number. For example, 'b1q3' is the third question in the first block, while 'b9q8' is the eighth question in the ninth block. We could use the dialogue boxes to perform all these **C**ompute commands, but this would be a laborious task. It is much easier to produce a series of syntax commands to do the work for us, and this approach is less likely to result in errors, as we can carefully check the syntax before running it. Here are the steps we could use to build up the syntax we need to perform these **C**ompute commands:

1. Using the **Compute Variable** dialogue box, enter the details needed to compute the new variable 'b1mean' for the block 1 mean (see Chapter 4, Section 6 for details of the **C**ompute command).

2. Click on the ⎡Paste⎤ button to paste the syntax commands into the Syntax Editor window (see below).

3. Select (highlight) this first block of text, copy it and then paste a copy of this block below the first. Leave a few blank lines between the first block and this second block.

4. Move the cursor to the start of the second block and use the **R**eplace function to change all instances of the string 'b1' to 'b2'; click on the **F**ind Next button, and then click the **R**eplace button repeatedly until all the changes are made. Do not use the **R**eplace All button, as this will replace all instances, including those in the first block.

5. Now repeat steps 3 and 4 until you have 10 blocks of syntax, each instructing SPSS to compute the mean of the 10 variables that make up that block. Block 1 will compute the variable 'b1mean', block 2 will compute the variable 'b2mean', and so on.

6. Carefully check the syntax for the **C**ompute commands. Make sure you have changed all variable names systematically and that you have a full stop at the end of each line.

7. Make sure that you have an **Execute** command (with a full stop) after the last **C**ompute.

8. Select all 10 **C**ompute commands and Click on the **Run Selection** button. The 10 new variables will be computed and appended to your data file.

These steps are illustrated below.

CHAPTER 13

This first block of syntax was produced using the **Paste** button on the **Compute** dialogue box.

This second block is a copy of the first. It is being edited to replace each instance of 'b1' with 'b2'.

Note the blank line we have inserted between blocks.

We are about to change 'b1q4' into 'b2q4' by clicking the **Replace** button. Don't use the **Replace All** button, as this will change every instance of 'b1' into 'b2', including those in the earlier blocks.

Saving syntax files

Once completed, a syntax file can be saved. If the Syntax window is the active window (i.e. if you are currently working in this window), you can simply save the contents of the window as a syntax file by selecting **Save As** from the **File** menu. SPSS will automatically add the suffix '.sps' to the end of the file name. We strongly recommend that you accept this default suffix.

It is a good idea to use the same root name for all the files relating to one project. For example, in the case of the adoption survey described in Chapter 4, the data file might be called 'Adopt.sav'. The output files produced from the analysis of this file might be saved as 'Adopt1.spv', 'Adopt2.spv' etc., and a syntax file for this research might be called 'Adopt.sps'. In this way, it is easy to see which files relate to each other. These files could then all be saved in a common folder in your file system, perhaps called 'Adoption Project Files' or something similar.

Executing syntax commands

Once you have written and saved your syntax commands, you can execute, or run them, either by highlighting the lines of syntax you want to execute and clicking on the **Run Selection** button, or by choosing one of the options from the <u>R</u>un menu. It is safer to highlight the commands and use the **Run Selection** button.

> We recommend that you get into the habit of executing syntax by highlighting the commands you want to run and clicking on the **Run Selection** button. This way you will only execute the lines you want.

Syntax errors

Once the syntax has been executed, any errors will be reported at the bottom of the Syntax window. These warnings are reasonably clear, and include a note of the line number at which the error occurs, so you shouldn't have too much problem tracking down the error in your file. If you have more than one error, it's a good idea to correct these one at a time, rerunning the syntax file after each error is corrected, as it is possible one error will generate several problems in the file.

The screenshot of the Syntax window (see below) shows an example of an error. In the second **Frequencies** command, we have deliberately misspelt the name of the variable ('seex' rather than 'sex') so that you can see what the error report looks like. SPSS reports that the error is on line 5 (which is also marked with an arrow) and explains that the variable name hasn't been defined. It even recomends you check the spelling – good advice in this case! This warning also appears in the Output window.

Selecting the correct data file

Another common error when performing data analyses using SPSS syntax is to run your syntax against the wrong data file. It is possible to have several different data files open in SPSS at the same time. This isn't something novice users are likely to do, but as you become more experienced, you may find yourself working on projects where you have several related data files, a number of which may be open simultaneously. In this situation, one of the first things you should do before running a syntax file is to check which data file is active. The active data file can be selected from a drop-down list in the Syntax window (see below), or it can be specified in a syntax command, which has the form **DATASET ACTIVATE Dataset1**.

> If you run your syntax file on the wrong data file, SPSS will normally report errors when it encounters undefined variables. However, if you have two data files that have common variable names, SPSS may not detect any errors and your mistake could go unnoticed. Be extra careful in this situation and consider including the **DATASET ACTIVATE** syntax line at the start of each block of syntax to reduce the risk of analysing the wrong data set.

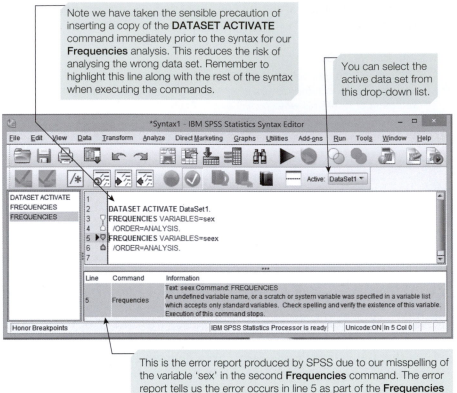

Note we have taken the sensible precaution of inserting a copy of the **DATASET ACTIVATE** command immediately prior to the syntax for our **Frequencies** analysis. This reduces the risk of analysing the wrong data set. Remember to highlight this line along with the rest of the syntax when executing the commands.

You can select the active data set from this drop-down list.

This is the error report produced by SPSS due to our misspelling of the variable 'sex' in the second **Frequencies** command. The error report tells us the error occurs in line 5 as part of the **Frequencies** command, and that the problem is an undefined variable name. We are advised to check the spelling of the variable name.

Section 2: SYNTAX EXAMPLES

One of the big advantages of being able to use SPSS syntax is that it enables you to benefit from the enormous number of helpful websites that provide short pieces of syntax to perform statistical analyses which cannot be undertaken using the dialogue boxes alone. One useful resource is the website of IBM, the company that now owns and markets SPSS. The IBM Knowledge Center for SPSS provides lots of examples of syntax routines. This is located at www-01.ibm.com/support/knowledgecenter. To illustrate how useful this resource is, we will now use syntax obtained from this site to compare correlation coefficients.

Comparing correlation coefficients

In Chapter 6, Section 5, we demonstrated how to compare two independent correlation coefficients in order to determine whether they were significantly different from one another. This required us to use formulae to compute Fisher's z-scores, which could then be compared against published tables of critical values. A much easier alternative is to use syntax to do these calculations for us. The section of syntax below is adapted from the IBM Knowledge Center (www-01.ibm.com/support/docview.wss?uid=swg21480038).

> * testing equality of independent correlations.
> * H0: R1 = R2; r1 & r2 are sample corr of x,y for groups 1 & 2 .
> * n1 and n2 are sample sizes for groups 1 and 2.
> Compute z1 = .5*ln((1+r1)/(1−r1)).
> Compute z2 = .5*ln((1+r2)/(1−r2)).
> Compute sezdiff = sqrt(1/(n1 − 3) + 1/(n2−3)).
> Compute ztest = (z1 − z2)/sezdiff.
> Compute alpha = 2*(1 − cdf.normal(abs(ztest),0,1)).
> Formats z1 to alpha (f8.3).
> List z1 to alpha.
> Execute.

The first three lines of this syntax program are comments to help us understand the calculation. The next four lines are **Compute** statements, and these are exactly equivalent to the formula given in Chapter 6. The fifth **Compute** command calculates the alpha value (the p value) for the calculated z-score, thus avoiding the need to use tables to look up the critical value. The **Formats** command ensures that the new variables are displayed to three decimal places. The **List** command displays the values for the new variables.

Before we can run this syntax, we need a simple data file. The file will consist of just one row of data containing four variables: the correlation coefficients for the two groups to be compared, and the sample size (n) for each of these two groups. The data file is shown below.

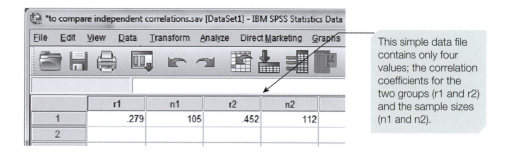

This simple data file contains only four values; the correlation coefficients for the two groups (r1 and r2) and the sample sizes (n1 and n2).

Set up this simple data file and save it, then type the syntax commands into a Syntax Editor window. Highlight the lines of syntax and select **Run**. You should see the output given below.

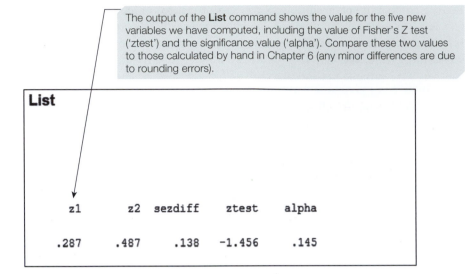

The output of the **List** command shows the value for the five new variables we have computed, including the value of Fisher's Z test ('ztest') and the significance value ('alpha'). Compare these two values to those calculated by hand in Chapter 6 (any minor differences are due to rounding errors).

List

z1	z2	sezdiff	ztest	alpha
.287	.487	.138	−1.456	.145

The syntax file we created to undertake this analysis demonstrates the use of the keyword **TO** in SPSS syntax. This keyword allows us to specify a list of consecutive variables. In the example above, we computed a total of five new variables, 'z1', 'z2', 'sezdiff', 'ztest' and 'alpha'. Because these are consecutive variables, occurring next to each other in the data file, we can specify all five with the syntax '**z1 to alpha**'. Thus, the syntax '**List z1 to alpha.**' lists all five variables, as seen in the output above. This can be a useful way of specifying a large number of variables very simply.

System variables

SPSS reserves several special variables, called 'system variables', for its own use. You rarely see these, but they can be useful when writing syntax. System variable names always commence with the special character '$'. One useful system variable is $casenum, which is the case number – the row number in your data file. You can use this system variable in <u>Compute</u> commands. For example, the following lines of syntax will create a new variable 'ParticipantNum' and set it equal to the case number.

```
Compute ParticipantNum = $casenum.
EXECUTE.
```

Type these lines of syntax into a Syntax window (don't forget the full stops) and then highlight and run them. You will find that the new variable has been added to the active data file. Note, however, that $casenum is always equal to the current case number, so it is important to use this syntax to produce the $casenum variable before doing anything that might change the order of the rows in the data file (for example, using the **Sort** command reorders the cases; see Chapter 4).

Another useful system variable is $sysmis, which SPSS uses to indicate a system missing value. System missing values appear as a dot in the appropriate cell of the data file. An example of the use of $sysmis is when creating a new variable. It is sometimes useful to initialise a new variable as missing, and then subsequently change this default value using **Recode** commands if certain conditions are met. An easy way to do this is with the system variable, $sysmis. The syntax is shown below. If you run this syntax, you will see the new variable is created and all values are set to system missing.

```
Compute NewVariable = $sysmis.
EXECUTE.
```

Section 3: GETTING HELP IN SPSS

It might seem odd to wait until the last chapter of this book before describing how to use the SPSS help system, but we hope that our instructions have provided all the assistance you have needed. However, you will need to make use of the help files provided with SPSS when trying to use functions or commands not covered in this book.

The Help button in dialogue boxes

Each dialogue box includes a **Help** button. Click on this button to open a page of help in your internet browser. This contains a mass of useful information, including a more detailed description of the statistical procedure and the options available for the command. This Help window will include a number of links to related content, including a link to the syntax for the current command, as described earlier.

This is the information provided when you click on the **Help** button in the **Independent-Samples T Test** dialogue box. Note that there are several pages of related help, which you can navigate using the left-hand pane of the window. Click on the small book icons to expand or collapse subheadings. The detailed information appears in the right-hand pane.

Click on this link to learn about the **Additional Features** of the **T-Test** command, which can only be accessed using syntax.

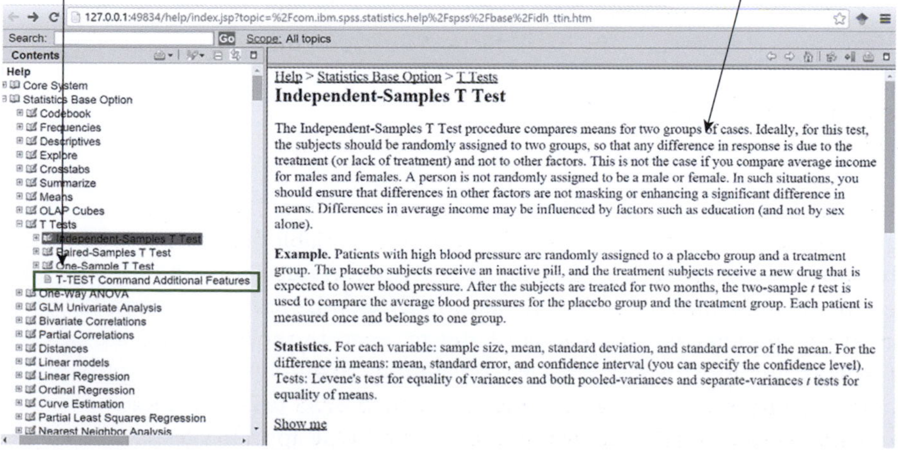

This page describes two special features of the **T-Test Command**, which can only be accessed using syntax. The second of these is quite useful as it allows us to quickly specify a large number of **Independent-Samples T-Tests** by using the **PAIRS subcommand**.

Click here to see the syntax for **the T-Test Command.**

This page provides a summary of the syntax for the **T-Test Command**, including the additional features such as those related to the **PAIRS Subcommand** described above.

Click on this link in the left-hand navigation pane to access more information about the **Pairs Subcommand**.

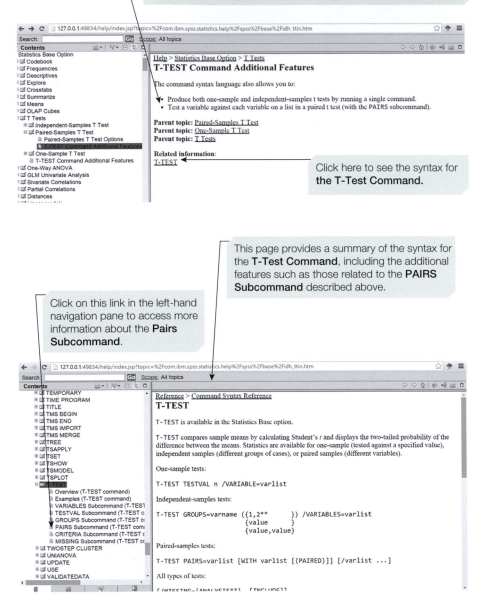

The **Pairs Subcommand** is an example of an additional feature only available through the use of syntax. If we undertake a **Paired-Samples T-Test** using the SPSS dialogue boxes (as described in Chapter 6), it is necessary to specify each pair of variables to be analysed. This can be time-consuming. Using syntax, it is possible to quickly specify a large number of pairings, for example pairing the first variable in a list with every other variable in the list, or pairing each variable in one list with each variable in another list. See below for details of these options.

This page describes how to use the **Pairs subcommand**.

Reference > Command Syntax Reference > T-TEST
PAIRS Subcommand (T-TEST command)

PAIRS requests paired-samples *t* tests.

- The minimum specification for a paired-samples test is PAIRS with an analysis list. Only numeric variables can be specified on the analysis list. The minimum analysis list is two variables.
- If keyword WITH is not specified, each variable in the list is compared with every other variable on the list.
- If keyword WITH is specified, every variable to the left of WITH is compared with every variable to the right of WITH. WITH can be used with PAIRED to obtain special pairing.
- To specify multiple analysis lists, use multiple PAIRS subcommands, each separated by a slash. Keyword PAIRS is required only for the first analysis list; a slash can be used to separate each additional analysis list.

(PAIRED). *Special pairing for paired-samples test.* PAIRED must be enclosed in parentheses and must be used with keyword WITH. When PAIRED is specified, the first variable before WITH is compared with the first variable after WITH, the second variable before WITH is compared with the second variable after WITH, and so forth. The same number of variables should be specified before and after WITH; unmatched variables are ignored and a warning message is issued. PAIRED generates an error message if keyword WITH is not specified on PAIRS.

Example

```
T-TEST  PAIRS=TEACHER CONSTRUC MANAGER.
T-TEST  PAIRS=TEACHER MANAGER WITH CONSTRUC ENGINEER.
T-TEST  PAIRS=TEACHER MANAGER WITH CONSTRUC ENGINEER (PAIRED).
```

- The first T-TEST compares *TEACHER* with *CONSTRUC*, *TEACHER* with *MANAGER*, and *CONSTRUC* with *MANAGER*.
- The second T-TEST compares *TEACHER* with *CONSTRUC*, *TEACHER* with *ENGINEER*, *MANAGER* with *CONSTRUC*, and *MANAGER* with *ENGINEER*. *TEACHER* is not compared with *MANAGER*, and *CONSTRUC* is not compared with *ENGINEER*.
- The third T-TEST compares *TEACHER* with *CONSTRUC* and *MANAGER* with *ENGINEER*.

The Help menu

You can also access help from the **Help** menu on each window. This gives access to several sources of information. To search for help on a particular topic, select **Topics**, and then enter a few keywords into the search box at the left of the window. For example, if you search for 'chi-square', SPSS will find a long list of related help files, which it will list in the left-hand pane of the window. Select from this list to read the help information (see below).

adoption_survey for 6th ed.sav [DataSet1] – IBM SPSS Statistics Data Editor

| ting | Graphs | Utilities | Add-ons | Window | Help |

| Topics |
| Tutorial |
| Case Studies |
| Working with R |
| Statistics Coach |
| Command Syntax Reference |
| SPSS Community |
| About... |
| Algorithms |
| IBM SPSS Products Home |
| Programmability |
| Diagnose... |

	adopted	q1	q2				q6	q7
.00	1.00	4.00	4.00				4.00	
.00	.00	4.00	1.00				3.00	
.00	1.00	2.00	3.00				2.00	
.00	.00	2.00	1.00				3.00	
.00	.00	4.00	5.00				2.00	
.00	.00	2.00	1.00				1.00	
.00	4.00	1.00	1.00				1.00	
.00	4.00	1.00	2.00				1.00	
.00	2.00	1.00	1.00				2.00	
.00	3.00	2.00	2.00				2.00	
.00	.00	5.00	4.00	5.00	5.00	5.00	5.00	

Click **Help** then select **Topics**. This gives access to the help system shown below.

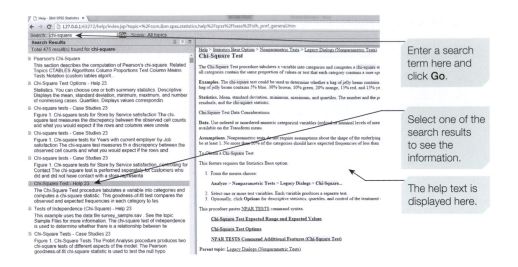

Other options in the **Help** menu include **Tutorial**, a step by step introduction to many of the features of SPSS, and **Command Syntax Reference,** which provides access to a pdf file containing further details of the syntax for each command. You might like to explore all these forms of help.

Statistics Coach

The Statistics Coach is designed to help you determine what type of analysis to do by asking a number of questions about your data and your hypothesis before suggesting a suitable statistical procedure. This can act as a useful reminder, but is no substitute for a basic knowledge of these procedures.

What's this?

When viewing output in the Output window, double-click on a table to select it. If the pivot table opens in a **Pivot Table Editor window**, you can right click on a heading and select **What's This?** from the drop-down menu. This will provide a short but useful description of the item. The example below shows the description of the **Levene's Test for Equality of Variance** in the **Pivot Table for the Independent Samples Test**.

Pivot Table Independent Samples Test

File   Edit   View   Insert   Pivot   Format   Help

SansSerif   9   B I U A

Independent Samples Test

		Levene's Test for Equality of Variances		t-test for Equality of Means					
								95% Confidence Interval of the Difference	
					df	Sig. (2-tailed)	Mean Difference	Std. Error Difference	Lower	Upper
q1	Equal variances assumed				17	.709	.29487	.77636	-1.34310	1.93284
	Equal variances not assumed			.361	8.702	.727	.29487	.81792	-1.56512	2.15486
q4	Equal variances assumed	.694	.416	-.081	18	.936	-.05495	.67879	-1.48104	1.37115
	Equal variances not assumed			-.077	10.765	.940	-.05495	.71438	-1.63150	1.52160

A homogeneity-of-variance test that is less dependent on the assumption of normality than most tests. For each case, it computes the absolute difference between the value of that case and its cell mean and performs a one-way analysis of variance on those differences.

Section 4: OPTION SETTINGS IN SPSS

There are a number of options that can be set in SPSS. These control such things as the appearance of the various windows, the way variables are listed in dialogue boxes, the appearance of output, and the location of files. Here, we describe how to access these options and highlight a few you might like to alter.

> If your screen looks different from the screenshots included in this book, this may be because some of these options settings are different. In particular, if your variables are always listed differently from ours, it may be that the **Variable Lists** options in your copy of SPSS are set differently to ours (see below).

Changing option settings

The option settings can be accessed from any of the various SPSS windows. Select **Edit** > **Options**. This will bring up the **Options** dialogue box (shown below). This dialogue box has a series of tabs across the top. Click on a tab to see that set of options.

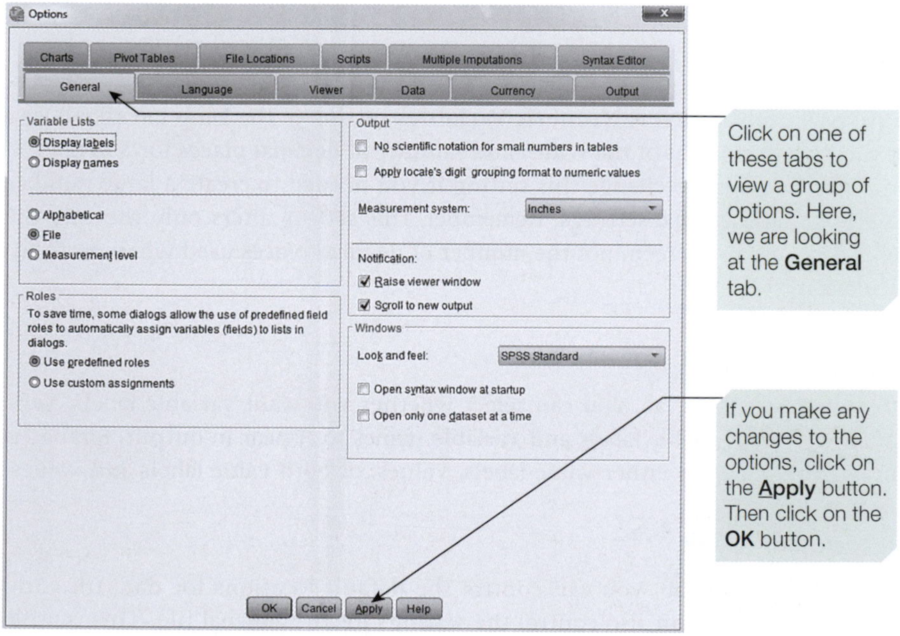

Click on one of these tabs to view a group of options. Here, we are looking at the **General** tab.

If you make any changes to the options, click on the **Apply** button. Then click on the **OK** button.

Some useful option settings

General tab

One of the most useful options in the **General** tab allows you to control how variables are listed in the dialogue boxes. By default, SPSS is set to the **Display labels** option. In this setting, SPSS lists the variable labels (with the variable name given in brackets). When working with complex data sets, the alternative **Display names** option is often better; this forces SPSS to list variables by name. The options on the **General** tab also allow you to control whether the variables are listed in **Alphabetical** order or in the order they are listed in the data file (**File**) or grouped by **Measurement level**. (It is worth noting that you can also choose between these various options when working in an SPSS dialogue box – just right click on the box that lists all the variables and select the options you require.)

Syntax Editor tab

In the **Syntax Editor** tab, you can change the colours applied to command names, subcommands and so on in the Syntax Editor window, and switch auto-complete on or off. You can also change where syntax is pasted into the Syntax window when you click the **Paste** button on a dialogue box (at the current cursor location or after the last command in the window).

Viewer tab

The tick box at the bottom left-hand corner of the **Viewer** tab controls whether the command syntax is written to the output file.

Data tab

The **Display Format for New Numeric Variables** section of the **Data** tab allows you to alter the default settings of the width and number of decimal places for a new variable. It might be useful to change this setting if you needed to create a large number of variables using the same settings. Remember, this setting alters only the way the number is displayed on screen, not the number of decimal places used when performing calculations.

Output Labels tab

From the **Output Labels** tab, you can select whether you want variable labels, variable names, or both variable labels and variable names to appear in output. Similarly, you can choose to display either value labels, values, or both value labels and values.

File Locations tab

On the **File Locations** tab, you can control the default locations for data files and other files in SPSS. You can also control the settings for the Journal file. This is a file that SPSS uses to keep a record of the syntax of all the operations you have undertaken in the current session.

Section 5: PRINTING FROM SPSS

Here we provide some information on how to print output, data and syntax files.

Printing output from the Output viewer window

To print from the Output viewer window, either click on the printer icon at the top of the window, or select **P̲rint** from the **F̲ile** menu. The option **A̲ll visible output** prints any output you could see by scrolling up or down in the Output window (i.e. not hidden output). Alternatively, you can print just the parts of the output you are interested in, using the **Selected output** option.

The **Page Set̲up** and **Page Attributes** options under the **F̲ile** menu allow you to control the paper size and orientation, the margins and to add footers and headers to your pages.

Printing data and syntax files

To obtain a printed copy of your data or syntax file, select **P̲rint** from the **F̲ile** menu of the appropriate window.

The **F̲onts** option under the **V̲iew** menu allows you to change the size and appearance of the font used to display and print the data.

Special output options for pivot tables

Most of the tables of results that appear in the Output viewer window are pivot tables. Double-clicking on a pivot table will select it, and either open a Formatting toolbar, or, in the case of more complex tables, will open the table in a new window. The tools in the Formatting toolbar can be used to adjust the appearance of the table prior to printing it. A huge number of options are available, including rotating the table (swapping rows and columns), adding or removing grid lines and scaling the table to fit the size of paper being used. Below, we describe a few of the most useful actions available from the Pivot Table window menu bar:

1. From the **P̲ivot** menu, select **T̲ranspose Rows and Columns** to swap the rows and columns of a table.

2. From the **F̲ormat** menu, select **T̲able Properties**. The tab-style dialogue box displayed will allow you to alter the appearance of the table. The Printing tab contains two useful options (**Rescale w̲ide table to fit page** and **R̲escale long table to fit page**), which force SPSS to automatically adjust the size of print so that the table will fit the page without being split.

3. Alternatively, select **TableLooks** from the **Format** menu and change the overall style of the table using one of a number of predesigned styles. See below for an example.

> Here we are going to edit this pivot table from the output of an independent samples t-test. First, double-click on the pivot table. This will open the table in the Pivot Table editor window (see below).

T-Test

[DataSet3] C:\Users\Richard\Documents\Backup of Lenovo 21 Jun 14\Documents\Documents\Publishing\Books\SPSS ed 6\Data files\adop

Group Statistics

	sex	N	Mean	Std. Deviation	Std. Error Mean
q1	Male	6	2.8333	1.72240	.70317
	Female	13	2.5385	1.50640	.41780

Independent Samples Test

		Levene's Test for Equality of Variances		t-test for Equality of Means					95% Confidence Interval of the Difference	
		F	Sig.	t	df	Sig. (2-tailed)	Mean Difference	Std. Error Difference	Lower	Upper
q1	Equal variances assumed	.469	.503	.380	17	.709	.29487	.77636	-1.34310	1.93284
	Equal variances not assumed			.361	8.702	.727	.29487	.81792	-1.56512	2.15486

> This is the Pivot Table editor window, which provides a number of tools to help change the appearance of the table. For example, click on **Format** and select **TableLooks**.

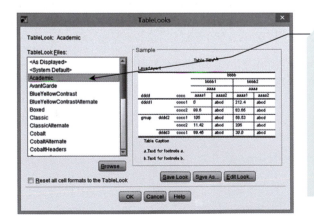

> In the TableLooks window, you can select from a number of different table styles. **Academic** is particularly useful.
>
> Select your preferred style and then click **OK**. The pivot table in the output file will be reformatted to match the new style. You can then copy and paste the reformatted table into your report.

4. From the **Format** menu select **Autofit**. This will resize the columns and rows of the table to a size that is appropriate for their contents. This usually makes the table slightly smaller and much neater.

Before using either of the rescale options (described in point 2 above), you could apply the **Autofit** option. This will remove any redundant spaces from the table before it is rescaled.

5. From the **Insert** menu, select **Caption**. This will allow you to insert a text caption inside the table.

6. Select a set of table cells by clicking and dragging over them. From the **Format** menu, select **Cell Properties**. Using the options under the three tabs of this dialogue box, you can set the size and colour of the font and background of the cells, how the content of the cells is aligned, and the format used to display the contents. Also under the **Format** menu, the **Set Data Cell Widths** menu item can be used to set the width of the cells.

7. Double-click on any text in the pivot table, including the table title or the row or column labels to edit the text. It is also possible to edit the contents of the cells in this way.

8. Close the Pivot Table Editor window to apply the changes you have made. The pivot table in the Output window will be updated to reflect these changes.

Once a pivot table is selected, it is possible to adjust the width of a column by clicking on and dragging the grid line dividing the columns. Double-clicking on a cell allows you to change the cell contents.

Section 6: INCORPORATING SPSS OUTPUT INTO OTHER DOCUMENTS

Once you have reformatted the pivot tables in your output, you will want to incorporate it into your word processed research report. If you are using Microsoft Word, this is simply a matter of copying and pasting the sections of the output. Follow the steps below.

CHAPTER 13

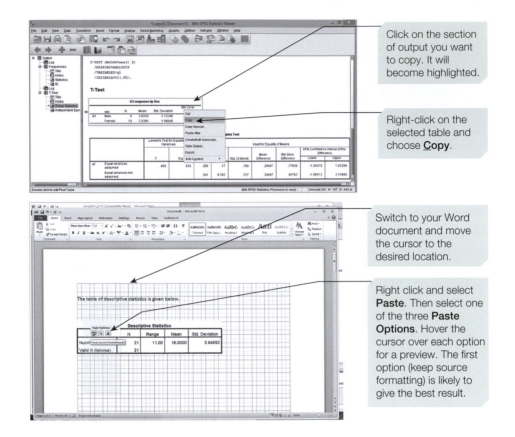

Click on the section of output you want to copy. It will become highlighted.

Right-click on the selected table and choose **Copy**.

Switch to your Word document and move the cursor to the desired location.

Right click and select **Paste**. Then select one of the three **Paste Options**. Hover the cursor over each option for a preview. The first option (keep source formatting) is likely to give the best result.

Exporting SPSS output

It is possible to export the SPSS output in one of several widely adopted file formats. For example, you can save the output as a Rich Text File, which can then be read into a word processor. This might be particularly useful if you need to send the output to someone who does not have access to a copy of SPSS. To do this, first select **File > Export**.

Click here to select the file format for the export.

Specify the name and location of the export file.

Click **OK** to export the output in the new format.

Section 7: SPSS AND EXCEL: IMPORTING AND EXPORTING DATA FILES

Many researchers use a spreadsheet program such as Excel to initially collate and tabulate their data. One reason for doing this is that most people will have access to an Excel compatible spreadsheet, whereas not everyone will be able to access SPSS. A further advantage is that it is sometimes easier to pre-process a large data file in a spreadsheet program than it is to use SPSS. Fortunately, it is easy to open Excel files in SPSS. Similarly, it is quite straightforward to save an SPSS file in an Excel file format. These import and export operations are illustrated below.

Import: opening an Excel file in SPSS

To illustrate how to open an Excel file in SPSS, we have created a simple Excel spreadsheet, shown below. The file contains some simple demographics and two variables, 'RT1' and 'RT2'. Note that in this case we have used the spreadsheet to compute 'MeanRT', the mean of 'RT1' and 'RT2'.

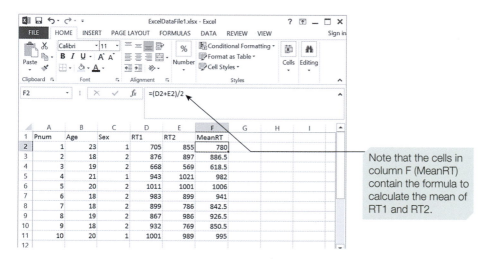

Note that the cells in column F (MeanRT) contain the formula to calculate the mean of RT1 and RT2.

We can now open this Excel file in SPSS. Switch to SPSS and click on the menu item **File** then follow the steps below.

Select **File**.

Select **Open**.

Select **Data**.

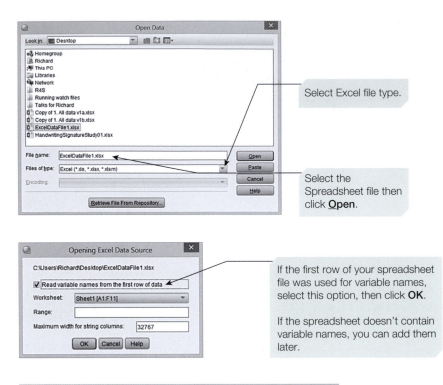

Select Excel file type.

Select the Spreadsheet file then click **Open**.

If the first row of your spreadsheet file was used for variable names, select this option, then click **OK**.

If the spreadsheet doesn't contain variable names, you can add them later.

The file has opened in SPSS. Note that SPSS has used the text from the first row of the Excel spreadsheet as variable names. Note also that the calculated values of the variable 'MeanRT' have been read into the data file.

Export: saving an SPSS file to Excel

It is also easy to save an SPSS data file as an Excel file.

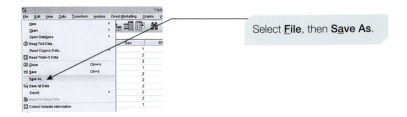

Select **File**, then **Save As**.

Select Excel file type and then click **Save**.

The file will be saved in Excel format with the variable names used as labels in the top row of the spreadsheet. In this way, it is easy to move files between SPSS and Excel.

Summary

- This chapter introduced SPSS syntax. We demonstrated how to use syntax files to control SPSS, and described some of the advantages of using syntax.

- Using syntax to control SPSS can enhance your productivity and gives you an invaluable record of your analysis. Syntax can also be used to repeat a set of analyses, for example after updating a data file. Using syntax to control your analysis can be particularly useful when working with large, complex data sets.

- This chapter also showed you how to access help files, including syntax help files.

- We also demonstrated some useful option settings in SPSS.

- The final sections of the chapter showed you how to print and export SPSS files, and how to incorporate the output into Microsoft Word documents.

- Finally, we demonstrated how to move data files between a spreadsheet program, such as Excel, and SPSS. This enables you to benefit from the best features of both programs.

CHAPTER 13

Appendix

All data files are available to download from he.palgrave.com/psychology/brace. We recommend that you enter the first few data files to become skilled at entering data and therefore include those for Chapters 4–7 here.

Data files for	Included here	Available from website
Data handling exercises	✓	✓
Log transformation exercise		✓
Data handling exercise for scales	✓	✓
One-sample *t*-test	✓	✓
Independent *t*-test	✓	✓
Paired *t*-test	✓	✓
Mann–Whitney U test	✓	✓
Wilcoxon matched-pairs signed-ranks test	✓	✓
Pearson's *r* correlation	✓	✓
Spearman's rho correlation	✓	✓
Chi-square test	✓	✓
McNemar test	✓	✓
One-way between-subjects ANOVA		✓
Two-way between-subjects ANOVA		✓
One-way within-subjects ANOVA		✓
Two-way within-subjects ANOVA		✓
Three-way mixed ANOVA		✓
Kruskal–Wallis test and Friedman test		✓
Multiple regression		✓
ANCOVA and MANOVA		✓
Discriminant analysis and logistic regression		✓
Factor analysis		✓

DATA FOR DATA HANDLING EXERCISES: CHAPTER 4, SECTIONS 1–9

id	sex	ethnicity	religion	adopted	q1	q2	q3	q4	q5	q6	q7	q8	q9	q10
1	2	2	3	1	4	4	4	5	2	4	3	5	2	2
2	1	2	3	0	4	1	5	5	1	3	2	3	1	5
3	2	4	2	1	2	3	2	2	1	2	1	1	1	1
4	2	3	2	0	2	1	1	3	3	3	3	1	1	1
5	2	2	6	0	4	5	3	4	4	2	4	5	4	3
6	2	5	5	0	2	1	9	1	2	1	1	1	1	1
7	1	4	3	4	1	1	1	2	1	1	1	3	2	5
8	1	1	6	4	1	2	2	1	1	1	2	2	3	1
9	2	2	3	2	1	1	2	1	1	2	1	1	1	1
10	2	3	3	2	2	1	2	3	2	2	3	2	2
11	2	4	5	0	5	4	5	5	5	5	5	5	5	5
12	1	4	5	1	4	4	3	2	4	3	4	3	4	3
13	2	4	3	1	3	3	3	3	2	3	3	2	3	4
14	1	1	6	2	2	3	5	4	2	3	4	1	3	5
15	1	3	3	1	9	1	2	1	1	1	1	2	3	2
16	2	4	1	4	1	2	1	2	2	2	1	2	2	2
17	2	5	2	0	5	4	4	4	3	4	3	4	5	5
18	1	1	3	2	5	4	9	4	4	3	3	2	4	4
19	2	1	2	4	1	1	1	2	1	2	2	1	1	1
20	2	2	3	9	1	2	3	2	3	2	2	2	3	3

DATA FOR DATA HANDLING EXERCISES: CHAPTER 4, SECTION 10

Qnum	q_a	q_b	q_c	q_d	q_e	q_f	q_g	q_h	q_i	q_j	q_k	q_l	q_m	q_n	q_o	q_p	q_q	q_r	q_s	q_t
1	4	2	3	4	4	4	2	2	2	4	2	3	3	5	4	3	5	3	3	5
2	2	2	6	3	4	4	1	2	3	4	2	2	4	4	5	3	3	3	3	2
3	4	2	4	4	5	5	2	2	2	5	3	2	3	2	5	2	3	3	3	4
4	4	2	4	5	5	5	1	1	2	5	2	1	1	3	5	1	2	2	3	5
5	4	2	5	4	5	4	1	2	2	3	2	2	5	4	2	2	2	4	4
6	4	2	3	3	4	3	2	3	2	4	3	2	3	2	4	3	3	3	4	4
7	5	1	5	4	5	5	1	2	2	5	2	1	2	4	5	2	2	2	4	4
8	5	2	5	5	4	4	2	2	3	5	3	2	2	5	5	1	3	3	3	4
9	4	1	5	5	4	4	2	1	2	5	1	1	3	5	5	2	4	1	1	5
10	5	2	5	5	5	5	1	2	2	4	2	2	3	1	5	3	3	3	3	4
11	4	2	3	4	5	5	1	2	2	4	2	2	2	4	4	2	2	2	4	4
12	4	1	4	4	4	4	1	2	2	5	2	1	2	4	2	2	2	4	4
13	4	1	3	4	5	5	2	1	1	5	1	3	2	2	4	2	2	3	5	5
14	4	1	3	4	4	4	1	2	2	4	1	1	2	3	1	4	3	3	4
15	4	3	3	4	4	4	1	3	2	5	2	2	3	4	2	3	3	3	4
16	5	2	5	5	5	5	1	2	2	5	2	1	2	5	4	1	3	1	4	4
17	4	3	4	4	5	2	2	3	3	4	5	2	5	4	4	2	4	3	3	3
18	2	2	3	3	5	4	1	3	2	4	4	3	4	2	5	2	2	4	3	2
19	4	2	5	5	5	3	1	3	3	5	1	2	3	2	4	1	3	1	4	4
20	4	2	5	5	5	5	1	2	2	5	2	1	3	5	5	2	2	2	5	5
21	4	1	4	4	4	4	2	2	2	5	1	3	2	3	4	2	3	2	3	3
22	4	2	3	4	4	3	2	2	2	4	3	4	3	4	4	3	3	3	2	4
23	4	2	5	5	5	5	1	2	1	5	1	1	2	5	5	2	2	2	3	5
24	5	1	4	5	5	5	1	1	1	5	1	1	1	3	4	2	3	3	3	3
25	5	1	5	5	5	5	1	3	3	4	3	1	5	2	5	2	4	2	4	4
26	3	2	3	4	4	4	2	3	2	4	2	2	3	4	2	2	3	3	3	3
27	2	4	2	2	2	1	4	4	5	1	5	5	5	4	2	5	5	5	2	1
28	3	2	3	4	4	4	3	3	4	3	3	4	5	3	3	4	4	3	2	2

Data continues on next page

Qnum	q_a	q_b	q_c	q_d	q_e	q_f	q_g	q_h	q_i	q_j	q_k	q_l	q_m	q_n	q_o	q_p	q_q	q_r	q_s	q_t
29	4	2	4	5	5	4	2	2	2	4	2	3	2	5	4	3	2	3	4	9
30	3	2	4	4	4	3	2	2	2	4	2	2	4	4	4	2	3	2	4	4
31	4	2	5	5	5	5	1	2	2	5	3	3	4	5	5	1	2	3	4	5
32	4	3	5	5	5	9	3	3	4	4	4	4	4	3	3	4	4	4	2	4
33	3	2	3	5	4	4	1	2	2	2	5	2	2	4	5	2	3	3	5	5
34	4	2	2	5	5	4	2	2	3	5	3	4	5	4	4	2	5	3	4	4
35	4	2	5	4	4	4	2	2	4	4	2	2	4	4	4	2	2	4	4	4
36	4	3	4	5	5	5	1	2	2	5	1	1	2	5	5	3	4	2	3	4
37	4	2	5	4	5	3	2	2	3	5	2	2	4	4	5	3	3	3	3	4
38	5	2	3	4	4	4	2	2	2	4	2	3	2	3	3	2	3	2	3	4
39	5	1	4	5	5	5	1	1	1	5	1	4	3	2	4	1	1	2	3	5
40	4	1	4	4	4	3	2	2	2	4	2	2	3	4	4	2	3	2	4	4
41	4	4	4	4	4	2	4	4	4	4	4	2	4	3	4	2	5	3	3	5
42	5	1	4	5	5	5	1	3	5	5	1	1	1	5	4	1	3	1	3	1
43	5	1	5	5	5	5	1	1	1	5	1	1	2	5	5	1	2	1	3	5
44	4	2	3	4	4	5	2	2	2	5	3	1	3	4	4	2	2	3	5	5
45	2	4	2	4	4	3	2	3	3	4	3	3	3	4	3	2	4	2	3	3
46	5	4	5	5	5	5	1	2	3	4	4	2	4	5	5	2	2	3	2	5
47	3	2	5	3	5	4	2	2	2	5	2	2	3	3	5	1	2	2	4	2
48	4	2	2	4	4	5	1	2	3	5	3	1	3	3	5	2	3	2	3	5
49	3	2	2	4	3	3	2	2	2	4	3	4	2	3	4	2	3	3	3	3
50	5	5	5	5	5	1	2	4	5	4	4	2	5	5	4	2	5	2	4	4

Appendix

DATA FOR ONE-SAMPLE *t*-TEST: CHAPTER 5, SECTION 2

Score
68.00
62.00
58.00
67.00
65.00
69.00
72.00
76.00
62.00
64.00
69.00
70.00
71.00
66.00
68.00
67.00
61.00
72.00
73.00
78.00

DATA FOR INDEPENDENT *t*-TEST: CHAPTER 5, SECTION 3

GROUP 1 = mnemonic condition 2 = no mnemonic condition	SCORE
1	20
1	18
1	14
1	18
1	17
1	11
1	20
1	18

Data continues on next page

GROUP 1 = mnemonic condition 2 = no mnemonic condition	SCORE
1	20
1	19
1	20
2	10
2	20
2	12
2	9
2	14
2	15
2	16
2	14
2	19
2	12

DATA FOR PAIRED *t*-TEST: CHAPTER 5, SECTION 4

LARGE SIZE DIFFERENCE	SMALL SIZE DIFFERENCE
936	878
923	1005
896	1010
1241	1365
1278	1422
871	1198
1360	1576
733	896
941	1573
1077	1261
1438	2237
1099	1325
1253	1591
1930	2742
1260	1357
1271	1963

Appendix

DATA FOR MANN–WHITNEY U TEST: CHAPTER 5, SECTION 6

SEX 1 = male 2 = female	RATING	SEX 1 = male 2 = female	RATING
1	4	2	4
1	6	2	2
1	5	2	7
1	8	2	4
1	5	2	6
1	2	2	7
1	4	2	5
1	4	2	2
1	5	2	6
1	7	2	6
1	5	2	6
1	4	2	6
1	3	2	3
1	3	2	5
1	5	2	7
1	3	2	4
1	3	2	6
1	8	2	6
1	6	2	7
1	4	2	8

DATA FOR WILCOXON MATCHED-PAIRS SIGNED-RANKS TEST: CHAPTER 5, SECTION 7

E-FIT RATING 1 (from memory)	E-FIT RATING 2 (from photograph)	E-FIT RATING 1 (from memory)	E-FIT RATING 2 (from photograph)
3	6	4	4
3	4	4	2
3	5	4	5
5	6	3	3
2	3	5	3
4	3	4	3
5	3	3	2
5	3	3	3
4	3	6	4
3	3	3	3
2	3	3	2
6	6	3	3
5	3	2	4
4	3	2	5
3	3	5	6
3	5	3	5
4	5	6	4
3	2	2	3
4	5	5	5
3	5	4	2
3	2	3	5
5	6	3	2
3	4	5	6
4	3	4	2

DATA FOR PEARSON'S *r* CORRELATION: CHAPTER 6, SECTION 3

AGE (in years)	CFF
41	34.9
43	30.5
25	35.75
42	32.3
51	28.0
27	42.2
27	35.1
48	33.5
58	25.0
52	31.0
58	23.2
50	26.8
44	32.0
53	29.3
26	35.9
65	30.5
35	31.9
29	32.0
25	39.9
49	33.0

DATA FOR SPEARMAN'S RHO CORRELATION: CHAPTER 6, SECTION 4

CONFI-DENCE	BELIEV-ABILITY	ATTRACT-IVENESS
4	4	2
4	3	3
4	6	4
4	6	4
4	4	3
4	4	4
4	3	2
5	5	4
4	4	3
6	5	4
4	6	4
4	5	5
4	4	3
6	5	4
5	5	4
4	5	3
2	4	3
6	4	4
3	5	3
3	3	3
2	5	5
5	5	4
5	6	4
5	4	4
4	5	4
5	5	4
5	5	4
4	4	5
4	4	4
3	5	4
5	6	4
5	5	4
1	5	3
5	5	4
5	5	4
5	6	4
5	5	5
4	5	4
4	5	4
4	5	4
5	5	4
4	5	4
5	5	3
4	4	2
5	6	5

CONFI-DENCE	BELIEV-ABILITY	ATTRACT-IVENESS
4	5	3
6	5	2
3	5	4
3	5	4
4	4	3
4	3	3
6	6	4
3	5	2
4	4	3
5	5	4
3	1	3
5	6	4
5	5	4
4	5	4
4	4	4
6	1	1
5	5	4
5	5	4
6	6	5
5	5	3
6	6	5
5	5	2
2	4	4
3	4	4
3	4	4
4	4	4
4	5	4
5	5	4
5	5	3
3	4	4
2	3	5
6	5	5
4	5	3
5	4	4
4	5	4
4	5	4
4	4	4
4	4	4
4	5	4
4	5	5
5	4	4
4	6	4
5	5	3
6	5	4

DATA FOR CHI-SQUARE TEST: CHAPTER 7, SECTION 4

BACKGROUND 1 = Asian 2 = Caucasian 3 = other	MOTHER'S EMPLOYMENT 1 = full time 2 = none 3 = part time	SCHOOL 1 = comprehensive 2 = private	TENDENCY TO ANOREXIA 1 = high 2 = low
2	1	1	1
2	1	1	1
2	1	1	1
2	3	1	1
2	3	2	1
2	3	2	1
2	2	2	1
2	2	2	1
2	2	2	1
2	1	2	1
2	1	2	1
2	1	2	1
2	3	2	1
2	3	2	1
2	3	2	1
2	3	2	1
2	2	2	1
2	2	2	1
2	2	2	1
2	2	2	1
2	3	2	1
2	3	2	1
1	3	2	1
1	1	2	1
1	1	2	1
1	1	2	1
3	2	2	1
3	3	2	1
3	2	2	1
3	2	2	1
3	1	2	1
3	1	2	1
3	1	2	1
3	1	2	1
3	1	2	1
3	2	2	1
3	2	2	1
3	2	2	1
2	2	1	2

Data continues on next page

BACKGROUND 1 = Asian 2 = Caucasian 3 = other	MOTHER'S EMPLOYMENT 1 = full time 2 = none 3 = part time	SCHOOL 1 = comprehensive 2 = private	TENDENCY TO ANOREXIA 1 = high 2 = low
2	1	1	2
2	1	1	2
2	3	1	2
2	3	1	2
2	2	1	2
2	2	1	2
2	2	1	2
2	2	1	2
2	3	1	2
2	3	1	2
2	3	1	2
2	3	1	2
2	3	1	2
2	3	1	2
2	3	1	2
2	3	1	2
2	2	1	2
2	2	1	2
2	2	1	2
2	3	1	2
2	3	1	2
2	2	1	2
2	2	1	2
2	2	1	2
2	2	1	2
2	3	1	2
2	1	1	2
2	1	1	2
2	1	2	2
2	1	2	2
2	1	2	2
2	1	2	2
2	1	2	2
2	1	2	2
2	1	2	2
1	1	2	2
1	1	2	2
3	1	2	2
3	1	2	2
3	1	2	2
3	1	2	2

DATA FOR MCNEMAR TEST: CHAPTER 7, SECTION 5

NORMAL HANDWRITING 1 = correct 2 = incorrect	HANDWRITING AS IF OPPOSITE SEX 1 = correct 2 = incorrect	NORMAL HANDWRITING 1 = correct 2 = incorrect	HANDWRITING AS IF OPPOSITE SEX 1 = correct 2 = incorrect
2	2	1	2
1	1	1	2
1	1	2	1
1	2	1	2
1	1	1	1
2	2	1	1
1	1	1	2
1	2	1	2
2	2	2	2
1	1	1	1
2	2	1	1
1	2	1	1
2	2	2	2
2	2	2	1
1	1	1	2
2	2	2	2
1	1	1	1
2	2	1	2
1	2	1	1
2	2	1	1
1	2	2	2
1	2	1	1
1	2	1	2
1	2	2	2
1	1		

Glossary

This glossary provides an explanation of many of the terms used in the book. We have used italics to indicate terms that have their own entry in the glossary. For further information about statistical or experimental design concepts, we encourage you to consult a statistics text.

ANCOVA (analysis of covariance)

An extension of analysis of variance (*ANOVA*) in which at least one covariate in included in the design. A covariate is a *variable* that has a statistical association with one of the *dependent variables*. ANCOVA allows us to estimate the impact of the *dependent variables* after allowing for the influence of the covariates.

ANOVA (analysis of variance)

An *inferential statistical test* that allows analysis of data from designs with more than two experimental *conditions* and/or with more than one *factor*. Often used to refer to the *experimental design* used to collect data suitable for analysis using this approach. ANOVA is appropriate for use with *parametric* data. The absence, however, of *nonparametric* equivalents for two or more factor designs means that ANOVA is often used in such circumstances. Fortunately, it is said to be fairly robust to violations of the assumptions for *parametric* tests, provided that the *cell* sizes are equal.

> Introduction to ANOVA
> One-way *between-subjects* ANOVA (see also *Kruskal–Wallis*)
> One-way *within-subjects* ANOVA (see also *Friedman*)
> Multi-way *between-subjects* ANOVA
> Multi-way *within-subjects* ANOVA
> Multi-way *mixed* ANOVA

Association

See *correlation* and *chi-square*.

Asymptotic significance

The *p* value calculated under the assumption that the *sample* is large and has an asymptotic distribution. For the vast majority of *inferential statistical tests*, the *p* value given by SPSS is the asymptotic significance. For many tests, SPSS now gives an option to also calculate the *exact significance*.

Bar chart

A graph used to display summary statistics such as the *mean* (in the case of a *scale* variable) or the *frequency* (in the case of a nominal variable). See also *chart*.

Between-subjects design

An *experimental design* in which all *factors* are between-subjects factors; that is, each participant contributes data to only one *level* of a factor (each participant only experiences one condition). See also *independent groups design* and *natural independent groups design*.

Binary logistic regression

See *logistic regression*.

Bivariate

An analysis involving two *variables,* for example, *correlation*. See also *univariate* and *multivariate*.

Bivariate regression

An inferential statistical procedure used to investigate a *linear relationship* between two *variables*. It can indicate the extent to which one variable can be explained or predicted by the other variable. See also *regression*.

Case

A case is the unit of analysis. In psychology, this is normally the data deriving from a single *participant*. An exception is in a *matched-subjects design*, when the pair of matched participants form the case. Each case should be entered into a separate row in the SPSS *Data window*. In some research, the cases will not be people. For example, we may be interested in the average academic attainment for pupils from different schools. Here, the cases would be the schools.

Cell

An element in the *Data Editor window* table, into which a value is entered. In *ANOVA* and *chi-square*, the combination of one *level* of one *factor* and one level of another factor. The cell size is the number of *cases* (normally *participants*) that fall into that cell.

Chart

The name that SPSS gives to a graph. A wide range of graph types is available from the **Graphs** *menu item*. In addition, the output of some statistical procedures include optional charts.

Chi-square

An *inferential statistical test* that is used to analyse *frequencies* of *nominal* data. Chi-square allows comparison between the observed frequencies and the pattern that would be expected by chance. In psychology, the multidimensional chi-square is most often used. It can be thought of as a test of association between two *variables*, or as a test of difference between two independent groups.

The chi-square distribution is used to assess *significance* for some other statistical tests, for example *Friedman* and *Kruskal–Wallis*.

Cleaning

See *data cleaning*.

Compute

An SPSS procedure that allows us to compute (calculate) a new *variable* based on one or more existing *variables*. The new *variable* is added to the data file.

Condition

See *level*.

Confidence interval

A pair of values that define a range within which we expect the *population parameter*, such as the *mean*, to fall. In the case of the 95% confidence interval, these values define the range within which there is a 95% probability that the parameter will fall.

Confounding variable

Any uncontrolled *variable* that changes systematically across the *levels* of the *independent variable* or *factor*. If a study includes a confounding variable, it is not possible to determine whether the results of an experiment are due to the *independent variable* alone, to the confounding variable alone, or to some *interaction* between those two variables.

Contingency table

Displays the *frequencies* or counts for the levels of one or more variables.

Correlation

Describes a *linear relationship*, or association, between two *variables* (measured on ordinal, interval or ratio *level of measurement*). *Pearson's r*, *Spearman's rho* and *Kendall's tau* are *inferential statistical tests* of correlation. See also *scattergram*.

Count

An SPSS procedure that allows us to count the number of times a particular value occurs, in one or more *variables*.

Covariate

See *ANCOVA*.

Criterion variable

The variable that is explained by the *predictor variable*/s in a *regression* analysis. Some sources use the term 'dependent variable' instead of criterion variable.

Data

A set of values. A data set is typically made up of a number of *variables*. In *quantitative research*, data are numeric.

Data cleaning

The process of checking the accuracy of a *data file* and correcting any errors that are found.

Data Editor window

The SPSS window in which data are entered and edited. It has the appearance, but not the functionality, of a spreadsheet window.

Data file

SPSS records a set of *data* in a data file. Data files in SPSS usually have the file extension '.sav'.

Data handling

A range of operations performed on the data after they have been entered into SPSS. The different types of data handling are accessed through the *menu items* **Data** and **Transform**. See also *compute, count, rank cases, recode, select cases, sort cases, split*.

Data transformation

In data transformation, each data value is replaced by a new value that is computed from the original value. A common data transformation is the *logarithmic transformation*.

Data View

In SPSS, the *Data Editor window* has two display settings. The Data View shows the data table, with the variables in columns and the cases in rows. See also *Variable View*.

Degrees of freedom

A value related to the number of *participant*s who took part in an experiment (t-*test*, *ANOVA*) or to the number of *factors* (*independent variable*s) in an experiment (ANOVA, *chi-square*). The degrees of freedom are required when using statistical tables of *significance*. Although SPSS gives the exact *p* value, degrees of freedom should still be reported as shown on the annotated output pages of those *inferential statistical tests*.

Dependent variable

The *variable* that is measured in an experiment, and whose values are said to depend on those of the *independent variable* (or *factor*).

Descriptive statistics

Procedures that allow you to describe data by summarising, displaying or illustrating them. Often used as a general term for summary descriptive statistics: *measures of central tendency* and *measures of dispersion*. Graphs (see *chart*) are descriptive statistics used to illustrate the data.

Dialogue box

A box that appears on the computer screen, normally after you have clicked on a sequence of *menu items*. SPSS uses dialogue boxes to allow you to control the details of a statistical procedure. Each chapter includes illustrations showing the dialogue boxes and explaining how to complete them.

Dichotomous variable

A *variable* that can only take one of two values, for example indicating the presence or absence of something.

Discriminant analysis

An inferential statistical procedure used to determine which *variables* predict membership of (or discriminate between) different categories of another *variable*.

Effect size

A measure of the magnitude of an effect. Can be expressed in the units used to measure the *dependent variable*, or in standardised units such as Cohen's *d*.

Equality of variance

Also referred to as *homogeneity of variance*. One of the requirements for using *parametric* statistical tests: the variance of the data for one variable should be relatively similar to that of the other variable(s) being analysed, even when they come from *populations* with different *means*.

Error bar graph

A graph in which the *mean* of each *condition* is plotted with a vertical bar that provides an indication of the magnitude of the error associated with the measurement of the *mean*, and hence an indication of how accurate the measurement is likely to be. In SPSS, we can use error bars to indicate several different measures of error, including *standard error, standard deviation* and *confidence interval*.

Exact significance

The *p* value calculated on the assumption that our data are a small *sample* of the *population* and/or do not have an asymptotic distribution. For many tests, SPSS now gives an option to calculate the exact significance in addition to the default *asymptotic significance*. Fisher's Exact test, an alternative in *chi-square*, only gives the exact *p* value.

Execute

Part of SPSS *syntax*. The execute command instructs SPSS to perform the command specified in the preceding lines of syntax.

Experimental design

Describes specific methods by which experiments are carried out and which are intended to prevent *participant irrelevant variable*s from *confounding* the experiment; for example, *repeated measures design*; two-way between-subjects *ANOVA*. Basic designs are described in Chapter 1, and other designs are described where relevant for particular statistical tests.

Experimental hypothesis

See *hypothesis*.

Factor

In *ANOVA*: another term for *independent variable*. The term 'factor' is used particularly when discussing *ANOVA* statistical tests and designs, whereas the term 'independent variable' is used more often for *two-sample designs*. See also *between-subjects design* and *within-subjects design*.

In *factor analysis*: a dimension (or a psychological construct) that underlies several measured *variables*.

Factor analysis

Statistical procedure used to identify whether a *factor* structure underlies *correlations* between a number of *variables*.

Factorability

Indicators of whether it is likely that there are any *factors* underlying a set of *variables* that are entered into a *factor analysis*.

F-ratio

The statistic obtained in *ANOVA* calculations. It can be described as the *variance* due to manipulation of the *factor* divided by the *variance* due to error.

Frequency/ies

The number of times a particular event or value occurs. Also an SPSS command available from the *menu item* **A**nalyze, which will produce tables of frequencies showing the number of times a particular value occurs in each *variable*. See also *bar chart*.

Friedman

A *nonparametric* equivalent of the one-way within-subjects *ANOVA*.

Graph

See *chart*.

Graphboard Template Chooser

A system that helps the user construct *graphs* by picking from a large collection of templates that can then be modified.

Grouping variable

SPSS uses this term for the *variable* that specifies two or more groups of *cases* to be compared. For *independent groups design,* the grouping variable is the *independent variable*. For example, in an experiment to compare the performance of participants in either quiet or noisy conditions, the grouping variable will be the independent variable, noise level. In other cases, the grouping variable is an independent variable that is not manipulated by the experimenter. For example, if we wish to compare the performance of men and women, the independent variable will be sex. Grouping variables are nominal variables. See *levels of measurement*.

Help

There are a number of different sources of help available within SPSS, including the **Help** menu and the Help button on most *dialogue boxes*.

Homogeneity of regression

An assumption of *ANCOVA* that the relationship between the *dependent variable* and the covariate is similar across all levels of the *independent variable*.

Homogeneity of variance

Also referred to as *equality of variance*. One of the requirements for using *parametric* statistical tests: the *variance* of the data for one *variable* should be relatively similar to that of the other variable(s) being analysed, even when they come from *populations* with different *means*.

Homogeneity of variance-covariance matrices

An assumption of *multivariate analysis of variance (MANOVA)*, which is an extension of the assumption of *homogeneity of variance*.

Hypothesis

A prediction about the outcome of a study. The experimental hypothesis predicts that a difference between *conditions* will occur, that a relationship will be found, or that an *interaction* will occur. The null hypothesis predicts that there will be no difference between conditions, that a relationship will not be found, or that an interaction will not occur.

Independent groups design

An *experimental design* in which each *participant* experiences only one *level* of the *independent variable*. Usually used for designs with two *levels* of one independent variable. See also *natural independent groups design* and *between-subjects design*s.

Independent variable

A *variable* either that is systematically manipulated by the experimenter to have different values (true experiments), or the values of which are chosen by the experimenter (*natural independent groups designs*). Each value of the independent variable is called a *level*. See also *factor*.

Inferential statistical tests

Procedures that allow you to draw inferences from the data collected. The outcome of an inferential statistical test estimates the probability of obtaining these data if the null hypothesis was true. If that probability is sufficiently small ($p \leq .05$ in psychology), the null hypothesis is rejected; otherwise it is retained. Various inferential statistics are covered in this book.

Interaction

An interaction is present between two *variables* if the effects of the two *variables* are not simply additive. For example, a high dose of drug A may impair performance more than a low dose, but drugs A and B may interact such that the effect of drug A is reversed in the presence of drug B.

Interaction graph

A *line graph* showing each *level* of two *factors*. The *dependent variable* is on the y-axis and the *levels* of one *factor* on the x-axis; the *levels* of a second *factor* are indicated by separate lines on the graph. See also *chart*.

Irrelevant variable

Any *variable* other than the *independent variable* (or *factor*) and the *dependent variable/s*. Good *experimental design* should ensure that irrelevant variables are controlled so that they do not become *confounding variables*.

Kendall's tau

An inferential statistical test of correlation used to analyse *nonparametric* data.

Kruskal–Wallis

A *nonparametric* equivalent of the one-way between-subjects *ANOVA*.

Level

An *independent variable* or *factor* will have two or more levels. For example, the factor temperature may have two levels: hot and cold. If there is only one *factor*, then its levels are equivalent to the *conditions* of the experiment. When there are two or more *factors*, the conditions are defined by the particular combination of the levels of the *factor* (for example, male participants tested under hot conditions).

Levels of measurement

The type of scale used to measure *variables*. Usually, four levels of measurement are described: *nominal*, *ordinal*, interval and ratio. The first two are classified as *nonparametric* levels of measurement, and the last two as *parametric* levels of measurement. SPSS uses the term *scale* to describe interval and ratio levels of measurement. See also *measure*.

Linear relationship

A relationship between two *variables* is said to be linear if the data points follow a straight line (or close to a straight line) when plotted in a *scattergram*.

Linear trend

Describes the situation in which the *mean* values from a *factor* with three or more *levels* follow a straight line; this can be assessed for significance. See also *quadratic trend*.

Line graph

A graph in which the points plotted are joined by a line. The points could each represent the *mean* of one sample, or they could represent the *frequency* of particular values in an SPSS *variable*. See also *interaction graph* and *chart*.

Logarithmic transformation

A *data transformation* in which each point in a data set is replaced with its logarithmic (either natural or common) value. Logarithmic transforms are typically applied to a data set to reduce the influence of *outliers* so the data more closely match the assumptions of a statistical procedure.

Logistic regression

A statistical procedure that examines the impact of a number of *predictor variables* on a categorical dependent variable. SPSS distinguishes between binary logistic regression in which the dependent variable has two categories, and multinomial logistic regression in which the dependent variable can have more than two categories.

Log transformation

See *logarithmic transformation*.

Mann–Whitney

An inferential statistical test used to analyse *nonparametric* data from *two-sample independent groups designs*.

Matched-subjects design

An *experimental design* in which each *participant* is matched closely with another participant, to give a participant pair. Each member of the pair is then allocated, by a random process, to different *levels* of the *independent variable*. Also called matched pairs design. It is a type of *related design*.

McNemar

An inferential statistical test used to analyse *nominal* data obtained by measuring a *dichotomous variable* for a *two-sample related design*.

Mean (M)

A *measure of central tendency*: the scores are summed and the total is divided by the number of scores.

Measure

SPSS uses the term measure, in the *Variable View*, to refer to the level of measurement for a *variable*. See *levels of measurement*.

Measure of central tendency

The average or typical score for a sample. See *mean*, *median* and *mode*.

Measure of dispersion

A measure of variability within a sample. See *range*, *standard deviation*, *standard error* and *variance*.

Median

A *measure of central tendency*: the scores are put into rank order and the middle score is the median.

Menu items

In SPSS, the menu items are the words in the highlighted bar across the top of the window, which give the user access to drop-down lists of options.

Missing values

A data set may be incomplete; for example, if some observations or measurements failed or if participants didn't respond to some questions. It is important to distinguish these missing data points from valid data. Missing values are the values SPSS has reserved for each variable to indicate that a data point is missing. These missing values can either be specified by the user (*user missing*) or automatically set by SPSS (*system missing*).

Mixed design

A design in which at least one *factor* is *between-subjects* and at least one is *within-subjects*. This is an aspect of the terminology used to describe *ANOVA* designs.

Mode

The most common value in a *sample* of scores: a *measure of central tendency*. If a *sample* of scores has more than one mode, SPSS shows the lowest value.

Multinominal logistic regression

See *logistic regression*.

Multiple regression

An inferential statistical procedure used to investigate *linear relationships* between three or more *variables*. Multiple regression can indicate the extent to which one variable can be explained or predicted by one or more of the other variables. See also *regression*.

Multivariate

Analysis of data in which either two or more *dependent variables* are measured while one or more factors are manipulated, for example, *multivariate analysis of variance*; or three or more *variables* are measured, for example *multiple regression*. See also *univariate*, *bivariate* and *dependent variable*.

Multivariate analysis of variance

An inferential statistical procedure used to analyse data collected using designs in which two or more *dependent variables* are measured, while one or more *factor*s are manipulated. See also *ANOVA*.

N

In statistics, the character '*N*' (uppercase) is typically used to indicate the size of a *population*, while '*n*' (lowercase) is used to indicate the *sample* size. SPSS uses '*N*' to refer to the number of cases being analysed

Natural independent groups design

An *independent groups design* or *between-subjects design* in which the groups are chosen by the experimenter from pre-existing (natural) groups. For example: male and female; smoker, ex-smoker and non-smoker. The results of natural groups studies cannot be used to draw conclusions about cause-and-effect relationships, but only about differences or associations that might be a result of variables other than those used to define the natural groups. Studies using a natural independent groups design are sometimes called 'quasi-experimental studies'.

Nominal

A *level of measurement* that yields nominal data, also referred to as 'categorical data', where the value does not imply anything other than a label; for example, 1 = male and 2 = female.

Nonparametric

A term used to denote:

1. nominal and ordinal *levels of measurement*

2. data that may be measured on ratio or interval scales but do not meet the other assumptions (equality of *variance* and normality of distribution) underlying *parametric* statistical tests

3. the *inferential statistical tests* used to analyse nonparametric data.

Nonparametric statistics make use of rank order, either of scores or the differences between scores, unlike *parametric* statistical tests. Because nonparametric tests make no assumptions about normality of distribution in the data, they are sometimes called 'distribution-free tests'.

Null hypothesis

See *hypothesis*.

Options

Options in *dialogue boxes* can be set to request additional statistics or control the appearance of *charts*. Also, selecting **Opti**o**ns** from the **Edit** *menu item* allows you to set options that will be applied more generally.

Ordinal

Ordinal data are data measured on a scale that only indicates rank and not absolute value. An example of an ordinal scale is academic performance measured by class rank. See also *levels of measurement*.

Outlier

A value recorded for a *variable* that is far from the majority of values.

Output window

See *Viewer window*.

P value

The *p* value is the probability of obtaining the observed results if the null hypothesis were true. In psychology, it is conventional to declare a result to be statistically significant if the *p* value is less than or equal to .05. See also *significance level*.

Parameters

A characteristic of an entire *population*, such as the *mean*. Normally, we estimate a *population* parameter based on the statistics of the *sample*.

Parametric

A term used to denote:

1. ratio and interval *levels of measurement*

2. data that are measured on one of those scales and also meet the two other requirements (equality of *variance* and normality of *distribution*) for parametric statistical tests

3. the *inferential statistical tests* used to analyse parametric data.

Parametric statistics make use of the actual values of scores in each *sample*, unlike *nonparametric* statistical tests.

Participant

People who take part in an experiment. Previously, the word 'subject' was used, and still is in many statistics books. The word 'subject' is often still used to describe *ANOVA* experimental designs and analyses (e.g. '2*2 within-subjects design') as in this book.

Participant irrelevant variable

Any *irrelevant variable* that is a property of the *participants* in an experiment. The term 'subject irrelevant variables' is sometimes still used.

Paste

In SPSS, the Paste button pastes the lines of *syntax* required to perform a command into the *Syntax Editor window*.

Pearson's *r*

An *inferential statistical test* of *correlation* used to analyse *parametric* data.

Pivot table

The name that SPSS gives to a table of results displayed in the *Output viewer window*. The appearance of a pivot table can be altered for the purposes of presentation in a report

Planned comparisons

A group of statistical tests used to compare particular *conditions* from *ANOVA* designs. Planned comparisons must be specified before data are collected. If used inappropriately, then the *Type I error* will be inflated. See also *unplanned comparisons*.

Population

The total set of all possible scores for a particular *variable*. See also *N*.

Power

The power of an inferential statistical procedure is the probability that it will yield a statistically significant result.

Predictor variable

The variable/s used in a *regression* analysis to explain another variable (the *criterion variable*). Some sources use the term independent variable/s instead of predictor variable/s.

Print

The content, or a selection, of all SPSS windows can be printed by selecting **Print** from the **File** *menu item* while the appropriate window is open.

Quadratic trend

Describes the situation in which the *mean* values from a *factor* with three or more *levels* follow a curved line (for example, a U-shape); this can be assessed for significance. See also *linear trend*.

Quantitative research

In psychology, describes research that involves the analysis of numeric data measured on any of the four *levels of measurement*. In contrast, qualitative research often involves the detailed analysis of non-numeric data, collected from small, non-random *samples*. SPSS is designed for use in quantitative research. Sometimes, 'quantitative data' is used to describe data measured on ratio, interval or ordinal scales, and the term 'qualitative data' is then used to describe data measured with nominal scales.

Range

A *measure of dispersion*: the scores are put into rank order and the lowest score is subtracted from the highest score.

Rank cases

An SPSS procedure that converts interval or ratio data into ordinal data. A new *variable* is added to the data file that gives the rank of one of the existing variables.

Recode

An SPSS procedure that allows the user to systematically change a particular value or range of values in a *variable*.

Regression

If two *variables* have been measured, *bivariate regression* can be used to allow prediction of a participant's score on one variable from their score on the other variable. If three or more variables have been measured, then *multiple regression* can be used to analyse the data. A regression line is the line drawn using the regression formula, and represents the 'best fit' to the data points in a *scattergram*.

Related designs

A term that includes *repeated measures* and *matched subjects designs*. Usually used for designs with two *levels* of one *independent variable*. See also *within-subjects designs*.

Repeated measures design

An *experimental design* in which each *participant* experiences every *level* of the *independent variable*. It is a type of *related design*.

Sample

A subset of a *population*. A smaller set of scores we hope is representative of the *population*. See also *N*.

Scale

In SPSS, describes interval and ratio *levels of measurement*.

Scattergram

Sometimes called a 'scattergraph', and in SPSS it is called a 'scatterplot'. Two variables are plotted, one on the x-axis the other on the y-axis, and a point is plotted for each case. Used to display the results of a *correlation* analysis. See also *chart*.

Select cases

SPSS procedure that allows the user to select a subsample of the *cases* on the data file. Cases can be selected on the basis of the values of a particular *variable*. Subsequent analyses will only be performed on the selected cases.

Sig

SPSS uses the shorthand 'sig' to indicate a *p value*. See also *significance level*.

Significance level

The outcome of an inferential statistical test estimates the probability of obtaining the observed results assuming the null *hypothesis* is true. If that probability is equal to or less than the significance level, the null hypothesis is rejected; otherwise it is retained. By convention in psychology, the significance level is set to .05.

Situational irrelevant variable

Any *irrelevant variable* that relates to the situation in which an experiment is carried out.

Skewed data

If a data *sample* is not normally distributed but has a 'tail' of *cases* that are either particularly low or particularly high compared to most of the scores, the *sample* is said to be skewed. Such a *sample* does not meet the assumption of normality of distribution. See *parametric*.

Sort cases

SPSS procedure by which the *cases* in the *Data window* can be sorted into a desired order based on the values of one or more *variables*.

Spearman's rho

An *inferential statistical test* of *correlation* used to analyse *nonparametric* data.

Sphericity

An assumption when performing a within-subjects or mixed *ANOVA* that the variances of the differences between all possible pairs of levels of a *within-subjects* factor are equal.

Split

SPSS procedure that allows the user to split the *cases* into two or more groups based on the values of a *grouping variable*; subsequent analyses will be performed separately for each group or the groups will be compared.

Standard deviation (*SD*)

A *measure of dispersion* that gives an indication of the average difference from the *mean*. SPSS uses the formula that is designed to estimate the standard deviation of a *population* based on a *sample* (i.e. $N - 1$ is used as the denominator rather than N).

Standard error (*SE*)

A *measure of dispersion* that is equal to the *standard deviation* divided by the square root of N. The full name is 'standard error of the *mean*'. (The 'standard error of differences between *means*' is obtained as part of calculations for the t-*test*; the 'standard error of the estimate' is used in regression.)

Statistics

A general term for procedures for summarising or displaying data (*descriptive statistics*) and for analysing data (*inferential statistical tests*). A characteristic of a *sample*, such as the *mean*, used to estimate the *population parameters*.

Syntax

The program language that can be used to directly control SPSS. For more experienced users, controlling SPSS in this way can sometimes be a useful alternative to using the *dialogue boxes*. Syntax commands may appear in the *Output window*. Syntax commands can be pasted into and edited in the *Syntax window*.

Syntax window

The Syntax Editor window can be used to write *syntax* files to control an analysis. Beginners will not need to use the Syntax window.

System missing

A *missing value* automatically assigned by SPSS. System missing values are shown as dots in the relevant data cells. See also *user missing*.

System variables

Variables reserved by SPSS. System variables have names starting with the '$' symbol.

t-test

An *inferential statistical test* used to analyse *parametric* data. The one-sample *t*-test compares the *mean* of a single *sample* with a known *population*, for example average IQ score. For *two-sample designs*, there are two versions, both comparing two *means*: the independent *t*-test for *independent groups designs*, and the paired *t*-test for *related designs*.

Transformation

See *data transformation*; *logarithmic transformation*.

Two-sample designs

Experimental designs with two *levels* of one *independent variable*. See also *independent groups design* and *related designs*.

Type I error

A Type I error occurs when the null *hypothesis* is rejected in error. If the *significance level* is set at .05 (the convention in psychology), we will make a Type I error on an average of 1 in 20 occasions. If the significance level is reduced, the chance of Type I errors will fall, but the Type II error rate will increase. Repeated, unplanned testing of a data set can also increase the Type I error rate. See also *planned* and *unplanned comparisons*.

Type II error

The situation in which the null *hypothesis* is retained in error. The Type II error rate depends partly on the *significance level* and partly on the power of the *inferential statistical test*.

Univariate

An analysis involving just one *dependent variable*, for example, *Mann–Whitney*, *paired t-test* and *ANOVA*. See also *bivariate* and *multivariate*.

Unplanned comparisons

A group of *inferential statistical tests* that may be used to make all the possible comparisons between *conditions* from *ANOVA* designs, as they control for the increased chance of obtaining *Type I errors*. See also *planned comparisons*.

User missing

A *missing value* assigned by the user. See also *system missing*.

Value label

The label assigned to a particular value of a *variable* in an SPSS data file. Value labels are particularly useful in the case of *nominal* variables. Value labels are included in the SPSS output and will help you to interpret your analysis.

Variable

In *experimental design*, anything that varies that can have different values at different times or for different *cases*. See also *confounding variable*, *dependent variable*, *independent variable* and *irrelevant variable*. A variable in SPSS is represented by a column in the *Data Editor window*.

Variable label

Explanatory label that you can give to an SPSS *variable* when you define it. The variable label is printed in the SPSS output and often is shown in *dialogue boxes*.

Variable name

Name given to an SPSS *variable* when it is defined. The variable name will appear at the top of the column in the *Data Editor window*, and may appear in the SPSS output.

Variable View

In SPSS, the *Data Editor window* has two display settings. The Variable View shows details of the settings for each variable in the data file. See also *Data View*.

Variance

A *measure of dispersion* equal to the square of the *standard deviation*. Equality of variance between the *samples* is one of the requirements for using *parametric* statistical tests. SPSS will test for equality of variance (e.g. when performing the independent t-*test*). A rule of thumb is that the larger variance should be no greater than three times the smaller variance.

Viewer window

Displays the output of statistical procedures in SPSS. Also referred to as the *Output window*.

Wilcoxon matched-pairs signed-ranks test

An *inferential statistical test* used to analyse *nonparametric* data from *two-sample related designs*.

Glossary

Within-subjects design

A design in which each *participant* experiences every *level* of every *factor* (or if there are *matched subjects*, in which each pair experiences every level of every factor). See also *repeated measures design* and *related designs*.

z-score

A way of expressing a score in terms of its relationship to the *mean* and *standard deviation* of the *sample*. A z-score of −2.5 represents a number that is 2.5 *standard deviations* below the *mean*.

References

For any text marked * earlier editions will also be useful.

APA (American Psychological Association) (2009) *Publication Manual of the American Psychological Association* (6th edn). Washington, DC: APA.

Bird, K.D. (2004) *Analysis of Variance via Confidence Intervals*. London: Sage.

Brysbaert, M. (2011) *Basic Statistics for Psychologists*. Basingstoke: Palgrave Macmillan.

*Cohen, J. (1988) *Statistical Power Analysis for the Behavioural Sciences* (2nd edn). New York: Academic Press.

Cole, D.A., Maxwell, S.E., Arvey, R. and Salas, E. (1994) How the power of MANOVA can both increase and decrease as a function of the intercorrelations among the dependent variables. *Psychological Bulletin*, 115(3), 465–74.

Cooper, C. (2010) *Individual Differences and Personality* (3rd edn). London: Hodder Education.

Field, A. (2005) *Discovering Statistics Using SPSS* (2nd edn). London: Sage.

Field, A. (2013) *Discovering Statistics Using SPSS* (4th edn). London: Sage.

Fife-Schaw, C. (2012) Questionnaire design. In G.M. Breakwell, J.A. Smith and D.B. Wright (eds) *Research Methods in Psychology* (4th edn), Chapter 6. London: Sage.

Fritz, C.O., Morris, P.E. and Richler, J.J. (2012) Effect size estimates: current use, calculations and interpretation. *Journal of Experimental Psychology: General*, 141(1), 2–18.

Giles, D.C. (2002) *Advanced Research Methods in Psychology*. Hove: Routledge.

Hartley, J. (1991) Sex differences in handwriting: a comment on Spear. *British Educational Research Journal*, 17(2), 141–5.

Hollin, C.R., Palmer, E.J. and Clark, D.A. (2003) The level of service inventory – revised profile of English prisoners: a needs analysis. *Criminal Justice and Behavior*, 30, 422–40.

Hong, E. and Karstensson, L. (2002) Antecedents of state test anxiety. *Contemporary Educational Psychology*, 27(2), 348–67.

Howell, D.C. (1987) *Statistical Methods for Psychology* (3rd edn). Belmont, CA: Duxbury Press.

*Howell, D.C. (2013) *Statistical Methods for Psychology* (8th edn), International Edition. Belmont, CA: Wadsworth, Cengage Learning.

John, O.P. and Benet-Martinez, V. (2014) Measurement. In H.T. Reis and C.M. Judd (eds) *Handbook of Research Methods in Social and Personality Psychology* (2nd edn), Chapter 18. Cambridge: Cambridge University Press.

Kemp, R.I., McManus, I.C. and Pigott, T. (1990) Sensitivity to the displacement of facial features in negative and inverted images. *Perception*, 19(4), 531–43.

Kline, P. (1994) *An Easy Guide to Factor Analysis*. London: Routledge.

Larsen, K.S. (1995) Environmental waste: recycling attitudes and correlates. *Journal of Social Psychology*, 135(1), 83–8.

Mackenzie Ross, S.J., Brewin, C.R., Curran, H.V. et al. (2010) Neuropsychological and psychiatric functioning in sheep farmers exposed to low levels of organophosphate pesticides. *Neurotoxicology and Teratology*, 32(4), 452–9.

Mason, R.J., Snelgar, R.S., Foster, D.H. et al. (1982) Abnormalities of chromatic and luminance critical flicker frequency in multiple sclerosis. *Investigative Ophthalmology & Visual Science*, 23, 246–52.

Miles, J.N.V. and Shevlin, M.E. (2001) *Applying Regression and Correlation: A Guide for Students and Researchers*. London: Sage.

Mulhern, G. and Greer, B. (2011) *Making Sense of Data and Statistics in Psychology* (2nd edn). Basingstoke: Palgrave Macmillan.

Newlands, P. (1997) Eyewitness interviewing: Does the cognitive interview fit the bill? Unpublished PhD thesis, University of Westminster, London.

Paterson, H.M., Kemp, R.I. and Forgas, J.P. (2009) Co-witnesses, confederates, and conformity: effects of discussion and delay on eyewitness memory. *Psychiatry, Psychology and Law*, 16(1), 112–24.

Rust, J. (2012) Psychometrics. In G.M. Breakwell, J.A. Smith and D.B. Wright (eds) *Research Methods in Psychology* (4th edn), Chapter 7. London: Sage.

Siegel, S. and Castellan, N.J. (1988) *Nonparametric Statistics for the Behavioral Sciences* (2nd edn). New York: McGraw-Hill.

Skinner, B.F. (1965) *Science and Human Behavior*. New York: The Free Press.

Stroop, J.R. (1935) Studies of interference in serial verbal reactions. *Journal of Experimental Psychology*, 18(6), 643–62.

*Tabachnick, B.G. and Fidell, L.S. (2014) *Using Multivariate Statistics* (6th edn), International Edition. Harlow: Pearson Education.

Towell, N., Burton, A. and Burton, E. (1994) The effects of two matched memory tasks on concurrent finger tapping. *Neuropsychologia*, 32(1), 125–9.

Towell, N., Kemp, R. and Pike, G. (1996) The effects of witness identity masking on memory and person perception. *Psychology, Crime and Law*, 2(4), 333–46.

Index

In this Index, numerals in italic format are page references for a glossary entry for the term.